More Praise for *Skills for Career Success*

"Whether you need a new job or better skills, *Skills for Care[...]* Elaine is as encouraging as a best friend but tough enough [...] success. This book is a lifeline for people who want to take control of their career."
—**Ken Blanchard, coauthor of** *The New One Minute Manager* **and** *Leading at a Higher Level*

"Elaine shows us that career success starts by building a strong foundation of lifelong learning. What's really unique in this book are challenge exercises for a variety of situations such as wanting to unstick a stalled career. No matter your career level or aspiration, Elaine will provide you with a road map for career success grounded in personal accountability for learning and development."
—**Tony Bingham, President and CEO, ATD**

"Looking for a way to kick your career up a notch? *Skills for Career Success* provides the road map you need to follow, the fifty-one critical skills you need to master, and six hundred activities you can use to build those skills. We're not talking amateur here. We're talking Olympic-level performer. Whether you want to coach others or coach yourself, this is the guidebook you need to have handy when you first set foot on the track . . . and when you return to it every day to stay in shape for the challenging days ahead."
—**Jim Kouzes, coauthor of** *The Leadership Challenge* **and Fellow, Doerr Institute for New Leaders, Rice University**

"Elaine Biech has performed an extraordinary feat: delivering a book of bite-size, just-in-time insights that are grounded in timeless wisdom about career and personal development. This is a must-have resource for young people beginning their careers—and the equivalent of a booster shot for professionals who are decades into their careers and still hungry to improve. Open this book to any page, and you'll learn something you can put to use right away."
—**John R. Ryan, President and CEO, Center for Creative Leadership**

"Wherever you are in your career—starting out, hitting the reset button, or gaining forward momentum for that next career step—you'll find practical advice in Elaine's book. You can go 'all in' on your personal development plan or simply try her fast daily tips."
—**Tacy M. Byham, PhD, CEO, DDI, and coauthor of** *Your First Leadership Job*

"Elaine Biech goes way beyond just career—this is a book about success in life itself. All professionals in the human capital area should absolutely know the contents of this book. This just could be all you need to deliver to your organization."
—**Dr. Bev Kaye, CEO, Bev Kaye & Company, and coauthor of** *Help Them Grow or Watch Them Go* **and** *Up Is Not the Only Way*

"Elaine leads the way as people remake themselves to keep pace with the evolving workplace of virtual work, shifting technology, and working outside the normal forty-hour week. Her diversification strategy will make you more marketable in this agile environment."
—**Rear Adm. (ret.) Gib Godwin, President, BriteWerx Inc.**

"This book is an essential and practical guide for achieving career success. Whether early in your career, seeking a career change, or striving for excellence on your current path, there is something for everyone."
—**Marcia J. Avedon, PhD, Executive Vice President and Chief Human Resources, Communications, and Marketing Officer, Trane Technologies**

"There's only one way to get the job you want: learn. It doesn't matter if you're a grocery clerk who wants to be the next assistant manager or a marketing director who wants to start your own firm. Elaine Biech shows you how to think differently about your professional development so you can learn your way to the career you deserve."
—**JD Dillon, Chief Learning Architect, Axonify, and founder and Principal, LearnGeek**

"Disruptions in our society, in our organizations, and yes, in our careers require powerful approaches to building and rebuilding the skills and readiness of our workforce. Elaine Biech brings a lifetime of experience in the world of learning, development, and careers to this must-read book."
—**Elliott Masie, Chair, The Learning CONSORTIUM**

"Elaine has done a masterful job of presenting the most important parts of developing your career: identifying what you want, creating a successful plan, developing the skills and character you need for success, and ensuring that you stay on track! Make this book your go-to guide for a successful career."
—**Marshall Goldsmith, Thinkers50 #1 Executive Coach and bestselling author of *Triggers* and *What Got You Here Won't Get You There***

"In these uncertain times, it's critical to focus on reevaluating skills and to be more intentional and deliberate about our career choices. Wherever you are in your career journey, this is a timely resource with an abundance of ideas, tips, and guidelines that will get you to the finish line."
—**Rita Bailey, founder and President, Up to Something, LLC, and former Director, University for People, Southwest Airlines**

"It's the most useful resource I've seen in years—the table of contents alone is worth the price of the book. It has all the essential topics to set priorities and build your skills to become a driver of your own success. The chapters about your personal style and knowing and improving upon your weaknesses are critical."
—**Mindy C. Meads, Board Chair, Sun Valley Culinary Institute; former CEO, Lands' End; and former co-CEO, Aeropostale**

"This is the perfect guide to coach others or to coach yourself for career success. Elaine shows you how to lay out a plan, gain experience, and tackle the skills necessary with a practical easy-to-implement design."
—**D. Kimo Kippen, founder of Aloha Learning Advisors, LLC, and former Chief Learning Officer and Vice President, Hilton**

"Now more than ever, employees need a guide to help them figure out their careers. Elaine Biech has written that guide. It will take them from 'What do I want to be when I grow up?' to 'I'm on the right track!'"
—**Jenny Dearborn, founder of Actionable Analytics Group and former Senior Vice President and Chief Learning Officer, SAP**

"A comprehensive reference to help anyone serious about personal and professional growth. Every chapter is chock-full of important considerations and questions with practical and real-life suggestions for the present along with strategies for the long run."
—**Pamela Schmidt, Executive Director, ISA—The Association of Learning Providers**

"This book is packed with the fifty-one skills you need for career success and more than six hundred ways to improve the skills to enhance your career. And the bonus chapters at the end double the value: building character, avoiding career derailment, and how managers develop employees. It's all here."
—**Jenn Labin, Chief Talent and Diversity Officer, Mentorcliq**

"Elaine is really in sync with her learners; she wants you to succeed. Figuring out who you are professionally and how to develop your career are vital to your success. Elaine will help you do that."
—**Rich Douglas, PhD, PCC, Principal, Rich Douglas Consulting, LLC**

"Elaine practices what she teaches and is an inspiration for integrity, service, and excellence. I was the beneficiary of her tireless efforts to help make others successful. This book is the next best thing to working with her in person. Her easy-to-read style provides a practical path for both personal and professional success."
—**William J. Shirey, PhD, President, ISE Consulting**

"Searching for ways to acquire the skills you need for a successful career? Look no further. Elaine provides tips for people in a hurry, practice sprints, strategies for the long run, and additional reading for the final stretch."
—**David M. R. Covey, bestselling coauthor of *Trap Tales***

SKILLS FOR CAREER SUCCESS

SKILLS FOR CAREER SUCCESS

Maximizing Your Potential at Work

ELAINE BIECH

Published with the Association
for Talent Development

Berrett–Koehler Publishers, Inc.

Berrett-Koehler Publishers, Inc.
1333 Broadway, Suite 1000
Oakland, CA 94612-1921
Tel: (510) 817-2277
Fax: (510) 817-2278
www.bkconnection.com

ORDERING INFORMATION

Quantity sales. Special discounts are available on quantity purchases by corporations, associations, and others. For details, contact the "Special Sales Department" at the Berrett-Koehler address above.

Individual sales. Berrett-Koehler publications are available through most bookstores. They can also be ordered directly from Berrett-Koehler: Tel: (800) 929-2929; Fax: (802) 864-7626; www.bkconnection.com.

Orders for college textbook / course adoption use. Please contact Berrett-Koehler: Tel: (800) 929-2929; Fax: (802) 864-7626.

Distributed to the U.S. trade and internationally by Penguin Random House Publisher Services.

Berrett-Koehler and the BK logo are registered trademarks of Berrett-Koehler Publishers, Inc.

Printed in the United States of America

Berrett-Koehler books are printed on long-lasting acid-free paper. When it is available, we choose paper that has been manufactured by environmentally responsible processes. These may include using trees grown in sustainable forests, incorporating recycled paper, minimizing chlorine in bleaching, or recycling the energy produced at the paper mill.

Library of Congress Cataloging-in-Publication Data

Names: Biech, Elaine, author.
Title: Skills for career success : maximizing your potential at work / Elaine Biech.
Description: First edition. | Oakland, CA : Berrett-Koehler Publishers, Inc., [2021] |
    Includes bibliographical references and index.
Identifiers: LCCN 2020037962 | ISBN 9781523091928 (paperback ; alk. paper) |
    ISBN 9781523091935 (adobe pdf) | ISBN 9781523091942 (epub)
Subjects: LCSH: Career development. | Vocational qualifications.
Classification: LCC HF5381 .B4245 2021 | DDC 650.1—dc23
LC record available at https://lccn.loc.gov/2020037962

First Edition
30 29 28 27 26 25 24 23 22 21 20   10 9 8 7 6 5 4 3 2 1

Set in Archer and Gotham by Westchester Publishing Services
Text designer: Maureen Forys, Happenstance Type-O-Rama
Cover designer: Adrian Morgan

For Shane and Thad
Who know the importance
of clearing life's hurdles

RACING TOWARD SUCCESS

Icons representing the **four steps** in part one of this book appear on the inside of the racetrack.

Icons representing **skill categories** in part two appear around the outside of the racetrack.

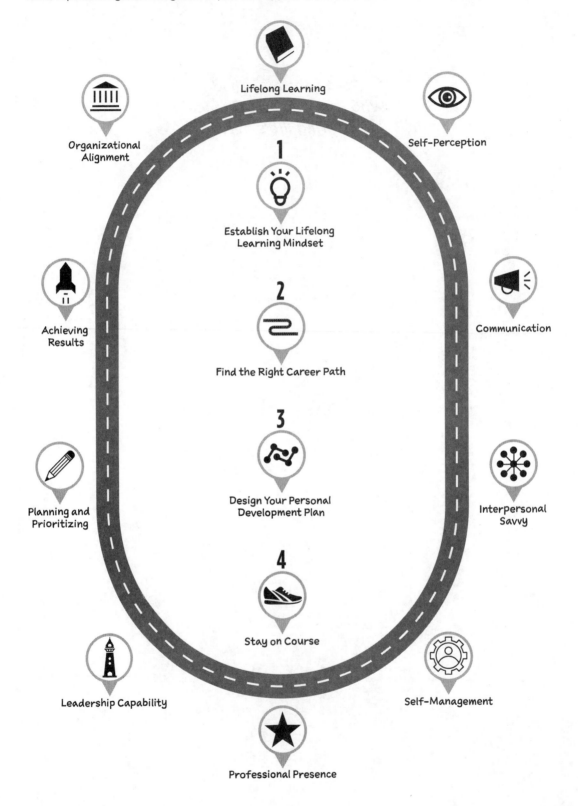

Lifelong Learning

Organizational Alignment

Self-Perception

1 Establish Your Lifelong Learning Mindset

Achieving Results

Communication

2 Find the Right Career Path

Planning and Prioritizing

Interpersonal Savvy

3 Design Your Personal Development Plan

4 Stay on Course

Leadership Capability

Self-Management

Professional Presence

CONTENTS

INTRODUCTION

Get Your Career on Track

In your hands you hold a plan to maximize your potential at work and create the career you desire.

You are responsible for your future. What you do today creates your tomorrow. It influences how you think, talk, and conduct yourself. What you learn and experience today forms the impetus for your successful career in the future. But how do you start? This book can help you identify your career vision and select ways to practice new skills, and it offers tips to stay the course.

Most important: This book is not intended to be read cover to cover.

- If you are trying to identify a career, start with Steps 1 and 2.
- If you know the career you have passion for, review Steps 3 and 4.
- If you have received feedback and you know what skills you need to improve, turn to Part Two to locate specific skills and start improving.
- If your career has stalled or derailed or plateaued, read Challenge 2.

- If you're working to improve your image, reputation, or character, start with Challenge 1.

- If you are a manager who wants to help your employees, go to Challenge 3.

Take control of your career now. I challenge you to turn to any page in this book and read a paragraph or two. I am quite certain that you will find a new idea or a reminder of something you can strengthen or improve.

There are many ideas in this book. All of them will work if you do. None of them will work if you don't. Take responsibility for your future and let the suggestions in this book inspire you to take the next steps toward your satisfying career.

Taking control of your career is hard work.

WHY THIS BOOK?

In most organizations, employees are accountable for their own development. Managing your own development and career is no longer an option. Some organizations may have employee journey maps or learning paths that lay out a predetermined learning plan for employees. Still, you should play an active role in managing your career. So how do you go about figuring out your own career path? No one cares more about your career than you do.

If you want to run a marathon, you must prepare for it. You would study what the experts do; you'd start running short sprints; you'd learn how to stretch; you'd begin to eat the right things; you'd put together a playlist that motivates you. And you'd create an overall plan and work at it for months before the race. There's a lot to do to win a race.

If you want to have a career that is meaningful and inspires you, you must prepare for it the same way you would a marathon. You might seek experts in your profession; you'd try some short sprints such as a job swap to experience the work; you'd learn with a stretch assignment; you'd begin a diet of learning the right things; you'd put together a "playlist" of strategies that motivate you to try new experiences. And you'd create an individual development plan (IDP) and anticipate working at it for months.

This book can help you tap into what you are passionate about, what skills you have, and what skills you need. You also need to look to the future to determine what skills will be required—that is, what will someone pay you for? And what's the gap between what you want to do, can do, and still need to learn to do? That's where you can make a difference for you. You can determine how to upskill and reskill your proficiency so that you can win the race to the career you desire.

Your career is the most valuable investment you can make in your life.

WHY NOW?

You may be reading this book for many reasons. Perhaps you are new to the workforce and are curious about what skills you'll need. You may be reading this book because your career has reached a plateau; perhaps you've received the results from your 360-degree assessment and need ideas to shore up several skills. You may also be reading this book because you see the future and know that your current career is in for turbulent times. Or, you may be reading this book because your current work is just not as exciting and invigorating as it once was. Whatever your reason, it is wise to step back and review who you are and who you want to be.

Remember to plan what you will need to do to achieve the career you desire. As the saying goes, it's not a sprint; your career development is a marathon.

This book will keep you on track to the finish line and beyond.

WHAT'S IN THIS BOOK?

First of all, remember that this book is *not* intended to be read from cover to cover. Start where it makes the most sense for where you are now.

Part One. Steps 1 through 4 contain general information about career development. You'll learn why it's critical to be a lifelong learner and to have a growth mindset. You'll find ideas for how to find the right career path for you and how to stay on course. You'll learn to write an IDP that is practical and useful to you.

Part Two. The skills presented here focus on how to develop your career. Ten categories present 51 skills that employees must have in order to be truly successful in their careers. For example, if you've received feedback from your supervisor during an appraisal meeting or from a 360-degree assessment that you need to improve your accountability, turn to Skill 43 to learn the measures of success, the hurdles you will need to overcome for improvement, and a dozen ways that you can start practicing.

This book is not meant to tell you everything you need to know about a skill or behavior. Instead, the 10 skill categories show how you can gain more insight about each skill and how you can obtain experiences that will lead you to improve them. Each of the 51 skills presents the key measures of success and mindset hurdles you'll need to overcome. These are followed by exercises that are divided into three sections:

- **Tips for People in a Hurry** are things you can do immediately or changes you can make to improve nearly instantly. Generally they are things you can do with no planning. You'll likely have to set aside some time, but most can be implemented without much more than a paper and pencil.

- **Practice Sprints** are tactics that can be implemented as reminders or actions you can take with a small amount of planning. In some cases they involve other people—for example, scheduling a meeting with your supervisor. A number of the tactics ask that you create a plan, but you will not likely need to do any research.

- **Strategies for the Long Run** are suggestions and plans that will help you develop your skills over time. They take longer than the tips and sprints but are more permanent. These are items that will be more difficult to do; some may push you out of your comfort zone and expect you to take a risk. You'll be expected to invest a longer period of time—days, weeks, or even months—to complete the development. These might be strategies that you add to your personal development plan.

Each of the 51 skills ends with a "Cross Training" section that points you to related topics in the book. "Reading for the Final Stretch" is a short list of books for further learning on each of the topics.

Part Three. The Challenges discussed in this section cover some important "extras." The first two Challenges address character and trip ups that can derail your career. The third Challenge is written for your manager—providing direction on how to support your career planning.

BEYOND THE BOOK

Online tools and downloadable resources can be found at https://ideas
.bkconnection.com/skillsforcareersuccess. These tools relate to the skills
and categories discussed in the book, including such things as interview
questions, self-assessments, worksheets, and planning sheets.

PART ONE

TAKE CHARGE OF YOUR CAREER

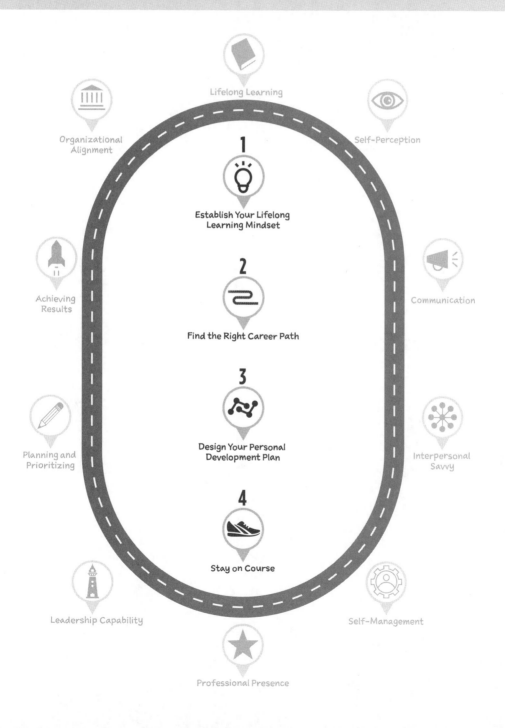

Lifelong Learning

Organizational Alignment

Self-Perception

1
Establish Your Lifelong Learning Mindset

Achieving Results

Communication

2
Find the Right Career Path

Planning and Prioritizing

Interpersonal Savvy

3
Design Your Personal Development Plan

4
Stay on Course

Leadership Capability

Self-Management

Professional Presence

Establish Your Lifelong-Learning Mindset

Benjamin Franklin is a model for lifelong learning. A founding father of America, he helped draft the Declaration of Independence and the U.S. Constitution; negotiated the 1783 Treaty of Paris, ending the Revolutionary War; invented bifocal glasses, the rocking chair, the Franklin stove, the American penny, the armonica (a glass musical instrument), and a flexible catheter; was the first postmaster general for the colonies; and organized the first successful American lending library. He also published *Poor Richard's Almanack* 25 consecutive years and the *Pennsylvania Gazette*, the most widely read paper in the colonies; he discovered the Gulf Stream; he invented the lightning rod based on his famous kite-and-key experiment; and he taught himself to swim, crafting his own wooden flippers.

In 1749 he wrote an article about education in Pennsylvania that resulted in establishing the Academy of Philadelphia, now the University of Pennsylvania. His self-education earned him honorary degrees from Harvard,

Yale, the University of Oxford, and the University of St. Andrews (Isaacson 2003).

Quite impressive for someone who was born the 15th of 17 children and dropped out of school at the age of 10. Franklin, who now graces the U.S. 100 dollar bill, accomplished all this based on self-learning through reading and experience.

What can we learn from Benjamin Franklin, perhaps one of the original lifelong learners? Franklin had a voracious appetite for learning, resulting in the accomplishment of a profuse number of major contributions to society. So how did he do it, and how does that translate into our world of lifelong learning today?

- **Set goals and track them.** Franklin set time to complete his "present study" or focus on his "virtues list" and tracked the results (Franklin 2016).
- **Create a plan.** Franklin created a plan for every day, following a similar schedule because he believed in the benefits of routine and healthy habits.
- **Schedule time to learn.** Franklin scheduled time to learn by getting up early in the morning and reading and writing for at least an hour, sometimes reading all night so that he could return a borrowed book.
- **Incorporate experiential learning when possible.** Franklin turned his concepts and hypotheses into experiments.
- **Reflect on what you're learning.** Franklin reflected on each day, asking, "What good have I done today?"
- **Balance your life and include rest and fun.** Franklin enjoyed laughter and leisure time with friends and family, including a two-hour lunch every day, although he did not allow it to take over time for learning.

LIFELONG LEARNING AND YOUR ORGANIZATION

According to the Association of Talent Development (ATD), lifelong learning is the "self-motivated, ongoing pursuit of knowledge for personal or professional reasons. It may occur formally or informally, intentionally, or incidentally." Lifelong learning is also known as continuous learning, agile learning, or learning drive. Lifelong learners are self-motivated, have insatiable curiosity, and practice intelligent risk taking. They continually seek knowledge and are open to learning new skills.

Lifelong learning is associated with two learning theories: cognitivism and constructivism. Cognitivism addresses the learning that occurs when you make sense of the relationship between what you know and what you are learning. Constructivism, on the other hand, proposes that learning comes from many sources, including life experiences, and that what you learn is dependent on your traits and how you internalize what you have learned.

Your organization is likely interested in lifelong learning not from a theoretical angle but from a much more practical perspective. Think about it. Your organization must keep up with the technology, economic, geographic, political, and demographic changes it is facing. It must be an agile organization. It comes as no surprise, then, that its employees must also be agile to support the organization. The organization is learning new things, so employees must also learn new things. Lifelong learning is a critical skill for organizations because learning and agility are the keys to remaining competitive.

An organization that values learning and hires employees who value continuous learning has a strong future. In return, learning organizations that help their employees shape the future directions of their careers encourage engagement. Today's organizations expect that employees will be accountable for their own development and that they will seek the support and resources they need.

Are you an employee who values lifelong learning? If so, you aren't alone. Recent research shows that employees want opportunities to learn and grow at work. They want their managers to coach them and to value them as both people and employees, and to help them understand and build their strengths (Gallup 2016). As a skilled employee you want to learn and gain skills to be more valuable to your organization. That is possible as a lifelong learner. You know that you have responsibility for meeting your development needs. The first step is knowing what it takes to be a lifelong learner.

LIFELONG LEARNERS

Who are lifelong learners? ATD's lifelong-learning research shows that organizations considered "high performers are more likely to make developing lifelong-learning behaviors a priority" (ATD 2018, 8). Actually, if the rate of change continues to accelerate, every employee will need to be a lifelong learner. According to the study, lifelong learners

- view learning as an exciting opportunity,
- are self-motivated,
- are self-aware and know their own interests,
- are open-minded,
- have an insatiable curiosity.

Are you a lifelong learner? You may be, but just haven't acknowledged it yet. Most of us learn for personal or professional development, but the two may not be distinctly different since developing personally can also improve your professional knowledge and skills, and vice versa. Besides, there doesn't need to be a reason to learn, since learning for the sake of learning can be a rewarding experience. When you read Franklin's story, you get a keen sense of that—Franklin loved to learn.

ADVANTAGES OF LIFELONG LEARNING

You are the key benefactor of lifelong learning, with advantages that span both your personal life and your professional life. Think of how you benefit personally first. Learning increases your confidence and self-esteem. It improves your quality of life and ensures a more satisfying life with your family and friends. It helps you be more flexible and increases your interpersonal and communication skills. It encourages your creativity and innovation and challenges your beliefs and opinions.

You benefit professionally by increasing your adaptability to change. If you are like most employees, you want to learn, develop, and grow. A culture of lifelong learning enhances your understanding of the world around you and your organization. It increases your readiness for opportunities. For employees, successful job performance is related to an individual's desire to learn. Lifelong learning will certainly improve your performance and your professional demeanor. It improves both your satisfaction with your work and your engagement level. Continuous learning will increase your opportunities for career advancement and will make it less likely that you will derail (see Challenge 2) from your career.

Although you and your colleagues may seem to benefit the most from lifelong learning, your organization also gains value from investing in a culture that supports lifelong learning. For example, employers want employees who can solve problems, communicate clearly, think critically, and collaborate with others; these skills are often a result of self-aware employees who are open to learning. ATD's (2018, 19) lifelong-learning research showed that the top five benefits to the organization include improved

- employee engagement levels,
- overall organizational performance,
- ability to retain talent,
- ability to meet changing business needs and objectives,
- business competitive ability.

Learning organizations are places "where people continually expand their capacity to create the results they truly desire, where new and expansive patterns of thinking are nurtured, where collective aspiration is set free, and where people are continually learning how to learn together" (Senge 2006, 3). *Harvard Business Review* describes the advantages of a learning organization as "improved innovation, agility, and organizational learning" (Groysberg et al. 2018, 49). Lifelong learning benefits you and your colleagues as well as delivers value to your organization.

PRACTICE LIFELONG LEARNING

Take a moment to think about all that you know and all that you still want to learn. I get exhausted just thinking about everything I need to know to do my job. This is what makes my work so exciting, but this sense is also what necessitates that each of us becomes a lifelong learner. Who determines whether you know enough? Know the right things? What you still should learn? Well it's you, of course. Lifelong learning isn't new—as Franklin showed us. What's new is the emphasis it is receiving in today's business environment.

I once read that most people achieve only a third of their potential. Successful professionals in any position achieve much more than a third of their potential because they continue to learn and develop. What do lifelong learners do?

- Lifelong learners assess where they are compared with where they want to be and determine a plan to get there.
- They improve their processes continuously. They identify new ways that are better and more efficient and implement them.
- They are on the cutting edge of their industries. They are aware of state-of-the-art practices as well as the fads of the day. They have knowledge of their professional organizations' journals and newsletters that helps keep them abreast of developments in the field.
- They understand the basics of the job and how to implement them in today's world.
- They ask questions and experiment to try new things.
- They seek resources, read, and apply their new knowledge.
- They share knowledge and teach others.
- They are in the know about their customers (internal and external) and keep up to date with all the things that are important to them.

Ask yourself how you stack up against these things that lifelong learners do. Remember, lifelong learning is an investment in you. If you won't invest in you, who will? Lifelong learning relies on your mindset, determination, and curiosity.

Yes, it takes a great deal to be your best: competencies, confidence, commitment. You can do it. Be all the things that you are capable of being. Thomas Edison once said, "If we did all the things we are capable of, we would literally astound ourselves." Go ahead. What's stopping you? Astound yourself. Find the passion in your life. Then learn all you can. Love what you do and do what you love.

DABBLE FIRST

Not sure you want to jump into this lifelong learning thing? Wondering what you might like to learn? If you want to experiment with learning opportunities to upgrade your knowledge and skills, try a couple of these examples for starting your lifelong learning:

- **Fulfill a dream.** Think back to your childhood dream. What did you want to be? Have you achieved your goal? It's never too late. Make a list of all the things you would like to learn—professionally and personally.

- **Go virtual.** Attend virtual learning events. Hundreds of virtual learning opportunities are available: both those that have a fee and those that are free. Try one out. You will probably learn something that you can use to help your next customer.

- **Attend a conference.** Everyone should attend at least one conference every year. You will learn a great deal and meet many people with whom you can create a valuable network. As much learning occurs in the hallways as it does in the education sessions.

- **Expand your network.** Network with others inside and outside your organization. You'll call on them when you have questions.

- **Start a podcast habit.** While driving to work or on a walk, listen to a podcast on an interesting topic.

- **Find a mentor.** Talk to a mentor or a coach to learn how they can help you.

- **Volunteer.** Identify a nonprofit, civic group, or school that could use help. You will learn in these situations, and it will look great on your résumé.

- **Take a class.** Enroll in a course that interests you. Check your training department for suggestions. Classes may be facilitated by your organization or by external vendors.

- **Try it out.** Experiment with tools and techniques you haven't used before. Ask your colleagues for suggestions.

Although dabbling isn't the systematic process I recommend you stay with to refine your skills for achieving career goals, it is a way to move into the learning mode. It will give you a chance to experience how enjoyable learning can be.

SKILLS THAT SUPPORT AGILE LIFELONG LEARNERS

Probably the most practical issue you should consider is how you can learn while you earn. That is, how can you learn from the experiences you have on a daily basis, and then how can you augment what you learn on the job? It requires an agile learner. According to George Hallenbeck (2016, 6), "Learning agile individuals are distinguished by their willingness and ability to learn from experience." But he stresses that they must also excel at applying what they learn. You need to apply what you learn before you can be certain that something was really learned. Learning agility can focus on a dozen different things. Individual learning agility can be viewed as four specific sets of behaviors:

- **Seeking skills**, or having the willingness to be immersed in new and challenging situations, include your ability to identify the boundaries of your comfort zone, risk-taking skills, and skills to expand your network.

- **Sensemaking skills** help you learn from experience by asking why, how, and why-not questions and include your ability to identify learning opportunities, to question your own beliefs and perspectives, and to prepare mentally and physically for learning.

- **Internalizing skills** require you to take time to reflect and to seek feedback and include your ability to reflect on and monitor your progress, your capacity to pursue and act on feedback, and your ability to identify experiences that promote self-awareness.

- **Applying skills** combine what was learned with past experiences and apply it to new challenging experiences. This is your ability to measure progress, to identify connections and consistencies, and to apply learning in planned and spontaneous situations (Hallenbeck 2016).

LEARNING OPPORTUNITIES

So where do these learning opportunities come from? Check around your organization and you will find learning options that fall into at least these four categories. You will explore these categories more fully in Steps 2 through 4:

- **On the job,** such as accessing online tutorials, job shadowing, or completing a job rotation.

- **Participating in courses, training programs, or certifications,** including taking an online course, attending an in-person learning event, or attaining a certification.

- **Informal daily options,** such as joining a managers' networking group, mentoring an intern, or conducting research on a future project.

- **Learning outside the organization,** which includes volunteering, speaking at a conference, or participating in an executive exchange.

Networking should also be called out as a unique learning opportunity for you. Networking takes place in many forms and in many places. Consider your needs for networking. Networks can be inside or outside your organization and can serve many purposes. To be effective, networks need to be developed, maintained, and leveraged. Networking requires an attitude of generosity—giving and helping first. Offer to support or build networks inside your organization and beyond. You can support your colleagues by introducing them to your network. You'll find more information about networking in Step 3.

 LEARNING TACTICS TO ENHANCE LEARNING FROM EXPERIENCE

Learning from challenging job experiences is essential for development. You can maximize your learning if the learning experience employs a variety of learning tactics (Dalton 2014). Most of us favor one or two learning tactics. You will learn more if you broaden the way you learn. As you think about how you learn, consider employing different tactics to enhance and expand your learning.

Learning tactics can be arranged in four categories. Here's a brief explanation and a list of strategies for each. Once you decide which one or two tactics you use least often, select one of the strategies listed under it and practice with it soon. A best practice for learning is to reflect on what happened and why. Reflect personally and also share your thoughts with someone else to hear another perspective.

Feeling Tactics are used by individuals who need to manage anxiety and uncertainty of new learning.

- ☐ Recall times when you were successful, even if you were uncomfortable.
- ☐ Pay attention when you feel frustrated in a situation; identify the source.
- ☐ Keep a journal and track your feelings when they interfere with learning.

Action Tactics are used by individuals who learn by doing.

- ☐ Commit to making something you've been procrastinating about happen this week.
- ☐ Take on a project with a tight schedule.
- ☐ Teach someone else a skill.

Thinking Tactics are used by those who prefer to work things out by themselves.

- ☐ Ask yourself what lessons you learned this week and list them.
- ☐ Look for patterns in similar situations and note where you have seen these before.
- ☐ Keep a journal to track progress on learning a skill.

Accessing Others' Tactics are used by those who like to seek advice, examples, or support.

- ☐ Find someone who will give you insight on a problem area in your life.

> ☐ Don't assume that your idea is the best one—obtain input from others.
>
> ☐ Pick a role model for a particular skill that you value, and observe and interview the person.

READY TO BECOME A LIFELONG LEARNER?

Lifelong learners are self-aware, have a desire to learn, are curious, and are willing to be vulnerable. Are you? Step back and take stock of where you are and where you want to be. Determine some measure of success, drive a stake in the ground, and head for it. You can establish measures that include both knowledge and skills. Next, identify a developmental plan for continued growth—even consider certification or returning to school. You'll learn how to do this in the next couple of chapters.

For now, let's look at actions that will support your learning plan. Let's walk through some possibilities that can serve as a foundation for your learning.

BUILD CONFIDENCE

Confident people have an aura about them that makes others want to be a part of what they are doing. They are admired by and inspire confidence in others. According to the Mayo Clinic, low self-esteem impacts almost every aspect of our lives (Neff, Hsieh, and Dejitterat 2005). I am certainly no confidence expert, but here are thoughts that are helpful to me: Think of self-confidence as something you can develop if you practice every day. It starts with being knowledgeable about your profession. Confidence is a great foundation and nothing builds confidence like knowing your stuff.

MIND YOUR MINDSET

Your mindset goes beyond the attitude you have toward your job, your organization, and the changes occurring around you. Face each day with a positive attitude, make and keep commitments, be authentic and approachable, and look out for your colleagues. This mindset brings out the best in you and those around you. Your expertise will shine through with a positive mindset that believes in the importance of what you do.

Lifelong learning requires a growth mindset, or the belief that people are able to increase their talent and ability through curiosity and learning. The growth mindset concept was pioneered by Carol Dweck (2013). Her research shows that employees with a growth mindset have a desire to learn and a tendency to embrace change, learn from criticism, and find inspiration in the success of others.

A report by McKinsey & Company (Brassey, Coates, and van Dam 2019) identifies seven mindset practices that can help you become a lifelong learner:

1. **Focus on growth** by ensuring you have a growth mindset as defined by Dweck. You must believe that there are no limitations to what you can learn.

2. **Become a serial master** by achieving mastery in several topics. As the world changes faster and people work later into life, you should develop different areas of expertise to retain relevancy.

3. **Stretch** outside your comfort zone to try new tasks, acquire new knowledge, and develop new skills.

4. **Build a personal brand and network** by understanding what skills you need, setting goals, understanding what you want to be known for, and building your network. Identify what differentiates you and prepares you for new opportunities.

5. **Own your personal development journey** by creating learning goals, measuring progress, working with mentors, seeking feedback, and making an investment. Explore which skills you require to take control of your own development.

6. **Discover** *ikigai* (Japanese for "the reason for being") and explore the four elements for your aligned future focus by discussing the intersection of doing what you love, what the world needs, what you are good at, and what you can be paid to do.

7. **Stay vital,** which requires you to make staying healthy a priority, including decisions about sleep, exercise, eating, meditation, and practicing a positive attitude.

PREPARE EARLY

Lifelong learning will help you plan for the future. Develop your skills and knowledge to maintain your place on the cutting edge. Staying in touch with the changes in and the excitement of your organization will keep you enthusiastic and passionate about what you do. We live in exciting times and changes are happening rapidly. This makes your job challenging and exciting. What can you do now to prepare for the future?

- Recognize that your development is your responsibility.
- Create an individual development plan (IDP) that is linked to your organization's strategy (Step 3).
- Build a professional learning network using social networks such as LinkedIn, Facebook, Twitter, and others.
- Participate in massive open online courses, commonly called MOOCs, or other virtual learning to get experience.
- Take an active role in an online community—perhaps become a community manager.
- Invest time to reflect on the work you do and what you need to start learning.

DEMONSTRATE COMMITMENT

Commitment is a pledge that binds you to completing an action or reaching a goal. Whether in your professional life or your personal life, it is a fundamental principle of success. Think of a commitment you've made. If you were totally committed, it may have been difficult. You may be wondering what kind of commitment you will need to make in this situation. It can go way beyond this chapter, but perhaps you can begin with a commitment to your organization, your profession, or to your own lifelong learning.

LEARN TO LEARN

Most organizations today are in a constant sea of change. Change from technology, customer expectations, new business models, consolidations, new service models, global competition, and a host of other changes force organizations to learn and change large systems with unimaginable speed. Arie de Geus, a business theorist, states, "The ability to learn faster than your competitors may be the only sustainable competitive advantage" (Senge 2006, 236). Employees who learn and grow at the same rate that their companies require are viewed as most valuable. This calls for employees who know how to learn. These four attributes have been found to put you in the right framework for learning:

- **Aspiration:** Focus on the positive aspects of learning something; eliminate the negative excuses for not learning.
- **Self-awareness:** Focus on the ability to see all that needs to be learned, instead of thinking that the skill and knowledge have already been accomplished.
- **Curiosity:** Focus on why the new content is interesting, as opposed to seeing it as boring.
- **Vulnerability:** Accept that mistakes are normal when learning, instead of thinking how poorly you are performing.

What can you do to enhance your aspiration, self-awareness, curiosity, or vulnerability?

UPHOLD YOUR ORGANIZATION

What does your organization need, and how can you support it? Your commitment starts with learning what's most important to your organization and how you can help. Begin by obtaining copies of your organization's strategic plan and business plan. Read through them and tie what you do to these two plans. Identify your contribution to your organization's success. What could you do better? What do you need to learn so that you can do a better job? Go the extra mile and get copies for your colleagues and create a dialogue at your next staff meeting about how your department could do more to contribute to the organization's success.

EMPLOYEES ARE ACCOUNTABLE FOR THEIR OWN DEVELOPMENT

All organizations support their employees' lifelong learning differently. Check with your supervisor or your organization's talent development department to determine what learning support is available to you and what you need to do. Tap into all the contacts you learn about; sometimes one department may not be aware of what another offers. You want to be informed of all your options. Explore your own learning environment that will encourage you to take accountability for your learning.

As you become more autonomous in determining the direction of your career, you will see that learning is a strategic enabler for you, your colleagues, and your organization. As a result, you will continue to see the value in becoming a lifelong learner. Remember to tie your learning to your organization's needs. This way it becomes a win-win for both you and your organization. In addition, your organization is more likely to go out of its way to provide you with the learning experience you need. Always ask for what you need (supported by the facts of how it aligns with your organization's goals). If you don't ask for what you need and want, the answer will always be no.

BARRIERS TO LIFELONG LEARNING

Obstacles may prevent your lifelong learning. The most common barrier is a personal lack of motivation for nonrequired learning. Related is that employees don't know how to self-direct their learning. The book that you are holding covers everything you need to know about self-directed learning. Both of these are your responsibilities. You can ensure that neither prevents you from being a lifelong learner.

Another common barrier is the organizational culture. If the culture does not support lifelong learning and your leaders are not modeling lifelong learning, it will be difficult to encourage employees to become lifelong learners. Again, this one is in your hands. If you are passionate about learning, like Franklin, you can set your own goals and your own pace to achieve anything that you want. Your future really is your decision.

What sets you apart from your colleagues? Behaviors, skills, and actions that you might not expect. Being an expert, a consummate professional, goes way beyond completing a project on time or being a good team player. As you read the rest of this book, you will learn about the skills required of an admired employee and the character you'll want to build to demonstrate your value as an employee. This book will offer you ideas of what you need to know and do to begin your journey to your preferred future.

Questions to Ponder

? How can you evaluate the skills and knowledge you have and compare them with what you still need?

? How might you invest in you—your skills, your knowledge, and your mindset—to better address your important role for your company or your client?

? How can you identify the skills required for building a trusted partnership with the managers in your organization?

? How can you do a better job of paying attention to what your department really needs?

? How can you be aware of your customers' changing needs and adapt to meet their needs?

? What do you need to do to be a lifelong learner?

Reading for the Final Stretch

→ *Learning Agility: Unlock the Lessons of Experience*, by George Hallenbeck

→ *Atomic Habits: An Easy and Proven Way to Build Good Habits and Break Bad Ones*, by James Clear

Unless you try to do something beyond what you have already mastered, you will never grow.

—RALPH WALDO EMERSON

STEP 2

Find the Right Career Path

What do you want to be when you grow up? Seriously! How would you like to spend the rest of your life? Ronda Davis, training manager at Tyler Technologies, describes herself as a techie who loves computers and technology. Her career began as a web application developer, writing code in programming languages and working with databases, and she never questioned her career choice.

To keep up with the ever-changing technology landscape, she joined a professional group, the Carolina Information Technology Professionals Group. During one of the meetings an officer announced that they needed a volunteer to teach a website design course at a local high school. It was challenging because the students had an opportunity to receive scholarships and internship opportunities by completing technical training for building computers, creating websites, and developing video games.

Her first thought was, *I develop website applications for a living. How hard could this challenge be?* She accepted the challenge and after teaching website design to 30 high schoolers for 12 weeks, she was hooked and wanted to switch careers. She wanted to teach adults. This volunteer opportunity uncovered her love of sharing technology with others. Along her journey into a talent development career she learned several lessons. She shares with you here what she learned on her path.

Lesson 1: Learn what you need to learn. You have to discover what you need to know, and this can be the most daunting step. After all, how do you know what you need to know if you do not know what you need to know? Ask yourself: What are the requirements of the role I hope to achieve? What knowledge, skills, and experience are required? What certifications are recommended?

Lesson 2: Connect with others. Regardless of the type of environment, it is beneficial to connect with others to continue learning, discover best practices, and find others who face similar challenges. Join professional groups for development and look for opportunities to connect with others in the industry. Participate in LinkedIn groups. Networking works!

Lesson 3: Accept opportunities. As you branch out, you may discover opportunities where you can contribute. Look for volunteer opportunities or other places where your skills would add value. Find opportunities where you can build experience and gain credibility for your accomplishments.

Lesson 4: Expand beyond. As you take on opportunities and learn on your own, do not be afraid to try new and different experiences, even ones that you may normally not consider. I took a 200-hour yoga teacher training course in 2014, and today I am a registered yoga teacher. Discover your area of expertise and how you can add value to others. Find what makes you unique!

Lesson 5: Keep learning! Set learning goals to propel your career forward. Follow blogs, take online classes, or present at conferences. While I enjoy sharing what I know, I learn much more from the conversations with participants during and after my presentations.

WHY PLAN YOUR CAREER?

Ronda's passion shows through, and it was all because she volunteered for a challenge that took her out of her comfort zone. You don't have to wait for a serendipitous event as Ronda did to find your passion. This chapter will help you begin to set a career path that is right for you. You will encounter Ronda's lessons throughout this book as you work through your own career plan. There are at least three reasons why you should begin to focus on your career.

Be prepared. Experts say that those of you who are entering the job market will make numerous career changes (not just jobs) during your lifetime of employment. This means that you need to stay on top of your career and be a part of planning where you go and what you do. It's important to gain new perspectives, knowledge, and skills that build on each other as the future or world changes.

Do what you love. Most of us spend 40–60 hours every week at work, which is about 2500 hours every year. That's a lot of time! To invest that much of yourself, you should enjoy your job and your chosen career. Taking time to deliberately plan your future can help you discover what you have passion for, which makes you more likely to succeed as you become more valuable to your current employer and those in the future.

Invest in yourself. We all need to be lifelong learners. You can do this by seeking out ways to stay informed of changes, new technology, and improved ways of doing business. You may be today's expert but can easily fall behind if you fail to keep up. Stay on top of what is happening in your field, invest in learning so that you are prepared for your next position, and become a lifelong learner.

TAKE CONTROL OF YOUR CAREER

No one cares more about your career than you do. Whether you are employed full time, are self-employed, have a part-time job, or are a member of the gig community, you need to take control of your career. No one else can manage your career, because only you know what you want. Oh, yes, you should definitely tap others for ideas, feedback, and recommendations, but only you will have the final say about what you want to do. College advisers, friends, career coaches, your supervisor, and the HR staff can provide guidance. But guidance is only something for you to think about. It is not a career plan. That's up to you.

You need to do some focused work on your career. Your work should energize and excite you. That means you need to clearly understand what excites and energizes you. What gives your life meaning? Once you know what you value, you need to explore your options. Don't think you are stuck climbing the typical career ladder. That is so 20th century. You shouldn't even stop at thinking your career is a job with a traditional company. How about starting your own business? Starting a side hustle? Subcontracting or freelancing? Your passion and understanding your desires will guide you. I'm not suggesting you should risk it all, but don't be afraid to try. Even if you fail, you will learn a lot and be better for trying. Finally, never stop learning and improving. I have to believe that's why you are reading this book right now. So let's get on with it.

What Do I Want to Be?

Lifelong learning is important to both you and your organization. Organizations are changing dramatically, which means that employees require new skill sets and knowledge. To flourish, you must be in a continuous learning mode. When you become a lifelong learner, you will be prepared for and thrive in the future no matter what comes your way. You will need to take ownership of your learning by knowing how to assess what you want to do, identify developmental needs, set goals, plan your strategy, select a diverse range of learning opportunities to support your career, and develop your career plan.

This chapter addresses ways to determine what you want to do and helps you set potential goals to achieve your intention. You will clarify the "potential" goals in a future chapter. In the meantime you will want to do some exploring.

Figuring out where you would like to take your career is an important step. If you already know what you want to do and have your dream career, you can breeze through this section. If that is the case, I imagine that you are reading this book to emphasize developing the skills that will increase your potential for more responsibility and future promotions.

The people who are happiest in their jobs have alignment: Their values are aligned with the organization's mission and values. They find meaning in what they do. They are engaged at work. Usually this occurs when individuals have a chance to use their strengths to do work that they like. What you like to do is not what I like to do. That's fortunate because we each have unique jobs that should match our preferences. Before we go too far, there are two clear messages that you need to internalize:

1. You will never find a job that is void of things that you don't like to do. You should like 80 percent of what you do on the job. And yes, you will still need to do the other 20 percent.

2. You are not free to develop only your strengths. Nope! No way! No matter what you heard someone say at a conference. Everyone has weaknesses, and your organization expects you to improve. It is paying you to tap into your strengths and to improve your weaknesses.

So if you are not currently working in your dream job, you are at one of many places in your career. Perhaps you've recently graduated and took a job because it was available, but it isn't a fit. Perhaps you have been in your career for a while and you want to switch to another career you've experienced as a volunteer or during a rotation in your organization. Perhaps you don't like what you are doing, but you have no idea what you want to do. Or perhaps you are facing a dozen other uncertainties. This chapter will be helpful to each of you, but in different ways. The goal is to provide resources, activities, and questions so that you can ponder what you'd like to do.

Identifying the Best You

Finding your mission, purpose, passion, perfect career, good-fit profession—heck, just finding a job you like! Must it be so difficult? No. Let's begin by figuring out what purpose or a good fit means to you. We'll review your past thoughts, what you enjoy doing, available career support, and assessments and tools for understanding yourself better, as well as several exercises.

What Do You Like to Do?

This messy exercise puts everything in a pile and then asks you to sort through it all. You can incorporate results from similar, previously performed exercises. Let's get it all out.

- First review any documentation you've completed about your personal vision and mission or perhaps you've identified your life's purpose. At some point you probably listed the values that were the most meaningful to you. You may have identified your brand or wrote a value proposition or even crafted a career story. Pull out all of those musings and reread them. If you haven't completed your personal core values, turn to the activity at https://ideas .bkconnection.com/skillsforcareersuccess and complete it. Highlight up to 10 values that are the most meaningful to you.

- Think back to everything you've done in the past few years: jobs, volunteer work, activities, family events, and special projects. List all of the tasks and responsibilities, separating them into two categories: what you liked and what you disliked about each. What themes seem to pop out? Highlight them.

- Make a list of all the things you are passionate about—or at least like: people characteristics, job activities, geographical descriptions, working conditions, responsibilities, hobbies you have, topics that interest you, books that you've read, people you follow on social media, podcasts you listen to, and what you do in your spare time. Now review that list and highlight up to 10 of your favorite things. What themes pop out? Are some words listed in more than one category?

- What legacy do you want to leave? How will the world be better because you lived here?

Now pull it all together. What five or six things seem to repeat themselves? What does that say about your purpose in life or your career passion? I decided when I turned 30 it was time to figure out what I wanted to be when I grew up. I completed exercises like those listed here. The theme that emerged for me was that I loved and was good at organizing. I also liked to write and read and didn't want a boss. That doesn't seem like much of a plan. But it was enough to focus on as I returned to college as an adult. The same will happen to you. If nothing seems to fit together, keep your notes. Two things will likely happen. First, you will begin to see connections, and second, you will create unexpected meaning out of it all.

Multiple Routes to Success

Many options are available to you. Don't close the door on any until you explore them. Your ability to create your own sustainable career path depends on how you view the changing world and how you view your options. There are endless possibilities if you are willing to reinvent yourself. If you already have a job, you could try one of these:

- Blend your skills for your current job with skills from other jobs or industries and create a new job or position. It happens every day.

- Move horizontally to another department.

- Retrofit your current job by adding new skills. If you are staying within your company but your job is being phased out, watch for how other jobs and positions are being redefined. Can you combine those skills with what you do now to create a new job?

- Find a solution that can be used to solve key problems, then invent the job that will solve it.

- Remain in your field and identify a different job.

The Good and the Bad

Identify your three greatest strengths and your three greatest weaknesses. Describe your ideal job. How do the three align? How do your strengths support your ideal job? How would your weaknesses have to be developed for your ideal job?

Three Questions to Ask Yourself

1. What am I good at, and what are those skills and talents?
2. What would someone pay me to do?
3. What do I have passion for and love to do?

Draw a Venn diagram of the three topics: talent, pay, and passion. Your purpose may be found where those three overlap.

Tools for You

Several categories of support are available for your career exploration: career support, personality assessments, and skills and strengths indicators. You can also gain information by conducting a strengths, weaknesses, opportunities, threats (SWOT) analysis.

Career support. Assessment tools, interviews, instruments, and counseling are all available to help you develop career plans. Resources and tools available to you for career exploration opportunities include:

- Online databases: industry websites, a national repository of occupational information—for example, the U.S. Department of Labor's O*NET

- In person: industry showcases, campus events

- Networks: interview people in the field or related to your industry or profession

- Professional publications

- Career counselor professionals

- Competency models for specific professions

- Occupation profiles, salary finders, skills matchers, and assessments

You may wish to tap into some of these to gain more information or to explore other options.

Personality assessments. If you are interested in understanding yourself better or getting another perspective on what your personality type might like to do, one of these instruments might illuminate other possibilities:

- DiSC (www.discprofile.com/what-is-disc/historyof-disc)

- Myers-Briggs Type Indicator (MBTI) (www.myersbriggs.org/my -mbti-personality-type/take-the-mbti-instrument)

- Keirsey Temperament Sorter (www.keirsey.com/default.aspx)

- Strong Interest Inventory (www.discoveryourpersonality.com /stronginterestinventorycareertest.html)

- Career Leader (www.careerleader.com/individuals.html)

- Interest Profiler (www.onetcenter.org/IP.html?p=3)

Skills and strengths indicators. Numerous resources are available to identify your skills and strengths. Depending on your needs, each of these will add information to what you have already uncovered about your passions and purpose:

- The O*NET Skills Search portal is a free tool that can help you understand what skills are best suited to which careers (www.onetonline.org/skills).

- StrengthsFinder 2.0 is the new version of the book *Now, Discover Your Strengths*. It is a comprehensive guide to hundreds of different strengths that an individual can possess (http://strengths.gallup.com).

- MindTools is a comprehensive career skills website that includes many resources about different skills, as well as a free career skills newsletter. Its comprehensive 15-question assessment evaluates your skill set in five different areas (www.mindtools.com).

- The MAPP career assessment is a 15-minute test that matches you with careers that fit your skills and strengths profile. In addition, the MAPP website also features a variety of resources to help get you started on your career planning journey (www.assessment.com).

- VIA Survey of Character Strengths is a 15-minute self-assessment that is based on Martin Seligman's research on happiness (www.viacharacter.org/www/Character-Strengths-Survey).

- The World of Work Map is an American College Testing (ACT) resource that links interests with various career fields (www.act.org/content/act/en/education-and-career-planning.html).

SWOT analysis. Perhaps you've used SWOT to explore projects or for strategic planning. Well, it works to provide insight as you narrow down a desired career too. For example, a strength may be that you are well organized, and a weakness may be that you have limited management experience. An opportunity may be that you have chosen a growth industry, and a threat may be recent budget cuts. You will find a SWOT worksheet at https://ideas.bkconnection.com/skillsforcareersuccess.

BUT LIFE ISN'T ALL WORK

You are not your career. You are not the work you do. But the work should add value to your life. Most of us spend our time in eight general categories of life. They are not equally important, nor should you think that you should spend an equal amount of time on each. You should make a conscious decision about what balancing life and work means. The eight categories that most people consider a part of a balanced life include:

- Fun—vacations, hobbies, pleasure reading, travel
- Relationships—friends, current or future life partner
- Career—job satisfaction, work, career path, education
- Family—children, parents, relatives
- Social—sports, activities, clubs
- Health—exercise, diet, vitamins
- Financial—savings, investments, home, retirement plan
- Creative—self-space, spiritual, artistic, community, sharing with others

As you are considering your future, you may want to weave some or all of these into your plan. Doing so will create a holistic approach to planning for your future. Use the "Balancing Career and Life Goals" worksheet found in part 4 of this book. If the categories listed do not work for you, change them to something more meaningful. You will find a printable graphic at https://ideas.bkconnection.com/skillsforcareersuccess to assist in your planning. What is most important is that you do not think only about your career while conducting your career planning. When thinking about your career and setting goals, consider other parts of your life—your whole life.

KEEP YOUR WORK SKILLS CURRENT BUT LOOK TO THE FUTURE

Before we dive into what you need to learn, take a look at the opportunities you have for learning right now, where you are, by simply looking at things from a different perspective. At the least, staying current ensures that you stay on top of change and new demands of your workplace. But in addition, you become more valuable to your employer because you will use your time effectively and build confidence with new tools or techniques. What can you do?

Have you taken advantage of the coaching offered by your manager? You've probably had career discussions (if not, set one up today) when your manager suggested that you could sharpen your skills. Think back: Have you turned down training opportunities? Have you been passed over for a promotion that went to someone with less experience? Have you turned down rotational opportunities to work in another department? All of these are hints that you might be falling behind your colleagues. Options to resolve your predicament can be found throughout this book. Which ones apply to you?

THINKING ABOUT CHANGING CAREERS?

Before you leave your current career, job, or organization, be sure you know why you want to change. Also, have a conversation with your manager. It is possible that your desires could lead to an interesting discussion with your manager. Sometimes supervisors don't tell their employees about future plans, and you might just be a part of a bigger plan. In addition, there may be another position in another department that matches your new career aspirations; it could be helpful if your manager knows about your interests. Even if you leave a job, company, or career, you should be clear about why. Make a list of why you are changing careers. Consider some of these:

- **Know what you want.** Be clear about the value you add and what you want that you don't have now. Interview others in the career you are considering. Ask what they like about the career but also learn more about the frustrations. Get more information before deciding on a career switch.

- **Find a way to test your prospective new career.** Could you try it out part time or during your vacation? Before you actually make the switch, is it possible to shadow someone in the position? If the career is within your current organization, is it possible to do a job rotation for a couple of months? Try before you buy.

- **Be confident and specific about the expertise you need.** Do you need a degree, certification, online classes? What do you need to learn, and how will you learn it? How much will it cost? When would you develop yourself?

- **Realize that you'll go backward before you go forward.** Be aware that your title and pay are not going to be at the level they are now. Are you willing to change your lifestyle? Again, do some research and recognize that as the newest entry into your chosen career you will probably start at the bottom.

- **Be prepared to invest time.** You will need time to learn about the career. You will need more time to build your network. You will need time to learn the tasks. You will need to find more time by getting up earlier, not watching television, or avoiding all but what's necessary on social media. The extra time needs to come from somewhere.

Changing careers is a big commitment. You should not be discouraged. Everyone should do what they have passion for. Just be realistic and don't take the change lightly.

NARROW DOWN YOUR DEVELOPMENT NEEDS

Review all of the activities you completed above. What does it say about your purpose or passion? You will next create development goals for skills that will support your passion. Creating goals for your development is important no matter where you are in your career:

- You may already be immersed in your desired career.
- You may have expected to be further along in your career than you are.
- You may want to switch careers but feel stuck.
- You already have your dream job but want to learn more or build skills.
- You have a dream job in your sights but need to figure out what you need to learn to reach it.

For any of these situations, your next step is to set goals for your development.

As you look at all the things you need to learn to reach your dream job or career, don't take on too much at once. If you are like most of us, you have probably received a wealth of information on potential areas for development from a feedback survey, formal or informal assessments, your colleagues' and supervisor's thoughts, and your own self-reflections. Hopefully you've narrowed down what you want to do, at least for the time being. At this point you should generate a list of your development needs.

SET POTENTIAL GOALS BASED ON YOUR DEVELOPMENT NEEDS

You use goals all the time. Goals focus time and energy and help ensure that your efforts result in the outcomes you want. You will create actionable goals to drive your development efforts. There are three kinds of goals you might use: behavioral goals, competency goals, and outcome goals. It's not important that you focus on the names of the goals; it is more important that you select the right strategy at the right time.

Use Behavioral Goals for Visible Change

A behavioral goal is aimed at changing a specific behavior. You will actually be able to see the change as it happens. For example, a goal to "stop interrupting others when they are talking to me" would be something that others could observe. People talking to you will notice that you interrupt them less until finally you stop doing it completely. You create a behavioral goal when changing a specific behavior will enhance your effectiveness. Usually this means that you have received very clear and specific feedback about something you do that others can see.

A behavioral goal may be a stepping-stone to further development. For example, you might set a goal to "speak up in meetings" as a stepping-stone to broader improvements of taking more initiative on the job. Behavioral goals should specify the time and place where the changed behavior will occur.

- "I will start every day by exchanging information with my colleagues."
- "In staff meetings I will add positive input and practical suggestions."

Use Competency Goals to Develop or Improve a Skill

A competency goal is aimed at creating or improving a related set of knowledge, skills, and attitudes. Competencies are broad areas of effectiveness such as "demonstrates business acumen" or "strategic thinking." Whereas a behavioral goal is specific and improvement is visible, a competency goal is broad, is pursued over a longer time frame, and includes the development of your knowledge, skills, and attitudes. Development may be invisible to others. You set competency goals when you identify needs in broad areas such as strategic thinking, decisiveness, interpersonal relationships, managing conflict, or managing time.

Competency goals prepare you to take on more responsibility and more complex jobs in the future, such as a specific job or promotion you desire. Due to their breadth and size, competency goals require patience, perseverance, and courage. Results may take time; you can invest a lot with little to show for it at first, but the results can be worth the effort. To make it more meaningful, write the goal with a label and an outcome that reminds you why the goal is important.

- "I will increase my attention to detail, which will minimize my tendency to let small tasks fall through the cracks."
- "I will enhance my political savvy, which will increase my working effectiveness with others."

Use Outcome Goals to Achieve a Specific Result

Behavioral goals are narrowly focused on visible behaviors. Competency goals are more broadly focused on sets of skills. Outcome goals can be the biggest, broadest, and most far-reaching of all. If your organization uses IDPs, they may appear as a short- or long-term goal. Outcome goals are most useful when you

- can describe the results you will have when you finish the goal,
- have a specific timeline in mind (which can be short or long),
- have your organization's commitment to the outcome.

A useful outcome goal is focused and specific. The danger in creating an outcome goal is that it may be too broad and describe some ideal set of outcomes, such as "a highly creative team" or "departments that collaborate smoothly" or "an organization that is a better place to work." These may be impressive—even needed—outcomes, but they are not effective outcome goals.

To make them more effective, assign a timeline to the goal. A time constraint defines how much can get done in the time allowed. You should also include milestones along the way that will tell you when and what progress will be made. Make your outcome goals more effective by including outcome measures, so that you'll know when the goal has been achieved. These outcome goals include a timeline, milestones, and an outcome measure:

- "By midyear, I will turn in 90 percent of all contracts on time by establishing an action list, assigning timelines for each project, and asking my supervisor for ways to work smarter."

- "Within one year I will feel ready to apply for a position at the next level by finishing my MBA and gaining skills my supervisor has identified."

DRAFT POTENTIAL GOALS

You are now ready to begin writing goals. You identified a focal area for your development. Now it is time to set specific, actionable goals that will drive your self-development in this area. Set three or four goals (fewer than three may not be challenging enough; more than four may be overwhelming). Depending on the nature of your improvement, your goals may be behavioral, competency, or outcome goals or a mix of all types. Think about it like this:

- **Behavioral:** What behaviors do I need to change? Or what new behaviors do I need to start doing?

- **Competency:** What skills and knowledge do I need to obtain? Or what shifts in my attitude or perspective need to happen?

- **Outcome:** What results(s) do I seek?

Next to each goal note how motivated you are to accomplish it, what the consequences will be, and how difficult it will be. If you have too many goals, this analysis may help you prioritize some over others. Play around with various ways of stating your goal until you get something that meets your needs and the criteria of the goal type you are setting. Once you have a satisfactory version, list your potential goals on an action plan or just a separate piece of paper. In the coming chapters you will get more clarity of these potential goals, identify strategies that will accomplish your goals, and establish a more thorough plan.

Questions to Ponder

? Have a private discussion with yourself. Do you love what you do—really love it? Do you jump out of bed on Monday morning and say, "Boy, did I miss you, job! I can't wait to see you again!" Think about your response. Do you love your job?

? Select a career buddy to discuss new ideas. Meet for lunch every week to work on your career plans. Who could you ask?

? Review career opportunities for employees in your organization. Some organizations have a dual career ladder path that allows upward mobility for employees who wish to stay in their technical area but without supervisory responsibilities. It's a good way to retain technical expertise. Is this something that interests you?

? What are you passionate about? What do you value the most? What dreams do you have for your future in five years? Ten years?

? Think back to your childhood dream. What did you want to be? Have you achieved your goal? It's never too late. Make a list of all the things you would like to learn—professionally and personally. Can you get in touch with that excited kid that's still inside you?

Reading for the Final Stretch

→ *Up Is Not the Only Way: Rethinking Career Mobility*, by Beverly Kaye and Lindy Williams

→ *Finding Your Element: How to Discover Your Talents and Passions and Transform Your Life*, by Ken Robinson

→ *What Color Is Your Parachute*, by Richard Bolles

→ *Man's Search for Meaning*, by Viktor Frankl

→ *Life's Great Question: Discover How You Contribute to the World*, by Tom Rath

Orville Wright didn't have a pilot's license.

—RICHARD TATE

Design Your Personal Development Plan

Each of you begins this chapter with your own realities. You may be looking for a different job. You may be considering staying with your current company but pursuing a different career. You may want to gain knowledge and skills so you can apply for a promotion. You may even be planning to join the gig economy and start your own business—or at least a side hustle. Whatever it is—up, over, or out—you need to have a plan. Your success requires one. Success will not appear based on a single event or luck. You need a plan to move you from where you are today to where you want to be in the future. It needs to be your plan.

Your personal success is within you. Only you can design your future and your personal development plan. You of course know Albert Einstein for his theory of general relativity, winning a Nobel Prize in physics in 1921, and devising the most recognized formula in the world, $E=mc^2$. But did you also know that his parents took him to a doctor because he was so late in talking? Did you know that as a child he rebelled against authority by throwing a chair at his instructor because he didn't like the instructor's style? Did you know that he was expelled from school and his parents were told "he would never amount to much"? Einstein's mother tutored him until he was allowed to return to school.

He was rejected for the Nobel Prize twice, and when he finally received it, it wasn't for his most important work, the theory of relativity. Instead, it was for his services to theoretical physics, and especially for his discovery of the law of the photoelectric effect. Einstein would not, as it turned out, ever win a Nobel Prize for his work on relativity and gravity, nor for anything other than the photoelectric effect. It didn't matter to him; he had his plan in place by then.

As you design your personal development plan, be sure to consider three things. First, don't let others' opinions of you today or in your past limit your desires of what you want to do. Second, don't let rejections prevent you from trying again. Third, remember one of my favorite quotes by George Eliot (pseudonym for Mary Ann Evans), "It's never too late to be what you might have been."

By this time you have assessed your skills, knowledge, traits, and experience. You should also have completed some foundational work by establishing a personal vision and mission. Hopefully you've conducted some work on your values. Perhaps you have feedback from a 360-degree multirater or a personality or career instrument. If so, you are ready to begin to put a plan together. It's time to start designing your personal development plan.

PLANNING FORMAT

Your plan could be in the form of an individual development plan (IDP), often using your organization's specific format. If so, you should be working with your supervisor, who will be there to support you. If your organization has an IDP format, it is probably in a digital format and connected with resources, courses, and how your organization defines its employee experience. If your organization does not have an IDP process, you can view a typical IDP in part 4 or download a copy at https://ideas.bkconnection.com/skillsforcareersuccess. If you are completing your career plan without the benefit of your organization or supervisor, you can create your plan using your favorite action plan format or the action plan at https://ideas.bkconnection.com/skillsforcareersuccess. Let's look at the plans in more detail.

IDP GUIDANCE FOR YOU

An IDP provides a blueprint for you and your organization since it records and tracks goals, identifies developmental strategies at a high level, and documents accomplishments. It generally identifies long- and short-term plans and provides an opportunity for supervisors to add their comments and support. It should emphasize opportunities to learn and grow and establishes performance goals and objectives. It ties your personal development to the organization's strategic goals.

The IDP provides a disciplined approach for thinking through your career goals, relating your development to your organization's long-term plans, and identifying specific actions for you to take. For you and your supervisor, a draft IDP is the basis for discussion and agreement on the plans for your development. Your development is a joint undertaking, and the IDP is a written plan reflecting your intention and your supervisor's intention for your career development. Like other plans, the IDP outlines objectives and planned milestones. It is a flexible guide that should be reviewed no less than semiannually and updated as necessary to reflect your current work situation and your organization's needs.

The IDP lists training, education, and development activities (formal and informal) that will help you develop the competencies needed to meet your goals. Once you know your performance goals and objectives, you begin the process of preparing an IDP. In most organizations, the basic process consists of three steps:

- Preparing the draft IDP
- Discussing your draft with your supervisor
- Finalizing your IDP

Preparing the Draft IDP

You should recognize that IDPs are intended to include far more than training and education courses and conference activities. In many instances, the most important learning activities are experiential in nature and include job rotations, developmental assignments, and special assignments. These assignments provide you with ways to learn new techniques or to perform different types of work. Opportunities may be individual efforts but are more often opportunities to participate or lead team projects, task forces, or special projects. These career-broadening on-the-job experiences are critical to your development.

Your responsibilities. To prepare, take these actions:

- Understand the requirements of and expectations for your development.

- Review your current position description and your performance appraisal.

- Understand the goals of your department and your organization's strategic plan.

- Conduct your self-assessment, including identifying your goals and competencies that require further development.

- Draft your proposed IDP online and submit it to your supervisor for discussion. Make the IDP as complete as possible. Include information about conferences, mandatory training, courses, vendors, dates, and costs.

- Assess potential longer-term needs and project training, education, and development activities for discussion with your supervisor.

Your supervisor's responsibilities. To prepare, your supervisor will take these actions:

- Review your performance appraisal to determine your development needs.

- Review your current position description to determine whether the position description is accurate and update if necessary. Identify training, education, and development needs.

- Determine any changes to your performance expectations in order to project training needs.

- Review other considerations (e.g., workload projections, known operational changes, employee history, uncompleted training requirements from previous years, mandatory training requirements, and corporate strategic considerations).

- Identify informal learning opportunities.

- Assess your potential for longer-term needs and project training, education, and development activities.
- Provide guidance to you.

Discussing Your Draft IDP with Your Supervisor

The discussion between you and your supervisor is essential. Your supervisor is responsible for providing you an environment where you can discuss your progress and your career plans, for initiating the discussion, and for identifying development opportunities.

A successful discussion includes:

- Mutual participation and understanding of the objectives for the new performance cycle. This is an opportunity to make sure both of you are on track regarding the developmental areas you will pursue.
- A review of specific performance, training, education, and development needs based on discussions of job responsibilities.
- A review of the draft IDP and agreement on the contents of the final IDP.

Finalizing Your IDP

Upon completion of your career development discussion with your supervisor, complete your IDP and submit it to your supervisor. After concurrence by your supervisor, the IDP is forwarded to the human resources department.

Your supervisor will identify and prioritize your training requirements. Although you are encouraged to suggest potential training opportunities, it is your supervisor's responsibility to formulate your training and development requirements and to assign priorities to the development requirements.

Timely completion and submission of your IDP will allow an integrated and systematic approach to the review of the organization's total training requirements. IDPs provide the foundation for establishing a consolidated and structured development program and budget to support training, education, and development activities.

Your IDP is for your organization. If your organization does not have an IDP process, you can create your own personal development plan or simply create your own action plan. Whether your organization uses IDPs or not, you will still want to identify strategies and your own action plan.

CHOOSE THE BEST STRATEGIES TO ACHIEVE YOUR GOALS

Whether you are using an IDP or your own personal development or action plan, one of the most useful things you can do is to identify strategies to reach your goals.

Having a clear and honest grasp of your needs for development and translating these into focused, achievable, important goals prepares you to take action. Begin thinking about the strategies you will employ to achieve your goals. Before you get too far down that road, however, it's time to bring some important other people into the process. This is vital, since the process of working on your goals and achieving them will involve others.

SEEK THE PERSPECTIVES OF OTHERS WHO CAN HELP YOU

Think about the people who will be involved in helping you focus on and achieve your goals and who will be affected by your self-development work. Your supervisor should be high on that list, as should your direct reports if you have any. Depending on the goals you have set, some of your peers may also make the list. Your goals may also bring family members into the picture.

Have a conversation about your goals. There are three main reasons for doing this. First, you can get another opinion on the goals you have chosen. Second, you can get ideas about strategies for pursuing your goals. Third, you can build support from others to help you as you work on your goals.

Since you will be talking with several people who may have different perspectives, you may hear differing, even contradictory, opinions. It is your task to sort through these different perspectives, make decisions about what to pay attention to, and use the differences to expand your vision of what you are about to do.

After talking with others about your goals and sorting through their reactions and input, you may find that you want to go back and revise one or more of your goal statements.

Your supervisor's perspective. Use this suggested agenda to structure your conversation with your supervisor:

- If your supervisor provided feedback on a survey, such as a 360-degree feedback survey, begin with a thank-you.

- Review your goals to make sure your supervisor is clear about what you will be pursuing.

- Reach a shared understanding of the benefits you, your team, and your organization will realize.

- Ask about resources that are available to you for working on your goals.

- Ask how your supervisor can support you as you work on your goals.

- Talk about receiving ongoing feedback from your supervisor.

- Create a set of check-in points and a timeline for completing your plan.

Take notes during your conversation and later go over your notes and record the key points for future reference.

Others' perspectives. Structure your conversations with peers, a coach, a trusted friend, or family members. These other people are likely to be less directly involved with or affected by your goals, which makes them potentially very helpful neutral observers. Here is a suggested agenda for talking with them:

- If they provided feedback on a survey, be sure to thank them.

- Describe your goals and ask for their reactions.

- Discuss how they might be affected as you pursue your goals.

- Ask them what concerns they have with your plan or whether they see any barriers.

- Talk about any ways they think they might be helpful or any ways they can support your efforts.

- Share your timeline for completion.

Once again, take notes and record the key points.

PLAN STRATEGIES TO ACHIEVE YOUR BEHAVIORAL GOALS

Recall that behavioral goals are observable by others and are the most precise and unambiguous. Other people can actually *see* the change in behavior as you make it, and you can measure your progress by tracking concrete actions. When you have achieved your goal, you will know it; however, this does not mean that changing your behavior will be easy. You cannot leave it to chance; you need to plan specific strategies to help you reach your behavioral goals:

- **Observe and model.** Think of someone who represents what you want to do, who is a role model. Observe that person modeling your desired new behavior. Modeling the behavior does not mean merely copying the behavior. You must make it your own as you practice it over time. This requires that you have some detailed understanding of what is involved in the behavior.

  > Observe details of the person's behavior; you need a detailed understanding of what makes the behavior desirable.

  > Make notes as you observe; this will help you remember details. What does the person do? How does the person do it? Where does the person do it? When does the person do it? Why does the person do it?

  > Identify three or four features of the behavior that are most important to you.

  > Identify times and places you plan to try out your new behavior.

- **Reward yourself.** Reward yourself for positive steps toward your goal. Determine what extrinsic and intrinsic rewards are meaningful to you. An extrinsic reward is something you treat yourself to, like a nice bottle of wine or a night out with your spouse or family. The key to making an extrinsic reward effective is timing. You must set a specific milestone to trigger the reward and then wait until the milestone is reached before giving yourself the reward. Intrinsic rewards include feelings of satisfaction, the warm glow of success, or the thrill of accomplishing something difficult.

> Identify the kind of extrinsic rewards you find meaningful: things and activities you value.

> Make a plan to stay motivated and decide on key milestones and achievements that deserve a reward.

- **Use social support.** Don't go it alone. Achieving your goals will be easier and more effective if you get other people involved. Even if your behavioral goal seems to be completely private, such as spending more time alone to reflect on the day's events, others will be affected by your change in behavior. When you change, others around you will notice and may have to change also.

  > Seek people who will listen even when you need to "vent." Ask whether they would be available from time to time to listen and talk.

  > Seek people who will be willing to give you feedback. Do they notice any change in your behavior? What effects are they noticing?

  > Consider asking someone to coach you. This should be someone you trust and respect so that you will be able to accept and make use of what they have to say.

PLAN STRATEGIES TO ACHIEVE YOUR COMPETENCY GOALS

A competency goal is a related set of knowledge, skills, and attitudes that is broader than a behavioral goal since it includes multiple behaviors. It also involves a longer time frame for achieving success. The strategies for behavioral goals also help you with competency goals. However, because a competency goal is broader and takes longer, you will need additional strategies for success:

- **Learn about the competency.** Entire books have been written about some major competencies: strategic thinking, effective delegation, influencing others, and resolving conflict are just a few examples of competencies. Entering the name of the competency you are pursuing in an online search engine will produce a wealth of resources for your consideration.

> Review this book for explanations and for resources.

> Ask others about books they can recommend for the competency. Consider reading more than one book since each book will have a particular point of view; it is helpful to get multiple points of view and create your own plan for success.

> Talk to experts. Identify someone you know who is especially skilled at the competency you are pursuing and schedule an interview. Ask what they consider to be key skills involved in the competency, how they developed their skills, and why the competency is important. Take notes.

> Learn about a competency by observing a role model. Ask yourself: What did I observe? What did I learn? What do I still need to learn? How do my observations influence my plan?

- **Develop skills and attain knowledge.** Start learning the skills and content you need. Certainly we all think about training as a way to learn and grow, but there are dozens of other ways to meet your developmental needs. How else can you grow and develop?

> Attend conferences.

> Explore online courses, recorded lectures, streaming documentaries, open source learning, online conferences and learning events, and education depositories.

> Ask your supervisor for developmental or stretch assignments.

> Ask to serve on a department or cross-functional team.

> Meet with your customers and learn more about what they do.

> Get a mentor; become a mentor. Both are learning experiences.

> Use a coach.

> Complete a rotational assignment. Rotations can occur inside or outside the organization; talk to your supervisor.

> Join a professional association or group to maintain your professional awareness.

> Study on your own. Read books or professional journals. Listen to books or podcasts while driving, especially while stuck in traffic.

> Teach or facilitate a class or workshop.

> Volunteer at a local nonprofit organization.

> Network with others in the organization, as well as those outside the organization.

- **Practice the competency.** As important as it is to learn about the competency you are pursuing, only practice will build the skills required to possess the competency.

  > Check the myriad practice options for many of the skills in this book.

  > Identify times and places in your current job where you can practice.

  > Practice new skills in settings outside the workplace, such as in volunteer organizations or during community events.

  > As your skill increases, look for additional opportunities to actually perform your new skill set. For example, taking on a task force or rotational assignment can provide you with a setting in which you can perform your new skills.

PLAN STRATEGIES TO ACHIEVE YOUR OUTCOME GOALS

Outcome goals are the biggest, broadest, and most far-reaching of all goal types. They are changes to improve overall performance. Outcome goals are complex, take time to achieve, and require good planning.

- **Get commitment from stakeholders.** Think of all the people who will be directly involved and who will have to make changes and adjustments in order for your outcome goal to be achieved. What will it take to get each of them committed to these changes? You'll need to tailor your influence tactics for each individual. Ask individuals what it will take to make the goal a reality. What changes and adjustments will *you* need to make? What will keep you motivated to stay on course?

- **Get an early win.** Because outcome goals take time to achieve, it is important to make visible progress early in the process. This focuses positive attention on the work and helps build momentum.

  > Identify components of the goal that can be put into action early on.

  > Plan how you can make the action visible to many, if not all, members of your stakeholder group.

  > Determine how you can parlay early wins to your advantage.

- **Monitor your progress.** An effective outcome goal by definition includes an outcome measure. Use your metrics to communicate to your stakeholders how things are going and to diagnose problems and make adjustments in your change efforts. Assuming things are going well, it is also appropriate to celebrate success!

  > Set up processes for getting the data needed to compare the progress of the work against the measures.

  > Establish milestones—key tasks or phases of work that indicate progress.

  > Track how well the processes you've put in place to achieve your outcome goal are working. For example, if you've set up weekly meetings as a way of coordinating work on a goal, do key people attend these meetings and do they find them useful?

Don't view your strategies and goals as a checklist to do and mark as completed. They are a part of the development process—one that should focus on the kinds of changes that excite you and lead you in the direction you have chosen and the career you want. Complete your strategies and achieve your goals. And along the way, constantly reevaluate whether you believe you are heading in the right direction. B. C. Forbes, founder of *Forbes* magazine, recommends that you "think not of yourself as the architect of your career, but as the sculptor. Expect to have to do a lot of hard hammering and chiseling and scraping and polishing" (Goodman 2016, 128).

DIVE DEEPER INTO SEVERAL STRATEGIES

You can learn from almost anything you do. If you have specific strategies you can shape actions around those strategies to gain knowledge, skills, practice, or experience. Let's consider two areas that may not be the first things you think about but can be meaningful and have results that extend beyond what you might initially consider: community service and networking.

Community service. Have you ever volunteered to support a nonprofit? Community service is work completed by a person or group of people that benefits others. It is often done near the area where you live, so your own community reaps the benefits of your work. You do not get paid to perform community service, but volunteer your time. Community service helps many groups: children, senior citizens, people with disabilities, even animals and the environment. There are numerous benefits to participating in community service, for you and others. It gives you a sense of satisfaction, helps improve your community, offers a way to meet new people, results in personal growth, and gives you a way to gain work experience and learn about other jobs.

If you select community service as a strategy, determine who you would like to help, whether you want it to be recurring or a onetime event, the kind of impact you would like to have, and what skill you would like to learn.

What could you do? General community service includes things like organizing a community blood drive, sending cards to soldiers serving overseas, reading books or letters to a person who is visually impaired, organizing an event or parade for Memorial Day, helping register people to vote, and helping deliver meals and gifts to patients at a local hospital.

Schools and youth programs need volunteers to tutor children during or after school, organize a Special Olympics event for teenagers, work at a summer camp for children who have lost a parent, coach a youth sports team, give music lessons to schoolchildren, serve as a teen crisis counselor, and organize a book drive for a school library.

Networking. Groups of people can help you develop in many forms and in many places. Networks can be inside or outside your organization and can serve many purposes. To be effective, networks need to be developed, maintained, and leveraged. Most important, your networking requires an attitude of generosity—giving and helping first.

You should build networks inside your organization and beyond. You can support members of your network by introducing them to others or sending them information that they can use. You can define informal networks that serve different purposes such as provide advice, help solve problems, enhance communication, or provide influence and credibility. You should have some networks that span department boundaries so that you are prepared to change positions, departments, and even locations.

Consider external networking. The obvious reason is to be prepared for other job opportunities. But other reasons exist too: obtaining fresh ideas to solve problems on the job, advancing your career, gaining new skills, raising your profile by being visible, and learning about best practices that could transfer to your job. Social media is also an integral part of your networking activities. Take time to determine your purpose for networking:

- Are you networking for personal or professional reasons?
- What problem are you trying to solve?
- What are your career aspirations?
- Where do you see yourself in three years?
- What skills, knowledge, or experience are you looking for?
- Where would you find this type of partner for networking?

Networking will be most valuable when you enter networking with authenticity, veracity, reliability, and willingness to find mutual value. You will reap personal and professional benefits. Personally it builds your self-esteem and confidence, expands your support network, encourages connections, develops personal relationships, and increases your visibility and recognition. Professionally you will increase your chances for promotion, gain professional skills and career advice, find more suitable jobs, and create a source to find answers to any question; it will also provide a place for you to express and discuss industry-related options and opinions.

Leveraging networking with integrity. Sometimes new networkers build a network and then do not use it. Adopting the right mindset—an abundance mentality—and finding the right balance make networking beneficial for both parties. You may be concerned about giving and gaining mutual value, which is difficult—especially when one person is at a higher status. In this instance, the person with the higher status may simply want an opportunity to invest in another person's career. If advice was offered, simply reporting on the results is appreciated. If you are networking with someone of higher status, remembering to say thank you is often all they need. Showing gratitude is a key part of leveraging networking with integrity (Azulay 2018).

Questions to Ponder

? Create your IDP. It should include short-term objectives, long-term objectives, a specific timeline, and resources that you need for support. How can your IDP ensure that you use your skills and talents at work? How can your IDP ensure that you are preparing yourself with future skills?

? What are you doing to expand your informal, social, and on-the-job experiences into your development routine?

Reading for the Final Stretch

→ *Change Now! Five Steps to Better Leadership*, by Peter Scisco, Cynthia McCauley, Jean Leslie, and Rob Elsey

→ *It's Never Too Late to Be What You Might Have Been*, by BJ Gallagher

You have brains in your head,
You have feet in your shoes.
You can steer yourself
Any direction you choose.

—DR. SEUSS

Stay on Course

The success of rapper 50 Cent is more than incredible. He was born in one of the bleaker neighborhoods in New York City, Queens' South Jamaica. He was raised by a single mother, a drug dealer, who was 15 when 50 Cent was born. She died when he was eight, and he was sent to live with his grandparents (Encyclopedia.com).

He endured substantial obstacles throughout his young life. Taking note of his mother's success, he started selling drugs when he was 12 years old. He was arrested several times, dropped out of high school, served time in prison, and by 19 was the neighborhood drug kingpin. 50 Cent lived everything that most rappers write about, but few actually experience: crime, imprisonment, stabbings, drugs, and shootings.

By the time he was 21 he was managing several profitable crack houses. And then his son was born—and he decided to switch careers. He tried boxing, then discovered his passion for music. His music appealed to many. Some of his fans liked his hoodlum posturing in his gritty-edged music, others gravitated to his rags-to-riches story, and yet others liked his raunchy rap lyrics. When he switched from a life of crime to music he changed his street name from Boo-Boo to 50 Cent, which he says is a metaphor for change.

Unlike the rappers that grew up in middle-class families, 50 Cent actually lived most of the content that he weaves into his music and that got him into trouble too. He's survived stabbings and a shooting that left him with nine bullets in his body. For the latter he had the fortitude to drive himself to the hospital.

50 Cent is talented for sure, and he believes in himself. He's won a Grammy Award, 13 Billboard Music Awards, 6 World Music Awards, 3 American Music Awards, and 4 Black Entertainment Television (BET) Awards.

So how can a ghetto rapper inspire you? 50 Cent's career started in what he knew best, as do most of ours. When he decided to change careers he cast about identifying other things he had passion for. When he made the change, he changed his name, and even that became a metaphor for his new persona. But along the way to becoming a multimillionaire with a promising new career, he would periodically sink back to depending on and using the street smarts he grew up with.

Many of us get caught up in a life that seems to have a preprogrammed approach. We do what we've done before, follow the role models that are familiar, and even if we experience some success, we find it hard to resist the lure that pulls us to what we're accustomed.

All of us cast about for our calling or passion at one time or another. And once we find it, we have a tendency to slip back to what we know best and feel comfortable with. When that happens, you need to be ready with a solid plan for your future and well-crafted goals that encourage you to keep going. And you need to believe in yourself.

That's what this chapter is about. Find your calling and stay on course. But be prepared to pivot, because obstacles will come your way.

At this point you have formulated an idea of what you want to do, identified your development needs, set goals, planned your strategy, and selected a diverse range of learning opportunities.

To stay on course you need to capture all that you've created and intend to accomplish in a written plan. As you pull things together for your plan, remember to review your original work in the past three steps. Set goals that work for you and create a plan that encourages you to stay on track.

Your career plan will help you stay focused. You should also look ahead to determine what might take you off course. You will run into obstacles and may need to make some course corrections.

Let's take a look at capturing your good ideas to develop a career plan. You will find a simple template at the end of this book and a downloadable copy at https://ideas.bkconnection.com/skillsforcareersuccess, or feel free to use your own. The earlier steps all prepared you to think about your career and plan for the future. I truly believe in the concept that writing down your plan increases the chances that you will accomplish it. Write it down to stay on course.

YOUR CAREER PLAN

The key items in your career plan should include your goals, actions you'll take to achieve those goals, and the development activities you believe you'll need to move forward. Let's walk through the Career Development Plan template located in part 4 of this book. A downloadable plan is located at https://ideas.bkconnection.com/skillsforcareersuccess. Whether you use it or your own format matters less than knowing what you will want to include.

Career focus and ideal job. It's important to start with your broad thoughts about your career. Even if you do not know exactly what you want to do, you should just begin by capturing your views at this point. Remember, a career plan should be somewhat fluid and evolving. Your ideas will grow and change as you learn more about yourself and the job market. Every time you participate in a development opportunity, you come face-to-face with new ideas and options. It all becomes clearer as you move through your career. The activities you completed earlier about what was important should have provided clues and helped you focus on where you stand regarding your career focus and your ideal job at this moment in time. It will change as you learn more. Finally, be sure that you are thinking about the future. What will your career and ideal job look like 10 years from now?

Values, traits, and strengths. Listing your values, character traits, and strengths will help you stay focused on who you are and your basic belief system. The activities in Step 2 and Step 3 provide you with the answers. It is not likely that your values and character will change—unless you are intentionally working on them (for good reasons, of course). Listing your strengths reminds you of the powerful assets you have working for you as you continue to develop. These attributes create the foundation on which you can build your career.

Principal goal. Identify your key, principal goal. It should be something that you can accomplish in one to two years. This is where you pull everything together to determine what your key goal is at this time. This will depend on your position today and where you want to be in a year or two. Examples of goals may include these:

- By May 15 I will complete the project management professional certification process and be ready to apply for a job in the marketing department.

- By midyear, I will have developed a business plan, marketing plan, and transition plan to start my consulting business.

- By October 1 of next year I will have completed leadership classes, special assignments, and coaching, preparing me to apply for a management position in my department.

Review your individual development plan for ideas.

Support goals. To achieve your principal goal typically requires supporting goals and actions. Each support goal should be written as a SMART goal. It should be specific, measurable, attainable, relevant, and time-bound. SMART goals are better understood by everyone and have a greater chance of being accomplished. An example could be:

- Read three industry journals to improve my knowledge of trends every month during the first quarter.

- Set accurate SMART goals without aid 100 percent of the time for my second-quarter career plan.

Objectives, strategies, and actions. Each support objective should be broken down into smaller strategies or actions. Strategies describe what you are going to do and when you are going to do it. Think about the sequential order of each goal and list a date by which you anticipate completing each. These strategies and actions should focus on your weaknesses and areas of improvement. Think about the skills you will need to fulfill the goal. Also consider the resources you can use to help you accomplish each strategy or action. Resources may include a person, a book, a course, your coach, a special assignment, or your network. This book is filled with ideas. You will also want to reference the time you will invest. Finally establish a completion date. Your timeline is important to ensure that you stay on track.

Required development. No matter what your goal, it is likely that you will need to improve your skills, knowledge, or attitudes. Identify what they are, if they are not already covered in your strategies and actions. For example, you may require a rotational assignment in another department to learn general information about another facet of your organization. Some of your development may be included as an action or strategy, but it is highly likely that you will need more development that is outside the goals you've set. This is the place to list any special development. This could also be a place to list a specific skill that affects many other skills, such as being politically savvy or increasing your flexibility.

Potential obstacles. Finally, you need to anticipate obstacles that may prevent your career plan from succeeding. Obstacles could include hundreds of things, such as a lack of support from your supervisor, your ego doesn't allow you to learn from your failures, or you chose goals that were too ambitious. Take time to explore things that could go wrong with your plan. You may need to redesign your plan or create a mitigation plan. Share your plan with a trusted colleague or your supervisor and ask for their input on your plan. The next section goes into obstacles in depth.

Use your Career Development Plan to monitor your progress. Monitoring your progress is important for two reasons. First, it will keep you focused and on track. Second, seeing what you are accomplishing increases your confidence and assures you that you are making progress.

ANTICIPATE OBSTACLES

The biggest reason that self-directed career development is unsuccessful is the failure to anticipate obstacles. Change and development are not easy. Having a clear sense of *what* makes it difficult is critical to success. Otherwise you leave yourself open to being blindsided by difficulties you could have avoided or overcome if you had seen them coming.

You can prevent some obstacles by reviewing your plan to ensure that:

- You are clear about your development needs.
- You have selected clearly defined, achievable goals.
- You have used available resources to help you identify ways to learn the skills required to achieve your goals.
- You have support and understanding from others.

Two more obstacles include self-doubt that you can actually achieve your dream, and the presence of competing commitments and values that redirect energy away from the change you want to make. Let's examine them.

Self-doubt. What has prevented you from reaching goals you've set in the past? Understanding past blocks and deciding how you will manage them is key to your development. Pull out a sheet of paper and explore how you can change this from an obstacle to an advantage.

- **Don't make excuses.** Reflect on the reasons why you haven't changed something you know you should have already changed. Now examine your goals. Which of these reasons might become your primary excuse for not accomplishing them? What can you do to increase the probability that your goals will be accomplished by reducing and managing the obstacles listed?

- **Head off self-doubt.** Sometimes recognition of your abilities grows into doubt. You may start out with somewhat lowered expectations, and then when you are met with setbacks you lower your expectations even further. After another setback or two, you could end up with expectations so low that they are getting in the way of reaching your goals. You become discouraged, all the effort seems wasted, and you may even give up entirely. It can happen at the other end of the scale too. A person with unrealistically high expectations can end up in the same situation because they never saw obstacles coming at all. Their expectations were too high and fragile and popped like a bubble when things got tough.

- **Right-size your expectations.** Don't take on more than you know is reasonable. Think about your goals and determine how realistic your outcomes are. What are you predicting? How much control do you have over the outcome of the prediction? What steps can you take if your prediction comes into question? Reflect on and write out any expectations or predictions you have made concerning the goal you are having trouble with. Identify ways in which your expectations are outside of your control. Right-size your expectations for a goal by recasting them as being under your control. Describe how you will adjust if you are not meeting your expectations. Rewrite your goal if necessary.

Competing commitments. Commitment is vital for self-directed career development. At first blush, it may seem that true commitment will inevitably lead to success. But this may not be true, because other, equally strong commitments may be in competition with your change.

These competing commitments can be hidden. Because they can be out of your awareness, they can create a major obstacle to success. The key is to become aware of commitments that may be competing with yours. Figure out how to get your various commitments to work together and not compete.

Competing commitment awareness. Use this exercise if you are having trouble pursuing one of your goals to which you are truly committed. The purpose is to bring to light a possible competing commitment that is in conflict with your goal and may prevent you from achieving the change your goal calls for.

1. Start with a piece of paper that you divide into three columns.

2. Think about the main actions or behaviors you need to achieve your goal. These are actions or behaviors you have formed a commitment to; therefore, complete the sentence "I am committed to ..." by writing the actions necessary for achieving your goal in column one. For example, "I am committed to listening actively to others."

3. Think about the things you do (or the things you fail to do) that seem to get in the way of your desired actions. List those things in column two. For example, "I interrupt others, anticipate what they will say, and respond before they finish."

4. Think about situations in which you act the way you described. Ask yourself, If I did or did not do these things, is there some uneasiness or fear I would feel? In other words, think about the negative emotions you might experience if you behaved the opposite of the actions you listed. Are you protecting yourself from the worry or fear you would feel if you acted the opposite? A competing commitment may be protecting you from negative emotions. It's hard to look at the things we do for self-protection, but that's a reason why competing commitments tend to be hidden.

5. Are you protecting yourself from the negative emotions of doing the opposite of your actions? Write your competing commitment in

column three—for example, "I am also committed to protecting myself from people thinking I am passive and not a take-charge leader."

6. Ask yourself, What do I assume would happen if I stopped worrying about or fearing the outcome? What do I think could happen? For example, "I assume that I would not be a forceful leader—I assume it's my job to take charge and make things happen, not just be a sympathetic listener."

Completing this activity will help you understand any competing objectives or beliefs you might have. You will still need to determine how you will balance any conflicting beliefs that may exist.

STAY ON TRACK; ADJUST AS NEEDED

You have a clear understanding of what you want to achieve, why you want to achieve it, and how to deal with various obstacles. As you put your plan into action, it is important to stay focused. You probably have dozens of other priorities and things that demand your attention. It will be tempting to let other priorities take over. How can you stay focused on your development goals? Try these suggestions to help you:

- **Make change part of your day.** Make your development part of your daily routine. If you can't do all you planned, at least spend a few minutes jotting down ideas or thoughts about your goals. Just the act of thinking about your goal can help.

  > Put your plan work on your daily to-do list.

  > Create a diary or a journal for recording your developmental work.

  > Include records of daily actions taken and space for a daily reflection on your desk or wherever you will see it.

- **Track your effect on others.** Your changes will have an effect on others who know you. Track your effect by observing their reactions to you as you try new behaviors and skills. Paying attention to your effect on others is an important reality check.

  > Observe others' reactions.

  > Ask others for feedback. This could be as simple as: "I'm trying to take more initiative. How am I doing?"

> Listen for feedback from everyone.

> Note observations and feedback in your journal.

- **Identify personal development resources.** Many resources exist for you to use. They will help keep you energized. Look around and learn what others are using. Look for tools that can help you stay focused, positive, and inspired. You'll want to do your own search, but here are a few to start with.

  > Self-help books are high on everyone's list. Classics everyone should read are *How to Win Friends and Influence People* and *The 7 Habits of Highly Effective People*. New to the list are *Girl, Wash Your Face* and *Principles*.

  > Self-help podcasts can be listened to at your convenience. Start with those by Tony Robbins or the Habit Coach.

  > Apps such as Timely for time management, Golden to broaden your skills, and HabitBull can help you stick to your career resolutions.

- **Seek help when you need it.** You don't have to do this without support. Look around you to determine who could help.

  > You could use an accountability partner.

  > Don't wait for your supervisor to schedule a meeting. Ask for time to discuss what you are doing and share what you need help with.

  > Friends can often provide insight that work colleagues can't or won't. Ask a friend.

- **Revise your plan if needed.** Sometimes even the best plans need some modification. This should not be taken lightly. If you find yourself modifying your plan every other week, you may be giving in to the temptation to make things easier. On the other hand, if achieving your goals seems easy, you may have chosen goals that were not challenging or meaningful.

  > If you are having trouble meeting deadlines, ask yourself: Are these deadlines honestly unreasonable, or would I rather just take it easy?

> If the deadlines you set are actually too hard to meet, modify your plan. Deadlines should be realistic but challenging (but remember, sometimes you just need a break!).

> If things are too difficult, you may need to break things down into smaller steps.

- **Deal with failures proactively.** Almost everyone experiences some kind of failure along the way. In fact, if you experience absolutely no failures along the way, you may also not experience any significant change. Remember that setbacks are part of the learning and development process.

  > Record instances of failure in your journal along with what you learned. This helps make setbacks pay off.

  > Reflect on failures by asking yourself: What part of my plan is working? What happened that brought about the setback? What can I do differently the next time? What has been most helpful to me about this setback?

- **Plan time to reflect.** Plan time every day for reflection. What did you learn from your successes today? What did you learn from your difficulties? What are you going to do about them? Be your own coach and improve your performance tomorrow. Here are a few items I've worked on in my career:

  > Listen actively.

  > Be more proactive.

  > Ignore limitations.

  > Let go of the past.

  > Stop procrastinating.

  > Read more often.

  > Improve body language.

  > Increase willpower.

CELEBRATE YOUR SUCCESS!

Celebration is more than an opportunity to reward yourself for excellent work. Celebration also opens the way for others to be rewarded for the part they have played in your success. Celebration anchors what you have accomplished; it makes your success tangible and memorable. It creates a foundation for future self-directed change. A celebration is a chance to say: I did it this time and I can do it again! Try some of these celebratory actions:

- Send thank-you notes to the people who supported you and be sure to include your supervisor.

- Do something wild and crazy such as ziplining or rent a convertible for the day.

- Treat yourself to something special such as a spa treatment, an extra round of golf, or those expensive running shoes you've wanted.

- Make your public celebration more about others than about yourself; for example, you could buy donuts or pizza for the office.

- Do something you don't have time to do anymore, such as reading a new fiction book, visiting your favorite art gallery, or binge watching horror movies on television.

- Record your feelings of success and accomplishment in your journal.

WHAT WE KNOW FOR SURE

You may be thinking, "I have no intention of changing careers or jobs or companies. I am happy." I hear what you are saying. However, if you anticipate being in the job market 10 years from now, you may want to reconsider. Think to the future. Develop your skills. Learn lots. And keep an eye on the future.

Here's a summary of what we know to be true about career development and success:

- Mentoring works to help you become your best.

- Networking with others is an important social learning activity.

- Providing feedback to each other is a way to learn from experience on the job.
- Reading this book, attending a class, or listening to a podcast are ways to learn formally.
- The world will continue to change; you need to change with it.
- Study the future to stay ahead of changes; subscribe to *Abundance Insider*, the blog of Peter Diamandis.
- Building your own inner agility is important.
- Good things take time.
- You may need to help your manager be a better coach to you.
- Do what you can to reduce complexity; the explosion of information is overwhelming to everyone.
- "Your job" isn't "yours"; it will change. Be prepared.
- Becoming multifaceted is key to career advancement.
- Successful people never stop learning.
- You are responsible for your own continuous learning and development to remain marketable.

What's the most important skill for the 21st century? Organizations want and need avid lifelong learners who can turn on a dime, learn and change easily, predict the skills they will need before they need them, and support their organizations with the knowledge, skills, and attitude that are needed on the spot.

Questions to Ponder

? What did I make better today?

? What do I want more of in life?

? What do I still need to learn?

? What is great about me?

? What are my blind spots?

? How do people view me differently than I view myself?

? Who has been my most trusted adviser? Is it time to have another discussion?

? Whom would I love—not just like—to mentor me? What's stopping me from asking?

? What inspires me?

? What's the most important lesson I've learned in life? Am I living what I've learned?

? To whom can I be a trusted adviser?

Reading for the Final Stretch

→ *Switchers: How Smart Professionals Change Careers and Seize Success*, by Dawn Graham

→ *Find Your Fit: A Practical Guide to Landing a Job You'll Love*, by Sue Kaiden

It takes courage to grow up and become who you really are.

—E.E. CUMMINGS

PART TWO

SKILLS FOR CAREER SUCCESS

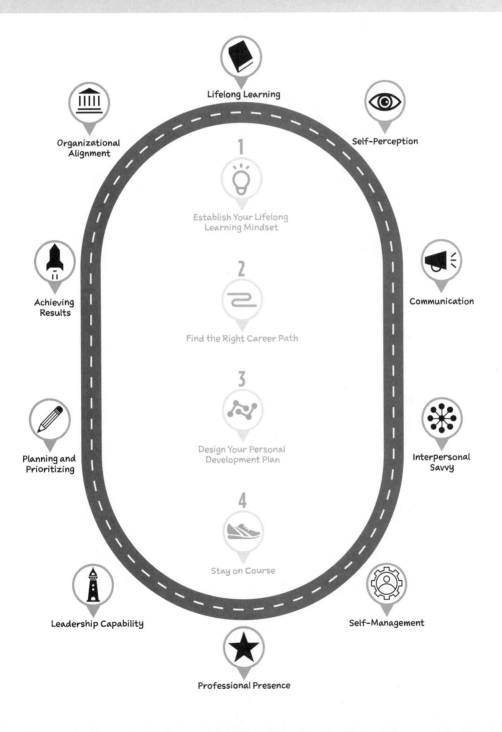

Lifelong Learning

Organizational Alignment

Self-Perception

1
Establish Your Lifelong Learning Mindset

Achieving Results

Communication

2
Find the Right Career Path

3
Design Your Personal Development Plan

Planning and Prioritizing

Interpersonal Savvy

4
Stay on Course

Leadership Capability

Self-Management

Professional Presence

Lifelong Learning

To paraphrase Alvin Toffler (1984), author of *Future Shock:* The illiterate of the 21st century will not be those who cannot read and write, but those who cannot learn, unlearn, and relearn. Our world is filled with people who have done exactly that.

Consider Michael Jordan, who is famous for saying, "I've missed more than 9000 shots in my career and I've lost almost 300 games." Thomas Edison dubbed his 10,000 failed lightbulb inventions not as failures, but that "I succeeded in proving that those 10,000 ways will not work. When I eliminated the ways that will not work, I will find the way that will work."

Winston Churchill failed the entrance exam for the Royal Military College twice. Abraham Lincoln lost eight elections, failed in business twice, and suffered a nervous breakdown. Malala Yousafzai did not give up even after the Taliban shot her in the face as she went to school. Vincent Van Gogh, one of the most influential painters in modern history, created over 2000 pieces of art but sold only one painting while alive.

J. K. Rowling, author of the Harry Potter book series, had a difficult childhood, endured a strenuous marriage that ended in divorce, and was diagnosed as clinically depressed. At 28 she was a single mother, jobless, and on state benefits. She moved to Edinburgh, Scotland, to be closer to her family and continued to work on her book.

Harry Potter and the Sorcerer's Stone was rejected by 12 major publishing houses and finally picked up by a small London literary house in 1996 owing to the insistence of the owner's daughter. Within eight years Rowling became the first author to become a billionaire.

Many of these examples show that success and failure are tied together. Rowling has said that she discovered her strong will for success and that her determination to continue to write, revise, and rewrite again led to the success. She learned how to make it work. Research by Angela Duckworth, author of *Grit: The Power of Passion and Perseverance*, reveals that people who reach the top of their fields are usually ferociously determined as well as self-directed. They have a strong desire to finish strong.

Those who intend to be the 21st century's successful literate must learn to learn. Sometimes called learning agility, this is the process of learning, unlearning, and relearning. This is true for many of those people who experienced major setbacks whom we now call successful. Success begins with knowing how to learn: having a growth mindset, creating your development strategy, learning from experience, accepting and implementing feedback, and taking advantage of formal learning opportunities.

Argue for your limitations and sure enough they're yours.

—RICHARD BACH

SKILL 1

Exhibit a Growth Mindset

A growth mindset is a distinguishing trait of people who believe that basic abilities can be developed through dedication and hard work. This differs from people who have a fixed mindset and believe that their traits are given and that their skills, abilities, and talent cannot be changed. Think of a growth mindset as the positive thinking of learning. A growth mindset is the belief that you can stretch yourself. You can develop and learn something beyond what you know and can do now. Both types of mindsets are just beliefs—albeit powerful beliefs. A growth mindset allows you to try new things, to accept challenges, to grow, and to achieve your dreams; a fixed mindset prevents you from attempting different options, prohibits you from accepting challenges, hinders your development, and gets in the way of the success you desire. You have a choice.

It's important because believing in yourself is the start to supporting a growth mindset that creates motivation, engagement, and productivity. People with a growth mindset believe that everyone can develop intelligence, talent, and skills and change their personality. Creating a growth mindset isn't always easy, but it leads to success for individuals and organizations. For example, Microsoft praises the concept and credits it for successes such as creating Learning Tools for OneNote, defining holographic computing, and moving team members into leadership roles even though they were not originally on that path (Dweck and Hogan 2016). A growth mindset is the key to learning more, performing better, appreciating yourself more, and enjoying what you do.

MASTERING THE SKILL

Hurdles to Overcome

- What negative messages do I tell myself about my ability to be better?
- How often do I feel threatened by others' success?
- How often do I avoid jobs or tasks that would be a stretch for me?
- Do I turn down projects or opportunities for fear of failure?

Your Path to Success

- Believe that your abilities can be developed through persistence
- View challenges as opportunities to learn and grow
- Be inspired by others who have attained their dreams
- Send positive messages that encourage you to try new things at which you want to excel
- Persevere at the skills you want to achieve and rarely give up
- View challenges and hurdles as options that motivate you

TIPS FOR PEOPLE IN A HURRY

- **Learn the power of "yet."** Carol Dweck (2017), author of *Mindset*, has stated that "yet" has become her favorite word. When facing something you don't know, tell yourself, "There is a better way to do this; I just don't know it—yet."

- **Learning isn't failing.** Stop berating yourself when you fail or make a mistake or fall short of meeting a goal; instead, absorb what you've learned. Business management guru Tom Peters says to "fail faster" so that you can learn more.

- **Define can-do.** Identify someone you know who has accomplished more in a lifetime than one might expect. Invite that person to coffee (your treat) and ask them what messages they send to themselves to create a can-do attitude.

PRACTICE SPRINTS

- **Attend to your KSAs.** The talent development profession focuses on three domains of development: knowledge, skills, and attitudes, often shortened to the KSAs. Knowledge is the information and facts that you recall to comprehend, analyze, or evaluate something. Skills are the mental or physical abilities you use to do a job or to complete daily tasks. Attitudes are the opinions and beliefs you have about a person, an issue, or an object. Make your own personal list of KSAs. To master a growth mindset, you first need to know what you want and need to learn. Make a list of the knowledge, skills, and attitudes you want to internalize and project. Define your ideal self. Then start to practice it. Behave as if you are already there.

- **To quit or not to quit.** Identify times when you thought you wanted to do something but quit before you achieved it or reached the end. It could be something personal or professional. Perhaps you dropped out of a class or ended involvement in a recurring recreational event (book club, baseball team). List as many as you can and then find 59 minutes to honestly answer these six questions:

  1. Why did you pursue the event initially?
  2. Why did you quit? What conversations did you have with yourself before you quit?
  3. What did you gain by quitting?
  4. What did you lose by quitting?

5. In hindsight, what could you have done differently before quitting?

6. What impact might you have had if you had stayed?

This activity is **not** always about staying. That would not be the correct venue. It is about recognizing why you quit or what you fear or what messages you are giving yourself. Once you are aware of what you believe, you are then able to make a better-informed decision about quitting or staying.

- **Make learning a habit.** A true lifelong learner learns all the time. Just thinking about that can be overwhelming. Start with a growth mind-set. Then try these tips to foster a habit to learn every day:

  > Link learning to something you do every day. For example, before checking your email, read a daily blog about leadership development.

  > Be specific about when, where, and how you begin your learning habit—for example, "I will read a leadership development blog every day before reviewing my email."

  > Monitor and track your conscientiousness. A checkmark on a calendar date when you are finished is simple, but can be very rewarding.

  > Start small in order to make it as easy as possible. B. J. Fogg, author of *Tiny Habits*, warns that if the habit is too large and requires a high level of motivation, it won't be sustained. Listening to a 60-minute podcast may be too much. Reading an 800-word blog can be a small and wise start.

  > Reward yourself during or immediately after. Perhaps in this instance you get a fresh cup of coffee to read the blog.

It's not easy to learn a new habit. And this example is very simple. But it is a place to start as you move on to something more complex, time-consuming, and presumptuous. Research shows the median time it takes a habit to be automated is 66 days. Perhaps give yourself a 30-day challenge to see if you can beat the odds. Then move on to something more difficult. You might, for example, begin by investing more time. You could read something written by classic management authors such as Peter Drucker or popular current authors such as Jim Collins.

STRATEGIES FOR THE LONG RUN

- **Adjust your attitude.** Your attitude is tightly related to your growth mindset. Attitudes are your emotions, beliefs, and opinions. Carl Jung explained attitude as a tendency expressed by evaluating anything with a degree of favor or disfavor, meaning that attitudes are often classified as positive or negative. Attitudes are formed as you experience life and create beliefs based on your upbringing, experiences, social adjustment, prejudices, and the beliefs of your friends, family, and colleagues. Attitudes have a powerful influence over your actions and can affect every part of your life as well as those around you. They can be difficult to change. If you are interested in adjusting your attitude—especially your growth mindset—try one of these tactics:

  > Clearly define the growth mindset goal you want to establish; paint a clear mental vision of what you'll do and say. Decide on reactions that will replace what you do now.

  > Your thoughts control how you feel, so be aware of how you think about situations: yes to a growth mindset, no to a fixed mindset.

  > Take responsibility for how you interpret what happens to you and how you respond. You can't choose what happens, but you can choose how to respond.

  > Identify what you can learn from every situation; doing so gives you an opportunity to practice a growth mindset in everything.

  > Keep your eye on your mindset goal. Don't let small daily slip-ups prevent you from making progress.

  Your attitude is all about what you tell yourself. What are you telling yourself about your ability to learn, grow, and develop? Is your attitude confident, optimistic, and encouraging? Are you sending positive messages to build a growth mindset attitude?

- **Stretch.** Decide what you'd like to learn on the job. Then create a plan for how you might learn it. Identify a stretch project or assignment you could do that not only will help you learn but also will help your organization. Be sure to include a plan for how you will track and monitor your progress, how long the stretch assignment will last, how your daily work will be covered, and how you will address setbacks. Identifying why you should invest time on the job is critical in order to sell your supervisor on the idea. You will need to provide a rationale for how investing your time will benefit the organization. Think in terms of multiples. How can learning the skills you've identified help your organization more than continuing to spend your time as you currently do? A stretch project should be something that is a developmental opportunity for you and a growth opportunity for your organization. Following this process for requesting and completing a stretch assignment may take a month or longer. Use it to help you focus on enhancing your growth mindset.

- **Own your beliefs.** Switching from a fixed mindset to a growth mindset isn't instantaneous, but it begins with challenging your own thoughts and acknowledging that you want a growth mindset. The next time you are faced with an opportunity to try something new, imagine what is going through your mind. Messages may be "People will think I'm stupid," "I'll make a fool of myself," or "This is too hard, way over my head, impossible to learn!" In the moment, stop, pause, identify these thoughts, and capture them in a note on your electronic device or on paper. Review this event later. If it happens often, collect several examples. When you are ready, create a list of all your current beliefs. Reflect on them, and next to each one identify the belief you would rather have. For example:

CURRENT BELIEF	PREFERRED BELIEF
• People will think I'm stupid • This is way over my head	• People will think I'm learning • I can learn anything I put my mind to

Next, begin to change your perspective. Keep your list close by and grade yourself on your belief. Are you creating the kind of growth mindset you want to own? It takes time to make these changes. For accountability, you may want to share what you are doing with someone who will discuss your progress with you.

CROSS TRAINING

You will find related ideas at these crossover skills:

- Set Goals
- Accept and Act on Feedback
- Practice Resiliency
- Make Key Decisions
- Lead Self

READING FOR THE FINAL STRETCH

- *Mindset: The New Psychology of Success*, by Carol Dweck
- *Grit: The Power of Passion and Perseverance*, by Angela Duckworth

SKILL 2

Create a Personal Development Strategy

Your personal development strategy is your opportunity to create a plan to acquire the knowledge, gain the skills, and practice the attitudes to reach your professional goals. Developing yourself, staying ahead of the changing demands of the workplace, and preparing for new opportunities that arise are your responsibilities. Your personal development strategy provides a blueprint for you to record and track your goals, identify development strategies, and document your accomplishments.

It's important because you are the only person who can take charge of your future. Your development strategy provides a disciplined approach to thinking through your career goals, relating your development to your organization's long-term plans, and identifying specific actions you can take. Your plan can provide a basis for discussion with your supervisor. Your supervisor can be supportive in helping you achieve your career goals; sharing your objectives and planned milestones with your supervisor opens the discussion. Show that you are not only interested in your development but also interested in supporting your organization.

MASTERING THE SKILL

Hurdles to Overcome

- How often do I ignore the need to learn because I am afraid of failure or want to appear perfect?
- What gaps in my knowledge and skills do I avoid developing?
- How overwhelmed am I by the amount of learning I need?
- Why have I ignored creating my personal development plan?
- How concerned am I that developing a plan and implementing it will take too much time?

Your Path to Success

- Accept that you are fully responsible for your development
- Identify specific skills you should develop to be better at your current job and to prepare you for future trends
- Establish clear, achievable development goals that energize you
- Learn where you can gain specific knowledge and skills both internal to your job and external to your workplace
- Be willing to ask for help from others
- Overcome barriers to achieve your development goals
- Identify development goals that align with your values
- Appreciate the value of linking your development to your organization's values

TIPS FOR PEOPLE IN A HURRY

- **My worth.** Look around your workplace and ask what you can do this year that will make you more valuable next year. Start a list.
- **More or less.** Identify what would make you happy to do more, to do less, or to do something differently.

- **SMART goals.** Practice writing SMART goals (specific, measurable, attainable, relevant, and time-bound) to ensure that the goals and objectives in your development plan take you where you desire. For now, write a SMART goal you will accomplish this week.

- **The appraisal says.** Review your most recent performance appraisal to determine your development needs.

PRACTICE SPRINTS

- **Can't do it alone.** Identify who controls your professional future. Your supervisor is of course the first person, but who else might influence whether you receive a promotion or a special project? Then decide how to improve your relationship with each of them and how you could spend time with them, such as being on the same committee. Ask them for development ideas.

- **Countless resources.** Your world is full of resources you can use to learn and achieve your personal development goals. Think broadly and make a list of all the ways you can acquire skills and knowledge. To get you started, general resources might include books, blogs, articles, journals, lectures, podcasts, YouTube videos, or social media. Resources available through your organization might include subject matter experts, respected leaders, coaches, mentors, online or face-to-face courses, shadowing others, special projects, or job rotations. Now narrow that list down to the best places to obtain the information you need.

- **Your values.** You'll be most satisfied when your development goals are aligned with your values. Name two or three things that you value the most about your current job. What would your daily sched-ule look like for your ideal day at work?

- **Dream job.** Identify your dream job. Start with a blank piece of paper and some colorful markers to draw a career path that will take you from where you are today to your dream job. Don't try to make the drawing pretty. Write words, draw stick figures, cross out ideas you discard. The idea is to just start thinking about it. Put your drawing away and pull it out in a month. What new ideas do you have?

- **Learning opportunities.** Mobile-enabled learning systems offer you the opportunity to learn anywhere, anytime. Learning can occur in an airport, in your hotel room, on the subway to work, or in a coffee shop. It may require some preplanning to download or upload the content you need or to obtain advice from a colleague or coach. Plan ahead and you can learn wherever you are.

STRATEGIES FOR THE LONG RUN

- **Write it down.** It's not enough to just think about your personal development strategy. You need to write it down. You will find a template at https://ideas.bkconnection.com/skillsforcareersuccess that will simplify this task. At a minimum you should incorporate these basic components:

  > Your personal and professional needs and wants

  > Specific long- and short-term goals

  > Development strategies to reach your goals

  > Resources you will tap into and if necessary the schedule and costs (such as for a class)

  > Start and completion dates

  > Alignment to your organization's/department's strategies and goals—to gain your supervisor's support

  Identify your priorities. You can't do it all at once, so decide a priority order based on appropriate sequence, urgency, and importance to you. Use your development strategy to guide your progress. Review your personal development strategy at least monthly, or more often to track milestones and accomplishments or to add new strategies and resources.

- **Enlist your supervisor.** Take your development plan to the next level by enlisting your supervisor's support. To prepare for your meeting, take the following actions:

  > Review your current position description and your performance appraisal.

  > Understand the goals of your department and your organization's strategic plan.

  > Review your proposed development and prepare to share it with your supervisor. Ensure it is as complete as possible.

  Plan to discuss what you see as your responsibilities and the support you'd like from your supervisor. Don't focus just on your needs but on how your development will benefit the organization as well. Ask about your organization's plans and how your development could support your organization's efforts.

- **Align with your values.** Although the goals you identified are written as SMART goals, they could be pretty dumb if they don't align with your values. Goals are usually written logically and intellectually. To be truly effective, your development goals should also come from your heart, what's important to you, and what feels right. Your values form the basis of what's important to you in your life. Values identify your passions and the motivations that are meaningful to you. You can examine your life from several perspectives, such as your career, relationships, personal, community, or others. If you've completed a values survey in the past, use it to clarify your values and to ensure that your development goals are aligned with your values. If not, a core values survey is located at https://ideas .bkconnection.com/skillsforcareersuccess. Complete it and compare the values that are important to you in your life with the development goals you've established.

- **Mind map you.** Create a mind map of the opportunities for personal growth. You will find an example of a mind map in part 4 and a downloadable copy at https://ideas.bkconnection.com/skillsforca- reersuccess.). Put "Opportunities to Develop" in the center circle. Begin to add ideas around the outside and place them inside the circles also. You may begin with several general categories such as "experiential activities," "training," and "nonwork." You may also list more specific categories such as "listening," "public speaking," and "email"—which might all roll up into the more general category of "communication." Don't forget creative, out-of-the-box ideas, such as learning to make cotton candy, enrolling in opera lessons, trying out for a play, taking a cooking class in Tuscany, or getting a real estate license. Use your mind map to create an individual development plan for yourself.

CROSS TRAINING

You will find related ideas at these crossover skills:

- Accept and Act on Feedback
- Set Goals
- Show Self-Awareness
- Exhibit Career Ambition
- Improve Weaknesses

READING FOR THE FINAL STRETCH

- *Stand Out*, by Dorie Clark
- *Unstoppable You*, by Patricia McLagan

SKILL 3

Learn from Experience

Learning from experience is sometimes called "learning agility," the rapid continuous learning that occurs based on experiences learners have. Based on a Center for Creative Leadership definition, it is a mindset and corresponding collection of practices that allow people to continually develop, grow, and utilize new strategies to equip themselves for increasingly complex problems.

It's important because the volatile, uncertain, complex, and ambiguous world in which we live requires us to master our ability to adapt and learn. Accessing the benefits of learning from experience is viewed as critical for success as you grow in responsibility. You will be skilled to handle new challenges and will be a valued addition to solving some of your organization's most daunting issues. Your organization will also reap the benefits as it becomes more flexible and more competitive.

MASTERING THE SKILL

Hurdles to Overcome

- How concerned am I about what others will think: Will they think I am incompetent?
- How much do I downplay what I learn every day?
- How often do my work priorities overtake time that I could be learning?
- What prevents me from experimenting, trying a new process, or accepting a new challenge?
- How often do I defend myself when challenged or given corrective feedback?

Your Path to Success

- Take the time to connect with and learn from those who can support your development strategy
- Observe the signals to learn from others, the environment, and your internal desires
- Accept responsibility for your own errors and grow from mistakes
- Try new approaches or make midcourse corrections
- Treat all situations as a chance to learn something
- Schedule and invest time to reflect on what you learn and how it can be implemented
- Take risks, remain flexible, and accept unfamiliar challenges
- Pursue experiences that could expand your perspective

TIPS FOR PEOPLE IN A HURRY

- **Review past experiences.** Think back to several times when you learned from experience. Any struggles or difficulties? What did you learn? Identify how you have implemented these lessons.

- **Find your passion.** You can't implement everything, but identify what you are most passionate about learning. Focus on strategies to gain related knowledge and skills.

- **Learn from discomfort.** Think of situations where you were just a little uncomfortable. Define what you were supposed to learn in that time and place.

- **Determine your risk level.** How likely are you to volunteer for a job or role where success is not guaranteed and where failure is possible? How do you feel about your response?

- **Find the "so what."** Hearing the "what" in a discussion meeting is generally easy. Try to determine the "so what" and also conclude the "now what" that is needed.

PRACTICE SPRINTS

- **Would Google hire you?** Laszlo Bock, former SVP of people operations at Google, shared that the number one thing Google wants in new employees is the ability to process on the fly by merging disparate bits of information. How are you learning the combined skills of flexibility, taking risks, gathering information, and making decisions in a lightning-fast way? How can you learn and practice those skills? Identify others in your organization who seem to possess these skills and interview them about how they acquired these skills.

- **Ask for more.** Ask your supervisor to assign you additional responsibilities. Ideally, request a project or task that is different from what you usually do. Identify the skills and knowledge you'll need to acquire to be successful. Track these skills as well as others you did not think of. Rate yourself on each skill. Share your rating with your supervisor and ask for your supervisor's level of agreement and feedback.

- **Try something new.** Try some recreational task outside of work that you've never done before: tennis, bowling, paddle boarding, reading poetry, swing dancing, or yoga. It should be a bit edgy and stressful for you. Track your thoughts and feelings before, during, and after the event. What does this tell you about your flexibility, level of risk, rate of experimentation, and ability to reflect? How does this relate to your behavior on the job? How could you improve this attribute?

- **Assess your skills.** Identify four colleagues who have a role or function in your workplace that is similar to yours. What skills do they have that you do not? What attributes do they possess that make them better at learning from experience than you? Identify how you can catch up.

STRATEGIES FOR THE LONG RUN

- **Assess your learning agility.** Warner Burke, of the Teachers College at Columbia University, identifies nine dimensions for learning agility: flexibility, speed (acting quickly), experimenting with behaviors, performance risk-taking (accepting new challenges), interpersonal risk-taking, collaborating, information gathering, seeking feedback, and reflecting (Burke, Roloff, and Mitchinson 2016). Rate yourself on each of the nine dimensions. Then for each dimension identify what you could learn on the job, what you could learn from others, and what you are unsure of how you might learn it. Meet with your coach, mentor, or accountability partner for a personal discussion to review your results. Ask for feedback that is honest, candid, and frank. Reflect on the discussion and create your plan to develop the attributes that will make you a more agile employee who learns from experience.

- **Volunteer.** Identify an opportunity with your professional association or a local community group, nonprofit, or religious group where you can give back to society and practice some of the skills you identified to develop. It affords you an opportunity to try out new skills, take risks, and experience unfamiliar challenges. Be sure to connect with someone who can give you feedback on your performance—especially about what you could have done differently.

- **Celebrate your mistakes.** It may be difficult to discuss your mistakes, but it is critical to learn from experiences. Identify the three most recent mistakes you've made on the job. Determine what you learned from them. Gather three colleagues together and share what you have concluded. Then ask for feedback from them as you listen carefully and take notes. Questions to ask include: Do you think I learned from these mistakes? Why or why not? What else should I have learned? What suggestions do you have for experimenting with new behaviors? What opportunities are available for me to practice? During this discussion you should practice acceptance of feedback, listening with an open mind. Do not become defensive—it will be hazardous to your career.

CROSS TRAINING

You will find related ideas at these crossover skills:

- Show Self-Awareness
- Practice Creativity, Innovation, and Appropriate Risk Taking
- Adapt to Situations
- Lead Self
- Practice Resiliency

READING FOR THE FINAL STRETCH

- *Learning Agility: Unlock the Lessons of Experience*, by George Hallenbeck

SKILL 4

Accept and Act on Feedback

A ccepting and implementing feedback is an imperative behavior for continued learning and growth. You may have heard someone say, "Feedback is a gift." It is a gift because someone took the time to help you learn and grow. If you are new to your job, feedback lets you know whether you are learning what you need to be successful. If you've hit a stumbling block, feedback gives you the information you need to evaluate the situation and get back on track. Sometimes feedback may not seem accurate to you, but you should still consider it because something caused a perception that led to feedback. Listen and check it out. Feedback is only helpful to you if you accept what you hear and implement what you can.

It's important because it provides information about progress, changes, or improvements. When progress isn't as good as you'd like, feedback can provide insight as to what you can do better or differently. If your progress is meeting expectations, positive feedback supports you, boosts your self-confidence, and encourages you to continue.

MASTERING THE SKILL

Hurdles to Overcome

- Why am I reluctant or fearful of receiving feedback?

- How willing am I to listen to someone who wants to provide advice?

- Why do I ignore feedback that could improve my performance or my relationships?

- How often have I received the same feedback from multiple people?

- What triggers prevent me from hearing and accepting feedback?

Your Path to Success

- Recognize the value and importance of feedback for learning

- Believe you can learn from everyone no matter who they are or what role they have

- Seek candid feedback on your performance, behaviors, and other attributes

- Respect those who go out of their way to provide you with both constructive and complimentary feedback

- Reflect on both feedback and your self-awareness for clearer understanding

- Accept feedback and change your behavior in response

TIPS FOR PEOPLE IN A HURRY

- **Get a little help from your friends.** List some of the things your friends and significant others have suggested need improving. Keep this feedback in mind as you go about your daily work.

- **Watch others.** Observe how others accept feedback. Put yourself in their place. What would you like to emulate? What would you do differently?

- **Bite your tongue.** The next time someone gives you feedback—positive or constructive—observe your yearning to speak before the other person is finished. Always wait until the other person is finished before responding.

- **Bolster your body language.** Be conscious of your body language the next time you receive feedback. What message is your body language sending?

PRACTICE SPRINTS

- **Initiate it.** Don't just accept feedback, initiate it. Ask for feedback from people whose opinion you respect and who will offer candid thoughts. Be sure it is someone who is able to observe your behavior and has an interest in your performance. Ask them to provide feedback on a specific behavior or task you perform. Practice listening, breathing, and accepting.

- **Gracious acceptance.** Make a list of all the behaviors you can demonstrate and the words you can say that show that you appreciate and accept the feedback someone gives you. Following your next feedback situation, review your list. How many of the items on the list did you use? How many do you wish you had implemented?

- **Feedback and development.** Share your personal development plan with three people and ask them for feedback. Schedule a separate meeting with each person. Ask them to tell you what they like about your plan, what they would add, what development ideas they have, and what opportunities you might be missing. Reflect on what they say and make appropriate changes to your plan.

- **Performance.** Review your most recent performance appraisal. What actions have you taken to make the suggested improvements? No matter what format, your performance review is feedback that you should act on. What do you need to implement? How can you make the changes? Inform your supervisor what you are doing and ask for feedback.

STRATEGIES FOR THE LONG RUN

- **Find feedback fellows for learning.** Identify six things you want to learn over the next six months. Then determine who would be the best people to provide you with feedback on the six items. Depending on what you choose, it could be one person for all six or six different people or a combination. Begin the process of learning using the input from your feedback fellows. At the end of the process, be sure to extend your appreciation for their help, telling them how you implemented the ideas they provided through their feedback.

- **Seek extended 360-degree feedback.** A 360-degree feedback survey provides you with the ultimate feedback. It lets you know how your colleagues, your supervisor, and sometimes your customers view your effectiveness. The feedback assists you in comparing what others believe your strengths and weaknesses are with what you believe they are. It can benefit you by increasing your self-awareness, build your confidence, and clarify the skills you need to work on the most. Ask your supervisor about your options.

- **Ask for a task.** Ask your supervisor to assign you a task that will help you accomplish your development goals. Ask if you can schedule specific feedback meetings with your supervisor so that you can learn and develop your skills. Once you've completed the task, provide feedback to your supervisor about the feedback sessions: what was helpful, what you have implemented, and what you would like to implement in the future.

- **Find a mentor.** Identify your purpose in having a mentor. Then create a list of questions and interview several individuals to find the best match. Your questions might include:

  > What key experiences led you to your current position?

  > Who or what had the most significant impact on your choice of this career?

  > What's the best part of your current position? The most frustrating part?

> If you were trying to dissuade me from aspiring to your position, what would you say?

> How would you advise someone like me to prepare for your job? What knowledge would I need? What experiences?

> What are the rewards of reaching your position? What are the disappointments?

> What mindset is required to reach your position?

> If you had to do it over, what would you do differently?

> What are your work/life balance issues and how do you deal with them?

> What experiences have you had that best prepared you for your position?

> What trends or challenges do you see for people in your position in the future?

> Whom do you most admire and why?

> Whom else should I talk with?

> Would you consider being my mentor? If yes, what's the next step? What could we both gain from a mentoring relationship?

> What should I have asked you about but didn't?

CROSS TRAINING

You will find related ideas at these crossover skills:

- Give and Receive Feedback
- Communicate Clearly
- Maintain Composure

READING FOR THE FINAL STRETCH

- *Ongoing Feedback: How to Get It, How to Use It*, by Karen Kirkland and Sam Manoogian

SKILL 5

Optimize Formal Learning Opportunities

Making the most of formal training is your opportunity to take advantage of focusing on a topic your organization thinks is critical for many (sometimes all) employees and for the organization. Formal learning is planned learning that uses activities within a structured learning setting and may include instructor-led classrooms, instructor-led online training, certificate or certification programs, workshops, webinars, and college courses. There is a curriculum, agenda, and objectives that occur within a preestablished time frame. Formal learning is often integrated with performance and other developmental activities. The goal is usually to develop employees for a change of behavior or improvement of skills. On the other hand, you may select and pay for your own formal learning by attending college classes or online webinars that you believe will enhance your learning goals.

It's important because your organization is giving you time to focus specifically on the learning that will occur. Generally, your organization has decided that the content of the formal learning experience is valuable enough to give you time to learn it. The benefits are that formal learning is expected to improve your performance, while at the same time it provides a structured baseline for all participants. You can optimize formal learning with how you prepare before, get involved during, and follow up after. It's important for you to know how you will implement what you learn.

MASTERING THE SKILL

Hurdles to Overcome

- Am I able to give a formal learning event my full attention?
- How well prepared am I for the learning?
- I have so much work to do; can I really afford to take time away from work to attend?
- Does this content address my career goals and my personal development plan?
- I was never a good student; what has changed?

Your Path to Success

- Have a strong desire to learn, grow, and broaden your knowledge and skills
- Take time to immerse yourself in a single topic
- Accept that you may be a beginner or student in order to explore new information and discover methods
- Act as a sponge around new ideas, concepts, and information
- Be open to others' perspectives
- Practice new skills as a novice
- Explore new ways to think about current behaviors and efforts
- Surround yourself with those who know more than you and learn from them

TIPS FOR PEOPLE IN A HURRY

- **Prepare.** No matter what format you use for formal learning, be sure you are prepared. Prepare physically by planning to manage your energy by taking breaks, drinking water, and planning for your comfort. Prepare mentally by deciding what you want to learn and how you will use it. Plan for how you will take notes.

- **Learn to.** When considering a learning event, don't just select it for what you will *learn about.* Instead, select it for what you will *learn to.* Ask yourself, "What will this course help me learn to do?" You can understand what the course is about, but what will you be able to do better, faster, and with more value for you?

- **Connect it.** Review your personal development strategy to decide what is in your plan that would be best served with formal learning. For example, it's hard to learn good communication skills from a book.

- **Get motivated.** Attending a formal learning event is a privilege, but sometimes you don't have the energy to invest. Determine the job relevance and the progress you will make on your goals. Focus on what you will learn that will make your life easier, your tasks faster, and your results better!

- **Get a referral.** If you are considering a formal learning event of any kind—online or in person, a certification program, or any other—talk to someone who has experienced it. Ask them what worked well, what was good, what was lacking, and whether they would recommend it.

PRACTICE SPRINTS

- **Online options.** If your organization doesn't provide courses in the content you need, check out some of these online course providers: Coursera, EdX, Khan Academy, Saylor, Udacity, and Udemy. Many are free or have a minimal charge.

- **Research options.** Use the format of the course to make your decision to attend. Determine the kind of developmental experience you can expect from a formal learning event you are considering. Ask whether there will be tests or homework, if you will be observed or videotaped during simulations, if the content is practical or theoretical, if you'll need to divulge anything about your shortcomings, or other concerns you might have based on the topic.

- **Before a learning event.** Meet with your supervisor to learn how the content connects to what you do on the job. Ask what your supervisor hopes you learn and what you should be able to do better or differently as a result of what you learn. Ask if there is anything specific that your supervisor has observed you not doing or not doing well that you can pay particular attention to during the course. You should leave this meeting with a clear understanding of the purpose of the course, its relevance to your job, and what your supervisor expects to change. As a result, set your own learning objectives. In addition, arrange for a colleague to take care of your work while you are out.

- **During a learning event.** Remember your purpose for attending the course. Do what you need to be mentally engaged: take breaks, drink plenty of water or other beverages, leave the room during breaks for a new perspective, and go outside to catch a breath of fresh air when you can. Connect with other participants during breaks if you attend a live session or through the chat function if an online course. Ask them what they appreciate most about the course. Get involved in the activities since the hands-on practice or discussion often reveals new content. Utilize your favorite note taking system. Ask questions for clarity or examples. If your question is not exactly on topic or is more personal, ask the instructor during a break or through a personal message if online.

  Finally, create an action plan that identifies what you will do when and where as a result of the course.

- **After a learning event.** Several steps will make the learning event helpful to you. Scan your notes and reflect on what you learned. Identify actions or follow up on resources you want to check out.

Review your development plan to determine how your new knowledge will affect next steps for you. You may need to change direction, add new tactics, or rethink your original plan. Meet with your supervisor to follow up on your discussion before the course. Also discuss new ideas or changes you'd like to implement. Share any barriers you perceive with transferring what you learned to the workplace. Share the action plan you created at the end of the learning event. Finally, make time to complete the assignments and recommendations, implement your personal goals, and invest in your development.

- **Insights from your coach or mentor.** After every formal learning event, you should speak with your coach or your mentor. Share what you learned and ask them for insight or what you are missing. Ask what obstacles they see in your intended change and how to make it more successful.

STRATEGIES FOR THE LONG RUN

- **Certification.** Degree programs are less important in many scenarios than professional certification. Identify any certification programs that may be different from but complementary to what you do. For example, achieving a project management professional certification may be extremely helpful if you manage programs, projects, or other ventures for your organization.

- **Learning with your brain.** Read a book that will help you understand what happens in your brain to learn and retain new content. John Medina's *Brain Rules: 12 Principles for Surviving and Thriving at Work, Home, and School* is an excellent choice. Think about your own learning preferences and how tapping into your brain to obtain the most benefits can benefit what you learn and retain.

- **Going to college.** Are you thinking about returning to college to either finish a degree or obtain a new one? This may be necessary if you are planning a career change or you need new skills or credentials to continue to progress. Don't make this decision lightly. It will be hard work, and it will be costly. You'll want to invest time in data gathering before making your decision. Consider these:

> Clarify your reasons for going to school.

> Make a list of the pros and cons.

> Find out if your employer offers educational assistance.

> Be realistic about the time commitment required.

> Identify how you will pay for tuition, books, and other expenses.

> Research programs and schools to find the right one for you.

> Decide if you want to attend part time or full time, or take online classes.

> Explore options to earn college credit for your prior learning or by testing out.

> Meet with a university employee who supports adult learners to get any additional questions answered.

CROSS TRAINING

You will find related ideas at these crossover skills:

- Manage Time
- Stay Organized
- Network with Others

READING FOR THE FINAL STRETCH

- *Brain Rules: 12 Principles for Surviving and Thriving at Work, Home, and School*, by John Medina
- *Preparing for Development: Making the Most of Formal Leadership Programs*, by Jennifer Martineau and Ellie Johnson

Self-Perception

I was a couple of months into my first real job as an accounting book-keeper in a small-town bank. It was 7 p.m. on a Friday evening—way past bankers' hours—and our books were not balancing. Everyone was panicking because no one was allowed to leave until the books balanced to the penny. That included bookkeepers, tellers, loan officers, and clerical staff. Even the cleaning staff were being held up because they couldn't wield their brooms and mops to clean away the mess of the day.

My boss, Marilyn, who was also our department head, was responsible for balancing the books daily. I had been assigned some menial job to double-check a list of figures. I was leaving the vault where the information was kept when I had to sidestep Marilyn, who was coming at me full speed. As she passed she asked, "Elaine, are we doing everything right? What ideas do you have?" I was focused on counting something, and, not wanting to forget where I was in the calculation, I chose not to speak but to simply shake my head. What I meant was, "I can't talk. I'm in the middle of counting."

Marilyn misinterpreted my head shaking as, "No, you are doing it wrong!" In that tense moment she let me know how she really felt about me, "You *never* think we are doing things right! You *always* have a better answer! If you think you can do a better job, you should just take over!" I had no idea I was perceived this way. And apparently she was referencing not only the balancing process but how I acted at other times too. I was shocked.

Several years later while working for a different organization, I participated in a workshop and completed a communication style assessment. Eight of my colleagues and friends anonymously completed the communication style surveys. During the workshop we learned about the four basic styles: controlling, analyzing, expressive, and collaborating. No style was better than the other, and each had its strengths and blind spots.

The facilitator had a raw sense of humor and was particularly hard on the controlling style, making jokes that they ate nails for breakfast and were always rushing so that automatic doors didn't open fast enough. He said that the negative side of the style was that they could appear domineering, insensitive, inhumane, ruthless, and critical. Of course, there were good things about the controlling style too. Controllers were organized, efficient, decisive, confident, direct, and results focused.

When we received our results from, as the facilitator liked to say, our "former friends," I was shocked to learn that I was perceived as a controlling style—and was located so far from center, I was almost off the chart! I argued that I was a loving mother, kind neighbor, and caring hospital volunteer; I couldn't be this domineering style! There must be a mistake. Well there was no mistake. I had to face again that I was not aware of how I came across to others. My self-perception needed to wake up!

To develop your self-perception, you need to know yourself, what you do well, and what you need to improve in order to happily meet your career aspirations. You need to be aware of your communication style and how you come across to others, then how to be flexible and adaptable as each situation requires. To accomplish all this, you'll need to have self-confidence and resiliency to make changes that you desire.

Step beyond your biases and be more aware of
how judgments may be holding you back.

—ELAINE BIECH

SKILL 6

Show Self-Awareness

Your self-awareness is the ability to understand and manage how your actions are perceived by others. Duval and Wicklund (1972) first proposed that self-awareness is actually made up of two parts. Internal self-awareness is your ability to understand your values, passions, and aspirations and how they align with your current surroundings, feelings, thoughts, and behaviors. External self-awareness is how well you identify how others perceive you. Although both are important, individuals who have a strong external self-awareness are viewed as more empathetic, more effective, and more successful. Highly self-aware people can objectively evaluate themselves, align their actions with their values, control their emotions, and accurately recognize how others view them.

It's important because the only way to improve your skills is by recognizing and accepting what you do well and what you need to improve. Professionally you become a better employee by understanding how others perceive your actions. Personally you will better understand what you are passionate about and why. You'll be able to align what you value to what you do, resulting in increased satisfaction and motivation. It is an important tool to ensure that you achieve your career aspirations and is even related to higher levels of overall happiness. Even with all these benefits, one study of about 5000 participants estimates that only 10–15 percent of us are actually self-aware (Eurich 2018).

MASTERING THE SKILL

Hurdles to Overcome

- How aware am I about my appearance, actions, communication, facial expressions, and limitations?
- How conscious am I about the impact my words and nonverbal behaviors have on others?
- How aware am I of acting out my feelings?
- How cognizant am I of any inner conflicts, contradictory beliefs, or inconstant values?
- How aware am I of how I want others to perceive me, my value, my contributions, or my performance?
- How happy am I with my current life circumstances? My health? My relationships? My professional situation? My finances?
- How mindful am I of myself in the moment?

Your Path to Success

- Overcome arrogance and defensiveness—key behaviors that prevent self-awareness
- Take the initiative to seek feedback from many individuals—don't wait for it
- Work with an awareness accountability partner
- Learn from mistakes
- Use reflection to be more self-aware

TIPS FOR PEOPLE IN A HURRY

- **Don't judge.** Listen to your colleagues and friends without evaluating or judging them. Articulate your feelings and how this helps to better understand and empathize with each person.

- **Focus on the what.** After a difficult discussion or conflict, review what happened in private. Think carefully about the discussion and what you could have done better. Stay focused on the "what," not the "why." "What" leads to thinking about positive future goals, whereas "why" can lead to inappropriate negative rationalization.

- **Note your effect.** Set a timer on your mobile phone for two hours. When the timer goes off, think back to what occurred during those 120 minutes. How often were you aware of your effect on others?

- **Name your motivators.** Think about what motivates you. How can you use these motivators to reach personal and professional goals? How valuable are these motivators to what you are doing today?

- **Learn every day.** On your drive/walk/ride home from work each day, ask yourself, "What's one thing that I learned about me today?"

PRACTICE SPRINTS

- **Make a date with you.** Schedule 30 distraction-free minutes of quiet time with yourself. During that time take notes about you, your day, how consistent you were during the past 24 hours, how inconsistent, what undermined your positive thoughts, and what could have been different. Determine if it is something you wish to change—or not.

- **Address frustration.** The next time you are frustrated, take a 10-minute timeout and focus on you. Take a nonjudgmental view of your thoughts and behaviors. Focus on the situation as well as on your reactions. What are you learning about you? What behaviors did you exhibit? What goals can you establish for your future improvement?

- **List your skills.** Make three lists of skills: skills you are good at, skills you know you should improve, and shortcomings that need lots of work. Leave blank space after each list and share the lists with several others. Ask them to add to each list. Once you receive feedback on your lists, schedule time with each person to discuss their lists. Ask them to explain their comments. During this discussion be aware of your behavior. Ask for ideas about how you could practice those skills and what other advice they could share with you. Be very aware that your body language conveys appreciation and acceptance. Do not make excuses. Thank them for their time.

- **Conduct a life audit.** Reflect on where you are personally, professionally, healthwise, financially, with relationships, and with other elements of your life. How satisfied are you compared with what you want? Determine what you want. Write down your goals and then go after them. Increase your awareness daily of where you are, where you want to be, and how you'll get there. Life audits are a great way to review where you've been and where you're going.

STRATEGIES FOR THE LONG RUN

- **Schedule a month of self-awareness.** Create a calendar on your handheld device or on paper. On each day note the topic for which you want to become more self-aware. Start the month with simple, uncomplicated items and become more complex, personal, and poignant throughout the month. For example:

  > Week one: pay attention to how often you are aware of yourself and what you are doing or saying. It could include things such as appearance, how often you speak, your use of language, or other things.

  > Week two: list a behavior each day, such as listening, making eye contact, interrupting others, saying thank you. Note what you think others thought of your behaviors.

  > Week three: pay attention to your feelings, such as joy, anger, disgust, fear, trust (or lack of trust), and sadness, as well as how your feelings may have affected others around you.

> Week four: focus on internal judgment calls you make each day. Step beyond your biases and be more aware of how these judgments may be holding you back.

> Review your notes. What did you learn about yourself? What behaviors will be helpful to your development and growth? What might you want to change? What values do you want to grow?

- **Complete a 360-degree assessment.** More than 85 percent of Fortune 500 companies use multirater feedback to develop their leaders (Folkman and Zenger, n.d.). Determine what your organization uses to help ensure that the feedback will align with your organization's needs. An anonymous instrument is best because those who provide the feedback will be more candid and honest than if they think you will see how each person rated you. Schedule a feedback session with the instrument's expert to gain the best feedback. Don't compare yourself against others; rather, focus on your highest scores and your lowest scores. Your highest are your strengths, and someone who understands the instrument should be able to help you determine how you might use those strengths to improve your weaknesses. Accept the scores without excuse and without defensiveness. Focus your attention on fixing fatal flaws, not just making minor improvements. Be sure to gain insights on identifying the most important competencies as well as practical suggestions for how to make the improvements. A good multirater will also have obtained input from you. And one of the most valuable parts is to determine how your ratings of yourself compared with the ratings of others who completed the feedback. Where do you think you are stronger or weaker than how others rated you? What does that mean for you from a self-awareness perspective?

- **Read a classic.** Read one of the classic books about personal improvement by authors such as Dale Carnegie, Napoleon Hill, Stephen Covey, Norman Vincent Peale, Viktor Frankl, Brian Tracy, Zig Ziglar, M. Scott Peck, or Brené Brown. What's the strongest message for you in the book? Identify three things you learned about yourself that you'd like to change. Establish specific measurable goal dates for achieving these personal improvements.

CROSS TRAINING

You will find related ideas at these crossover skills:

- Communicate Clearly
- Exhibit a Growth Mindset
- Learn from Experience
- Exhibit Self-Control
- Maintain Composure

- Appreciate People and Differences
- Build and Manage Relationships
- Accept and Act on Feedback

READING FOR THE FINAL STRETCH

- *Mindfulness: A Practical Guide,* by Tessa Watt

SKILL 7

Exhibit Career Ambition

Your career ambition is the desire to identify and achieve career goals. It means that you have a desire to do what it takes to move from a current role to other positions with the ultimate goal to develop into a more valuable employee. To be successful, you need to take initiative to make things happen—the opposite of wishing for a promotion and waiting for something to happen. Career drive demonstrates ambition, goal orientation, initiative, and exertion of the effort required to succeed. Often the focus is placed on one particular job or position and the drive becomes more specific. Ambitious employees learn what is required for the positions and begin to gain skills and knowledge. What is sometimes forgotten is that employees also need the right attitude—positive, persistent, confident, determined, and collaborative.

It's important because employees who have career drive are more likely to accomplish their goals and achieve their career dreams. Along the way you will go through development stages and mature as a person, thus growing personally as well as professionally. You will be respected by others in your organization and gain a reputation for having a good work ethic, being able to solve problems, and being a source of good advice. Having an ambitious career drive will keep you humble because you will constantly see room for improvement. Most important is that you are likely to have a sense of purpose in your life, a critical part of self-perception.

MASTERING THE SKILL

Hurdles to Overcome

- What career path do I want to pursue?
- How clear am I about what I want from my career?
- How do I measure my career drive and what motivates it?
- What job is actually right for my next step?
- How much am I willing to sacrifice to reach my ideal career?
- How ready am I for the rapid changes that occur in my organization and the world in general?

Your Path to Success

- Envision the ultimate career
- Be determined to succeed
- Set goals and make things happen to achieve the goals
- Take initiative to pursue and even create opportunities
- Sell your skills and potential to others
- Be realistic about your value to your organization
- Recognize that successful career pursuit takes more than a résumé of task accomplishments and longevity at an organization; it also requires charisma, diligence, collaboration, teamwork, communication, tolerance, influence, ethics, perseverance, optimism, and much more

TIPS FOR PEOPLE IN A HURRY

- **Stop sabotaging.** Think about how you may be standing in the way of your own success. Are you negative? Do you wallow in the past? Do you have a victim mindset? Do you avoid risk? Do you send yourself unsuccessful messages? Do you compare yourself with others and cry unfair comparison? Decide if you are sabotaging your career options. Identify new habits you'll put in place of the bad habits.

- **Don't ignore your needs.** Identify your challenges and address them. Your credibility will suffer if you do not address your weaknesses. Set a goal to improve one weakness.

- **Focus on results.** Help your supervisors see that you have your mind set on results. Few managers want to know all the trials and tribulations you faced while finalizing a project, negotiating a deal, or installing a new system. Spend more time communicating how much money you saved the company or how happy customers are.

- **Learn over coffee.** If you know individuals in the career you are considering, invite them for coffee (your treat) to discuss what a typical day on the job is like. Ask questions such as, "What's the best and worst part of the work?" "What do you recommend I do to prepare for this career?" "What would you want to see on the résumé of someone who is outstanding in this career?"

- **Be mindful of a career in overdrive.** It is possible to have too much career drive, and it could hold you back. You could be seen as excessively ambitious without substance. If you suspect this, think back to how you accepted past career advice.

PRACTICE SPRINTS

- **How strong are your skills?** Think about the career you'd like. Are your skills really strong in this area? Don't let your ego prevent you from asking yourself and others. If the answer is less than 100 percent, seek guidance for potential areas of improvement.

- **Explore real skills.** Seth Godin (2019) uses five descriptors to define the "real skills" of a successful career:

  1. Self-control: once you've decided that something is important, being able to persist toward the goal without letting distractions or bad habits stop you.

  2. Productivity: having the ability and commitment to accomplish the task.

  3. Wisdom: learning from experience those things that are difficult to learn from books.

  4. Perception: the ability to see things before others see them.

  5. Influence: the capacity to persuade others to do what they might not do on their own.

  Review these five "real skills" of a job and determine how you would define them. What have you done that demonstrates you have these skills? How would you rate yourself on each? Be hard on your rating. What can you do to gain more experience to develop each? Ask your supervisor for suggestions and for an opportunity to get experience on the job.

- **Showcase your strengths.** Don't assume that senior people know all you are doing for your organization. First, make sure you are willing to take on high-visibility projects with promotable outcomes. Then, make it easy for them to be your advocates. There's a fine line between bragging and informing, so don't take it to the extreme. But it is important to keep them aware of your strengths and accomplishments. For example, you can involve senior people by asking them for insights or opinions about a project. If they provide input, you have a rationale for keeping them informed.

- **Ask for more.** If you are happy with the organization where you work and want to develop your career there, work with your supervisor and others to get opportunities to build your skill set. Show that you are ambitious and want to help your organization achieve its goals. Meet with your supervisor and ask for support in your development on the road to the ideal career. Ask for problems to solve, projects to lead, and assignments to complete. Ask for developmental opportunities that will provide the experience you need, including participating in a job rotation, leading cross-functional teams, filling in temporarily for someone, getting on-the-job training, obtaining a mentor, or receiving career coaching.

STRATEGIES FOR THE LONG RUN

- **Lay out a plan.** Make a list of all the things you need to do to reach your career goal. Lay them out on a timeline with specific dates. Break each goal down into smaller objectives. Identify the resources you'll need for each step, name who can help you achieve each objective, and specify what you'll need to learn prior to each goal and how you'll learn it. Also list potential obstacles and what you may need to do to overcome them.

- **Find your sweet spot.** Career experts look for the sweet spot that creates your ideal career. It is the intersection of three areas: what you're good at, what the marketplace needs, and what you enjoy doing. You can begin the exploration by drawing a Venn diagram with the three areas intersecting. Use these suggestions to complete each:

  > **What do you do well?** Think in terms of skills, experiences, and interests—not the jobs you've held. This opens more options for you. Are you a good communicator? Are you good at sales? Do you like to write? Are you a good coach? Do you like planning?

  > **What's the demand in the market?** Identify whether there are jobs advertised that are similar to what you envision. Review job boards or talk to a career counselor.

  > **What do you enjoy?** In this case it might be a good idea to examine the differences between areas. For example, do you enjoy working alone or on a team? Do you prefer creative tasks or analyzing numbers? Do you prefer to be outside or at a desk?

- **Call a career coach.** If you are not sure why you seem to be stuck in a job, planning a major career change, or just not making the progress you think you should be making, it may be time to call a career coach.

Career coaches can provide assessments to help you pinpoint the kind of work and workplace that are a good fit for you. They can help you obtain constructive feedback about what you are doing well and where you need to improve. In general, career coaches can take the mystery out of career searches and can provide career confidence, insight, and encouragement.

CROSS TRAINING

You will find related ideas at these crossover skills:

- Create a Personal Development Strategy
- Exhibit a Growth Mindset
- Be Resourceful
- Sell Ideas
- Network with Others
- Advocate for Self
- Plan and Organize Tasks
- Model Corporate Expectations

READING FOR THE FINAL STRETCH

- *Up Is Not the Only Way: Rethinking Career Mobility*, by Beverly Kaye, Lindy Williams, and Lynn Cowart

SKILL 8

Understand Personal Style

Your personal style is the key to understanding why it is easy to get along with some people but oh so difficult to get along with others. Two well-known style assessment instruments are the DiSC Personality Profile and the Myers-Briggs Type Indicator (MBTI). We are all unique, all different. Because of this, our needs, goals, and desires often clash with those of others. Without a clear understanding that these differences are natural, we may label them negatively—"I'm right; you're wrong!"—when in reality it is merely a styles clash.

It's important because everything we do is relationship based, whether it's personal or on the job. In general, your ability to move into others' comfort zones sets the stage for positive relationships—both professionally and personally. Knowing your style improves your communication, builds work and personal relationships, and helps you appreciate the differences of others. Understanding others' natural strengths helps you understand what each colleague could do easily and happily. Implementing the value of style is critical to self-perception. A clarification—the concept about style is *not* about labeling people; we use words to convey meaning and understanding.

Hurdles to Overcome

- What do others say about my personal style?

- How do I think my style is perceived?

- How skilled am I at understanding others' personal styles?

- How knowledgeable am I about how my style affects others as they make decisions, view time, deal with stress, and perform many other daily activities?

- How prepared am I to adapt to a different style that's more comfortable to others as they address activities that are important to both of us?

Your Path to Success

- Accurately describe your own personal style

- Appreciate and accept the attributes of different styles

- Gain skills to move into others' "comfort zones" to improve understanding

- Understand how to build trust between different styles

TIPS FOR PEOPLE IN A HURRY

- **Gain personal perspective.** Ask for feedback from people around you. Gain different perspectives about how you communicate with others.

- **Look for clues.** Consider the colleagues with whom you work. What clues do they provide about their preferences and how they would each like to be treated? Identify how you could approach each person to improve your communication with them.

- **Match behavior.** Style is based on behaviors that you can see. Begin to notice others' behaviors such as voice tone (loud, soft, passionate, friendly), speech speed (fast or slow), expressions (intense, controlled, animated, smiles), eye contact (direct, minimal, fleeting, welcoming), and gestures (pointed, few, big movement, approachable). Each of these provides clues about the individual's style. Once you start to recognize these style clues, they will become natural and you will automatically match styles for better understanding. You don't need to remember all the labels; just begin to match the behavior of others to help them feel more comfortable.

- **Practice proficiency.** The personal style concept is something anyone can learn and practice. The concept is one of the most important ways to have an impact on the people you communicate with daily. Meet with someone who understands the concept and can give you a quick overview.

PRACTICE SPRINTS

- **Learn styles jargon.** Several instruments are available to assess styles. The theory is the same in all. The only difference is that the style names change. These four styles listed are based on work by David W. Merrill and Roger H. Reid (1994) and others:

  1. If you have a controlling (dominance) style, you likely place high demands on yourself and others. You are probably emotionally reserved and tend to be decisive and results oriented, giving guidance to everyone.

  2. If you have an expressive (influence) style, you are enthusiastic, creative, and intuitive and like being around people. You may easily get bored and tend to go off on tangents.

  3. If you have an analytical (conscientiousness) style, you tend toward perfectionism and prefer to have logical discussions filled with details. You tend to keep feelings to yourself.

  4. If you lean toward a collaborative (steadiness) style, you put a high value on people and friendships. You are a true team player and often go out of your way to avoid offending others. You have opinions but are not inclined to push for them.

Learn if your organization uses one particular instrument. Understanding others' styles and why you get along with some people more easily than others is critical to your success. Use the style names that are common to your organization.

ADAPT TO STYLES

Two continuums or scales are combined in a two-by-two grid to create the four styles. The power scale goes from take-charge to easygoing, and the formality scale goes from task oriented to people oriented. The four styles that are created are displayed in figure 1 and defined here:

- Controlling styles are at the farther ends of the take-charge and task scales.
- Expressing styles are at the farther ends of the take-charge and people-oriented scales.
- Analytical styles are at the farther ends of the easygoing and task scales.
- Collaborative styles are at the farther ends of the easygoing and people-oriented scales.

To be the most successful with the concept of styles, you can begin to practice how to adapt to each of the ends of the grid. For example, to adapt to those that are

- more take-charge than you: speed up your speaking, limit details, state your position clearly and concisely, take more risks, and be assertive.
- more easygoing than you: slow down and relax, ask more questions, pursue alternatives, take time to listen, and give them time to consider the issue.

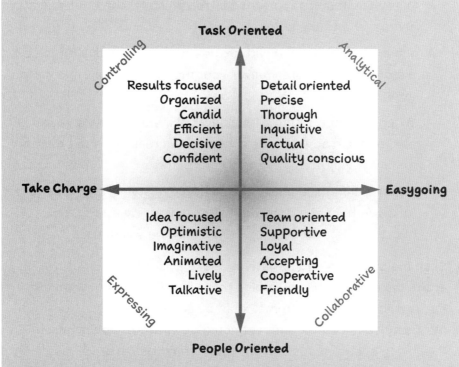

Figure 1. Four communication styles

- more task oriented than you: stick to business, get organized, avoid wild ideas and conversation, be more logical, and minimize small talk.

- more people oriented than you: respond to their ideas, refer to people by name and learn more about them, be tolerant, respond to small talk, and have fun.

- **Get into others' comfort zones.** Although everyone exhibits characteristics from all style types, each of us prefers one style type, and our behaviors reflect this preference. No one style is better or worse than the others. Each style brings with it a unique set of strengths and limitations. Make a list of all your colleagues with whom you would like an improved relationship. Identify what you believe their personal styles are. Then using this guide, identify two things you could do to improve communication with each:

> When communicating with controlling styles, be brief, specific, candid, and to the point.

> When communicating with expressive styles, stick with the big picture, avoid details, deliver your message rapidly, and make it exciting.

> When communicating with analytical styles, prepare your comments in advance, be accurate and realistic, and provide tangible evidence to support your points.

> When communicating with collaborative styles, take time to get to know them and draw out their opinions by asking "how" questions. Be sure to show how everyone will benefit.

- **Examine positives and negatives.** Make a list of all the positive attributes of each style. Examine the list and identify how taking each attribute to the extreme could be seen as negative. For example, being candid and confident could be viewed as being insensitive; being spontaneous and animated could be perceived as being flaky; being cautious and accurate could be viewed as nitpicky; and being sensitive and agreeable could be seen as being gullible. Positives can easily become negatives.

- **Opposites don't always attract.** Whenever you bring a group of people together, there are bound to be style differences. Understanding and valuing those differences can strengthen a personal relationship or a team's effectiveness. We generally get along with those who have a similar style to ours. Without understanding personal styles, it can be most difficult to get along with those who are our exact opposites: Controlling styles and collaborating styles are opposites. Analytical styles and expressive styles are opposites. Identify someone who is your exact opposite and have a friendly discussion about how you each view the other's behaviors. If you need to work together, create a plan to do that with ease.

- **Test it.** One of the most important things you can do is to take a reliable and validated personality test. The DiSC is one of the oldest and most trusted. How do the results corroborate how you view yourself? How do the results contradict with how you view yourself? Discuss your results with someone who will provide candid feedback to you.

- **Compare your intentions with others' perceptions.** We judge ourselves by what's on the inside, but others judge us by what they view on the outside. Create a page with three columns. In the first column, list your internal characteristics or what you "intend." In the second column, across from each characteristic in the first column, list your external characteristics or what others "perceive." For example, what you intend is to help people, but what others perceive is that you tell others what to do and come across as bossy. In the third column, determine what is causing the discrepancies. In the example you might identify that the wording of your helpful suggestions is too short and could be more of a two-way conversation. Once you have your list, discuss it with someone who will give you candid feedback about your observations. Ask for additional suggestions.

- **Change for life.** Meet with several people you know to identify what adaptions you need to make when communicating with others. Develop your plan for how you will make these changes. Select several people who seem to get along with different types and create your style sounding board. Ask them if you can connect with each to help you on your journey, to provide answers, to ask you the difficult questions, and to challenge you to grow and improve your personal styles skills.

CROSS TRAINING

You will find related ideas at these crossover skills:

- Resolve Conflict
- Influence, Persuade, and Negotiate
- Appreciate People and Differences
- Communicate Clearly
- Build and Manage Relationships
- Compassion (character trait)

READING FOR THE FINAL STRETCH

- *People Styles at Work . . . and Beyond: Making Bad Relationships Good and Good Relationships Better*, by Robert Bolton and Dorothy Bolton

SKILL 9

Improve Weaknesses

mproving your weaknesses begins with your desire. The more you learn about yourself, the more you will likely want to improve. You may realize that a large percentage of your thoughts, beliefs, convictions, and arguments are reflections of what you experienced in the past, assimilated based on former relationships, or sometimes are even just reactions to what you are feeling in the moment. Science has shown that some of our memories are unreliable, but we've told our untrue stories so often in our minds that we've built strong neuron bridges of false truths in our brains. We also tend to overestimate our strengths and underestimate our weaknesses, and our brains can't tell the difference between the truth and a lie. Theories exist about finding jobs that play to your strengths. Your goal should be to identify a job that engages three to five of your top strengths, but you still need to improve your weaknesses. You can be the most brilliant cybersecurity professional, but if you can't communicate your ideas, you likely won't be happy or successful in your profession.

It's important because being flexible and changing your perspective and your behaviors impacts your ability to learn and grow. If you cannot be flexible enough to make changes, you may be experiencing a blind spot. That blind spot may be preventing you from receiving a promotion, building a solid relationship, or achieving a lifetime goal. The breakthrough occurs once you are aware of it, accept it, and take steps to change yourself to create the person you want to be. Don't be surprised—meaningful change is hard to do.

MASTERING THE SKILL

Hurdles to Overcome

- How open and accepting am I to the feedback I receive from others?

- How tightly do I cling to my opinions? How set am I in my own ways?

- How often do I place blame because I believe my job focuses on my weaknesses, not my strengths?

- How well do I adapt to others' needs, styles, and requests?

- Am I aware of the triggers that set me off, how I respond, and what I'd like to do differently?

Your Path to Success

- Accept that there is a good chance that your intuitions and assumptions about your skills are incorrect

- Take time to confirm data and facts before pursuing a path

- Try new approaches or methods eagerly

- Display an openness to feedback and others' ideas

- Be coachable and have a strong desire to grow and learn

- Believe that it's important to understand both your strengths and your weaknesses

- Make adjustments in your personal behavior

TIPS FOR PEOPLE IN A HURRY

- **Are you really the expert?** Most of what we react to throughout the day is not something that we can be 100 percent sure of. Stop being the expert. Take a deep breath and ask yourself, "What can I learn from this discussion? How can this improve me and my thought process?"

- **I could be wrong.** Simply starting sentences with "I could be incorrect" increases your probability of accepting others' thoughts and being open to additional data. The result is that your brain will be curious and accepting of new ideas and may identify better, more innovative concepts.

- **Don't overestimate.** Most people overestimate their strengths. What strengths are you overestimating?

- **What's holding you back?** Think back to feedback you've received in the past 12 months from friends, family, colleagues, supervisors, and others—even in the heat of an argument. What similarities exist across all of them? Create a list for pondering.

- **Strengths or weaknesses?** Finding a job that focuses on your strengths is wise, but it is highly unlikely that you will find a job that avoids all your weaknesses. Even Tom Rath, author of *Strengths Finder 2.0*, suggests that you find your passion but also that you improve what you don't do well in order to affect your results. Does your current job play to your strengths? If yes, what are the basic weaknesses you need to improve to be effective?

PRACTICE SPRINTS

- **Discover your blind spots.** This four-step plan will help you uncover your blind spots:

  1. Begin by questioning where your life is now and whether you are moving in the direction you want. You are where you are because of choices you made. What beliefs got you here?

2. As Marshall Goldsmith's book suggests, what got you here won't get you there. So next identify what beliefs, attitudes, and behaviors you may need to change in order to get you to where you want to be.

3. Determine how your ego may be preventing you from moving forward. What beliefs are you reluctant to release that may be holding you prisoner in your own life? What can you do to change your beliefs?

4. Compile your notes and meet with someone you trust to give you no-nonsense advice about what you need to do.

Summarize by identifying what problems you created for yourself. Remember, it is not about changing YOU; it's about understanding your behaviors and perspectives so that you can adjust them.

- **Force field your change.** Think of what you want to change, and complete a force field analysis, a tool designed by Kurt Lewin. Name your target at the top of a piece of paper. List all the forces that are working to prevent the change you desire on the right side. List all the forces that work in favor of the change you desire on the left side. Now identify how you can make the driving forces stronger. Next identify how you can weaken or eliminate the restraining forces. You can download a force field analysis template at https://ideas.bkconnection.com/skillsforcareersuccess.

- **Go public.** Decide on your change and identify your goal. Establish two or three actions that will support the change. Tell two or three people about your goals and your actions, and ask if they would be willing to keep you on track.

- **Use a 4 by 4 forum.** One way you can identify your blind spots is to write down four positive words and four negative words that describe you. In addition, ask four colleagues, four friends, and four family members to do the same. Once you gather all the data, look for similarities and differences. Does everyone view the same positives and negatives? Or do some see the positives as negatives? What things do you see as positive but others see as negative? Or vice versa? Be sure to get back to everyone with a thank-you. If you want to take a risk, let them know what you plan to do differently.

- **You don't know what you don't know.** Joseph Luft and Harry Ingham created a technique called the Johari Window to help you uncover your blind spots. Your blind spots are at the intersection of how you perceive yourself and how others perceive you. The problem with blind spots is that you don't know what you don't know, and that can create problems for you. Most blind spots are based on assumptions. Generally they include the inability to accurately assess your skills, your beliefs that encourage you to take sides rather than see what you are missing, emotional blindness that clouds your perceptions, and believing that you are always right. In order to change, you need to discover these unknown unknowns—your blind spots. You can find a model of the Johari Window at https://ideas.bkconnection.com/skillsforcareer success. Review the four panes of the Johari Window: the arena, the facade, the blind spots, and the unknown.

- **Let a professional do it.** If you need additional support to probe and challenge you to see things from a different perspective in order to uncover your bias, prejudices, and blind spots, consider working with a mentor, coach, or psychologist. We all behave, think, and react automatically. We often respond without thinking and may be in a daze as we hurry from one important idea to another. It may take a professional to shake us out of our daily stupor. Many assume that introspection can improve awareness as we try to learn what we need to change. Yet research by Eurich (2018) shows that introspection isn't always helpful, because we may not do it right. If you're serious about making change, connect with a professional to get started.

- **Improve over lunch.** Identify someone with whom you've had a strained relationship. It could be someone from your personal or professional life. Invite the individual to lunch and suggest that you'd like to do what you can to repair the relationship. Take full responsibility, and accept how the individual may see the differences. Ask the individual to identify specific changes you should make and to suggest recommendations for how to make the changes. Offer your thanks. Ask for time to put a plan together and whether the person would be willing to meet with you again to review and make recommendations about your plan.

CROSS TRAINING

You will find related ideas at these crossover skills:

- Model Corporate Expectations
- Accept and Act on Feedback
- Learn from Experience
- Practice Resiliency

- Adapt to Situations
- Show Self-Awareness
- Flexibility (character trait)

READING FOR THE FINAL STRETCH

- *Managing Transitions: Making the Most of Change*, by William Bridges
- *Triggers: Creating Behavior That Lasts, Becoming the Person You Want to Be*, by Marshall Goldsmith

Display Self-Confidence

Your self-confidence is the ability to be secure in who you are and the skills and knowledge that you have. Self-confidence means that you are self-assured that you can make a valuable contribution to the situation whether as a member of a team, as a part of an organization, or in a solo situation where the results rest with you. Self-confident people recognize and value their own talents and competencies. You believe in and appreciate what you know and can do without being arrogant or bragging about it. Unfortunately too much self-confidence can easily appear to be cockiness or conceit. You need to demonstrate self-confidence without appearing egotistical. That can be difficult.

It's important because self-confidence underscores many other skills you need in your professional life. In some ways self-confidence can be an umbrella label for many other skills. For example, confidence in your strengths helps you tap into courage and determination when faced with a challenge. Self-confidence can also help you understand your limitations and how to adjust by tapping into your strengths. Self-confidence grows in a positive environment where you receive constructive feedback and where you have an opportunity to make decisions and set goals. Self-confident employees are considered more often for special projects, promotions, developmental opportunities, and other organizational honors.

Hurdles to Overcome

- How do I feel about my standing within my peers and colleagues?
- How easily do I sell my ideas to groups?
- How do I value my worth and contribution?
- How comprehensive is my work, ensuring accuracy, timeliness, and completeness?
- How do I react to opposition and resistance?
- How rational are my decisions, actions, and projects?
- How satisfied am I with my career results?

Your Path to Success

- Recognize and appreciate your own skills, talents, and competencies
- Be able to judge your status and standing with respect to the environment
- Experience the satisfaction of position among others
- Willingly express your ideas in groups
- Project dignity, compassion, and assurance
- Readily accept constructive criticism
- Be courageous about upholding a decision when you're certain it is accurate
- Understand the value of building and maintaining relationships
- Be humble and accepting about errors and omissions

TIPS FOR PEOPLE IN A HURRY

- **Be a volunteer.** Doing good for others is good for society and good for your soul. It is also good for gaining self-confidence.

- **Everyone's a critic.** Prepare for critics. We live in a competitive world, and thus it is likely that your project will receive criticism. Be sure to separate the emotional criticism (jealousy, dislike, possessiveness, one-upmanship) from the rational criticism, which is actually filled with helpful improvements. Know the difference.

- **Failure and confidence are an unlikely couple.** Learn from failure. You've heard it before, and it's repeated here because it's important. Learning from your failure is part a. Part b recognizes that failure can also be a confidence booster. Think of all the things you know now that you didn't know before. It's all in your perspective.

- **Who are you hanging out with?** Take care with the colleagues you spend time with. Sometimes a low self-confidence can be resolved simply by hanging out with positive people—those who will encourage you.

PRACTICE SPRINTS

- **Find a self-confident role model.** Low self-confidence can be destructive. It becomes a vicious cycle because if you have low self-confidence you are probably critical of yourself, don't feel you have anything to contribute, and fear even offering suggestions. This negativity leads to even lower self-confidence. What to do? Find a positive self-confident role model quickly. Connect your work to that individual. Be available to support them, work with them, and find your direction again. In return, they will reward you and demonstrate what it takes to be self-confident, show compassion, and help to silence your inner critic.

- **Learn the secrets to self-confidence.** Interview three of the most self-confident people you know. Imagine that you are a talk show host gathering information for your audience. Learn how self-confident each feels; it is often true that self-confident people don't think about the level of their confidence because they are too busy doing what needs to be done.

- **Tamp down the pride.** Although you've been reading about how to build self-confidence, it is possible that you have too much confidence that is not backed by skills, expertise, and talent. If that's the case, you'll need to learn why that's true. Learn what you are doing that makes it appear that you are coming across as egotistical. Ask someone to observe you in meetings and to write down what they see that could lead to this perception. Even better, find out if you could be recorded during a meeting or other event. View it and observe your actions. Sometimes overconfidence is a part of your personal style. Whatever it is, plan how you can adapt your behavior and communication to project what you desire. Truly self-confident people are flexible enough to make the change.

- **Refresh your résumé.** Take time to update your résumé. In doing so, observe all the new skills and knowledge you are adding to it. Each new experience adds to your list of talents. Your accomplishments should help you understand why you should be self-confident.

STRATEGIES FOR THE LONG RUN

- **Take on a project.** Ask your supervisor to provide you with a small project that's yours to manage, lead, and complete. While you are helping your organization complete a project, you are also building your self-confidence.

- **Teach another.** You can build your own self-confidence by building someone else's self-confidence. Sound complicated? It isn't. Coach a recent hire or someone junior to you to help the new hire learn about the job, understand the organization, gain experience, and gain skills. Use these strategies to nurture the new hire's self-confidence:

  > Offer praise and acknowledgment for all accomplishments.

  > Avoid correcting everything; it could harm confidence.

> Give your learner choices.

> Encourage the learner to establish attainable goals.

> Display a positive attitude throughout the relationship.

> Encourage your learner to constantly try to do better.

> Build on your learner's strengths before moving on to something that is completely unfamiliar.

> Encourage your learner to select one thing to improve and then provide the support to do so.

Throughout this coaching experience, think with a dual focus. You are building your self-confidence as you build the new hire's self-confidence. Now consider, what are you doing for your learner that you can implement for yourself? You are finding and managing experiences for your learner. How can you find the same kind of experiences for you? How can you establish your own attainable goals? Where can you go to receive encouragement and acknowledgment for your accomplishments?

- **Think positively.** Confidence is a result of being tested and comes from trying new approaches in positive, supportive environments. How supportive are those thoughts you experience every day? You average about 65,000 thoughts daily. Unfortunately, many of them may be negative. Your mind is trying to protect you from all the bad things in this world. However, those negative thoughts can also draw on your self-confidence. Start every day with 10 pennies in one pocket. Every time you think a negative thought, remove a penny and put it in a different pocket. Of course, you can't stop yourself from thinking negative thoughts. In fact, for self-preservation, you wouldn't want to. The exercise can help you be aware of the kinds of thoughts that may not be a boon to your self-confidence.

CROSS TRAINING

You will find related ideas at these crossover skills:

- Lead Others
- Maintain Composure
- Make Key Decisions
- Exhibit a Professional Image
- Courage (character trait)

READING FOR THE FINAL STRETCH

- *The Gifts of Imperfection: Let Go of Who You Think You're Supposed to Be and Embrace Who You Are*, by Brené Brown
- *The Confidence Code*, by Katty Kay and Claire Shipman

SKILL 11

Practice Resiliency

Resiliency is the ability to recover quickly after adversity strikes or you experience a failure. Resiliency is a skill we can all learn. It isn't about zipping through life unscathed or avoiding everyday challenges. No, quite the opposite; it's about experiencing life's natural obstacles to their fullest, learning from them, and continuing to live a joyful, positive life. Your resiliency allows you to be knocked down by life and, rather than wallow in your misery, get back up and be positive and ready to move forward. Many people use the term "bounce back" to define resilience. Resilient people are often viewed as calm, optimistic, and balanced.

It's important because it contributes to your professional success and your personal health. Resiliency leads to improved learning, higher productivity, and reduced absences. Resilient people are more involved in their communities and families. Higher resilience is even related to increased physical and mental health, such as less depression and greater resistance to stress. A positive emotional state, a part of resiliency, leads to a heathy immune system, so individuals can fight infection more effectively. Resilient people tend to have a positive perspective of the future, and they invest their energy to change the things that they control.

Hurdles to Overcome

- How well do I cope with stress at work and at home?

- How do I choose to react to unforeseen issues and problems?

- How optimistic am I in general?

- How skilled am I with implementing a practical problem-solving model?

Your Path to Success

- Overcome defeat or failure by making realistic plans and moving forward

- Move on after stressful conversations without deliberating about them

- Take care of yourself physically, mentally, and socially

- Be aware of yourself, your surroundings, and your interactions with people

- Value connections with other people

- Accept change and manage it as a welcome challenge

- Value a sense of humor

- Demonstrate optimism

TIPS FOR PEOPLE IN A HURRY

- **Plan time to recharge.** Find time to get away from the stresses of work, even if it's just a walk around the block. Ignore the unimportant work that can wait for another time. Do something that is more stimulating and refreshing.

- **Take care of your mind and body.** You know the drill: get enough sleep, eat healthy, exercise, and learn to manage stress. Taking care of you means you will be better prepared to deal with challenges that come your way.

- **Build relationships.** Strong personal and work relationships lead to a happier, healthier, more stress-free lifestyle. Build a support system of individuals you can count on to be there when you need them.

- **Learn something new.** Whether at work or at home, expanding your skills is important to keep your mind active and interested in life.

PRACTICE SPRINTS

- **Find meaning.** Make the work that you do meaningful. You spend too many hours of your life at a job to be doing something that isn't meaningful and satisfying. MIT Sloan research found five reasons that people found their work meaningful (Bailey and Madden 2016):

  1. The work needs to matter to others, and needs to have impact and relevance.

  2. The work must have moments that cause employees to feel challenged, motivated, and engaged—not necessarily always happy, but valuable to others.

  3. Meaningfulness does not need to be constant; in fact, it seems to be more important when the meaningful moments occur episodically, sometimes when they have the least control and when they least expect it.

  4. Meaningfulness was often experienced while reflecting on experiences, sometimes years later.

  5. Employees need to have a sense of a job well done.

  These five features of meaningful work go beyond a generic feeling of engagement. Think about meaning from three perspectives. What does your organization do to help you find meaningfulness? What does the work do to help you find meaning? And how do your interactions with others help you find meaning? What can you do to strengthen meaning in each perspective? What can you do to decrease meaninglessness from each perspective? How does meaning in your work relate to resiliency for you?

- **Connect.** Consider how you can use your network to build a strong support base. Your network can be critical when you need support, are looking for a job, or just need someone to talk to. Building a network is good, but making the connections personal doubles its value. Make a list of people you depend on from your personal or professional network. Select someone from that list and identify something you could do for that individual.

- **Get ahead of change.** Talk to your supervisor about anticipated changes the organization will face. How can you prepare yourself and your colleagues for these changes? Even with a fair warning, resiliency will be required. Host several groups in your own work area to discuss how everyone can be better prepared for the change—specifically what everyone can do to be ready to practice resiliency.

  1. What do you anticipate will stop or go away?
  2. What is something new that you anticipate will start?
  3. How can you make any transitions easier for your department?
  4. What positive experiences do you and your colleagues expect?

STRATEGIES FOR THE LONG RUN

- **Double the benefits.** You already know that managing stress is an important part of being a resilient employee. You could double your resilience rewards by teaching a stress management class. First, you would benefit by learning all the intricacies of managing your own stress. Second, the entire organization would benefit as you make the knowledge available to others.

- **Show your stuff.** Take on a project with a short timeline but a critical outcome from your boss or your boss's boss. It will give you an opportunity to live under pressure with a project that is very important. Track the times you tapped into your ability to be resilient. What did you do well? What do you need to improve?

- **Assess your resilience.** The Center for Creative Leadership assesses resilience based on nine topics. How well do you accept change? Continue to learn? Empower yourself? Have a sense of purpose? Separate yourself from your work? Develop personal and professional networks? Use reflection to grow? Keep your skills up to speed for future changes? Balance your financial situation?

  > What do your responses tell you about your resiliency?

  > What resiliency strengths can you rely on during change?

  > What areas should you develop to become more resilient?

  Identify the top three areas you need to improve and create an action plan to improve each. You can download an action plan template at https://ideas.bkconnection.com/skillsforcareersuccess.

CROSS TRAINING

You will find related ideas at these crossover skills:

- Plan and Organize Tasks
- Be Resourceful
- Maintain Composure
- Adapt to Situations
- Set Goals
- Flexibility (character trait)

READING FOR THE FINAL STRETCH

- *Micro-Resilience: Minor Shifts for Major Boosts in Focus, Drive, and Energy*, by Bonnie St. John and Allen Haines
- *A Year of Resilience: 52 Ideas to Be More Resilient and Stay Afloat throughout the Year*, by Maureen Orey

Communication

Jonathan Fraser became owner of the Memphis-based home and business security firm EntreLeader in 2006. He followed his father, who began the business in the early 1970s. But if he expected a smooth transition from his former role as an airline flight officer, it wasn't to be. Tragically, his father died of cancer in 2008. The company was stunned by the loss.

The global recession that began that year was another blow. Without its founder, and facing a severe economic downturn, the business stumbled, and workers lost heart and retreated into their own emotional bunkers. Jonathan himself was focused on keeping the company afloat and spent little time informing people about what was happening to the company.

Searching for a way to right the ship, Jonathan came across a business article that outlined the communication strategies used by successful companies. That article focused his attention and made him realize that his tenure at the company was in some ways marked by his own withdrawal from his workers—understandable when grief and economic pressures might drive a leader to isolate and shore up defenses.

Jonathan realized that his lack of communication added to workers' anxieties. Bolstered by what he'd learned, Jonathan put three deceptively elemental but undeniably useful communication tactics to work. He started a simple newsletter to keep his team informed not only about the business but also about what was happening among staff. It was a way to carry on the personal relationship his father had with his workers.

Next came monthly get-togethers. That took some experimenting, because people felt more like hunkering down at home than staying after hours at work. When the gatherings were moved to Friday afternoons and included entertaining activities (like ping-pong) and good food, workers started to look forward to spending time with each other. Connections that had been pushed away in response to tragic and overwhelming circumstances resurfaced.

Third, Jonathan scheduled regular Monday meetings with his team. The format was a stand-up fifteen-minute meeting in which successes and problems were reported, customer responses were shared, and congratulations were given for jobs well done.

It took about six months, but Jonathan's mindful communication practices began to heal the company's grief and relieve individuals' anxiety. He credits those simple but powerful communication practices not just for saving the business but for growing it by increasing camaraderie and trust, and by improving customer service.

Communication is your ticket to success,
if you pay attention and learn to do it effectively.

—THEO GOLD

Communicate Clearly

Your communication, the one skill you can't ignore, is the transmission of a message from a sender to a receiver. As figure 2 shows, the sender uses a medium to send the message, which goes through the sender's and the receiver's filters before the receiver decodes the message. The receiver's interpretation of the message becomes part of the feedback to the sender. Many places exist for problems to occur, including these examples. The environment can enhance or block communication. The filters, the biases or opinions based on past experiences, can create misunderstandings. We've been communicating since we were born, so you'd think we'd be experts by now. We're not. The skill or lack of skill of the sender and the receiver can cause them to use incorrect words or value-laden meanings, misstate or misinterpret the message, or incorporate unintended meanings. Communication is much more than talking. It also includes skills such as listening, asking questions, interpreting body language, and encouraging others to contribute.

Even though it is difficult, it's important to get communication right because it is the basis of so many other skills. It is essential for forming friendships, creating a productive and efficient workplace, building a team,

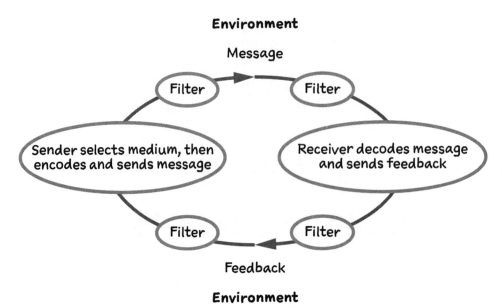

Figure 2. The communication process.

increasing customer satisfaction, growing the bottom line, and just about anything you want to do. However, the most important reason to hone your communication skills is that it is readily visible to everyone you work with: how clear and complete your messages are, how carefully you listen to and interpret messages from everyone, and how interested you are in building personal and professional relationships.

MASTERING THE SKILL

Hurdles to Overcome

- How aware am I of sending unclear or inappropriate messages?
- How often do I cut people off midsentence or begin to think of my response instead of listening to the whole message?
- What kind of negative messages do my facial expressions and my body language send when I am speaking or listening?
- What judgmental thoughts do I have about others when I should be listening to understand their perspective?

- Do I write off communication skills as too mundane or too basic?

- How often do I use the excuse "that's just who I am" to avoid making improvements?

- Do I overwhelm listeners with information they don't need?

Your Path to Success

- Ensure that your communication meets the 6 Cs: clear, correct, complete, concise, coherent, and courteous

- Customize your communication based on what you know others need, what motivates them, and what interests them

- Engage in active listening techniques and strive to understand others' perspectives to build relationships, understand expectations, make better decisions, gain knowledge, and reach mutual agreement with others

- Ensure congruency between your verbal messages and your nonverbal messages

- Select responses carefully using positive, objective words, inclusive neutral language, and accurate pronunciations

- Know which medium you should use, with whom, and when

TIPS FOR PEOPLE IN A HURRY

- **Observe nonverbal behavior.** Get in touch with nonverbal behavior by noticing what people do that influences their communication. Ask friends for feedback about what messages your eye contact, posture, hand gestures, or other body motions send while you are talking or listening.

- **WAIT.** Focus on you for a defined 90 minutes in a group. What percentage of the time are you speaking? What percentage are you listening? What does this say about you? Remember the acronym WAIT, which stands for Why Am I Talking?

- **Connect with others.** Study how people connect with others through communication. How do they connect with their thoughts? How do they connect with their feelings?

- **Compare communication techniques.** Identify a good communicator in your department and a personal friend who is a good communicator. Observe both and identify what they do that makes you feel they are good communicators. Are their techniques the same or different?

- **Review the process.** Review the communication process in figure 2. Use a green pen to mark the parts that are your strengths. Use a red pen to mark the parts that are your weaknesses. Use a yellow pen to mark those parts that could use some improvement.

PRACTICE SPRINTS

- **Compelling communication.** Consider a recent communication when you didn't gain the listener's attention as you had hoped. Ask yourself a couple of questions about the communication. Did you offer a reason the listener should invest time? Was the message unique, inspiring, or exciting to capture attention? What "proof" did you provide, such as a story, data, or examples, to relate your message?

- **Barriers to benefits.** List all the barriers that could prevent effective communication. This could include interpersonal such as body language; thinking of what you'll say next instead of listening; language such as different meanings for words; physical barriers such as distance or noise; perceptual such as disinterest or previous experiences; emotional such as lack of trust; or cultural, gender, or other differences. Which of these barriers are unique to you, and what can you do to change the barrier into a benefit?

- **Beyond active listening.** Based on work by Carl Rogers, active listening is often touted as the ideal, but there are levels beyond. *Active listening* demonstrates a high level of interaction with the speaker, such as asking questions to increase understanding and observing speakers' body language for underlying messages. Go beyond with *clarification listening* by paraphrasing the message in different words to increase understanding. *Empathetic listening* can be used to confirm whether your intuition about the speaker's feelings is correct.

- **Email audit.** Email three colleagues or friends. Ask them to identify three of your personal communication strengths and one communication weakness. How consistent were their responses? Compile your results and create a communication improvement plan. Think about how you could build on your strengths to improve your communication weaknesses. Share your plan with your coach or supervisor and ask for additional feedback.

STRATEGIES FOR THE LONG RUN

- **Select the best medium.** Examine your choices for delivering messages and whether you have used the best method based on each message. Methods for sending messages include voice, reports, email, or others. You need to decide what method to use based on whether the message is meant to be one-way or two-way, with immediate or delayed feedback, or to one person or more. Immediate feedback, for example, requires one-to-one, large or small meetings, video conferences, phone calls, or word of mouth. Delayed feedback could include intranet, newsletters, corporate communication, social media, reports, emails, or texting. Don't become overly reliant on one medium. Before determining the best method of communication, consider these parameters:

  1. One-way or two-way message
  2. Kind of message—routine and open to anyone or confidential
  3. The length of the message
  4. Whether it requires a response
  5. Urgency
  6. Requirements for a record of distribution

7. Size and the distribution of the recipients

8. Relationship of the sender and the receiver

9. Available technology

Create a plan for how you'll use this information in the future.

- **Learn a second language.** The ability to speak a second or third language is becoming more and more important for the globalized world. Learn a new language or brush up on your language skills using these resources:

  1. BBC Languages is provided by the BBC.
  2. Duolingo is a gamified learning process where you learn by translating content.
  3. Live Mocha is one of the newest online language learning communities.
  4. Memrise offers an innovative memorizing system for learning new languages.

  To make it more fun, enlist a colleague or friend to learn a language with you.

- **Question power.** Expand your communication experiences with the kinds of questions you ask. Experiment with three kinds of questions:

  > Clarifying questions ensure that you understand what's been communicated, add information, and define accuracy. They might begin with who, what, where, when, or how—for example, "Let me clarify, how many were involved?" or "Where might you find additional information?" *Why* questions can also be used with care, since they are often oriented in the past without providing much new information. They may also suggest a judgment call.

  > Open-ended questions draw people into a discussion and encourage them to expand their ideas—for example, "What do you think will happen next?" Open-ended questions can't be answered with a simple yes or no.

> Probing questions introduce new ideas and invite reflection on the topic. They can be helpful during problem-solving discussions and foster ownership of outcomes—for example, "Can you think of how you might be adding to the confusion?"

Before an important future communication, identify the questions you'd like to ask. What kinds of questions should you use more often?

CROSS TRAINING

You will find related ideas at these crossover skills:

- Practice Political Savvy
- Sell Ideas
- Lead Self
- Appreciate People and Differences

READING FOR THE FINAL STRETCH

- *Communicate with Confidence: How to Say It Right the First Time and Every Time*, by Dianna Booher

SKILL 13

Give and Receive Feedback

Your ability to give and receive feedback is both a responsibility and a privilege. When you receive feedback, be appreciative that the individual had the courage to share perceptions with you. Even if you believe the feedback to be misguided or wrong, it's important to show appreciation. You don't have to agree with all the feedback, but listen carefully because the individual's perception is there for a reason. When you give feedback, ensure it is authentic, specific, candid, and judgment-free. Be empathetic and compassionate. A good guideline is to ask if you can give feedback first. There is no reason to catch them off guard—or perhaps this really is a bad time. The goal is to help others learn and grow.

It's important because feedback is one of the most important ways that we receive the information and insight that help us develop, improve, and advance. We learn how others experience us and what would make our relationships more effective. Feedback is like the wiggly needle on a compass. Even though it is quivering back and forth, it knows where north is and will point us in that direction. The same is true with feedback. Feedback can be the compass that starts you on the right path.

MASTERING THE SKILL

Hurdles to Overcome

- How reluctant am I to share feedback?
- Why do I put off telling someone about something that concerns me?
- How often is my feedback vague, judgmental, or based on inappropriate humor or a generality such as "always" or "never"?
- How concerned am I that giving feedback will make me appear as a know-it-all?
- What causes me to become defensive or argumentative when someone gives me feedback?
- Why do I tighten up or hold my breath when someone gives me feedback?

Your Path to Success

- Recognize the value of the feedback you give to others
- Provide feedback to others that is specific, candid, appropriate, and timed close to the action
- Give feedback that defines the impact of the action
- Deliver both positive and negative feedback
- Listen carefully and respect anyone who offers you feedback
- Take time to think about the feedback and ask for suggestions to improve
- Be willing to change your behavior based on feedback

TIPS FOR PEOPLE IN A HURRY

- **Practice feedback.** Identify someone whose work you admire. Tell them. Provide positive feedback that is specific and direct. Express your feelings.

- **Say thank you.** Remember to thank everyone who gives you feedback.

- **End with feedback.** At your next meeting, suggest taking the last couple of minutes for everyone to shout out a thank-you to someone else in the room for what they did.

- **Begin a Feedback Friday.** Initiate a movement in your office that encourages everyone to practice giving feedback—especially on Fridays. Reflect on what you learn about feedback.

PRACTICE SPRINTS

- **The best.** Consider the best feedback you ever received. What made it the best? How can you implement some of the same techniques when giving feedback?

- **The worst.** Think about the worst feedback you ever received. How did it make you feel? What made it bad? What behaviors or tactics were used that you want to remember to never use?

- **Least expect it.** Identify someone to give feedback to who least expects it, such as the person who empties your waste basket or the person who makes the coffee. Remember to be specific, candid, and appropriate. Select a different person every day for a week. What responses did you get? Which words did you use that made the greatest impact? What did you learn from this exercise that you can use in the future?

- **Don't let your feedback flop.** Ensure your feedback to others is successful, not a failure. Do this by addressing the issues, not the individuals. Ensure that you provide feedback regularly; this makes it easier when something serious must be addressed. Deliver corrective feedback in private and positive feedback in public. Be specific and focus on outcomes, not weaknesses. Ask how you can help.

STRATEGIES FOR THE LONG RUN

- **Feedback buddy.** Identify a colleague with whom you can practice giving feedback. Begin by meeting over coffee and practice on each other. Next, move to role-playing positive feedback that you would each like to give someone else. Deliver the feedback to the individuals. Share the results with your buddy. Finally, role-play a scenario in which you each need to give constructive feedback to someone. Deliver the feedback and again share the results with your buddy. Ask each other what went well, what you could have done better, and what changes you would make next time.

- **Real situation.** Identify a real situation in which you need to give constructive feedback. Practice what you'll say using this template:

  - "When you . . ."   Describe the behavior
  - "I become . . ."   How it affects you or the impact caused
  - Wait for a response   Since it's likely the person will want to say something
  - "I wish that you . . ."   Specify change and how it will make a difference
  - "What's your idea?"   Listen and be prepared to consider alternatives

  Deliver the feedback and reflect on how well the discussion went. What would you improve before you provide feedback again?

- **Good, bad, and ugly.** Are you receiving feedback on a regular basis? Exchanging feedback is a process and not a single event. Identify 6–10 people you would like to receive feedback from on a regular basis. You may want to ask them how they define a "regular basis." Once the feedback starts pouring in, track it. Categorize the good, the bad, and the ugly and create plans to expand the good and to improve the rest.

CROSS TRAINING

You will find related ideas at these crossover skills:

- Accept and Act on Feedback
- Maintain Composure
- Communicate Clearly
- Compassion (character trait)

READING FOR THE FINAL STRETCH

- *Feedback: Why We Fear It, How to Fix It*, by M. Tamra Chandler

Influence, Persuade, and Negotiate

nfluencing, persuading, and negotiating are three situations requiring different communication skills. The Greek philosopher Aristotle identified three essentials for persuasive communication that stand the test of time: reason, credibility, and emotion. Influencing and persuasion mean to win others over, not defeat them. Don't think of using persuasion for solving a major difference, such as in a debate. Instead, consider all the times you persuade others to think as you do, to go along with your plan, or even just to take a break from work. To succeed at negotiating, which is slightly different from influencing, you need to do two things: first, clearly evaluate each person's priorities, interests, and alternatives; and second, determine how to "enlarge the pie" of options for the other person.

It's important because you have multiple opportunities to persuade colleagues, customers, subordinates, and leaders in your organization and in your personal life. Your ability to influence others and negotiate will help you communicate better, enhance teamwork, and complete tasks through others more effectively. Understanding the basics and a few techniques can also help you be more observant of others as they attempt to persuade you.

MASTERING THE SKILL

Hurdles to Overcome

- How often do I try to influence or persuade someone without preparation or determining what is important to the other person?

- How do my emotions affect my ability to influence others or negotiate?

- How often does my lack of respect for, disappointment of, or dislike of others prevent me from being successful in working with them?

- Why do I have to give up something to gain commitment from someone else?

- How often do I advocate for a solution without understanding the needs of others?

Your Path to Success

- Value your need to use persuasion and influencing techniques to gain agreement, commitment, or buy-in from others

- Understand how personal style is helpful as you influence others—especially as it relates to their emotions

- Realize the importance of getting attention and understanding others' needs before trying to influence them or negotiate

- Inspire and promote a vision upward, downward, and across department boundaries

- Use collaboration and transparency to work with others

- Accomplish your tasks by finding common ground among a group

- Know what's negotiable in each situation you are in

- Readily pursue the most important outcome or valuable reward in a negotiation

TIPS FOR PEOPLE IN A HURRY

- **Observe others.** People are trying to influence you, persuade you, or negotiate with you every day. During your next such experience, list what they did. For example, how did they get your attention? What did they do to appeal to what is important to you? How did they establish the need? Did they paint a picture of the future? Tell you about the next steps? What else?

- **Look for email influencers.** Review your emails. How many were trying to influence you to do something? What tactics did others use to persuade you?

- **See their side.** Success in influencing, persuading, and negotiating requires that you deeply understand the other person's point of view. Know what's in it for them. Think of examples.

- **Try flea market bargaining.** Visit a flea market or a garage sale to increase your confidence when negotiating. Take a chance and ask for more or less. Then be quiet and listen for a response.

PRACTICE SPRINTS

- **Take a class.** Identify a class that would benefit your skills. Any of the three—persuasion, negotiation, or influence—will be beneficial for you.

- **Personal Practice.** Influencing skills work at home too. Review the content here about techniques for influencing and personal styles. Use that information to persuade your significant other to do something you'd like to do this weekend but your significant other doesn't want to do. When you've completed your discussion, share what you were doing and ask for feedback about what worked and what you should improve.

- **Read about it.** Read a book about personal styles used to influence. *People Styles at Work . . . and Beyond*, by Robert and Dorothy Bolton, is a good one to start with. Understanding people and their styles should be one of your foundational skills.

- **Know when to fold 'em.** Negotiation is a daily occurrence for you personally or at work, from planning where to go to dinner to buying a car to trying to get a store to accept a return without a sales slip. The topic has been well studied and researched and comes down to six to nine steps (depending on the expert's model). Read these steps and use them to plan your next negotiation:

  1. Before negotiating, decide what you will do if you do not reach an agreement. This is called your best alternative to a negotiated agreement—or BATNA to those familiar with the jargon. It's the lowest value acceptable to you. Also estimate what you suspect the other party's BATNA will be. Decide if you can live with an adverse outcome.

  2. Identify any underlying issues that may be important to you and to the other person.

  3. Evaluate how important all issues are to you and to the other person so that you can prepare for trade-offs. Of course, you may not have the necessary information about the other person, but it creates a list of items you need to learn about.

  4. Assess the bargaining zone or the area where there might be a middle ground between highest and lowest dollar value or other negotiables.

  5. Identify where trade-offs exist. A fixed-pie mindset prevents people from making wise trade-offs. You may need to suggest a novel trade-off.

  6. Assess the possibility that you or the other person may be affected by irrational thoughts, pride, the fixed-pie bias, overconfidence, or other issues.

STRATEGIES FOR THE LONG RUN

- **Ponder persuasion principles.** There are a couple dozen persuasion and influence techniques and principles; most are influenced by the research of Robert Cialdini and the writing of Dale Carnegie. Here are Cialdini's six key principles. Review them, and if you are interested in more information, read one of the books listed at the end of this skill.

> Reciprocity: Do something for another without conditions or expectations of a returned favor.

> Commitment to consistency: A person who performs a small favor is highly likely to perform a larger one in the future.

> Social proof: People will do what other people appear to be doing.

> Authority: Individuals defer to those in authority.

> Likability: It's easier to persuade someone who has more in common with us.

> Scarcity: A shortage of something can be a powerful motivator.

Which of these principles makes the most sense to you? What can you do differently to tap into this research?

- **Use personal styles to persuade.** Recognizing and understanding the four basic personal styles may be the most practical and useful tool for influencing. The knowledge is the basis for the skills needed to know how to best appeal to each in a persuasive setting. Moving into the other person's comfort zone requires flexibility to influence. You should also use a tool to determine your own styles. Here's a quick overview of the four styles. Imagine you are influencing someone from each general category. Think of a current project you are working on. How would you prepare to influence, persuade, or negotiate with each type?

> Analytical (conscientiousness) people tend toward perfectionism and deal in logic and details. They tend to keep feelings to themselves. When influencing them, it's helpful to prepare the case in advance and be accurate and realistic. It is important to provide tangible evidence to support major points.

> Collaborative (steadiness) people put a high value on people and friendships. They go out of their way not to offend. Despite

having opinions, they are not inclined to say what's on their mind. To influence them, draw out their opinions by asking "how" questions and showing how everyone will benefit.

> Controlling (drivers) can make high demands on themselves and others and tend to be emotionally reserved. They are decisive and results oriented, and they like to give guidance to everyone. When influencing drivers, be brief, specific, candid, and to the point.

> Expressing (influence) people are social types. They are enthusiastic, creative, and intuitive but have little tolerance for those unlike themselves. Easily bored, they tend to go off on tangents. When influencing this type, it is useful to stick with the big picture, avoid details, and make it exciting.

Similar examples could also be matched to the MBTI's 16 personality types.

- **Practice on a project.** Meet with your mentor or supervisor and request a project or other experience in which you have to collaborate across organizational boundaries with individuals and groups that have competing priorities to yours. After starting the project, schedule regular meetings with your mentor or someone who can coach you through the process. Track what you learn during the experience.

- **Build your negotiation knowledge.** Ask your manager if you can participate on a short-term purchasing team that negotiates a contract for your organization, such as space, supplies, furniture, equipment, services, or other raw materials your organization purchases.

CROSS TRAINING

You will find related ideas at these crossover skills:

- Display Self-Confidence
- Resolve Conflict
- Understand Personal Style
- Demonstrate Problem-Solving Ability
- Sell Ideas

READING FOR THE FINAL STRETCH

- *Influence: Gaining Commitment, Getting Results*, by Harold Scharlatt and Roland Smith
- *How to Win Friends and Influence People*, by Dale Carnegie
- *Influence: The Psychology of Persuasion*, by Robert B. Cialdini

SKILL 15

Speak in Public

Public speaking has always been feared—even more so than death! Yes, speaking instills anxiety in most of us, but speaking to groups is something that you will need to do throughout your career. In order to make improvements, you need to consider two things. First, you need to compare your perception of your presentation skills with your listeners' perceptions of your presentation skills. Only then will you know if what you are experiencing is the same as what your listeners are experiencing. Second, it takes more time than you might imagine to be fully prepared to deliver a presentation. Good speakers make it look so easy! Behind all that perfection is a ton of preparation.

It's important to be a good public speaker because presentations are one of the key ways that most organizations share information with large audiences. You will miss out on project and promotion opportunities if you lack public speaking skills.

MASTERING THE SKILL

Hurdles to Overcome

- How often do I attend more to the communication content rather than how it connects emotionally with my audience?

- What could I possibly speak about that would interest anyone?

- How can I possibly overcome my nervousness? Is it worth it?

- Why would I want to memorize a speech and stand in front of a group that doesn't want to hear my message?

- Why do presenters think that an audience wants to hear them drone on and on?

Your Path to Success

- Recognize the huge difference that preparation makes before delivering a presentation

- Use stories, images, and examples to convey your ideas

- Develop and structure an effective presentation based on audiences' needs

- Select opening and closing techniques that captivate and motivate an audience

- Use a variety of patterns to organize presentations and convey messages

- Prepare and manage the presentation environment for success

- Practice your presentation

- Determine the best technique for using notes

- Design visual aids that support your presentation and enhance your message

- Manage question-and-answer sessions, including time allowed

- Acknowledge and address your specific anxiety concerns

TIPS FOR PEOPLE IN A HURRY

- **Use an "um" counter.** The next time you present, ask someone to count the fillers you use, what they are, and how many times you use each. Fillers include um, er, ah, and like.

- **Assess the 6 presentation Ps.** Consider the 6 presentation Ps and rate yourself on each: pitch, pace, pauses, projection, pronunciation, and passion.

- **Meet your new presenter.** When you meet new people, consciously note how you feel about them on first impression. Analyze how much comes from facial expressions, eye contact, gestures, tone of voice, distracting factors, dress, and so forth. What was positive? Negative? What does this tell you about what to do during your next presentation?

- **Emphasize the right word.** Select a sentence from your next presentation. The first sentence is a good one. Or use this sentence: Now is the time for change. Read it aloud, emphasizing a different word each time. Notice the difference in the meaning of the sentence depending on which word you emphasized? Observe this in your daily communication.

PRACTICE SPRINTS

- **Practice.** Identify training opportunities in your organization, starting with a brown bag lunch presentation to get experience speaking to a group. Ask someone to sit in the audience who will specifically observe and give feedback to you. Tell the person to look for things like nervous gestures or pacing. If possible, have your presentation recorded so that you can observe and critique your performance. Identify what you like and what you'd like to change.

- **Assess your speaking skills.** You will find a personal assessment about your speaking skills at https://ideas.bkconnection.com /skillsforcareersuccess. Complete the assessment to decide where to start. You may wish to make several copies of the assessment and ask others you trust to rate and comment on your skills. Review the differences between your responses and the responses of others. Look for similar themes.

- **Toast to the masters**. Identify and join a Toastmasters group to practice public speaking. A benefit of this well-established group is that you will receive valuable candid feedback.

- **Fail to prepare and you may as well prepare to fail.** Preparing to deliver a presentation is like preparing for a race. It requires a preparation process, planning, practice, and perseverance. You would prepare for a race by asking several questions. How long is it? What are the logistics? What's the best way to prepare? How much time should I invest? You will ask similar questions to prepare for a presentation. You can find a detailed checklist with 15 steps to prepare for a presentation at https://ideas.bkconnection.com/skillsforcareersuccess.

- **Make eye contact.** Eye contact is an important skill for presenters because it permits you to read whether the audience understands what you are presenting and helps you identify whether individuals have questions or want to make a comment. Eye contact demonstrates credibility and believability. It helps you bond with your audience with a show of sincerity. It shows that you are interested in the audience. It can also suggest a transition or help you make a point. Interestingly, good eye contact also shows that you will use fewer fillers. Observe the eye contact that you make in general conversation. How long do you maintain eye contact without breaking away? Do you hold eye contact until the end of a thought? Does your eye contact vary when you or the other person is speaking?

STRATEGIES FOR THE LONG RUN

- **Open and close it.** Many experts believe that the opening to your presentation is the most important part. In fact, some feel that you have just 90 seconds to make a statement while your audience critiques how you're dressed and evaluates how you sound. You want to grab their attention quickly and positively. Examples of openings include presenting a startling statistic, quoting an authority, or presenting a challenge. If your opening is the most important part of your presentation, your closing is the second most important part. An effective closing will summarize the main ideas, focus on the purpose, and provide a sense of completion. A good closure will do all of this simply—sometimes in one sentence. On the other hand, a powerful closing will do all of this and be memorable. Review your openings and closings and compare them with the information about powerful openings and closings at https://ideas.bkconnection.com/skillsforcareersuccess.

- **Sweaty palms, parched throat.** Nervousness is nothing more than a fear reflex. It is natural and occurs because your body is getting ready for fight or flight. Nervousness may be displayed in numerous ways: pacing or swaying, fidgeting with a pen, jingling change in your pocket, perspiring, shaking, clearing your throat, grimacing, tensing up, and dozens of other things. However, if you have interesting content, your participants will never notice that you are nervous. The number one rule regarding nervousness is, Do not tell your participants that you are nervous. If you don't tell them, chances are your participants will never know. You can't eliminate nervousness. In fact, you don't really want to eliminate it. The flow of adrenaline is what pushes Olympic contenders to go a bit faster, a bit longer to win the gold. You do, however, want to redirect all that nervous energy in ways that it can help you win at presenting. "Addressing Nervousness" at https://ideas.bkconnection.com/skillsforcareersuccess provides ideas for how you can redirect your nervous energy.

- **Get organized.** Generally, the purpose of your presentation will lend itself to an organizational pattern for your presentation. You, of course, need to add an opening and a closing. The organizational pattern provides you with a structure for the body of your presentation. Select an organizational pattern that maximizes the understanding of your message. Typical patterns include:

  > Chronological order to relate a story, give history, or describe something

  > Topical or logical order to classify or when main points have a pattern

- Spatial pattern to create clarity when describing a regional area or item

- Comparison and contrast to identify advantages/disadvantages or to learn about an unknown by comparing with the known

- Effect to cause to analyze what caused something

- Cause to effect to predict an effect or give the audience a sequential account

- Pros and cons to decrease the value of opposing positions (best for persuasion)

- Problem/solution to enlist the audience to support a new course of action

- Most important to least important to inform or persuade about a topic that has numerous aspects

- Goals to action to create the sense of "possibility"

CROSS TRAINING

You will find related ideas at these crossover skills:

- Display Self-Confidence
- Exhibit a Professional Image
- Maintain Composure

READING FOR THE FINAL STRETCH

- *Speak with Confidence! Powerful Presentations That Inform, Inspire, and Persuade*, by Dianna Booher

SKILL 16

Write Proficiently

Your writing ability is critical for practical reasons as well as the impression it sends. Practically it ensures good communication, prevents errors, ensures accurate records, and builds relationships with those internal and external to an organization. Your writing ability also sends an impression of your total value to the company. True or not, good writers are viewed as credible, intelligent, courteous, and confident. All of this adds up to your ability to be more influential. To achieve this, your written communication must be clear, accurate, and organized around a purpose. You should proof everything prior to disseminating it to check your spelling, grammar, correct word use, and tone.

It's important because your written communication is often a permanent record of both your competence and your conscientiousness. Your written documents may be an early predictor of your chances for a promotion. Your organization knows that good writing skills ensure effective business communication and prevent misunderstandings and rework. Good writing skills can save your organization money, time, and its reputation.

MASTERING THE SKILL

Hurdles to Overcome

- How often do I send out materials and content that I should have edited or asked someone else to edit for me?

- Why should I waste time considering the messages I email for tone, spelling, accuracy, and word choice?

- I didn't major in English—how do I find time to learn good writing skills at this point?

Your Path to Success

- Understand that you need to organize your written materials for the audience

- Constantly improve your vocabulary and grammar

- Be a passionate reader to constantly be in touch with expert writers

- Pay attention to detail in order to observe subtle changes

- Be willing to have your work critiqued

- Recognize that improving your writing skills is important to your organization

TIPS FOR PEOPLE IN A HURRY

- **Verify with visuals.** When possible, use graphics, sketches, graphs, or other visuals to send a clear message.

- **Conquer careless cursive.** Spelling, punctuation, and grammar must be flawless. Nothing says "I'm careless" more than sloppy writing.

- **Start strong.** Don't introduce your introduction. Begin a report or even a correspondence with a strong statement to gain attention.

- **Get tough on grammar.** Invest in a grammar proofreading tool (such as Grammarly) that picks up spelling and grammar mistakes. After repeatedly seeing your errors, you'll learn where your weaknesses lie.

- **Hey is not OK.** Although email is an informal communication method, research by Perkbox Insights reveals that "Hey" tops the list of irritating greetings. What's preferred? "Hi," "Hello," "Good morning /afternoon," and good old-fashioned "Dear."

- **Keep it short and simple.** The most valuable writing tip is to use short sentences and simple words.

PRACTICE SPRINTS

- **Sniff test.** Review all your written communication, including emails, proposals, and reports. Do you start with a clear objective and what readers should take away from the communication? Is the writing streamlined so that it is clear and concise? Does your communication state what readers should know or do as a result of reading the communication? To make it easy to comprehend, follow a simple format of starting with the facts, following with supportive details, and closing with a call to action.

- **Email expertise.** Email is one of the most informal communication techniques; however, the convenience and ease of email mean you must be careful to ensure that your message sends the right tone. Problems can occur when the recipient's interpretation of the tone doesn't match the intention of the sender. Read every email over carefully word-for-word before pressing "send." Send your message more quickly by making your content glance-able since it will likely be read on a screen and your readers are likely distracted and busy. Subheads, bullets, and tables help.

- **Editing cheat sheet.** Learn to edit your own writing, although it isn't easy. Ask any author. The best way to start is to create a personalized cheat sheet of things to look for. Begin by listing items that the pros look for, such as these:

1. Use an active voice; conduct a search on words such as *be-* verbs.

2. Eliminate unnecessary words such as adverbs or adjectives or phrases such as "there are" or "that you."

3. Remove all clichés.

4. Read the completed work aloud to find long sentences or convoluted concepts.

5. Identify and remove overused words such as "get," "make," or "very."

6. Include transition words to help the message flow, such as "so," "initially," "however," and others.

Next, add specific things that you need to eliminate from your own writing. Use this cheat sheet to review your written work and identify areas to improve, and then make those changes before delivering your work to your readers.

- **Start with "you."** Begin most communication messages with the word "you" or something about the recipient, such as "You are absolutely right" or "Your questions are just what we needed." It personalizes your message immediately, increases the chance that it grabs your reader's attention, and puts them ahead of you. Many people begin by saying something like, "I want to thank you for . . ." It would be much better to start with "Thank you for . . ."

STRATEGIES FOR THE LONG RUN

- **Good news, bad news protocol.** Correspondence can deliver good news or bad news. Good news follows three steps: The opening paragraph should state the news and why it is good. The middle provides details such as reassurance or how the actions will be implemented. The closing repeats the good news and adds congratulations or another positive statement.

Correspondence that delivers bad news uses a format that softens the message without delaying or avoiding the bad news. It starts by setting up the news in a way it can be heard and understood. It usually includes reasons and alternatives. Avoid using words and phrases like "unfortunately." This type of correspondence also follows three steps: The opening paragraph refers to the situation by stating the request, advising about any action, and making a neutral statement about the situation. The middle states the bad news with details and alternatives. It begins with the details or reasons (for example, "one of the expectations"), states the bad news as clearly as possible, and adds potential alternatives. The closing incorporates a neutral or positive statement, offers additional information, and expresses appreciation for the recipient's part in what happened.

- **Writing class.** Register for a business writing class. Your company may offer one or recommend one that is top notch. Even if your organization will not pay for the class, you should still register and pay for it yourself. If there is one area you should invest in you, it's in a writing skills class. Good writing skills are difficult to attain from a book. You need an instructor who will give you candid and practical feedback.

- **Remote communication.** It is difficult to be a remote colleague. No matter which end you are on, as it relates to remoteness, you can set a high standard for effective written communication. When you have a concern about a colleague's reaction or emotional response, choose a phone call or video chat. Consider the sensitivity of the message before sending an email and consider whether a phone call would be more appropriate. Avoid using writing to convey humor or sarcasm; at best the message will be lost, and at worst the message could be misconstrued as negative. Be attentive to time differences. The best plan works with a general agreement to switch off from one location to the other.

CROSS TRAINING

You will find related ideas at these crossover skills:

- Communicate Clearly
- Stay Organized
- Exhibit Technology, Analytics, and Data Knowledge
- Lead Ventures

READING FOR THE FINAL STRETCH

- *Presenting Data Effectively: Communicating Your Findings for Maximum Impact*, by Stephanie Evergreen
- *The Associated Press Stylebook*, by the Associated Press

Interpersonal Savvy

When Mary Barra took over as CEO of General Motors in 2014, the company was facing a crisis: GM had issued 84 safety recalls that caused the deaths of hundreds of drivers and passengers. Instead of making excuses, she decided to be an "influence for good." She recalled almost 30 million vehicles and believed it would be wrong to put the situation behind the company. Instead she said she wanted to put this painful experience permanently in the company's collective memory. This action was the first of many that changed the hearts and minds of GM employees and customers, enabling them to overcome a troublesome period. Although this was a huge decision, Mary emphasizes many smaller actions that have made her a beloved as well as effective leader.

In April 2020, *Fortune* named Mary as one of the 25 greatest leaders amid the COVID-19 pandemic. She placed at number nine on the list. GM was the first big American automaker to commit its idle assembly lines to the fight against COVID-19. U.S. Department of Health and Human Services awarded GM a $489 million contract to deliver 30,000 ventilators.

In addition, Mary made a strong public statement over the George Floyd killing, saying she was impatient and disgusted—words that came from her heart, not the marketing department. In response, she created an inclusion advisory board. In 2019 she was one of a few CEOs who had pushed the

Business Roundtable to adopt a new, more inclusive statement of corporate purpose.

Mary believes it's important to build relationships, which she does by asking for feedback from her staff. She appreciates the differences individuals bring to the organization and holds meetings to collaborate on ideas and resolve conflict, not to just to disseminate information. She believes interpersonal relationships are rooted in aligned values, and recommends that whether you're acquiring a company or hiring a new person for your team, it's wise to spend time determining whether your values match. She suggests asking what values are important and why, and then listening carefully.

Mary believes in sharing credit and is the first to give credit to her mentors throughout her career who ingrained in her the importance of appealing to both the intellectual and emotional side of her employees. As an engineer, Mary's logical reasoning is natural, but her mentors have encouraged her to be attuned to what people care about too. To her, interpersonal savvy is caring about others' fears and aspirations. Mary advises everyone who wants to advance their careers to find mentors, coaches, and advisers who can help identify missing interpersonal skills that need polishing and then implement their recommendations.

Treat them all the same by treating them differently.

—STEPHEN COVEY

SKILL 17

Build and Manage Relationships

Your ability to build and manage relationships will lead to a strong network of allies in your department and throughout the organization. Your professional success needs to exist on multiple levels. That kind of success is impossible unless you know how to build relationships at every level and across departments. Making people feel comfortable and building connections is the start of relationship building. You must also be positive and respectful, offer support, accept others where they are, and invest time in the relationships.

It's important because everything in an organization is accomplished by many people, so relationships are critical. If you struggle with relationships, you may not notice how others think about you until a small relationship mishap expands into a conflict. You can't afford for that to happen. You need to master building and managing relationships to ensure that others trust you and have confidence in you and your competency. Well-managed relationships are important to your organization too in order to accomplish its goals.

MASTERING THE SKILL

Hurdles to Overcome

- How aware am I of my inability to manage relationships?
- Why do people have difficulty trusting me and building a relationship with me?
- What do others have that I don't that makes them popular?
- Why don't I have friends?

Your Path to Success

- Have a sense of humor that respects others
- Advocate for others
- Put others at ease with your warmth and pleasantness
- Build positive and productive internal and external working relationships
- Work across department boundaries
- Proactively gain trust and respect from your colleagues and customers
- Work to understand what others might be thinking or feeling before making decisions or discussing tasks
- Maintain credibility in the eyes of employees throughout your organization
- Reach out to others to engage them in a common cause

TIPS FOR PEOPLE IN A HURRY

- **Get real.** Take time to be honest with yourself. How do you really feel about the people you work with? How important are they to you? Do you care about them? Their feelings? Or do you think about how they can help you get to the next step in your career? Don't share this with anyone, but be honest with yourself.

- **Make the rounds**. One of the easiest things you can do that makes a big difference in relationships is to walk around your department every morning to say hello. Start this habit immediately.

- **Smile more.** Unfortunately, only a third of us smile naturally, a third of us don't smile, and a third of us are considered smile neutral. If you fall into one of the last two categories, make an effort to smile more. Smiling builds trust and encourages others to want to get to know you better.

- **Treat a team member to coffee.** Invite someone from your team with whom you'd like to build a relationship to coffee (your treat). Make it a goal to learn three new things about your teammate.

PRACTICE SPRINTS

- **Your relationships.** Create a plan to actively manage the relationships you've built at work. Decide where those relationships exist and what is needed to build and manage them. It could be as simple as meeting with them on a regular basis or remembering to ask about their families. It could be sharing advanced information about your plans and asking them for suggestions or what role they would like to play. It could be initiating a long overdue apology or seeking out someone you haven't connected with in a while.

- **Like and learn.** Building relationships can take time, and it's obvious that they pay off in the long term. You can reap an immediate return by identifying one thing you could learn from several people you want to build relationships with. It could be personal or professional. What does each have to offer? Most will be proud to share their knowledge with you. You'll learn and build a relationship at the same time.

- **Newest employees.** Volunteer to help onboard the newest employees in your organization. It could be someone in your department, but you may actually learn more if the employee is in a different department. Invest yourself in this task—and on the side, note what you do that helps to build a relationship with the new employee. Go the extra mile and help individuals build relationships for the times when you are not available. Help employees by introducing them to other employees, finding lunch partners, showing them where the supply room and cafeteria are located, and recommending the best nearby restaurants. Take the time to get to know new employees during your onboarding activities. Stay in touch and continue the relationships. What are the pros and cons of developing relationships in other departments?

- **Networking group.** Establish a networking group in your organization so that others can also build relationships across the organization. It can begin informally, and perhaps meet for lunch twice a month. Identify a purpose so that everyone has a reason to continue to stay involved.

STRATEGIES FOR THE LONG RUN

- **Out on a limb.** Identify someone with whom you have a strained relationship. Invite that person to give you feedback on what you need to do to improve your relationship. Remember, once you ask, be sure to listen, be positive, and thank the individual. Think about what was said. Reflect. Decide what you will do. With the person's permission, continue to build the relationship.

- **Relationship checklist.** What does it take to build relationships? Create a checklist of all the things you believe help initiate, develop, and maintain relationships. Hundreds of items could be on this list; however, remember that your list should be designed for you and your situation. Have someone you trust review your list for anything that you've forgotten. Use these examples to get you started:

  > Listen without judging.
  > Understand other people and their unique characteristics.
  > Take the first step to get to know others better.

> Initiate conversations—have a list of discussion starters available.

> Learn three nonwork items about everyone, such as hobbies, children, interests.

> Treat people equitably; different people have different needs.

> Share something about yourself.

> Practice reliability and accountability.

- **New buddies.** Identify three to five people in your organization with whom you should build relationships. A lack of time often prevents us from taking the first step to introduce ourselves and begin the relationship. The reasons for the relationship could be that they have a future corporate perspective similar to yours or that you share similar interests outside of work. In some cases you may want to partner for strategic reasons that will benefit your department and your organization. If this is the reason, what are you waiting for?

CROSS TRAINING

You will find related ideas at these crossover skills:

- Influence, Persuade, and Negotiate
- Collaborate with Others
- Lead Others
- Be Accountable

READING FOR THE FINAL STRETCH

- *Interpersonal Savvy: Building and Maintaining Solid Working Relationships*, by the Center for Creative Leadership authors
- *Power Questions: Build Relationships, Win New Business, and Influence Others*, by Andrew Sobel and Jerold Panas

SKILL 18

Collaborate with Others

Your ability to collaborate with others is another one of those skills that aren't in any training manual but are required in order to accomplish your work. Collaboration isn't new, but it has gained new prominence as we reinvent how we work together. Collaboration means that you have the ability to think beyond yourself and have a team-oriented mindset. You have likely collaborated with others in many ways: on a baseball team, in a voluntary fund-raising group, as a member of a chorus or band, and even in a group of friends. Collaboration is required whenever a group of people are mutually dependent on each other to achieve a common goal.

It's important because as humans we do almost everything in teams. Collaboration helps your organization by taking advantage of everyone's ideas, increasing communication, and tapping into a broad array of skills and knowledge. Collaboration is crucial to your organization because it engages employees, escalates agility, increases productivity, generates innovative ideas, increases buy-in, and accelerates business results. The organization values employees who collaborate with others.

MASTERING THE SKILL

Hurdles to Overcome

- Why don't people listen to me when I have the answer?

- Why should I work in a group and give all my good ideas away?

- How can we think we are productive when we are meeting all the time?

- How aware am I that I come across as the curmudgeon in our team?

- What's the benefit when I am more productive working alone?

- How aware am I that I see my colleagues as competitors?

Your Path to Success

- Work with others to get things completed without creating disagreements

- Diplomatically and tactfully reference concerns and difficult events

- Get the job done even when you have no control over others or the tasks

- Gain cooperation and support when working with your colleagues from other functions and departments

- Give graciously and take with gratitude

- Admit your own mistakes, taking full responsibility

- Compromise to move the team forward

- Forgive others' mistakes and jump in to support where you can

TIPS FOR PEOPLE IN A HURRY

- **We versus I.** Attend to how often you use the word "we" as opposed to "I." Be aware, because others are.

- **Credit.** Do you give credit to others often enough? Stay focused on who is doing what for an entire day. Decide what you can do to ensure everyone is receiving the recognition they deserve.

- **Team trust.** Speak well of your team—when you don't, you will appear petty.

- **One collaboration at a time.** If you find that being collaborative isn't easy, think of it in stages. Select one person to be your collaboration colleague and work on the skills to build a collaborative relationship with that person.

- **Beyond work.** Socializing with colleagues outside of work is a great way to build a relationship of trust and understanding.

PRACTICE SPRINTS

- **Find a cause.** Collaboration happens more readily and naturally when a compelling and exciting mission is the central focus. What is the exciting cause that draws you in? How well do you think others have defined the purpose of your collaboration? If there is no clear cause that you can define, take the lead to ask those collaborating on the project. What do they see as your purpose? How do they define the goal? What is their vision for the result? Having a clearly defined cause will engage and energize more people.

- **Invite involvement.** The next time your group is working together, observe those that don't seem to be as connected as the rest. Ask them for their ideas and thoughts about the direction the group is heading. Learn what they bring to the project or to your work group and how they can contribute. Gain their support and cooperation to increase productivity and improve results. Make a habit of looking around every group you are in to determine who isn't contributing and how you can engage them.

- **Span boundaries.** Identify a problem that your department has with another department in your organization. Ask your supervisor for support in forming a cross-functional team to identify how to resolve the problem.

- **Check your tools.** Technology has had a big impact on our ability to collaborate within an office and virtually. Are you taking advantage of the right tools to collaborate? Consider file sharing, instant messaging, video conferencing, and social media. If you are not using these tools, learn more about what's available in your organization.

STRATEGIES FOR THE LONG RUN

- **Collaboration challenge.** Although collaboration is viewed as a way to increase productivity and engage employees, there can be some challenges. Many of these challenges focus on the balance between individuals and teams. Several areas include recognition, goal setting, level of participation, position titles, decision making, and division of work. Collaboration can be difficult for people who have a strong sense of individuality and have likely been rewarded for what they contribute. If you have a strong personality, it may be difficult to overcome your desire to resist. Recognize that collaboration will not solve all business problems, so there will still be a need for your individual contribution. Still, if you want to progress in your current organization and it has been decided that collaboration will maximize its success, you'll need to make a decision. Meet with your mentor to mull over your options. Perhaps you need to ask your supervisor for a balance of team and your individual participation. Perhaps you need a coach to help you understand how to be more collaborative. A 360-degree feedback instrument could provide feedback from different people. Use any of these options to determine how to overcome your collaboration challenge.

- **Team building.** A team intervention, often called team building, may help to move your work group into a more collaborative space. If collaborating is difficult for you and others on the team, seek an opportunity to have your team attend a one-to-two-day offsite workshop to explore how you can all work together to obtain more productive results.

- **Volunteer project.** Take on a project that will give you an opportunity to practice collaboration skills. You have several options. One option is to ask your supervisor to assign you to a high-visibility team or project in which you work across your organization's boundaries. A second option is to volunteer for a committee for a community group such as your local civic league or at your church or school (for example, working at a bake sale). During your volunteer time, observe your interactions with others. How would you evaluate your collaboration skills? What do you still need to learn?

- **Value of dialogue.** To truly understand others, research the value of dialogue, a discussion between two or more people defined by openness, honesty, and genuine listening. In brief, guidelines for dialogue include these guiding principles:

  > Participants must "suspend" their assumptions.

  > Participants must regard one another as colleagues.

  > They should be located in a private and comfortable location.

  > They should eliminate all distractions and allow enough time (an hour or more).

  Dialogue was popularized by David Bohn, a contemporary quantum physicist, and Peter Senge, MIT professor and author, to help people be more aware of input and learn how to best meet everyone's needs. Dialogue is not easy to learn.

CROSS TRAINING

You will find related ideas at these crossover skills:

- Build and Manage Relationships
- Lead Others
- Be Resourceful
- Manage Projects

READING FOR THE FINAL STRETCH

- *Give and Take: Why Helping Others Drives Our Success*, by Adam Grant
- *Five Dysfunctions of a Team*, by Patrick Lencioni
- *Connection Culture: The Competitive Advantage of Shared Identity, Empathy, and Understanding at Work*, by Michael Lee Stallard, Jason Pankau, and Katharine Stallard

SKILL 19

Appreciate People and Differences

Your ability to appreciate people and their differences is key to effective communication and your ability to be effective on the job. Routine or natural behaviors can be misinterpreted and cause unexpected problems when you work with others whose backgrounds are different from yours. Exhibiting empathy through acceptance allows you to put yourself in someone else's shoes without making judgments about them or the situation. It conveys respect for others, their views, and what they have experienced. It is often wise to acknowledge the differences that others bring based on their culture, experience, personal background, and what is currently happening.

It's important because accepting and appreciating people and differences allows you to suspend judgment and avoid disagreements until you have a clear understanding of the situation. This understanding demonstrates that you want to be fair. To be successful, you need to be aware of your own assumptions, interpretations, and biases. It is also important because diversity brings fresh ideas and a multifaceted view to the work environment. Cross-cultural communication skills are essential to build alignment and synergy. Accepting people and differences creates an equal opportunity workplace, in which a diverse set of individuals are empowered to excel. Inclusion and respect for everyone in the workplace benefit performance and working conditions.

MASTERING THE SKILL

Hurdles to Overcome

- How aware am I of judgmental messages I have in my brain when I really should be listening to the message?

- What is it that prevents me from appreciating people that are different from me?

- Why is it uncomfortable to work with people who are not like me?

Your Path to Success

- Accept and work effectively with people who differ in race, gender, age, nationality, culture, or background

- Be conscious of your biases and values without favoring them over another's

- Demonstrate patience by allowing others to talk without interruptions

- Ask questions to show you are interested in learning more about others' unique situations

- Confirm your clear understanding by reflecting back both content and emotions during a discussion of differences without disagreeing

- Bring out the best in people you work with

- Remain open minded and tolerant of others' idiosyncrasies, shortcomings, and faults

- Avoid assumptions of others based on race, religion, gender, or nationality

- Enhance your organizational results by leveraging everyone's unique talents and perspectives

- Respect values of all employees from different backgrounds

- Appreciate the opportunity and challenge of working in cultures different from your own

- Increase awareness of your personal assumptions, interpretations, and biases and how they might be clouding your thoughts and feelings

TIPS FOR PEOPLE IN A HURRY

- **Identify triggers.** When you experience a judgmental thought, determine what trigger set it off. Try to catch yourself the next time you experience a trigger, pause, and decide what thought you could put in its place.

- **Try empathy.** Clarifying, understanding, and relating to the views and perspectives of others toward situations that occur in the workplace are valuable skills. Work toward compassion.

- **Hunt for exclusion.** Sometimes exclusionary practices exist, but we are so used to them that we don't recognize them as such. Look for exclusionary practices that may exist in your organization. What can you do about them?

- **Develop an inclusion plan.** Write your personal inclusion plan. Include your own vision, your mission, and the values that reflect your beliefs. Include the behaviors you will demonstrate that exemplify your inclusion values.

PRACTICE SPRINTS

- **Humor awareness.** What a culture determines to be funny can vary greatly. Humor can help calm people in new situations; however, if perceived by others as inappropriate, it implies disrespect instead.

Humor is often told from the teller's worldview without enough understanding of the other person's viewpoint. To understand a joke, the other person must understand the context as well. Recognize that in a new situation, it is probably better to avoid using humor.

- **Culture and business norms.** Standards in business differ from culture to culture, from how to physically and verbally meet and interact to how an organization approaches selling or delivering value to customers. Cultural views on negotiating can focus on win-win or win-lose outcomes. Some cultures approach decision making for what's best for individuals, and others for what's best for everyone. Some cultures stifle emotions and work from a logical framework in their decision making. Emotional cultures do not avoid expressing emotion and will often do so spontaneously, believing it is acceptable and helpful. Open a discussion with someone who has different business norms from yours. Use the dialogue skills found in the "Collaborate with Others" skill, suspending judgment and truly trying to see business norms from another culture.

- **Ethnic fair.** Most large cities have ethnic festivals. Attend several to learn the history, talk to other participants, and sample the food. Arm yourself with some powerful questions to help you understand the people better: What are the biggest differences/similarities between your culture and ours? How do our differences affect relationships? How do the differences affect workplace actions and inclusions? If you had a magic wand and could change anything, what would it be?

- **Celebrate.** Join your organization's committee that identifies, acknowledges, and celebrates holidays of different cultures.

- **First impressions game.** Try this the next time you attend a social event. Use John Maxwell's (2010) concept (from *The 21 Indispensable Qualities of a Leader*) and put a "10" on everyone's head that you meet. How do you do that? Expect the best of them. Expect that they will be the most interesting person you meet all night. Learn and use their names. Be positive. Be curious. Focus on their interests. Finally, be sure to treat them as a "10." You will be known as the best party attendee—not that that is your goal. Your goal is to practice making everyone feel like the most important person at the social event.

STRATEGIES FOR THE LONG RUN

- **Culture immersion.** Request an assignment in another culture so that you can live and work with people who are unlike you. If your organization doesn't have this kind of opportunity, join a group that can offer you a short-term service project in a foreign country.

- **Diverse mentoring.** Select someone who has a different background from yours. Ask if they would mentor you about their perspectives, assumptions, upbringing, and other things that make them unique. Plan to meet weekly for at least three months. Trust will need to be built for candid conversation to occur. It sometimes takes a while for discussion to get down-and-dirty to uncover real truths and feelings.

- **Self-awareness.** You observe and evaluate things differently than others with whom you work. What is considered acceptable behavior in your culture may be inappropriate in another. Problems arise when you use your meanings to understand others' realities. If you increase your self-awareness, you will be able to recognize the influence that your experiences have had on shaping your perspective. You will be able to accept this mindset as yours. To be more self-aware, you'll need to become more

  > conscious of your own biases and values without favoring them over another's,

  > aware of how your values and biases affect others,

  > comfortable with cultural differences,

  > aware of your attitude, beliefs, and behaviors that may be oppressive to others.

  Determine how you can become more self-aware on each of these four points.

- **Your cultural background.** Study your own cultural background. Discuss your family history with older relatives. How does your identity influence you and your behaviors? Your preferences? Your perspectives? How does this affect your biases toward others and actions at work? How does your cultural upbringing make you more effective or less effective on the job? What influences how you accept people and differences? What do you think you should change?

CROSS TRAINING

You will find related ideas at these crossover skills:

- Communicate Clearly
- Show Self-Awareness
- Build and Manage Relationships
- Adapt to Situations

READING FOR THE FINAL STRETCH

- *Leading with Cultural Intelligence: The Real Secret to Success,* by David Livermore

Resolve Conflict

Your ability to resolve conflict is a skill that will be useful more often than you would like. When you hear the word "conflict" you may immediately think about the negative aspects: anger, fear, stubbornness. But conflict has a positive side too. When you have the skills for resolution, it is possible to uncover new ideas, deepen relationships, grow, and especially find a way forward that meets everyone's needs. To resolve conflict, you will need to understand each person's reaction to conflict. Understanding how this behavior fits into different conflict management styles is critical to recognizing its effect on a situation. When faced with conflict, people have different responses. Kenneth Thomas and Ralph Kilmann's Conflict Model is the most widely used and defines five different ways for responding to conflict. Their research is based on two dimensions: cooperativeness and assertiveness.

It's important because people have fundamental differences in how they see things. When differences exist, conflict is likely and must be resolved. Conflict that is avoided or handled poorly wastes time, money, and talent. Effectively resolved, conflict opens the door for improved relationships and opportunities to incorporate divergent perspectives to achieve more.

Hurdles to Overcome

- What causes my discomfort when someone expresses emotions?
- Why do I want to hide when someone disagrees with me?
- What purpose is served in listening to people spout off about something they can't control?
- How often do I let off steam without a good reason?
- How often do I forget to get to the bottom of the issue before attacking back?

Your Path to Success

- View conflict as an opportunity for additional information
- Accept responsibility for your part in a conflict
- Proactively work to resolve conflicts
- Focus on the big picture and ways to compromise to identify solutions that work for all
- Take the time to gather all the facts before you try to resolve the conflict

TIPS FOR PEOPLE IN A HURRY

- **Importance.** Think about your last conflict. What was it that made you think it was important enough to cause a conflict? Does it still seem that important?
- **Win-win.** You've probably heard of a win-win approach to conflict. What does that mean to you, and how have you seen people employ a win-win approach?
- **Root cause.** A root cause is the core issue that sets in motion the cause-and-effect that leads to a problem—generally the beginning

of the mess. Think about a conflict you've witnessed recently. What was the root cause? Did the resolution determine the root cause? Why? What difference does reaching the root cause make?

- **Your response.** Based on Thomas-Kilmann's model, which of the five responses (competing, accommodating, avoiding, collaborating, and compromising) do you use most often when faced with conflict? How satisfied are you with that?

- **The value of listening.** One of the most valuable skills for effective conflict resolution is your ability to listen—not just hear but listen for understanding. Ask yourself, "What am I learning?"

PRACTICE SPRINTS

- **Expect emotion.** Conflict is often based in emotions, and professionals find ways to be comfortable with emotions. Start by appreciating that emotions provide important data that defines what's behind the words you hear. Is it anger? Sadness? Fear? Frustration? Emotions are clues for how to address the conflict. Pay attention to the tone of voice, body language, stance, and gestures. How do they support the message you heard? Name the emotions when you can—for example, "You seem frustrated about . . . Can you tell me more about it?"

- **Defuse anger.** If you are ever the target of another person's anger, you will want to be able to defuse that anger. Angry people do not listen very well, but that doesn't mean you shouldn't try. Try some of these tactics that allow a slow calmness to occur:

    1. Acknowledge the anger by listening to identify the cause.

    2. Avoid personalizing the anger as your own.

    3. Identify the facts of the complaint.

    4. Show empathy and avoid defensiveness.

    5. Ask relevant, clarifying questions to ensure you understand the anger.

6. Try a logical approach; if that doesn't work, find something to agree on, such as the facts or at the least the person's right to be angry.

7. Explain what can be done, indicating a specific time and date.

Once you've done the most you can, try to confirm an agreement. Ask the other person to specify the agreement, including any dates and responsibilities. If all else fails, defer the conversation for another time.

- **Employ conflict strategies.** Many strategies exist to manage and resolve conflict. Learn several of these strategies so that you are ready when a conflict arises:

  1. Use I-messages rather than you-messages since you-messages are perceived as blaming.

  2. Address conflict directly; don't try to avoid the discussion.

  3. Avoid words such as "always" and "never" since these words are exaggerations and rarely true.

  4. Consider what you know about the other person in terms of behaviors and personality, since it will help you know what to expect.

  5. Think about your relationship and history with the individuals, their personality style, and general behavior patterns to help you anticipate potential reactions.

  6. Focus on what you need to talk about. Identifying the central issue maintains focus and prevents you from slipping into other matters.

  7. Communicate concerns in a clear, specific, and neutral way, avoiding raising your voice or dramatic hand gestures.

  8. Make sure to focus on the behavior, not the person.

- **Take a pause.** When you sense a conflict coming on, teach yourself to take a deep breath and pause. Listen and ask why you need to talk. Should you ask a question instead? Then you can always say, "I need to think about this; when is a good time for us to continue this discussion?"

STRATEGIES FOR THE LONG RUN

- **Learn the Thomas-Kilmann Model.** Kenneth Thomas and Ralph Kilmann's Conflict Model is the most widely used and defines five different ways for responding to conflict (Thomas and Kilmann 1974):

  1. **Competing:** Using a competitive response, individuals seek to satisfy their own needs without regard to, and often at the expense of, others involved.

  2. **Accommodating:** Accommodators neglect their own concerns to satisfy the concerns of another person.

  3. **Avoiding:** In this response, individuals do not address conflict. They do not seek to satisfy their own interests or the interests of others.

  4. **Collaborating:** Collaborators work with others to find a solution that fully satisfies all interests.

  5. **Compromising:** Compromisers seek to partially satisfy all participants.

  None of the five responses to conflict is inherently superior or inferior. Sometimes one response is more effective than another depending on the situation. For example, a competitive approach is better than a collaborative approach for handling an emergency. A person's response to conflict is a learned behavior, and it changes as the person gains life experience. Understanding your own preferred response to conflict and its positive and negative effects is valuable to managing conflict.

- **Consider anger management.** If you have difficulty controlling yourself during conflict, consider taking an anger management class. Since you may hear about them during a newscast, they sound worse than they actually are. The course will help you develop healthy ways to express your frustration. It will also help you examine your triggers and adjust how you view situations.

- **Experience mediation.** If you know two people who have been in conflict mode for a period of time, offer to mediate a solution between them. Before doing so, read a couple of resources such as those suggested at the end of this section.

CROSS TRAINING

You will find related ideas at these crossover skills:

- Influence, Persuade, and Negotiate
- Maintain Composure

- Collaborate with Others
- Courage (character trait)

READING FOR THE FINAL STRETCH

- *The Mindful Guide to Conflict Resolution: How to Thoughtfully Handle Difficult Situations, Conversations, and Personalities*, by Rosalie Puiman
- *Resolving Conflict: Ten Steps for Turning Negatives to Positives*, by Harold Scharlatt

SKILL 21

Network with Others

Your networking skills can accelerate your career success. Networking provides you an opportunity to connect with like-minded professionals to exchange information and develop professional contacts. You have a valuable opportunity to meet new individuals who can be helpful to you. By broadening your circle of acquaintances, you can learn about job opportunities and trends in your industry. Professional networking can occur online one-to-one or in groups, in a physical location where people come together to meet other professionals, or in a one-on-one scenario where you ask someone to introduce you to someone else.

It's important because networking increases your ability to learn from those you meet as well as connect with others who can support your career development. Many people think of networking mainly to find a job or get career advice. There are other reasons. Networking will help you develop all of your skills, especially listening, asking questions, and refining your interpersonal skills. It will ensure that you stay on top of the latest industry trends, meet prospective mentors or customers, stay in touch with the job market, and have access to resources that can foster your development. Networking gives you credibility and builds your self-esteem. All of these skills benefit your organization too. A better-informed you means a better-informed organization.

MASTERING THE SKILL

Hurdles to Overcome

- How aware am I of doing the majority of talking?
- What value does networking bring to me?
- How would I even know how to start, what to say, or why I would network?
- Why have my attempts to sell people on my ideas been rebuffed?

Your Path to Success

- Live an attitude of give first and take only when you need something
- Present an authentic, sincere presence and a desire to help those you meet
- Genuinely appreciate any recommendations or information you receive
- Show respect by asking thoughtful questions and showing you are interested in others
- Complete your homework to know who you are networking with—and know that the more influential the person, the more research is required

TIPS FOR PEOPLE IN A HURRY

- **Get a goal.** Identify your key purpose for networking. Create your networking goal. Write it down.
- **Give abundantly.** Networking will be more successful if you do not keep score. Take on an abundance mentality of someone who is

always willing to connect and share what you can. It could be a book recommendation or an introduction to another professional.

- **Always say thank you!** After any networking meeting or event, note who you spoke with so that you can *immediately* email or send a handwritten note to thank them for their ideas, time, or whatever else is appropriate. You'll stand head and shoulders above others who are too busy to write thank-you notes.

- **Listen.** Be a listener first (and most); be a discusser second (and least). Listening prepares you to know what ideas, tips, and advice you can provide to be a good giver.

PRACTICE SPRINTS

- **Develop a networking plan.** What's your five-year goal? What goals have you set to reach that goal, say in two years, one year, and 90 days? If you haven't already written these goals, do it now. Next to each of your goals identify two or three people who can help you reach these goals. They can be people who are already in your network or people you do not know. No idea who to list? Conduct a bit of research with people you know or resources on the intranet. See? You are networking already! Determine how you will connect with each person. If you need someone to introduce you to another person, make that a part of your plan. Finally, clarify what you need to learn from everyone with whom you network. Do you need specific information? Do you need ideas or confirmation about your ideas? Do you need an introduction to someone else? Make your needs a part of your networking plan.

- **Network at work.** Ask for an assignment that will put you in the middle of people who are connected to the dream job you'd like. Interested in working in the marketing department? Ask for a rotation there. Before you ask, be sure to prove to yourself that your rotation assignment will also help your organization. Then be ready to explain it to your manager.

- **Not the most—just the best.** Networking is not about compiling the longest list of contacts (that's selling) but rather about compiling the best list of contacts. When networking, think in terms of who will be the best (even if you have no idea of how you might connect with the individual). Make a list and post it where you will see it every day: on your mirror, your desktop, or your tablet. Make this your networking wish list.

- **Let go the leeches.** At times you will connect with some people only to learn that they are takers—leeches who are looking for how much they can get out of you. It's OK to stop networking. In fact, it's a smart move. This is not the same as those you've networked with to help, knowing that they can't share because they are still learning. That's different. They are your network followers whom you joyfully help. On the other hand, let go of those who ask for favors again and again and often don't even thank you (my pet peeve).

STRATEGIES FOR THE LONG RUN

- **Develop power contacts.** You may have heard someone say that all contacts are equal. That may be true, but some are more than equal. Someone who is a leader in your profession or who has published several books (not self-published) with large publishers or who has an esteemed title deserves more than a sniff of your time to nurture a relationship before you connect. You should build up to the actual contact and then after you connect invest time to reinforce the connection. You can reference the individual when you post a message or blog. You can inform others about what the person is doing or market something. Build these relationships.

- **Master networking skills.** If you decide to initiate a plan to network, master a few skills first so that you don't waste your time and hurt your chances with potential contacts. Review these skills and characteristics. Identify those that you are already skilled at and those that you need to shore up. Once you have completed your self-assessment, share your results with someone you trust for their perception. Then set to work creating an action plan. You can find a template at https://ideas.bkconnection.com/skillsforcareersuccess to create your plan.

> **Be authentic.** As Oscar Wilde said, "Be yourself; everyone else is already taken." If you are only in it to take, you will be found out.

> **Remember names.** Networking is about building relationships, and remembering names is the first important step.

> **Ask interesting questions.** Networking is about getting others to talk. Ask questions that uncover the passion in others: What excites you? What's the best thing that's happened to you this week? What are you looking forward to this year?

> **Listen.** Networking is a mutually beneficial relationship, making it more important to listen than to talk. You will build trust by listening.

> **Practice diplomacy and tact.** Networking requires you to be discreet, sensitive, and insightful. Choose your words carefully. Watch your body language and think before you speak. Don't brag!

> **Maintain a positive attitude.** Demonstrate a positive outlook every moment. Let it come through in your words, tone, body language, and view on life. Be inspiring and motivating.

> **Give.** Focus on the other person and don't expect anything in return. This is not trading; it is building and maintaining connections for shared mutual gains. Plan how you can help others succeed.

> **Create a plan.** Investing in building your network will deliver a return. You have to do the planning, and it starts with identifying your networking goals.

> **Follow up.** The best networking occurs after the networking is over. Follow up immediately and say thank you. If you promised to send a resource or connect someone, do it as soon as possible. Make your follow-up personal in order to continue to build the relationship.

- **Monitor and maintain your network.** Networking may be difficult to start, but it can also get out of hand quickly. You need to invest the time to monitor and maintain a vibrant network. Ensure that you have solid goals in mind. Maintain integrity in your networking by being sure that you are giving at least as much as you are getting. Effective monitoring occurs when you screen those who are in your network to determine if they still meet your intended goals. At times, hard decisions may need to be made. Due to limited time you may need to eliminate some people. In other cases, you might decide to minimize time with people who are "takers," waste your time, drain your energy, or create a negative atmosphere. Maintaining a vibrant network is equally important and occurs when you add new people to take the places of those who were eliminated. You will be a successful networker if you make it a priority to meet a diverse array of people. Schedule networking regularly. Build and constantly maintain your network. Instead of reaching out to others only during a time of need, a vibrant network affords you the ability to have contacts available all the time. Maintaining a vibrant network requires both giving and asking. It means being available when someone wants to "run an idea past you" or asks for an introduction. Maintaining a network also occurs when you ask for support or ideas or connections. Networking needs to be mutually beneficial. It takes time to maintain your vibrant network.

CROSS TRAINING

You will find related ideas at these crossover skills:

- Understand Personal Style
- Communicate Clearly
- Advocate for Self

READING FOR THE FINAL STRETCH

- *Networking for People Who Hate Networking*, by Devora Zack

Self-Management

Karen Kaplan knows a little about self-management. It starts with making the best effort every day at the task at hand. It relies on saying "Yes" to the opportunity of challenging assignments. It includes exhibiting self-control and staying composed under pressure. It means managing your time and staying organized. And in Karen's case it meant starting at the bottom and managing yourself in a way that satisfies your values and accomplishes the results that are satisfying to you.

Karen wasn't really qualified for her first job at Hill Holliday, an advertising agency. She was hired as a receptionist. Some people would have just taken that and after a few years perhaps moved on to another job. But not her. She realized that her job gave her facetime with people at all levels of the organization. It's said she kept every business card handed to her.

Then she expanded her responsibilities into the firm's secretarial pool (despite not being able to type) and then on to the account management department. She continued to expand her skillset, watching and learning, rising to eventually become CEO. Her experience in so many different company functions and the lessons she took from each one give her a tremendous knowledge of the company and how its parts fit together and how the people in those functions work together. She is recognized as one of the top women in the marketing field.

Karen's story sounds like an implausible, latter-day Horatio Alger rags-to-riches tale. But get beneath the surface and you find a woman dedicated to becoming the best she can be at whatever role she occupies. The advertising business can be volatile and prone to disruption. Karen's view is to learn by leaning into change. She champions continuous learning at the company, which uses rotating assignments and more recently launched an effort to raise the digital skills of all employees.

Now that she serves at the top role of the organization, you would think Karen's ambition, learning, and self-improvement might slow down. You would be wrong. She says that there are good CEOs and better CEOs, and she plans on making herself one of the latter.

If people are doubting how far you can go,
go so far that you can't hear them anymore.

—MICHELE RUIZ

Maintain Composure

Your ability to remain composed under pressure is likely not going unnoticed. When things go awry, we turn to those quick-thinking, grounded people who appear to be able to handle anything. You can prepare to be one of those people. Tensions and pressures are inevitable in your organization, but your reaction to them is entirely your own choice. You might be surprised to know that this is a skill you can learn.

It's important to stay composed under pressure because you are less likely to suffer the effects of stress, anxiety, and worry. Your ability to remain calm leads to better health and a higher level of productivity. Your organization needs people who can remain composed during chaos because others will look to you for leadership and feel less anxious as well.

MASTERING THE SKILL

Hurdles to Overcome

- How often do I miss out on an opportunity because I don't want to look like a fool?

- How often do I play the victim or blame others?

- How often do I lose my cool and say things I shouldn't?

- Why am I easily overwhelmed, which results in withdrawal and frustration?

Your Path to Success

- Demonstrate a positive, mature attitude

- Manage stress for yourself and those around you

- Represent the voice of reason during a crisis or emergency

- Demonstrate your ability to adjust on the fly when necessary

- Think quickly during change

- Remain capable and resilient during high-pressure situations

- Maintain respect and courtesy for all during crises, including your colleagues, contractors, and customers

- Admit readily when you don't know something

TIPS FOR PEOPLE IN A HURRY

- **Practice positivity.** When you are under pressure, thinking of something positive distracts your brain from dwelling on the negative situation you are facing.

- **Take a deep breath.** Next time you sense an unexpected stressor heading your way, close your eyes and take four deep breaths.

- **Expect the unexpected.** Life is full of surprises—some good, some not. Make expecting the unexpected a part of your mantra, and remember to see each new pressure as an opportunity to try something new.

- **Take a break.** Train yourself so that when a crisis occurs you can say, "I need time to think through this. Can we regroup at . . . ?"

PRACTICE SPRINTS

- **Try being an anti-perfectionist.** Sometimes a tendency toward perfectionism causes a lack of composure. Treat yourself to a new way of thinking—although it will take some practice. Try one of these:

  1. Learn and practice the 80/20 rule: 80 percent is good enough.
  2. Evaluate your standards; think of your ideals as guides, not absolutes.
  3. Examine your goals and expectations and adjust them to be more realistic.
  4. Practice saying no more often.
  5. Challenge the perfectionist voice in your head; will the earth stop spinning?

  Practice one of these for a week. What's the result?

- **Name it.** Neuroscience has recently shown that remaining calm under pressure is not an innate trait but a skill that anyone can learn. When your brain senses a threat or crisis, it causes a "fight or flight" reaction. This perception causes your brain to secrete hormones that tell your nervous system to prepare to take action. Your breath gets short, your body floods your muscles with blood, and your peripheral vision goes away. You are caught in a feedback loop between your brain and your body. To interrupt the feedback loop, scientists have discovered that naming it will reduce the "fight or flight" signals. You need to reflect on your feelings and name them. It's best if you can label the emotion positively. For example, instead of fear, anticipation; instead of worry, concern; instead of dread, caution; and so forth. This frees up energy allowing you to think more clearly about the issue rather than worrying. Plan to label your next pressure.

- **Find your focus.** In a crisis or even semi-crisis situation you can feel out of control. To regain your composure, emphasize the positive and focus on what you can control. Studies of people who have been prisoners of war and special-forces instructors who dealt with unimaginable situations had one thing in common: they were optimistic. Starting with the positive allows you to stay calm and focus on what you can do. A feeling of control can make all the difference. Think about a situation in which you might feel out of control. What message could you tell yourself that will put you back in control?

STRATEGIES FOR THE LONG RUN

- **Practice perspective.** Keep requests, crises, emergencies, and disasters of all sorts in perspective. Easier said than done? Yes. Try one or two of these suggestions over the next month or two. The more you practice something, the more automatic it becomes.

  > Try to imagine the best and worst things that could happen, and you will probably see that even the worst isn't that bad.

  > Focus on the reality. So if it's just one two-hour problem in seven days, that's 2 out of 168 hours, or only about 1 percent of your time.

  > Remind yourself of all that is going well. Just how significant is this?

  > Turn it into an opportunity to learn. Ask yourself, "What can I learn from this?"

  > Practice some deep breathing exercises and imagine yourself in your favorite, most relaxing location.

- **Wing It.** Here's a process you can practice now so that you'll be prepared to use it when the time arises. Imagine you've been asked to give an impromptu speech. How could this happen? Many things may occur that could lead to you giving an impromptu presentation: the planned speaker got stuck in traffic or you are the expert in a situation that requires a presenter. Here's a QUICK plan to help you think through what you will say. If you have been asked to present, it is most likely because you are seen as an expert. You probably have lots of content; it just needs to be organized. Follow this QUICK step plan:

> Q—Quietly take a moment to get organized. If possible, get away by yourself.

> U—Uncover the purpose to keep you focused.

> I—Identify the three major points you will make and add supporting evidence.

> C—Conclude with a call to action, quote, or referral back to the purpose.

> K—Kick-start your presentation with a story that you've told many times.

If you can't slip away, follow the QUICK step plan while sitting quietly in the audience. When it comes to the three points, first, second, and third will work. Another common organization structure is the past, present, and future. Walk to the podium, stage, or front with enthusiasm and confidence, knowing that the audience is delighted that you saved the day! Take a deep breath, take a look around at your fans, and begin to tell your story. If you want to, grab a pen and paper (even a napkin or envelope) to jot down notes. Identify a few single words that will keep you organized and remind you of the key points and support/examples. Identify a few comments, stories, or examples that relate to the audience. Do not make excuses, apologize, or try to fill time. Once you have finished, enjoy the applause—you deserve it!

- **Take care of you.** It often comes down to your health. So think of the solution as taking care of the holistic you. The usual are on the list: exercise, get enough sleep, and eat a healthy diet. Add to this practice mediation or mindfulness, generate positive thoughts, and increase omega-3 consumption by eating more fish and nuts.

CROSS TRAINING

You will find related ideas at these crossover skills:

- Display Self-Confidence
- Exhibit Self-Control
- Courage (character trait)
- Practice Resiliency

READING FOR THE FINAL STRETCH

- *Flow: The Psychology of Optimum Experience,* by Mihaly Csikszentmihalyi

Exhibit Self-Control

Your self-control is your ability to govern your physical, emotional, and psychological actions and desires. Self-control can be improved with practice. The ability for self-control is located in the prefrontal cortex of your brain. It is the planning, decision-making, and problem-solving part of the brain that allows you to evaluate alternatives and avoid doing things you might later regret. Studies show that self-control is an innate ability that changes over a lifetime and can be improved with practice.

It's important because self-control allows you to regulate your behavior and your comments to prevent conflict and achieve your goals. Self-control can improve your decision-making ability and your ability to focus. It also plays a role in your emotional happiness and well-being and helps to solve trust issues. People who display self-control appear to have higher self-esteem, better physical and mental health, and better relationships.

MASTERING THE SKILL

Hurdles to Overcome

- How often do I disagree or add my ideas and information before it is appropriate to do so?

- Why do I find it difficult to concentrate on what is being said when I have something to add or when I disagree with the message?

- How often do I let my emotions get in the way of a professional exchange, and how is that affecting my reputation?

- What is that buzzing in my head that prevents me from hearing the message when someone criticizes me?

Your Path to Success

- Show that you are comfortable with silence; it is not necessary for someone to be talking all the time

- Manage criticism effectively without feeling threatened or getting defensive

- Demonstrate composure in difficult situations

- Contribute to solving the problem instead of complaining

- Stay focused and self-disciplined

- Deal effectively with those who are resistant

TIPS FOR PEOPLE IN A HURRY

- **Silence is good.** If you are uncomfortable with silence, determine why; silence gives the other person a chance to continue and you a chance to gather your thoughts.

- **Go for a walk.** Instead of losing your cool and saying something you'll wish you hadn't, go for a walk around the block or to a different floor in the building. If someone expects a response, just ask them to hold that thought until you get back. You will return with a response that you've thought through.

- **Manage your time**. It's easy to lose self-control if you are overscheduled. Check your calendar. If you are overbooked, practice saying no, or at least "not now."

- **Practice caution.** Self-control that is displayed as listening quietly can be confused with accepting someone's ideas or perspectives. Self-control doesn't mean you should hold back your opinion. You should allow sufficient time to uncover data and seek clarity with an open mind.

PRACTICE SPRINTS

- **Interrupt your interruptions.** If you find yourself interrupting or being impatient, try something different that will stop it from occurring. Sometimes it takes drastic measures. For example, you could give the other person permission to call you out for interrupting. Practice focusing on the words the other person is saying, rather than what you want to say. Challenge yourself to be able to repeat the final sentence someone says. Start a habit of pausing after someone is talking to formulate your thoughts. It takes practice and patience to change interruptions.

- **Count to 10.** The old saying of count to 10 really does work. If you don't like counting, create your own delaying tactic; you need about 60 seconds to regain control. Get a cup of coffee; scribble a note in your notebook; look out the window. Don't say anything for 60 seconds. Then respond.

- **Talk it out.** Take time to talk about what happened with someone who observed the interaction. Ask what you need to do and how you can make that change. Listen carefully. Take notes. Respond affirmatively and ask, "What else?" Don't disagree or make excuses; you may not get another chance with this person.

- **Let the oxygen flow.** Improve the oxygen flow to your brain by inhaling through your nose as you slowly count to four. Hold your breath as you count to four again. Then exhale as you count to eight, ensuring you push out all the remaining air. Repeat two more times. Practice this breathing process on a regular basis so that it becomes almost automatic.

STRATEGIES FOR THE LONG RUN

- **Count 'em.** Think back to the last dozen times you lost your cool. Identify the reason or trigger that started it. Was it a specific person or kind of person? Were you criticized or attacked? Were you angry or surprised? Was it about authority or money? Finish your list and then group the reasons into a couple of categories. Once you have the groupings, ask what these groups trigger in you. Is it ego? Lack of confidence? Will it cause more work? How do you wish you had responded? Write the words down and say them aloud. For the next month track every time you lack self-control. What was the situation? How did you respond? At the end of the month determine if you are more self-aware before you respond. How can you manage your responses better?

- **Craft a rational plan.** It can be difficult to keep things in perspective. Daily situations seem to get crazier every day. You can approach these unexpected events differently. Try not to get caught up in the frenzy of the moment. Instead, put a rational plan together—it's something you know how to do. What's the goal? What are the objectives that will get you to the goal? What's the timeline, and who can do what by when? Thinking about a rational plan to resolve whatever has happened will prevent you from reacting negatively and will put your energy into something more productive. Remember, success is all about Plan B.

- **Keep a gratitude journal.** Try starting a gratitude journal to curb your self-control. Keeping a gratitude journal has been touted by some researchers as nearly a miracle cure, and not so much by others. When you look into it, you find that there are research-based tips that help to reap the greatest rewards from journaling. (Who'd have guessed?) When done correctly, keeping a gratitude journal is shown to reduce illnesses, improve sleep, increase happiness, lower symptoms of depression, lower stress, boost generosity, and even lower your risk of heart disease. Follow these tips for the best results (many agree you should see results in 21 days):

> Don't just go through the motions; enhance journaling by making a conscious decision to become more grateful.

> Make it personal, focusing on people more than things.

> Consider what your life would be like without certain blessings.

> Elaborate in detail about a particular person, thing, or relationship rather than a long list of superficial items.

> Record events that were pleasant and unexpected.

> Writing once or twice per week is more beneficial than daily journaling.

CROSS TRAINING

You will find related ideas at these crossover skills:

- Maintain Composure
- Show Self-Awareness
- Advocate for Self
- Humility (character trait)

READING FOR THE FINAL STRETCH

- *Emotional Intelligence: Why It Can Matter More than IQ*, by Daniel Goleman
- *Triggers: Creating Behavior That Lasts, Becoming the Person You Want to Be*, by Marshall Goldsmith

Manage Time

Your time is the most valuable commodity you have. Managing it ensures productivity, creativity, and results. Time management is your ability to plan and control the time you spend on specific activities. The key purpose of time management is to increase effectiveness, efficiency, and the productivity of a task. Managing your time doesn't necessarily mean juggling the most commitments. Instead, think of it as working intentionally to achieve what's most important.

It's important because, when done correctly, it ensures that you will accomplish more in a shorter time period. Well-managed time ultimately uncovers and frees up time that you can use in other ways. Side benefits of good time management include less stress, increased focus, respect of others, and, of course, time that you can use in any way that you choose.

Hurdles to Overcome

- Why am I always behind schedule?

- How can I be expected to get all this done with disruptions from email, phone calls, coworker interruptions, and unscheduled changes?

- How can I do my work when everything is urgent and important?

- Why isn't multitasking working for me?

Your Path to Success

- Establish priorities and focus on the most important tasks first

- Set short- and long-term goals

- Avoid time wasters, distractors, and time robbers

- Do distasteful jobs first

- Avoid procrastination or delaying decisions

- Say no or refuse nonpriority work

- Ensure your meetings are productive

- Appropriately allow or stop interruptions

TIPS FOR PEOPLE IN A HURRY

- **Monitor your screen time.** This will take you no time at all but will provide real-time data. Most mobile devices have available apps that measure, display, and communicate how much time you spend in front of a screen. Track your screen time for a couple of weeks. Is this how you want to spend your time?

- **Schedule email**. You do not need to respond to email the moment it pops into your inbox. On the other hand, you don't want to ignore it for long periods of time either. You can be more efficient if you choose when you'll read and respond to email. For example, you could try addressing email at 9 a.m. and at 2 p.m. or just before you go home.

- **Slow down.** Fred Rogers, of Mr. Rogers's fame, had a framed quote on his studio wall that said, "L'essentiel est invisible pour les yeux" (What's essential is invisible to the eye). Take time to slow down and enjoy the being. If you don't have time to slow down, ask if this is how you want to spend your time.

- **Block distractions.** Stay focused and accomplish more by finding your favorite way to block distractions. Different things work better for different people. It could be using a headset, using your computer's do-not-disturb function, silencing your phone, or hiding away in an unoccupied conference room.

PRACTICE SPRINTS

- **Track your time.** Do you know how you really spend your time? Few of us do. Buy an app or create your own method to log your time. For ease, measure it in 15-minute intervals. You'll find a template at https://ideas.bkconnection.com/skillsforcareersuccess if you wish to use it. Evaluate your data at the end of one week. If you think it was an unusual week, track your time for another week. Then compare. How much time are you spending in each category? What surprised you? What pleased you? What do you want to change? Compare how you are spending your time with how you want to spend your time. Is it what you desire?

- **Follow the 80/20 rule.** Set priorities on your list using the Pareto 80/20 principle, which states that 80 percent of your results will come from 20 percent of your tasks. Identify the most important tasks, which will be the most valuable use of your time. Those are your priorities.

- **Control your combined calendar.** Begin to block time for activities you don't seem to have time for. Begin by having only one calendar for business and personal. This avoids double booking or forgetting events in one part of your life when you are immersed in the other.

Color code events for additional separation. Professionally that might be writing and planning time. Personally it might be spending time with your children or volunteering in your community. Schedule it. If you don't, it may not happen.

STRATEGIES FOR THE LONG RUN

- **Your day.** Examine how you spend your day and take advantage of the best time to do different things. For example, arrive early. This is not to advocate for spending more time at work, but often 30 minutes at the beginning of your day to get organized can make you feel in control for the rest of the day. Save the last 15 minutes of your day to plan for the next day by listing important tasks, deadlines, and scheduled meetings. In between, engineer your schedule based on your energy level throughout the day. If you're energetic in the morning, complete your most demanding or creative projects then; if you experience downtime in the afternoon, use it for routine tasks such as expense reports. Anticipate the unanticipated by scheduling some flextime for crises that may pop up throughout the day. Finally, the last thing you can do on Friday is to organize your upcoming week. You will feel organized and ready to go Monday morning.

- **Time-managed meetings.** One of the biggest time wasters can be meetings if they aren't planned well and don't use attendees' time well. Sometimes we spend so much time in meetings that we don't have time to do other important tasks. Meetings are important, but the majority could be more efficient. Attend someone else's meeting to gather ideas for what to do before, during, and after meetings to make them more efficient and effective.

- **A hijacked day.** Many things can prevent you from being organized, but one of the most recurring is that we allow other people and activities to hijack our days. You may have started with a list of important things you needed to complete. Then at the end of the day you felt like you didn't get anything done. You probably completed lots of low-priority activities or filled in for your boss at a meeting or helped your colleagues do something. But your priorities languished. What can you do? Establish a plan for the day and stick to it. Determine what's using your time and find a way to stop it. Try these suggestions:

1. Turn your email notification off so you don't hear the ding every time something pops into your inbox.

2. Close your door if you have one—but at least post a sign that announces you're working on an important project.

3. Stop trying to multitask. Experts tell us we are much less efficient when we work on more than one thing at a time.

4. Set a defined amount of time, say 45 minutes, for an important project and don't stop until the time is up. Treat yourself at the end with a walk around your floor or a phone call you've been looking forward to.

Monitor and track the results each day. How many days were you able to complete your most important tasks?

CROSS TRAINING

You will find related ideas at these crossover skills:

- Stay Organized
- Understand Personal Style
- Balance Life
- Set Goals

READING FOR THE FINAL STRETCH

- *175 Ways to Get More Done in Less Time*, by David Cottrell
- *Eat That Frog: 21 Great Ways to Stop Procrastinating and Get More Done in Less Time*, by Brian Tracy

SKILL 25

Stay Organized

Your ability to stay organized is a skill that will pay off over and over. There are different degrees of getting and staying organized. You need to be organized to get anything done, and you need to stay organized to succeed in life. It's not something you can do once and forget. What's the alternative? Disorganization causes stress, leads to frustration, and makes life much more difficult. Keep in mind that it is not just about having an orderly desk or sorting things into lists—although that helps. It is about defining the meaning of and importance to other things and putting them in order based on what makes them important to the bigger picture.

It's important because being organized saves time, prevents frustration, increases productivity, ensures you reach goals, and ultimately saves money. It reduces stress from daily and chronic chaos. It also protects your professional reputation, which can be ruined by just losing one essential paper or forgetting one vital meeting.

MASTERING THE SKILL

Hurdles to Overcome

- Why can't I ever find things?
- Why can't I ever finish my to-do list?
- How am I supposed to get my work done when things just pile up around me?
- What's the big deal? I've never been organized, so why would I want to start now?

Your Path to Success

- Commit to your own success, determined
- Be available and prepared when needed
- Practice self-discipline in your efforts to stay on task
- Maintain a clean desk and manage paperwork
- Use technology effectively to track information and schedules
- Take pride in being on time with quality results

TIPS FOR PEOPLE IN A HURRY

- **Do, delegate, or dump.** This tried-and-true technique is a time management and organizational tool. Touch each email or piece of paper once and place it into one of three piles: what you need to do, what belongs to someone else, or what can be thrown away.

- **Capture your sleepy ideas.** Do you ever wake up in the middle of the night with a great idea, only to have it vanish in the morning? That's how our brains work. Keep a pen and paper next to your bed to capture those great ideas. Bonus idea—get a pen that lights up.

- **Organize your to-do list.** Keep a list of your tasks. Separate them into categories such as home, work, and committee, or today, this week, and this month. Find a system that works for you.

- **Declutter your desk.** Organize your desk. Pick each item up once and do one of these: put it where it belongs, create a place, or toss it. Then keep it clutter-free.

- **Don't check it.** When you travel, be sure to keep everything you need for the first 24 hours, such as your clothes, PowerPoint presentation, contact information, or any meeting notes or materials, in your carry-on luggage. If your luggage is delayed, you can at least get through the first day.

PRACTICE SPRINTS

- **Right now.** You may want to be more organized but don't know where to start. Whenever that happens, take a breath, pause, and ask yourself, "What is the most important task for me to complete right now?"

- **On time.** Timeliness projects professionalism and organization skills. People who are late project incompetence and a lack of integrity. Adopt an on-time attitude. Then live up to it. To be more timely, begin adding 25 percent to the time you estimated to get anywhere. Prepare ahead—for example, at home, lay out your clothes, briefcase, and materials the night before, or for an evening event, as soon as your get home. At the office, set reminders and gather what you need for a meeting in the morning. Lay out stacks of materials for each event of the day so you can grab and go.

- **No more "one more."** Do you try to squeeze one more task in before you leave to go to a meeting or to lunch with a colleague? Organized people rarely fall prey to the "one more thing" syndrome. They don't try to squeeze in one more email or one more conversation or one more phone call. If you think you do this, be aware of when it occurs and stop it in its tracks. The result is that you will feel more organized, be more put together, be on time, and be in control.

- **Have an organized vision.** Create a vision for your "organized life" that identifies what you want your life to look like once you are as organized as possible. Picture it in your head and why it matters to you. Define what "organized" looks like. What will you do? What won't you do? Define exactly what you stand to gain if you achieve this organized vision and what you will lose if you don't.

- **Put it away.** Visit a retail or office supply store and load up on plastic bins, shelves, baskets, or boxes; colored file folders, pencil cups, a bulletin board, utensil holders, or anything else you think your office could use. Determine an approach that makes sense. Make your workspace work for you. Hire an organization consultant to get you started if you need to. Get rid of things you don't need and identify the best place for everything. Once you put your system into play, always return things to their rightful place. Everything will be in its place and you won't waste time looking for them. Keeping your physical and your virtual workspace space organized will help you stay focused.

- **Correct the problem.** Begin to look for patterns that might prevent you from being organized or being on time. Then correct them. For example, if you regularly forget your phone charger, buy a spare to keep in your car or at work. If you travel a lot and forget to pack items for your Dopp kit or makeup bag, duplicate all the items and keep one kit already packed in your suitcase. If you regularly look for your keys, place a hook by the door and make it a habit to hang your keys every time you return. Place items in the same place every time so that you know where they are when you want them or know with a glance that they are missing. If your gas gauge creeps near empty, causing a panic on the freeway, make a promise to never allow the gas tank in your car to drop below 25 percent.

CROSS TRAINING

You will find related ideas at these crossover skills:

- Manage Time
- Show Self-Awareness
- Plan and Organize Tasks
- Be Accountable

READING FOR THE FINAL STRETCH

- *Indistractable: How to Control Your Attention and Choose Your Life*, by Nir Eyal
- *Awaken the Giant Within*, by Tony Robbins

SKILL 26

Balance Life

Your ability to balance your life—personal and professional—requires that you first define your priorities and values. Your values serve as the foundation to support your lifestyle. Balance is not equality. Balancing your life means giving the appropriate amount of time and attention (of your choice) to each area of your life. What must you do to balance your career, relationships, personal needs, community, family, health, finances, fun, or others?

It's important because leading a balanced lifestyle provides many benefits—some that you may not even be aware of. Balance improves your general health and well-being, reduces your stress, improves your mental state, and helps boost your energy. You probably know that exercise can improve your mood, but social connections can do the same. Balance isn't just a feel-good concept—people who have achieved balance claim to be more empathetic, more productive, and more creative and are better able to empower and motivate others. Finally, people claim to be more satisfied with who they are and what they are doing. Try it!

MASTERING THE SKILL

Hurdles to Overcome

- How aware am I of doing things that do not add quality to my life?

- How many things am I doing out of habit that I should shed?

- How can I always be behind with not enough time to do everything?

- What's wrong with leaving every night at five o'clock when I've given my eight hours?

- What's wrong with working late every night since I hold myself to a high standard?

Your Path to Success

- Accept that you can't do everything, and do not feel guilty about it

- Establish your priorities for home as well as your priorities for work, and constantly reevaluate them for your total life

- View your balanced life as an important part of being a good employee

- Say no when appropriate

- Simplify all parts of your personal life and professional life

- Invest time to reenergize, reflect, and have fun outside of work

TIPS FOR PEOPLE IN A HURRY

- **Not one and done.** Balance isn't something that you establish once and then maintain. It changes depending on where you are in life and what's most important to you at the time. What influences your balance right now?

- **Here's to your health.** Your health should be a part of your balance. Stay healthy with the right nutrition, exercise, and sleep. Of course, you know that, but make it a part of your life balance—especially if you have a high-pressure job.

- **Define success.** "How do you define success?" is a favorite interview question. Think about what's most important to you. How would you answer that question in an interview? If your spouse or significant other asked you? If your child asked you? If your mother asked you? Now how do you answer it for yourself? Is your life balanced for your desired success?

- **What's your pace?** What would it mean to live life at your own pace? If this is an intriguing question, use it to start a conversation with someone.

PRACTICE SPRINTS

- **Explore your other options.** Most community colleges or recreation centers offer a long list of courses that cover everything from biking to jewelry making to yoga. Check out what's available that might fit into your plans for a more balanced life. It's more fun with another person, so invite someone from your organization or a friend to join you in some balanced fun!

- **Just say no.** The inability to say no is often the culprit behind an unbalanced life. This can be hard for many of us. Sometimes you know you must say no. Then again, there are other times when you don't want to say no. Here are some alternatives. Try one or two that you might want to make a part of your repertoire. This will help to prevent you from squeezing too much into a too-short time period.

  1. Explore other possibilities: "What you've asked isn't possible; tell me your ultimate goal and let's explore other possible ways to attack this."

  2. Offer alternatives: "I can't attend your meeting. Could I send someone to sit in and get the information?"

  3. Give a rain check: "I can't attend your meeting this week, but I am available next week."

  4. Provide a reason for a delay: "I am wrapping up a deal for the organization, but I can give it a shot next week."

- **Use values for better balance.** In both the "Find the Right Career Path" section and skill number 2, "Create a Personal Development Strategy," you are asked to define and examine your values to better align your development goals. Do it now if you haven't already. Your values should also be the basis for your plan for better balance. In fact, your values should be the foundation for all that you do. Use the values worksheet located at https://ideas.bkconnection.com/skillsforcareersuccess to identify your most important values and compare them with how you spend your time. How can you plan a better-balanced life based on the values that are most important to you?

STRATEGIES FOR THE LONG RUN

- **Balance your life goals.** Think of your life as a pie, with each piece representing a different category. You can define your personal categories any way you wish. I use these eight categories:

  > Fun—vacations, hobbies, pleasure reading, travel

  > Relationship—friends, current or future life partner

  > Career—job satisfaction, work, career path, education

  > Family—children, parents, relatives

  > Social—sports, activities, clubs, community, volunteering

  > Health—exercise, diet, vitamins, sleep

  > Financial—savings, investments, home, retirement plan

  > Creative—self-space, spiritual, artistic, sharing with others

  Assign an approximate percentage of your waking time to each. This gives you a guideline to determine if you are living your values. Identify a goal that you wish to reach in each of the categories. For example, if you have been telling yourself you need to get in shape, you may wish to create a goal such as, "By January 31, I will go for a 30 minute walk three times each week." You may also wish to rate your satisfaction with each category on a 1–7 scale. Feel free to change these categories to something more meaningful for you.

You can print this activity at https://ideas.bkconnection.com /skillsforcareersuccess.

- **Use a life coach.** Hire a life coach who will counsel and encourage you to review a range of professional and personal issues. A coach can help you identify, clarify, and create a vision for what you want, as well as encourage your self-discovery and growth. If you've already established a plan, you can use a coach's expertise to modify your goals as needed to ensure your goals, personality, and vision fit you well.

- **Stop doing.** Like most people, you probably want to increase the amount of time you spend on some part of your life. Since we all have exactly the same 10,080 minutes in every week, you'll probably need to determine where those minutes or hours will come from. You will probably need to stop doing something. Try this. Make a list of all the items you'd like to stop doing. Go through each item to identify which you could stop doing and which you would like to reduce the amount of time you spend doing it and by how much. Put an action plan together (a template is located at https://ideas.bkconnection.com /skillsforcareersuccess), complete with a listing of who will do what by when and a realistic timeline. As a secondary step, determine a plan for not filling in your time with other items that are not part of your strategy for the long run. It is always possible to slip back into what was previously comfortable. What do you need to let go permanently?

CROSS TRAINING

You will find related ideas at these crossover skills:

- Set Goals
- Network with Others
- Be Resourceful
- Show Self-Awareness

READING FOR THE FINAL STRETCH

- *Eat Sleep Work Repeat: 30 Hacks for Bringing Joy to Your Job*, by Bruce Daisley

Professional Presence

What were your expectations when you were hired for your first job? Do a great job and you'll be rewarded appropriately? Unfortunately, recognition and reinforcement aren't always proportionate to an employee's performance. Your professional presence plays a big role in whether you receive the recognition you deserve, whether your priorities are funded, and whether you are a respected and visible voice in your organization.

Some organizations have a culture that respects its employees. Employees are treated politely, are encouraged to express opinions and ideas, and are recognized for their contributions. In other situations, managers play favorites, have superior attitudes, and don't communicate or listen.

Charlotte Ashlock, currently an editor for Berrett-Koehler Publishers (BK), has experienced both kinds of cultures.

She says that she started working for BK, and although she liked the culture, she was frustrated with the huge amount of time she had to invest in attending organizational decision-making meetings. She just wanted to do her job. Then she took a job with a tech company where she got her wish. She wasn't expected to "waste" time on discussions, wasn't involved in meetings, and had the luxury of just keeping her head down and completing her work.

She conducted research that she believed gave the organization a strong competitive advantage; she benchmarked the competition, gathered data, and reviewed products. She believed her research provided a way for the tech company to leapfrog its competition. All the while she was researching and writing her report, she was not visible to the tech company's leadership. She was also not advocating for her project, and with no visibility, few knew the value her ideas could potentially bring to the organization. She turned in her report, and a few months later she was laid off. She doesn't believe the report was ever read.

She returned to BK as an editor, but this time with an appreciation for how vital meetings are and how important it is to understand what the other functions do. She values learning about how their priorities align with hers and BK's goals. She appreciates that others want to hear her opinions and ideas. And she realizes the value in promoting herself and her work, as well as the need to be politically savvy. She says, if you don't advocate for your work, who will?

Do you feel icky when talking about selling yourself or advocating for your priorities? Charlotte suggests that if you have negative vibes about playing politics or selling yourself, replace the nomenclature. Instead of "selling" and "politics," define your goals in terms of a cause. Don't "sell" your projects or promote yourself; "champion a cause" to make your organization better. Don't view it as "playing politics" but "championing" something bigger than yourself to make the world a better place.

Shaping your professional presence requires that you practice political savvy and advocate for yourself. Exhibit a professional image that projects confidence and optimism, that reflects both your organization's interests and your personal values, and that projects professionalism in how you look and what you say. You need to adapt to situations as they arise and always model your organization's expectations. And you need to stay visible.

You are free to choose,
but the choices you make today will determine
what you will have, be, and do in the tomorrow of your life.

—ZIG ZIGLAR

Practice Political Savvy

Y our political savvy is your ability to understand how your organization works beyond the org chart that you see on paper. It requires you to have a deeper understanding of who the influencers are that can support or reject a project. Influencers aren't always people with titles; they are also the informal leaders in your organization—those whom people ask for advice and whom leaders listen to. Political savvy requires that you take time to understand others and their needs, think before you speak, and implement your networking and influencing skills. This knowledge can be used to effect positive actions that support your career, your professional objectives, and your organization.

It's important because political savvy is based on trust and builds trust throughout your organization. Being politically savvy is useful to you to ensure your own career advancement as well as to demonstrate how you can support others. To get things done, you must be aware of the political dimensions in your organization as well as the political savvy practices that get things done.

Hurdles to Overcome

- How can I make a difference when there is never buy-in for my ideas?

- Why should I bother with others since most people just want to see how quickly they can climb the corporate ladder?

- How do I stop myself from spouting off about the wrong topics at the most inopportune times?

- Politics is so nasty, underhanded, and sneaky; why should I be involved with it at all?

Your Path to Success

- Practice proficiency for building relationships and developing contacts throughout the organization, including superiors

- Maintain political awareness

- Exhibit trustworthiness, sincerity, integrity, respect, authenticity, and candor

- Truly understand your organization and its vision so that you can predict its requirements and provide support

- Be perceptive of others as you take the time to understand, care, and help those in your organization

- Use a broad array of information about individuals and your organization to enhance your personal goals as well as your organization's objectives

TIPS FOR PEOPLE IN A HURRY

- **Know your influencers.** Know who can advance or block your career progress. It's not just obvious influencers but also informal leaders and gatekeepers. Treat everyone with genuine respect.

- **Think first.** You know you should think before you speak (or act). It is one of the most important skills if you wish to be viewed as politically astute.

- **Observe others.** Identify those whom you respect for their authenticity, integrity, and ability to get the job done with praise from leadership. What skills do you observe? What approaches do they use? Whom do they network with? How do they behave? What can you learn from them?

- **Pinpoint political people.** Identify people who are obviously political. What behaviors do they exhibit that you admire or dislike? Do they annoy or amuse you in any way? How do you address them? What behaviors do you want to imitate or reject? Do you perceive any ulterior motives? What's missing in their behavior? What do you want to project?

PRACTICE SPRINTS

- **Thrive, not just survive.** Your ability to thrive in today's workplace depends on your political awareness and savvy. Most skills that fall under the political savvy definition can be combined into the three major categories listed here. Review this list and check those that you believe you need to improve.

  1. Understanding your organization: observing changes your organization makes and why, and attending to nonverbal clues about what's going on below the surface

  2. Understanding yourself: being self-aware of your behaviors and knowing which ones you need to adjust to inspire trust, build integrity, and demonstrate authenticity

  3. Networking: building relationships across department boundaries and with superiors and always showing a sensitivity and a willingness to help others

- **Know where to influence.** Developing your influence requires thoughtful planning. Begin to connect your work with the rest of the organization. Whom do you need to help you achieve the results you need? And the opposite, who can you help achieve their objectives?

- **Turn frustration to facilitation.** Think about the person in your organization who frustrates you the most. It may be someone who prevents you from obtaining information or supplies when you need them. Replay your last few encounters with this person. What rationale does the individual give you for the action? How could you adjust to meet this individual's requirements? What goals does this person have? How could you help the individual meet these goals? How well do you know this person? How could you get to know the individual better? Meet with someone you trust to share the situation and to get ideas for turning your frustration around and getting the person to facilitate your requests better.

- **Help others.** Don't let your job description define who you are. See it as the minimum that you do. Always be on the alert for how you can help others grow, develop, and excel on the job. Political savvy is not just about what you gain but also about helping others advance too. Live a life of giving, and you will learn that the more you give and help others, the more you will be helped yourself. It is not something you keep score of; it is not an I-helped-her-now-she-owes-me game. You will experience help from many directions. Even more valuable is that you will achieve a reputation for being someone who can be trusted, is sincere, has integrity, and is respected and authentic. You will gain status as an influencer for the organization and that gets leadership's appreciation.

STRATEGIES FOR THE LONG RUN

- **Hone political savvy.** Having political savvy means that you are an influencer in your organization. Becoming an influencer requires two skill tracks and the ability to bring them together at the right time. The first skill track is how you support others and help them to succeed. It includes behaviors such as creating a sincere and authentic relationship with others; offering support, advice, and assistance; saying yes more often; being a good listener; going out of your way to help; and making mutually beneficial introductions. The second skill track is how you project your own success. It includes actions such as making an effort to meet senior-level employees, refusing to gossip, networking across department boundaries, thinking before you act, declining to complain about the organization and its leaders, and keeping your good works in front of leadership. The key is to balance the two skill tracks. How balanced are you? Make a list of actions you've completed in the last 30 days that show how you helped others. Make a second list of actions you've completed in the last 30 days that show how you project your own career success. What do the two lists say about you? What can you do to ratchet up both? Create a six-month plan and review it with your mentor.

- **Manage up.** Building your ability and self-confidence to communicate with senior leaders is a benefit of political savvy. It begins with building a trusting relationship and rapport with your supervisor. Keep your boss informed with all necessary information. Be proactive and inform your boss where struggles are occurring and where things are going well. Don't allow your boss to be blindsided. Open communication should lead you to anticipate what your boss will need and how you can provide support before you are asked. Managing up goes beyond your boss by having open and candid discussions with other senior leaders. It includes your ability to answer questions or advise senior leaders based on expertise and experience that you have. Again, work with your boss to help you understand what's needed in these situations and how to put both of you in a positive light. What's your manage-up plan? How can you begin to make your boss's job easier?

- **Become a board member.** Serve on a board for a community non-profit organization to study how other organizations manage. Who are the influencers and what do they do? What motivates individuals and how do they interact across department lines? How well do individuals navigate change and how does their political savvy change? Discuss anything you don't understand with members of the organization. The board chair will also be able to shed light on the interactions. What are you learning that you could implement at your organization?

CROSS TRAINING

You will find related ideas at these crossover skills:

- Network with Others
- Build and Manage Relationships
- Model Corporate Expectations
- Promote the Organization's Vision and Values
- Advocate for Self

READING FOR THE FINAL STRETCH

- *Empowering Yourself: The Organizational Game Revealed*, 2nd ed., by Harvey Coleman

Exhibit a Professional Image

Your professional image is what you project with your demeanor, appearance, and poise. You are always on. Your image is also portrayed in how you respond to others and how they speak about you. As you can imagine, it covers dozens of aspects from the clothes you wear to the words you choose to your telephone etiquette and how you treat others, no matter what their role, job, or position. Professionals take the initiative to set the standard to look, sound, and act their best. An important element of your professional image is your ability to communicate ideas, knowledge, and information. You will be expected to explain decisions and reasoning, invite questions, lead meetings, set agendas, and influence others. You need to communicate professionally to be heard and respected.

It's important because you are constantly projecting messages that others interpret. They are tuning in to who you are. Your image sends messages that extend beyond your communication. The image you project makes others decide to view you as professional or not. Whether you like it or not, you are constantly sending messages of your professionalism that are being judged by others. Since you have 100 percent control of this message, why not send your preferred image?

MASTERING THE SKILL

Hurdles to Overcome

- How aware am I of the negative images I give off when I get upset, complain about management, swear, or ignore someone?
- Why should I pay attention to all that professional image stuff; aren't I here to get a job done?
- What am I supposed to do when I get upset; isn't letting off steam healthy?
- Who cares what I wear or look like; does it affect the quality of my work?

Your Path to Success

- Increase your awareness of the language, responses to others, and conversation topics you use
- Be aware of your physical appearance, dress, grooming, voice, manners, mannerisms, and views
- Maintain an optimistic outlook, projecting confidence and poise
- Be reliable, responsible, and accountable to complete work on time and with quality
- Reflect your company's interests and your values
- Allow for mistakes and manage emotions; cope with stress
- Overcome setbacks but learn from them and understand that organizations can be complicated
- Take initiative and responsibility for problems that are not yours

TIPS FOR PEOPLE IN A HURRY

- **The power of image.** Whether you like it or not, image is powerful. Examine those colleagues who are the most respected. Be honest with yourself. How does your image compare with theirs? Compare dress, grooming, mannerisms, speech, word choice, and interaction with others.

- **Manage your digital presence.** Check all social media. Did you post pictures of your weekend fun that are less than professional—even harmful to your career? Did you post rude comments about someone? Even if you only intended to share your pictures and comments with your friends at work, you may be preventing future career opportunities. Do what's necessary today.

- **Look in the mirror.** A recent survey found that 51 percent of employers admitted to making a decision not to employ someone because the employers didn't like the way the applicant looked. Check your professional image. Would you hire you?

- **Help someone today.** Take initiative to help someone today. It doesn't matter whether it's a big or little task—making a sincere offer will help build your professional image.

- **Make a good first impression.** There is never a second chance for a first impression. What could help you make a good first impression?

PRACTICE SPRINTS

- **Dress for success.** Although the book with this title is from the previous century, it is still important that you determine appropriate attire for different settings and situations. If you are presenting a training program to a group or a proposal to a potential client, your attire should be one notch up. For example, if you expect men to wear slacks and a sport jacket, wear a suit. If you expect women to wear dresses, wear a dress and jacket or a suit. Around the office, wear what everyone else wears, paying particular attention to what your supervisor wears. If you are scheduled to give a presentation to senior leadership, dress appropriately; if you aren't sure what to wear, ask your supervisor for advice. First impressions count. What do you need to change to be dressed for success?

- **Professional presence.** Your communication must begin with credibility and personal presence. In her book *Creating Personal Presence*, Dianna Booher (2011, 177) writes, "Your presence involves your physical, mental, and emotional essence, as well as character. It encompasses what others think or feel about you, based on their interactions with you over time. When that feeling turns out to be favorable, you earn trust and credibility." To build professional presence and credibility, begin by knowing how to form a strategic message. This includes

  > stating the conclusion first and then building the case to support it,

  > delivering the strategic context and significant details,

  > using appropriate positive language,

  > asking thought-provoking questions,

  > presenting a point of view,

  > ensuring your points are memorable. (Booher 2014)

  Demonstrate credibility nonverbally by maintaining a confident posture, following acceptable appearance norms, and being respectful. The ultimate goal is to build rapport with everyone. Think about your strategic messages. How closely do they follow Booher's formula? If not, what do you need to change? Meet with a communications expert from your training department or your marketing department to help you with your professional messaging and presence.

- **Change "but" to "and."** Changing a single word in your vocabulary can make a difference in how people perceive you. Instead of saying, "I like that idea, *but* here's something . . ." you could say, "I like that idea, *and* here's something . . ." Try it. It's almost magic. "But" is a word that sets people up for a disagreement; "and" is a word that suggests inclusivity.

- **Take a positivity break.** Do you find the faults in others' statements, correct what they say, identify flaws in processes, or disagree with their plans? Do others consider you negative? Take a positivity challenge for a week. During that week, track the number of negative statements you make and the number of positive statements you make. If you are brave, you'll ask a colleague to track them for you. If you are very negative, you may not even hear negative statements. If that's the case, you may need a trusted friend to help. At the end of each day examine your count: how many negative statements and how many positive statements? Set a goal for yourself each day, such as 10 percent fewer negative statements and 10 percent more positive statements for the next day. This activity may not clear up all your negativity, but it will make you more aware and it will begin to show up in the positive image you'd prefer to project. A positive attitude toward your work, your colleagues, and the world in general will benefit your professional image.

STRATEGIES FOR THE LONG RUN

- **Ask for more.** Once you've been in a position long enough to meet all expectations, ask for more responsibility. Inform your supervisor that you believe you understand the daily tasks of your job and you are eager to learn more that would help your department and the organization. Ask how you can help with anything that is on your supervisor's list of to-dos. These guidelines may help you:

  1. Be certain that your supervisor believes you are exceeding all requirements in your current job.

  2. Define your expectations for "more responsibility." Are you aware of a project that is bogged down? Do you want to learn specific skills? Have you identified something your organization requires that you can help with?

  3. Use a regularly scheduled career development meeting to present your offer, or if you don't have a meeting scheduled, email your supervisor to schedule one.

4. Identify your expectations for the meeting, such as how you will keep the discussion positive, how you'll share the constructive aspects of your job, why you want more responsibility, and how you'll demonstrate being confident (without being cocky).

5. During the meeting, get right to your request. Keep the discussion upbeat. It's unlikely that your supervisor will have something in mind on the spot, but it is wise for you to close your meeting by suggesting a time for a decision. You might say, "Would it work if I check back next week?" If you are comfortable you could even suggest a specific date.

6. As soon as you return to your workspace, email your supervisor to say thank you for taking the time and that you look forward to the next steps. Taking initiative is a skill most employers would like increased in their employees!

- **Learn to manage stress.** How did you manage the most recent stressful situation you experienced? Responding poorly can ruin your professional image. How do you wish you would cope with stress? Register for a stress management class either through your training department or through your local community college. Try to select one that lasts over a longer period of time, giving you a chance to experiment with the techniques you are taught and to get feedback.

- **Aim for 1 degree each week.** At 211 degrees, water is hot. At 212 degrees, it boils. Boiling water produces steam that can power a battleship, be used as a sterilizer for surgery, or turn a turbine to produce electricity for a city. Only one degree makes the difference. Think about what one extra degree of effort might do for you. Review all the aspects for building your professional presence in this section, such as your dress, the words you choose, your responses to others, requesting more work, your mannerisms, your respect for others, and more. Make a list of all the items that could use more effort from you. Under each item, list one to three things you could do that take a small amount of effort—one degree—to improve. Make a commitment to improve one thing by one degree each week. List one of the items on your calendar, one per week. Remember, sometimes it takes only one degree to separate the best from the rest.

CROSS TRAINING

You will find related ideas at these crossover skills:

- Be Accountable
- Make Key Decisions
- Display Self-Confidence

- Show Self-Awareness
- Communicate Clearly
- Maintain Composure

READING FOR THE FINAL STRETCH

- *Creating Personal Presence: Look, Talk, Think, and Act Like a Leader*, by Dianna Booher

Advocate for Self

Your ability to advocate for yourself means understanding how to ask for what you need candidly and respectfully. This is not empty bragging or arrogant demands. None of us gets everything we want, but there are times when you won't get it simply because you didn't ask. You might ask for many things. A promotion or a raise probably comes to mind first, but they aren't the key things. Your ability to advocate for your development may be most at stake. Are you able to advocate for the kind of learning experiences you need? Are you being considered for the high-visibility team that has been based on your six months of research? Did you get approval to take the course that would help you be more efficient? Do your skill and knowledge better match a different position in your department? All of these are reasons to practice advocating for yourself.

It's important because everyone is overworked and overwhelmed with more to do than they have time for—including your boss. That means your boss isn't likely to know everything about all of your colleagues, and so your advocacy will be valuable information. Advocating for the best use of your skills can increase your productivity and engagement. It also helps your organization to have the best candidate in the best position to achieve its strategic imperative.

MASTERING THE SKILL

Hurdles to Overcome

- How well do I sell myself without bragging?
- How objectively do I value my contribution and value to the organization?
- How satisfied am I with the recognition I am given?
- How sure am I that my superiors know the value of what I contribute to the organization?
- How often do I allow my emotions to overtake my rational judgement?
- How often do I come across as arrogant, demanding, or aggressive?

Your Path to Success

- Appreciate the value your skills and knowledge provide to the organization
- Have a clear and unbiased opinion of your contribution
- Balance your self-confidence with appreciation for others' contributions
- Have a realistic appreciation for what the organization needs from you
- Maintain a level head as you plan what you expect from others
- Clearly ask for what you want after you've done a thorough preparation
- Accept rejection professionally
- Accept negative responses as your opportunity to improve your request in the future

TIPS FOR PEOPLE IN A HURRY

- **Believe in you.** Advocate for yourself; always be 100 percent on your own side. Promoting yourself can be intimidating. But you need to believe in you. If you don't, why should anyone else?

- **Leave out emotions.** Advocating isn't about your feelings. It's about what you deserve. Keep all conversations calm, focused, and unemotional.

- **Ask for what you want.** Don't ask for less than you want, thinking it will be more appealing. The person you are asking doesn't know you're asking for less. You aren't likely to get more, so have the courage to ask for what you want. If you ask for less, you'll get less; if you ask for more, you just might get it.

- **Timing is everything.** Before you plan a big request, think about your timing. If your department is wrestling with problems, the people you need to approach are probably distracted. So unless your request will help solve the problem, find a better time. Of course, if your request is time-sensitive, don't wait too long or you will miss the opportunity.

PRACTICE SPRINTS

- **Get over yourself.** Don't assume that everyone knows what a great job you are doing; what results you are getting; how often people come to you for help, guidance, or training; or what value you produce that is above and beyond your job description. "They should know" doesn't work. You need to tell them. You are the only person who is central to all your accomplishments—like the hub of a wheel. The people or projects you interact with are like the spokes, and when it is all put together you create a wheel that helps move the organization forward. You are the only person who knows all that you do. No one else is privy to your contributions, so you can't assume that your bosses spend time thinking about what a good job you are doing. Get over yourself and tell them candidly but without arrogance.

- **"No" may mean "not now."** Rejection can require an attitude shift from you. Think back to what you requested. Was your request for something appropriate? Do you have the respect of the person you spoke with? Perhaps you are focused on the wrong things or don't have a clear view of how the person values (or doesn't value) your contribution. Perhaps the timing isn't right. The person is swamped with a new project. The organization is chaotic over a merger. In those cases, asking again after something changes could garner a "yes." Think about children: they ask for toys and treats, if they can stay up longer, and if they can use their tablets for another hour. They hear "no" often, but it doesn't stop them from asking again. The more "asks," the greater their chances of getting a "yes." This is not approval to be a pest, but do get comfortable with the word "no." Sometimes it just means "not now."

- **Be memorable.** Do you stand out? Sometimes advocating for yourself means that you must stand out in a way that is both positive and attention-getting. The person who always makes a deadline and is also cheerful. The person who is the most gifted in the company and takes plenty of time to talk to the cleaning crew. Being memorable means that you balance your expertise with a desire to learn from everyone, that you weigh your options when deciding what you want to be remembered for. Your reputation is yours to shape. What is your reputation in your organization? What will make you memorable so that you don't have to work so hard to make your case? Instead, your reputation precedes you, so the person knows you would only ask for something that is appropriate for the organization and for you.

- **What's in it for them?** Preparing to ask for anything will be dead in the water unless you have figured out what's in it for the person you are asking. Think about what's most important to this individual. Are numbers down in the department? If so, how will your request increase them? Is the department short staffed? If so, how will your request make it more efficient? Is the person responsible for a high-visibility project? If so, how will your request help to guarantee the results? Also examine what most interests the individual: a pet project, a need to improve a relationship with another department, a desire to lead a different team? How can your proposal help them achieve their goals?

- **Career at stake.** In his book *Empowering Yourself*, Harvey Coleman states that your career advancement is based on a combination of these: 10 percent on your performance, or the daily results you deliver; 30 percent on your personal brand, or what others think of you; and 60 percent on who knows what you do. Whether you agree with Coleman's percentages or not, his research shows that your career is dependent on much more than your daily results. How do you rate yourself on each of the three requirements for career performance?

STRATEGIES FOR THE LONG RUN

- **Keep your bosses informed.** It is never too early to begin thinking about your long-term career moves. One of the most important is regular communication with those who can influence your career advancement. That includes your boss, your boss's boss, your boss's colleagues, influential colleagues, and your organization's informal leaders. Here's where you can put your networking skills to good use. What's useful to keep them informed?

  > Maintain records of the results you've accomplished and the effect on the organization—not just your daily task list.

  > Make your boss aware of your accomplishments—not by bragging about them but by sharing data to show you care how the organization benefits.

  > Set goals for yourself and break them down into small steps to create a path to your goal and share how you're doing.

  > Enlist a mentor to help you decipher how you need to advocate for yourself.

  > Ask your network to advocate for you.

- **Schedule a request.** Plan far enough in advance so that you can schedule a meeting. Make sure it is a good time for the person to whom you'll present your request. Schedule for an in-person meeting. This helps ensure that you'll have the individual's undivided attention and that you'll be able to read body language. Plan what you'll say and what you will ask for—specifically. To help with your success, implement these dos and don'ts:

  > **Do**

  - ☐ Be thoroughly prepared—draft a game plan with who, what, how, and when to make it an easy "yes"
  - ☐ Know who you are pitching to—tailor your presentation to appeal to the individual's personal style
  - ☐ Be confident, not cocky
  - ☐ Follow your meeting with a brief but sincere thank-you note

  > **Don't**

  - ☐ Talk too much—provide the best related example, not the most examples
  - ☐ Take all the credit for your accomplishments—share the glory with your team and use "we"
  - ☐ Allow your emotions to get in the way
  - ☐ Create extra work for the other person for planning or researching your request—have it done before you meet

- **Know your value.** Before advocating for yourself, be sure that you know what value you bring to your organization. It may surprise you to learn that your value to the company should be approximately three times your salary. You can start by listing the knowledge and skills you bring. What do you know better than anyone else in the organization? Research your value in the market for your position, industry, and location. You may not be able to produce specific numbers, unless you are in sales, but you still should be able to discuss your value to the organization. Your perception is just one facet. How do others feel about your contributions to the organization? Have you earned a reputation as someone who takes initiative, solves the tough problems, or builds teams? What others value about you counts—a lot. You'll have to include your accomplishments. Be sure that you've been tracking them and that you've included data that supports each and the ROI to the organization of each. Your value is calculated on your contributions, dependability, and accomplishments. What's your value?

- **Use caution.** Tooting your own horn may be a step backward if not handled appropriately. Like everything else, you need to conduct a thorough analysis of why you need to assert yourself. Think about the advantages and drawbacks. Be sure to properly advocate for the right reasons. One way to think about it is that you are assessing yourself from an internal perspective or view of yourself, your abilities, and contributions. Others will have an external view of you. Be honest about how others will view you and your request before you jump in to advocate for something you believe you can or should do.

CROSS TRAINING

You will find related ideas at these crossover skills:

- Display Self-Confidence
- Be Accountable
- Practice Political Savvy
- Network with Others
- Understand Personal Style

READING FOR THE FINAL STRETCH

- *Ask Outrageously! The Secret to Getting What You Really Want*, by Linda Byars Swindling
- *Empowering Yourself: The Organizational Game Revealed*, 2nd ed., by Harvey Coleman

Adapt to Situations

Your ability to adapt to new situations is vital to accepting whatever change comes your way. Mishaps, modifications, conversions, and issues are a part of the natural flow of work. Your employer will appreciate your willingness to take things in stride and your desire to fill in wherever and whenever the need dictates. Adapting requires employees who can solve problems, envision the future, and plan a path forward. The path is rarely smooth or straight, and flexibility is required to traverse the road into the future. Adaptability requires access to a range of behaviors that enable you to experiment and adjust as things change.

It's important because change is inevitable. The ability to adapt and adjust to situations is a requirement if you want to be viewed as a professional who supports your organization through good times and bad. Flexibility and adaptability can be learned and must be practiced for your personal success.

MASTERING THE SKILL

Hurdles to Overcome

- What causes me to play the blame game when something goes wrong?

- How often do I embrace or avoid risk?

- Why have I made "you can't teach an old dog new tricks" my mantra?

- Why adjust when that's the way we've always done it?

Your Path to Success

- Recognize the value you bring to support your organization in an ever-changing world

- Show excitement for the new skills you will learn as your organization grows and evolves

- Be positive about new directions your department makes

- View adaptability and flexibility as two skills you can acquire to keep you on the cutting edge

- Accept appropriate feedback to ensure that you are open to future possibilities

- Recognize the value of transparency and making facts and truth the basis of workplace communication

- Combine different options to create new methods and novel associations

- Be perceptive and have a sense that a different approach is required

- Manage multiple priorities and tasks

- Listen to others' ideas and be open to trying something different

TIPS FOR PEOPLE IN A HURRY

- **Contribute.** As situations change and require your flexibility, share your thoughts and energy for what needs to be adjusted. Contribute your experience and expertise. Don't be just a spectator.

- **Have a change of plans.** Think back to the last change of plans you and your family faced. How did you adjust? How did you help others adjust?

- **Be curious.** Before you react to a new situation or a modification to a current process, ask lots of questions to explore the actual adjustment that will be required.

- **Do it differently.** Change your routine for a day. Eat something different for breakfast. Take a different form of transportation or route to work. Start your day earlier or later. Meet with different people. Work from a different desk. Change the time you check email. Visit a different part of your building. How comfortable (or not) was your day? Why?

- **Adapt.** Adaptable people are tolerant, learners, resilient, sensitive, energetic, positive, respectful, and vulnerable. Are you?

PRACTICE SPRINTS

- **Try flexibility.** Practice adapting by setting goals for yourself that will require you to be flexible in the environment. Select either a personal or a professional environment. For example, personally you could volunteer to chair a committee at your church or civic league or travel to a city you've never visited without a specific plan. Professionally you could chair a department team or offer to experiment with a new process or method your department is considering. How did it feel to be faced with a situation in which you have no experience but yet were expected to respond or produce something? How did you react to the expectations you faced? What lessons did you learn?

- **Learn a different lingo.** Ask your supervisor for a temporary assign-ment to a department that is different from yours. This experience will put you in a situation where you face ambiguity and uncertainty. It could be valuable to you and your department if the other de-partment is either an internal customer or supplier to your depart-ment. Every department has its own way of doing things, its own jargon, and its own measures. When the differences between two departments are very different, it can cause problems. Spending time in another department benefits your department because learning the differences can help with communication and prevent potential difficulties. It benefits you because you learn how to adapt to unplanned situations as well as what you could do better next time.

- **Understand your reactions.** Make a list of people you work with. Half of your list should be people who you think are easy to work with and the other half should be people who you think are difficult to work with. Generally those who are easy to work with have styles that are similar to yours, and the ones who are difficult have a style that is different from—sometimes even the opposite of—your style. Note how each person makes decisions (how much information they need or what is important), how they communicate (fast or slow, details or big picture), and what message they send (people- or task-oriented). Compare your styles, and it is likely that those whom you work with more easily will be more like you. Now, the most important part is to determine how you can adapt to the others. How can you get into their comfort zone? How can you make them feel more comfortable working with you?

- **Immerse yourself.** Join a new group or activity that is just a little outside your usual norms. After your first event, review what hap-pened and how you responded. Can you compare it to some other time you were placed in a similar situation—perhaps something that occurred early in your college days? What do you wish you had done differently? How can you turn those wishes into a tactic for the next time you find yourself in a similar situation?

STRATEGIES FOR THE LONG RUN

- **Chase a challenge.** Identify a situation in your department that causes problems. Ask your manager if you can form a team to address the challenge. Use a practical problem-solving model. Pay particular attention to who will need to adapt and how they will need to adapt. Have a discussion with each person, encouraging their input and involvement about making the adjustment work for the department. What did you learn about others' ability to adapt? What actions did you take that seemed to work best? How can you transfer these skills to become your consistent way to adapt to new situations?

- **Be a Plan B person.** Get in the habit of having a Plan B ready—or at least considered. Contingency planning isn't just for major disasters. Your contingency plan, whether on paper or in your head, should include scenarios that may arise and what should happen in each case. It should include what will trigger putting your Plan B into action and what that strategy will be. Details should include who needs to know, who has responsibility, and what a notional timeline would look like. Of course, you don't need a plan for everything you do, but you should consider your key projects or actions when there is some risk. Success is all about Plan B.

- **Adapt 3 ways.** The Center for Creative Leadership has identified three types of flexibility that help you adapt. Which do you think you do well, and which do you believe you need to improve?

  1. **Cognitive flexibility** means that you can see when something no longer works, use different approaches, connect unrelated things, and create order out of chaos.

  2. **Emotional flexibility** means that you have a way to address your own emotions and those of others in order to maintain progress when some may be complaining or resisting.

  3. **Dispositional flexibility** means that you remain optimistic and realistic at the same time, accept ambiguity, and see change as an opportunity.

NOT "BUSINESS AS USUAL"

In times of uncertainty, how do you adjust and adapt? Reflect on two or three recent changes at work or in your personal life. Take a few minutes to jot down how you felt, what you did to adapt, and how you responded to others in each case. In what ways were your responses similar? How were they different? Also consider your behaviors from the perspective of others. If your colleagues or family members saw you, what words might they use to describe you? Adaptability is a skill that can be learned and practiced. Read through the following list of qualities and perspectives and put a check beside any items that describe you during times of change.

- ☐ Change direction with smoothness and timeliness
- ☐ Spring back quickly after a setback
- ☐ Avoid procrastinating and learn quickly
- ☐ Revise plans
- ☐ Consider others' concerns during adjustments
- ☐ View change as an opportunity
- ☐ Quickly master new technology, vocabulary, and operating rules
- ☐ Seek corrective feedback to improve
- ☐ Recognize my strengths and weaknesses fairly accurately
- ☐ Adjust my style to changing situations

How many boxes did you check? Are you surprised by your answers? Are you as adaptable and flexible as you thought? What plan can you make to improve?

CROSS TRAINING

You will find related ideas at these crossover skills:

- Influence, Persuade, and Negotiate
- Exhibit Self-Control
- Champion and Manage Change
- Be Resourceful
- Sell Ideas
- Understand Personal Style

READING FOR THE FINAL STRETCH

- *Change Anything: The New Science of Personal Success*, by Kerry Patterson, Joseph Grenny, David Maxfield, Ron McMillan, and Al Switzler
- *Adaptability: Responding Effectively to Change*, by Allan Calarco and Joan Gurvis

SKILL 31

Model Corporate Expectations

Your actions must meet corporate expectations. Organizations hire employees to help them make or save money and to achieve their missions. In exchange for your time and salary, your employer expects several basic behaviors from you: doing your best, having a positive attitude, showing initiative, accepting feedback, and being willing to learn. Organizations may have additional expectations, depending on the industry and your position as well as the kind of work you are doing. For example, some organizations have expectations that you will be a good team player, requiring you to be willing to help others, share your ideas for improvements, and encourage other team members.

It's important because everyone is hired and paid to help the organization be successful. When basic expectations are in place, your organization has the resources, time, and financial ability to develop you and your career to its fullest. The more successful your organization is, the more successful you can be.

Hurdles to Overcome

- How aware am I of the negative statements I make about my organization?

- How can I get my job done if I don't outmaneuver others as we all compete for the same resources—isn't it "every man for himself"?

- How can I change my attitude? Isn't that just who I am?

- Why should I worry about whether my organization is successful— what is it doing for me?

- My job is the pits; why should I care about being nice or the quality of my work?

Your Path to Success

- View self as part of the larger organization

- Display a positive, respectful, cooperative attitude, doing what needs to be done

- Seize opportunities and take initiative; perform your job above acceptable standards

- Commit to producing timely results and maintain good attendance

- Conduct yourself in a professional way, even when away from work

- Follow your organization's policies and procedures when dealing with issues

- Constantly demonstrate honesty and integrity

- Represent your organization in a responsible manner

TIPS FOR PEOPLE IN A HURRY

- **Take initiative.** One expectation that is on everyone's list is taking initiative. What does that mean to you? What does it mean to your boss? How do you demonstrate taking initiative? Is it enough?

- **Hustle to make headway.** How willing are you to jump in and do what's necessary? Move boxes? Enter data? Empty wastebaskets? Research shows that those who willingly and happily do what's needed learn more and are more likely to succeed than those who won't.

- **Say something nice.** Organizations need support too—especially from their employees. What's the last positive thing you said about your organization and your work?

- **Demonstrate commitment.** What does commitment to your organization and your team mean? What have you done in the past week to show commitment?

PRACTICE SPRINTS

- **Attitude, attitude, attitude.** The message heard from managers over and over is: Give us an employee with the right attitude, and we can ensure them a successful career. Julie, a senior manager in the pharmaceutical industry, said, "My fellow managers all agree that the right attitude is more important than education and experience. I can teach someone with a great attitude. I can't change a person who comes across arrogant or has been difficult with my admin." Examine your own attitude. Only you can change it. A poor attitude can only be detrimental to your career. How does your attitude need to change toward your organization, leadership, your boss, your colleagues, and your job?

- **Tangible expectations.** Make your organization's expectations tangible. Make a list of all the basic expectations you believe your organization has of you, such as cooperative, committed, respectful, dependable, and takes initiative. Share the list with your supervisor and ask about anything you left off the list. Next make each expectation tangible to what you do—list specific behaviors that you can see or hear. For example, for dependable, you could list things such as arrives at work on time, finishes every assignment on schedule, exceeds quality expectations for every task, or fulfills every promise to colleagues. Use this list as a reminder as well as a way to monitor your behaviors. Review your list after one week. How'd you do? What do you need to do better?

- **Willing to learn.** Due to the uncertainty and ambiguity about the future of work, the most important skill for the 21st century is the ability to learn. Equally important to employers is your willingness to learn. You have both the ability and the willingness to learn. Sometimes nuances get in the way of your willingness to learn, such as a dislike of authority, an aversion to taking advice, thinking you know better, an inability to learn from your mistakes, unwillingness to accept additional responsibility, or others. Check your willingness to learn. Do any of these reasons to not learn resonate with you? If they do, it may be wise to check your ignorance at the door—and come on in to learn as much as you can.

- **New employees.** How does your organization communicate its standards, expectations, and cultural norms to new employees? Is it adequate? How could you help?

- **Just do it!** Analysis paralysis? Perfectionist? Procrastinator? Lack of enthusiasm? No longer committed? Fear of failure? There can be no excuses in professionalism. Be proactive. Don't wait for someone to tell you to find a solution, start the machinery, or take a shortcut. Take the initiative before being told. Initiative is an essential skill. It is what distinguishes a leader from a follower. There are plenty of excellent employees who are happy to follow directions, but initiative is powerful. Initiative changes the world. Who has taken initiative that has changed your world? Mahatma Gandhi, Martin Luther King Jr., Mother Teresa, and George Washington all took initiative that changed our world. Are you making an excuse or taking initiative? Identify what taking initiative means to you. Be a self-starter.

STRATEGIES FOR THE LONG RUN

- **Practice initiative at home.** Don't think that just modeling your organization's expectations at work guarantees your professional image. It doesn't. You need to practice at home too. Start with taking initiative. Look around your home; where is taking initiative needed? Emptying the dishwasher? Taking out the trash? Sweeping the garage? Adding ketchup to the grocery list when you finish the last drop? Keeping the car's gas tank filled? Yes, there are hundreds of little things you could do to practice home initiative. No idea where to start? Ask your spouse, children, or significant other for ideas.

- **The why of expectations.** Do some research to determine why your organization's expectations are important. Start by reviewing your organization's values, vision, and mission. How do the expectations support these important statements? Next, interview several leaders. What's important to them? What keeps them up at night? What's on their bookshelves? What's their business philosophy? Ask questions and observe them. Find out what hopes they have for your organization. Circle back to the expectations. How will your organization's expectations of you help to meet organizational goals? How do you fit in? How can you demonstrate that you are a part of making your organization successful?

- **Surpass standards.** Don't get bogged down by negatives in your workplace. You are better than that. Your ability to model your organization's expectations will be easy if you have established your own, higher standards. Think of your organization's expectations as only the start for you: Positive? Of course! Respectful? Naturally! Cooperative? Certainly! How can you go above and beyond the standard expectations established by your organization? Set your own standards that take you to the next level. You can set an example that others will observe and follow. Share your enthusiasm and energy for higher standards with others. Seeing your actions and commitment will encourage them to discover and establish their own standards. Your behaviors and attitude will have a lasting impact on those who are a part of it. Remember, your organization's standard expectations are only a start for you. You can exceed them and find passion in your work.

- **Expected expectations.** A compiled list of what employers expect from you includes these nine listed most often: positive attitude, dependability, initiative, cooperation, commitment, enthusiasm, honesty, accepts feedback, and continual learning. Review this list and identify the three that you need to improve the most. Define each to clarify what it means to you and your job. Work with your mentor or coach to identify practical ideas about how you could practice these behaviors and what might prevent you from being your best in these areas. In addition, ask for support to monitor your progress.

CROSS TRAINING

You will find related ideas at these crossover skills:

- Improve Weaknesses
- Show Self-Awareness
- Exhibit a Professional Image
- Be Accountable

READING FOR THE FINAL STRETCH

- *12 Choices That Lead to Your Success*, by David Cottrell

Leadership Capability

W hat is a leader?

Leaders set direction, create an inspiring vision, and create the opportunity for their teams to win. Warren Bennis said that "Managers are people who do things right and leaders are people who do the right thing" (Bennis and Nanus 2003, 20). I take the second half of Bennis's definition one step further. I believe that leaders help themselves *and* others do the right things.

Dennis Padilla, former director of contracts and grants at the Office of Naval Research, shared a story that is one of those things that happens in an instant but makes an impression on you for life.

Dennis and the Chief of Naval Research, a Navy Admiral, had just left a high-level meeting of critical national importance. They were headed down a stairwell with the admiral leading and Dennis following as they continued to discuss the issue that needed to be resolved. All of a sudden the admiral made a quick, clipped move, and Dennis almost crashed into him.

The admiral, it turns out, had seen something on the step and walked back up one step in order to retrieve it. The admiral did not stop talking about the dilemma that still needed a solution and didn't comment on what he was doing, but stooped down to retrieve a PayDay candy bar wrapper that someone had dropped on the step. He then turned again, continued his dialog, and proceeded down the stairwell.

The admiral was highly regarded by all. Following his retirement from the navy, he served as associate provost and professor of engineering at West Virginia University before being selected in 1997 as academic dean and provost at the Naval Academy, the first alumnus in history to do so.

Here was a respected U.S. Navy admiral, discussing a critical national issue while racing down a set of stairs, who abruptly stoops down to pick up someone else's litter. It's a simple act of doing the right thing. It's a small deed—doing the right thing.

What's fascinating about this story is that I remember it often. When I last spoke with Dennis to ensure that I got the story's details correct, he said that he too often thinks of this leadership example. It's a small thing from someone of great stature. Small things often create lasting impressions on many.

What is a leader? Whether you are leading yourself, others, or a project, focus on doing the right things—no matter how small. Leaders help themselves and others do the right things.

Brains, like hearts, go where they are appreciated.

—ROBERT MCNAMARA

SKILL 32

Lead Self

Your leadership skills are critical whether you have a designated leadership role or you are an informal leader in your organization. It begins with how you lead your own life and focuses on behaviors that create your foundation for leadership. You need to listen to yourself to reveal your values, personal purpose, and vision that you have for yourself. Harvard's Ronald Heifetz and Marty Linsky (2002) describe it as your ability to simultaneously stand on the balcony and observe yourself on the dance floor. Spending time alone to think about your day, how you reacted to events, how what you are doing aligns with your purpose, and how passionate you are about your daily accomplishments all help to divulge how you are leading yourself. Solitude creates clarity.

It's important because you need the foundational skills of leading yourself in order to know how to lead others. Some experts believe that you can't be a great leader unless you learn to lead yourself first. Good leadership—no matter what role you play—begins with knowing who you are and who you want to be.

MASTERING THE SKILL

Hurdles to Overcome

- How aware am I about the differences between managing and leading, and do I even care?

- What career choices am I making right now with my negativity, short-term focus, lack of purpose, and frustrations?

- How can I be sure that this work is aligned to my purpose?

Your Path to Success

- Set a good example by energizing others with your commitment and passion

- Model a good work ethic and energy to improve

- Take control of your thoughts and be honest with yourself

- Model credibility and integrity by being transparent, open, and authentic

- Create and live your personal vision and purpose

- Exhibit passion about your purpose and find ways to help your organization succeed

- Genuinely enjoy responsibility

- Have self-confidence that doesn't require constant praise and reinforcement

TIPS FOR PEOPLE IN A HURRY

- **Journal to learn.** Start a leadership journal. Many opportunities for learning and skill practice exist through journaling. Capturing your thoughts and feelings in a journal allows you to review it at a later date—much like taking a snapshot.

- **What did you model?** Fifteen minutes before you end your day, think back to what you did today. How did you lead yourself? What did you learn? How pleased (or not) are you with your actions?

- **Discover solitude.** Spend time thinking about your day and how satisfied, passionate, energized, and happy you are.

- **The company you keep.** Your friends influence your emotions, your decisions, and what you do. You can choose the colleagues that surround you at work. Do the colleagues you hang with at work elevate you? Inspire you? Boost your self-confidence? Model the excellent leader you want to be?

- **Childhood passion.** What did you love to do when you were a child? How does it connect to who you are today? How does it connect to how you want to lead yourself today?

PRACTICE SPRINTS

- **Favorite leaders.** Think about your favorite leaders, such as those in your community or organization or famous leaders. Identify the specific traits and behaviors that you most admire. Are these traits and behaviors ones that you wish to be a part of your leadership repertoire? List them in your journal and beside each behavior compare yourself with your favorite leader. How can you build the skills and knowledge to become a better leader like your favorite leaders?

- **Book a visit.** Visit a large local bookstore. Go to the leadership section and pull five books off the shelf that address the self-leadership challenges you face. Get a cup of coffee. Page through the books and jot down 10 new things you learned about leading. Be prepared to share these ideas with your coach. How will you implement what you learned?

- **Lead yourself.** What in the world does it mean to lead yourself? You need to determine that for you. No one else can do it. Here are a few items to consider: keep learning, control your thoughts, take initiative, deliver what you promise, exceed expectations, demonstrate character, build trust and integrity, share credit, and know who you are. Your turn—make your list of how you will lead yourself.

⊕ TRUST—THE LEADERSHIP STARTING POINT

A strong foundation of trust is one of the quickest ways to establish that you are worthy of being a leader. Listed are actions that you can take to build trust. Rate yourself on these actions. How well did you do? How consistent are you? If any of these skills need to be improved, begin today.

- ☐ Ensure that your words and actions are congruent; avoid mixed messages.
- ☐ Act in ways that support the values of your organization.
- ☐ When having difficulty with another coworker or team member, go directly to that individual to discuss the situation. Be a straight shooter, discussing issues with that person rather than with others about the person.
- ☐ Be a sounding board on sensitive issues for others. Demonstrate strong listening capability.
- ☐ Share your own opinions and perspectives, even when they are different from the majority view. Avoid being a "yes" person.
- ☐ Keep your focus on the big picture and the shared goals of the organization.
- ☐ Accept accountability for your own actions and the results of those actions.
- ☐ Avoid blaming others. Instead, focus on what can be done to fix the situation.

- **Mistakes are a gift.** Teddy Roosevelt stated, "He who makes no mistakes, makes no progress." Observe how you react to mistakes. The times that you learned the most were often the times when you made a mistake. Do you admit to your mistakes? Do you apologize when appropriate? Are you defensive? Ask a trusted friend's opinion as well. If you react badly or make no mistakes at all, you may be considered as "unteachable" to those above you. Take on a perspective of being a lifelong learner. Make mistakes. Accept the feedback. Apologize when appropriate. Learn to lead from your mistakes.

- **Notable quotables.** Turn to your journal to capture quotes that inspire you. They may be quotes you jot down from an article or book you read; they may be words spoken by someone on the radio; they may be quotes from some of your favorite heroes and speakers, such as Abraham Lincoln or Martin Luther King Jr.; they may come from actors or actresses; they may be cartoons you rip out of the Sunday comic section; they may be something your grandmother always said; they may be ads with catchy phrases; or they may be phrases that you say. Whatever they are and wherever they come from, begin your quote notes today. Continue to add to them. Review them. Reread them. If they inspired you once, they will again. And if they inspire you, they will inspire someone else.

STRATEGIES FOR THE LONG RUN

- **Attend a conference.** Identify a conference that would be appropriate for the kinds of skills you need to learn. They may or may not be related to your industry. For example, if you are a leader with a large coaching responsibility, there are several excellent coaching conferences across the nation. It might also be useful for you to attend a conference that digs into your interpersonal skills—yes, it may be uncomfortable, but you will learn so much about how others view you and what you can improve.

- **Substitute for someone.** If someone is away for a period of time for a vacation or work-related travel, volunteer to substitute for the individual who is out. Ask for and be prepared for lots of feedback, improvement suggestions, and corrective recommendations. It isn't easy to be thrown into a situation like this, but you will learn a great deal about yourself, your skills, and what it takes to do other jobs. Ensure that your supervisor is involved, not just to give you permission to take on the responsibility but to provide additional feedback and to be ready to coach you through some of the difficult spots. What did you learn about how you lead yourself?

- **Uncover your purpose and passion.** Spend time every day thinking about your purpose. It could be over your first cup of coffee or on your ride home at the end of the day. You will continue to refine your life's purpose over the years. Get in the habit of reviewing your day and how it contributed to or prohibited your purpose. Some people find that they are in the wrong career or industry. If possible, identify a purpose partner—someone who shares your sense of purpose. It's easier to stay focused when you are surrounded by others who share what's important to you. Find your purpose; find your passion.

- **What do others see?** It's difficult to see yourself as others see you. Schedule time for a personality assessment. Absorb the results. It will help you understand why you do what you do. Some of your personality preferences help you achieve what you desire; others get in your way. We judge ourselves by what's inside, our intentions. Others judge us by what they see on the outside, our behaviors. Sometimes our intentions and our behaviors are not in perfect alignment. A personality assessment will provide the details you need to make more of what you do what you intended to do. And yes, once you are aware of your behaviors that get in the way of success, you can change them.

CROSS TRAINING

You will find related ideas at these crossover skills:

- Accept and Act on Feedback
- Promote the Organization's Vision and Values
- Model Corporate Expectations
- Network with Others
- Show Self-Awareness

READING FOR THE FINAL STRETCH

- *Dare to Lead: Brave Work. Tough Conversations. Whole Hearts*, by Brené Brown
- *Communicate Like a Leader: Connecting Strategically to Coach, Inspire, and Get Things Done*, by Dianna Booher
- *For Your Improvement*, by Michael Lombardo and Robert Eichinger
- *The Leadership Challenge: How to Make Extraordinary Things Happen in Organizations*, by James Kouzes and Barry Posner

SKILL 33

Lead Others

Your ability to lead others is a topic on which an entire library of books has been written, which confirms how important it is. To effectively lead others requires modeling behaviors that motivate, engage, and inspire others. Good leaders help their team members feel connected to their organization and their organization's vision. An important part is mentoring and coaching team members to develop the skills that will advance their careers and also giving them experience by delegating appropriately.

It's important because your ability to lead others is likely to make or break your career. Yes, there are other career paths you can take in which you stay in your expertise lane and do not manage or lead others. Still, the skills that are mentioned in this section will be important to you because even if you don't lead a team, you will definitely be a team member on numerous teams during your career. So it's important that you learn to be a good team member too. Your organization needs teams to meet its goals, encourage employee engagement, and produce a higher quality of products and services than if everyone was working alone.

Hurdles to Overcome

- Aren't mentoring and coaching my team just an excuse for HR to shirk its duties?

- How can I be expected to motivate and delegate to others when I haven't figured it out myself?

- Coach and mentor? Where do I find the time?

- How aware am I about my beliefs that teamwork, empowerment, delegation, and motivation aren't effective to get the work done?

- If I want it done right, I need to do it myself—what am I supposed to do?

Your Path to Success

- Motivate others to perform their best by creating a compelling vision of the future

- Inspire commitment to your team and engagement to your organization

- Draw others together to envision future possibilities and to engage to achieve them

- Model behaviors that empower and engage others

- Connect others' vision and passion to the team and your organization

- Recognize and reward others' contributions

- Mentor and coach your team to build their skills and your organization's capacity

- Delegate work that provides substantial responsibility and benefits to the individual

TIPS FOR PEOPLE IN A HURRY

- **Identify your team's passion.** What excites your team members? What inspires and motivates them? To what do they aspire? Do you know?

- **Be other-focused.** Observe your interactions with others over the next week—both at work and at home. Note the amount of time that your interchange is focused on them and how much is focused on you. Tip the scale in their favor if it isn't already.

- **Ponder this quote.** John Madden said, "Coaches have to watch for what they don't want to see and listen for what they don't want to hear." When leading others, you need to watch for what you don't want to see and listen for what you don't want to hear. Make a list of items that you have heard and seen recently that you know need to be addressed.

- **Set an example.** When others view you and your team, what do they see? What are you doing that sends a message? What example do you set?

- **Develop others.** Think about ways you can develop others on your team.

PRACTICE SPRINTS

- **Prepare to lead a team.** What can you do before you take on your first team? Consider these ideas. Partner with someone who has experience leading teams, where you could be an observer. You could be a team member and have regularly scheduled coaching sessions with the leader. Attend a leadership class. Purchase an online leadership course.

- **Set clear expectations.** Obtain input from your team to create a list of performance and overall expectations for your team and specifically for individuals. The list should include how they deal with you and others. Update your list regularly as new issues emerge or the environment changes. Coach team members. Encourage your team to attend training. Personally meet with individuals regularly to discuss expectations. Keep them involved and engaged.

- **Cultivate objectivity.** Cultivate an attitude of objectivity in dealing with your team. Once a team member problem is identified, it is theirs to solve. Paternalism, favoritism, and condescension are poor excuses for positively developing employees. You owe employees the opportunity to:

    1. Hear what you believe is unacceptable behavior directly
    2. Receive guidance on the way the organization wants individuals to behave
    3. Be offered an opportunity to demonstrate acceptable behavior
    4. Decide how to proceed and to face the consequences of that decision

    One of the biggest mistakes leaders make is to personalize an issue and become upset, angry, or disappointed with a person. While it's human to feel that way sometimes, it's important to remember that dignity requires that we honor a person's choices. Help where appropriate to do so, but don't take responsibility for a team member's misconduct. If you are not as objective as you think you should be, use a leadership journal to record what you believe you are doing, how you feel about it, what you need to change, and how you will measure your success at making changes.

- **Inspire commitment.** Commitment, sometimes called engagement, means that employees are willing to give their discretionary energy to support the organization's success. David Ulrich, coauthor of *Leadership Brand*, contends that commitment is a part of the value proposition between an employee and the organization. The employee who is willing to give value should get value back. Your leadership role as a coach gives you an opportunity to have this discussion with those you are leading. A guide at https://ideas .bkconnection.com/skillsforcareersuccess will define what you can provide to increase employee commitment. Inspiring commitment and obtaining engagement is a critical leadership skill. Find a coworker whom you trust and review the guide to determine how both of you can implement this action. Then coach each other to excellence in this critical leadership talent.

- **Deal to delegate.** Delegation is the process of assigning a responsibility from one person to another. Delegation is not just giving orders. Delegation means transferring a task along with responsibility and authority. Delegation has many advantages. It is motivational, builds trust, is an effective time management technique, builds a positive work environment, builds a strong team, develops others, and enhances solid management practices. Delegate tasks that will provide maximum benefit for employees and the team. Delegating the parts of your job that offer challenges and opportunities for growth is usually motivating. Delegate tasks that can be performed more than once, research that is clearly defined, statistical analysis that needs focused effort, representation at a meeting, or many other things. Avoid delegating crises or high-pressure assignments, any situation where success will be difficult, or tasks that are in a trial period. There are four steps to the delegation process: preparation, communication, monitoring, and evaluation. Identify something you can delegate to one of your team members and walk through the four-step delegation process. Afterward, evaluate your delegation skills to determine what you need to do better.

- **Recognition—pass it on.** Find a quiet place and think of times when you felt most valued by your organization. What was the situation? What did others do to create the climate where you felt valued? What contributions did you make, and how were you recognized? How would you describe the impact on you?

  Pause and think about your responses. Now think about today. What contributions are your fellow team members currently making? What would you lose if they were not present? How often do you tell them you appreciate their contributions? How often do you recognize their progress? List the people whose progress, contribution, and achievement you have been somewhat negligent in recognizing. Think about how you are going to rectify this. Begin a plan now.

- **Check your research.** Many organizations conduct engagement research. Learn about the most recent engagement research your organization has conducted. What were the findings? If you have multiple-year data, what are the trends? What has been done? What can you learn from your organization's data?

- **Encourage development plans.** Encourage all of your employees to create their own development plans. You should have developed yours, so share it with them as a model of what they can do to develop their own. Coach them through the process.

STRATEGIES FOR THE LONG RUN

- **Take a class.** One of the most important courses you can take is how to be a good leader. Many more skills than I can cover in this section are required. Some are located in other parts of this book. Here's a short list of what I think every leader should master: communication, coaching and developing others, inspiring commitment and engagement, motivation, accountability, managing change, influence, negotiation, self-awareness, providing feedback, visioning, solving problems, making decisions, delegating, empowering, managing meetings, managing time, organizing, networking, planning strategically, building teams, aligning with the organization, and yes, modeling all of these behaviors. Study leadership. Take a class.

- **Effective coaching.** Turn to https://ideas.bkconnection.com/skills forcareersuccess for a list of effective coaching characteristics. Rate yourself following the instructions. Share your results with your supervisor and obtain additional feedback from your coach. You could also share this list with your team and ask them for the items they think you do well and those they'd like you to do more often or better. After receiving feedback from others, select the three characteristics that need the most improvement and create an action plan for developing your skills.

- **Motivate all.** You can't motivate people; motivation is internal. It is your job to create an environment that encourages self-motivation and inspires employees or team members to be excited and satisfied with their roles and contribution. How do you create that environment? You'll need to learn what works best for individuals—each will be different. These suggestions can start your thinking: learn about their interests; plan more one-on-one time with each; find creative ways to provide positive feedback; ensure they all have the resources required to do their jobs exceptionally well; develop their skills and knowledge; involve them in decisions; ask for their input; gamify your most important tasks for friendly competition; create stretch goals; provide challenging work; appreciate their differences; lead with a vision; practice transparency; and trust them. Select one or two things you could experiment with and try them with your team.

- **Develop a future leader mindset.** Cultivating the full potential of others is especially difficult when you are also required to deliver business results. Still, it is critical to find time to develop the "high potentials" for the organization. Begin to think of the high potentials on your team as a corporate asset. Top talent belongs to your organization, not a specific team or department. View them as "on loan" to your team. While it may be difficult to give up the best and brightest on your team, you can't hold on to high potentials to pursue short-term goals. Sometimes the best development opportunities are found in another experience. Think about the individuals on your team that may be high potentials. Make a list of all the developmental opportunities that would be good for them—both inside and outside your team. Continue to maintain that list and find growth opportunities for each of your high potentials. This is a positive future leader mindset.

- **So you're going to be a mentor!** Good for you! But what the heck does a mentor do? There will be plenty to do, but just in case there is a lull, I have a guide to help you. Turn to https://ideas .bkconnection.com/skillsforcareersuccess to find questions that you can use to begin discussions early in the process, at the midpoint, and near the end. Plan to be the best mentor ever.

- **Coach and stretch your team.** Identify stretch assignments and rotational assignments that will develop your team members. Stretch assignments are those opportunities that are just outside the individual's area of expertise and comfort zone. Rotational assignments move employees into an area for a designated time to gain experience. Both stretch assignments and rotational assignments are likely to be in an area of the organization where the employee has little or no experience. These assignments are intended to broaden employees' knowledge of the business and enhance their skill set. Create the list of stretch and rotational assignments for your team members and share it with your supervisor to identify how your ideas can be implemented.

- **Volunteer to develop others.** Many organizations would welcome your skills to coach and develop others. Check with your local Boys Club, Girls Club, Big Brothers, Big Sisters, 4-H, Boy Scouts, Girl Scouts, or other locally supported civic groups.

CROSS TRAINING

You will find related ideas at these crossover skills:

- Build and Manage Relationships
- Give and Receive Feedback
- Plan and Organize Tasks
- Champion and Manage Change

READING FOR THE FINAL STRETCH

- *Compass: Your Guide for Leadership Development and Coaching*, by Peter Scisco, Elaine Biech, and George Hallenbeck
- *Monday Morning Leadership: 8 Mentoring Sessions You Can't Afford to Miss*, by David Cottrell
- *Be the Boss Everyone Wants to Work For: A Guide for New Leaders*, by William Gentry
- *A Coach's Guide to Developing Exemplary Leaders*, by James Kouzes, Barry Posner, and Elaine Biech

Lead Ventures

Your ability to lead ventures and projects is the ultimate leadership skill. You'll be able to use many skills to ensure your success. You need to know how to lead productive meetings. You will have a team that will help you complete your project, so you will need to help the team create a strategy and to work as a team to implement it. That strategy needs to align with your organization's mission. The project will give you an opportunity to ensure that your team members see how their work aligns with the goals of the organization. As you lead projects you'll use many other skills you've learned in other sections of this book, such as clear communication, delegation, decisiveness, problem solving, setting goals, motivation, organization, and many others.

It's important because your organization depends on various projects and ventures to get its products and services to its customers. A productive team ensures that the organization is producing the best product with the most efficiency and productivity. Teamwork is important to you because it provides learning opportunities for you and your team. Leading successful ventures benefits the organization and the team members by promoting workplace synergy.

MASTERING THE SKILL

Hurdles to Overcome

- How aware am I of my inappropriate team behavior?
- How can I have time to plan for the future when I barely have enough time to get my work done every day?
- Can't our leaders see that meetings are just an excuse for a gabfest and a big waste of time?

Your Path to Success

- Manage meetings and groups for productive results
- Understand the need to lead and manage productive teams for results
- Create and implement strategy
- Clarify and align to your organization's vision, mission, and goals as well as ensure your team members have clear, shared priorities
- Develop objectives and business strategies with implementation plans
- Update plans to reflect changes

TIPS FOR PEOPLE IN A HURRY

- **Meeting mettle.** Think of the last three meetings you attended. What did you contribute? What could you have done better?
- **Teaming tenacity.** What teams were you on in high school or college? Debate, choir, band, football, soccer, field hockey? What made your teams great? What gave them tenacity and resolve to win? What could you transfer to your organizational team?
- **Personal strategy.** What tools and information did you use to create a personal strategy, such as which school to attend, which apartment to rent, and which car to purchase? How could you use those

same processes, tools, and information-gathering action for creating a strategy for your current organizational venture?

- **Minimalist meeting.** Calling a meeting? Think efficient and make it small. Invite only those who need to be there for only the amount of time that is required. Try a stand-up 15-minute meeting.

PRACTICE SPRINTS

- **Invite yourself.** Ask to sit in on another leader's meeting. Observe the leader's process, communication, and body language. What can you learn from it? Be sure to thank the individual for allowing you to observe.

- **Build a winning team.** Great teams cultivate a culture that encourages constant improvement. People on these teams don't hold back; they are not political, and they do not miss opportunities to get better. Help your team members to know what it is like to participate on such a team, to know how great it feels. It can be one of the most fulfilling experiences you can have. Winning teams make team members better professionals and help them continue to grow and develop. Have you been inspired when witnessing a sports team that is moved by something greater? It's when the individual players surrender to become part of a greater whole that amplifies their individual contributions. What are the characteristics of winning teams? A list of 10 winning team characteristics is located at https://ideas.bkconnection.com/skillsforcareersuccess. Give this list of 10 characteristics to your team and have them rate the team as a whole on each of the characteristics. On which two or three characteristics did your team score the strongest? Give everyone a high five on those. On which characteristics did your team score the lowest? As a team, identify three things you can all do that will lead to a more winning team.

- **Learn strategic planning.** Your organization likely conducts a strategic planning session every year to review or create its vision, mission, and strategic goals. These events are usually attended by the organization's leadership. Let your manager know that you would like to be involved in your organization's strategic planning efforts. You may not be able to attend the event itself unless you volunteer to help, such as by taking notes or by supporting data gathering ahead of time. If this isn't possible, once a new strategy has been developed, encourage leadership to hold a town hall meeting to share the details. Ask for specific emphasis on the vision, values, and mission.

- **First team meeting.** Everyone should leave the first team meeting with a clear understanding of the team's purpose, the goals, timeline, who is on the team and why, the process to complete the work, what team norms are expected, the communication process, the decision-making process, and how meetings will be documented. How will you accomplish all of these during your first meeting? Meet with your coach for some practical tips, guidelines, and templates for how to accomplish everything.

STRATEGIES FOR THE LONG RUN

- **Effective and efficient meetings.** Leading a project or any venture requires you to call and lead a number of meetings. The first step is to determine if a meeting is really required or if there is a more efficient way to accomplish what you need to complete. Meetings are important, but the majority could be more productive. Meeting management guidelines at https://ideas.bkconnection.com/skillsfor careersuccess provide ideas for what to do before, during, and after a meeting to make them more efficient and effective. Practice them every time. If some of these time-honored tools are not practiced at your organization, learn why not. Learn if the entire department or organization would be willing to try them with your help.

- **Build a playground.** Find a community project in which your team could volunteer to complete something in a couple of days. Involve the entire team in developing the strategy. It could be to build a playground, make small repairs to homes for the elderly, or complete a clean-up project. Spend time at the end of each day to review "what we did well" and "what we would like to do better" as a team.

- **Volunteer for a nonprofit.** Volunteer to facilitate a strategic planning session or to guide a strategic planning effort for a nonprofit, professional association, church, local community group, or another organization in your local area.

CROSS TRAINING

You will find related ideas at these crossover skills:

- Manage Time
- Plan and Organize Tasks
- Stay Organized
- Set Goals
- Practice Systems Thinking
- Make Key Decisions

READING FOR THE FINAL STRETCH

- *The Leadership Challenge: How to Make Extraordinary Things Happen in Organizations*, by James Kouzes and Barry Posner
- *Pfeiffer Book of Successful Team Building Tools*, by Elaine Biech
- *The New Extraordinary Leader: Turning Good Managers into Great Leaders*, by John Zenger and Joseph Folkman

Planning and Prioritizing

Today 900 million people do not have access to clean drinking water, and 3.4 million people die annually due to waterborne diseases. According to the United Nations, half the population will have a limited water supply by 2025 (Diamandis and Kotler 2020).

Enter Dean Kamen. Peter Diamandis describes Dean Kamen as a nerd Batman in a denim work shirt. But Kamen's invention does more than save Gotham City. Dean is the inventor of the Slingshot, a waist-high white box that can produce about eight gallons of water per hour using approximately the same amount of solar energy used to power a hair dryer (Diamandis and Kotler 2020). Obviously this isn't Dean's first invention. He has over 440 patents for various inventions, including robotic prosthetics, all-terrain wheelchairs, and insulin pumps.

Dean solved a worldwide water problem by setting goals and planning and organizing the tasks required. But he faced another problem: how to distribute the Slingshot to remote areas that needed it. He was resourceful. In 2012 when Coca-Cola approached Dean to build a unique soda fountain, he agreed if Coca-Cola would use its global distribution network to deliver the Slingshot to rural areas of Latin America and Africa, providing clean water for years. The whole project fits with Coca-Cola's long-term plan to replenish 100 percent of the water used in its beverages.

The partnership between Dean and Coca-Cola is an excellent example of systems thinking, setting goals, and being resourceful to solve a worldwide problem.

Be thankful for problems. If they weren't so hard,
someone with less ability might have your job!

—UNKNOWN

SKILL 35

Practice Systems Thinking

Your ability to use systems thinking will help you throughout your career. Systems thinking is a philosophy requiring a holistic approach. It focuses on the way everything within a single system interrelates and how every system is a part of another, larger system. Since systems thinking is a framework that is built on the interconnectedness of things, it does not break them down into separate parts before analysis. Systems thinking helps you see the impact of feedback that affects how a system behaves. It is helpful when you solve problems that require you to analyze situations in order to explain unexpected effects.

It's important because systems thinking broadens your thinking, providing you with new ways to view and articulate a problem. Systems thinking demonstrates that every choice you make will impact another part of the system. By anticipating various impacts and the trade-offs when planning or solving problems, you can make a more informed choice for the organization as a whole.

MASTERING THE SKILL

Hurdles to Overcome

- How aware am I of ignoring other parts of the organization when I solve a problem in my area?

- Isn't each department required to address its own area to the best of its ability?

- What can I do beyond my area—should I feel responsible to address the broader organization?

- Why isn't it the C-suite's responsibility to think about the organization's systems?

Your Path to Success

- Understand your organization from both a big-picture view and a detailed view

- View the interconnectedness of various parts of your organization and how they each impact one another

- Take a holistic approach to understand what's best for your organization when considering new initiatives

- Understand the rationale your organization makes for various investments

- Appreciate the role other departments play with respect to your department

TIPS FOR PEOPLE IN A HURRY

- **Enhanced by systems thinking?** What organizational approaches, processes, or methods do you think would be enhanced by a systems perspective?

- **Learn about your organization.** If you need to learn more about the other parts of your organization, where can you start?

- **Change your job.** Imagine one thing you could change about your job that would make it easier for you. What other parts of your organization would be affected? How?

- **Why not systems thinking?** Systems thinking is not common among employees. Why do you think that is?

PRACTICE SPRINTS

- **Systems thinking book.** Read Peter Senge's *Fifth Discipline*. Although heavy reading at times, this is a breakthrough in thinking and has become a modern-day classic. If you don't want to read all of it, examine the chapters that focus on systems thinking. Discuss the book with your boss. What are you missing about the concept?

- **New hobby.** Take up a new hobby or sport. Observe the support systems you require to allow you to adjust to this hobby—for example, how do you find time, who helps you with other responsibilities, what lifestyle changes have you made? Everything you do is a part of a system. When something changes, it affects everything else. Support system adjustments are required for successful changes to occur—even with the start of a hobby. Think about how this relates to the support systems required to allow changes to occur efficiently in your department or throughout your organization.

- **Leader interview.** Generally senior leaders have a broader perspective of the organization. It is likely one of the skills that got them where they are today. Work with your manager to gain access to one of the executive/senior leaders in your organization. Invite the leader to attend one of your department meetings the next time the individual is available. Inform the leader that you would like to create a discussion in your department about strategic alignment. If an in-person visit isn't possible, you could set up a video conference or telephone call. Ask your team members to assist you in identifying questions to ask the leader. Here are some suggested questions to get started:

1. What factors in the environment are forcing change for our organization?

2. What challenges does our organization face this year?

3. What global issues will affect our organization's future?

4. What business strategies will require support from our department?

5. What competencies will be required to support the business strategies?

6. What do you see happening with our customer base?

7. What excites you about the organization's future?

After the interview, summarize what you learned and determine how the responses and discussion broadened your perspective of your organization's system. How can this information help you be a more informed systems thinker?

- **Organizational map.** Draw a map of your organization and how tasks, information flow, products, communication, and groups relate to each other. Where are things running smoothly? Where do bottlenecks exist? Imagine changing one part of the work flow and predict what else would change throughout the organization. Share your map with two other people from different departments. What insight could they share?

STRATEGIES FOR THE LONG RUN

- **Systems thinking tools.** There are many tools for systems thinking, but this list can get you started. Begin to study systems thinking in depth to uncover more information about each of these. You may want to sponsor an employee round table where you each take one of the concepts and get together to share what you learned and how they all fit together.

  > **Interconnectedness** requires a shift in mindset, away from linear to a circular process where everything is reliant on something else.

> **Synthesis** is the combining of two or more things to create something new. This is the opposite of analysis, where concepts are pulled apart for study.

> **Emergence** is the outcome that occurs based on the self-organization of parts that come together.

> **Feedback loops** occur causing flow between the elements of a system because everything is interconnected. The goal is to have feedback loops that are reinforcing and balancing the entire system.

> **Causality** is the ability to see how things influence each other within the system.

Like systems thinking, these tools are meaningful when you examine them together, perhaps in a systems mapping exercise. There are many ways to map a system, but the fundamental principles are universal. What are the things in the system, and how do they interconnect and act in a complex system?

- **Employee exchange.** With the support of your supervisor, identify several job swaps—that is, two, four, or six employees who could be paired to swap jobs for a day to understand the other's role in the system. The next day, facilitate a discussion between them to determine the outcome, what they learned about the other's job, and how both jobs relate to the big picture. How does each job depend on the other? What feedback loops occur? What cause-and-effect situations exist? Where does synthesis occur?

- **Input/output.** A system is a collection of interactive parts that together produce the desired goal. That means a system is made up of smaller parts, and if one of those parts changes, it affects the entire system. Your organization is a system, and when something changes in one department, it affects the entire system. A high-functioning system has the ability to constantly exchange feedback throughout its parts so they remain aligned. Customers—either internal or external—are the recipients of the systems process. Think about how the system in your department works, and fill in the input/output chart in figure 3 for a visual representation of the system.

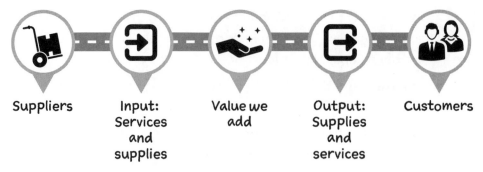

Suppliers | Input: Services and supplies | Value we add | Output: Supplies and services | Customers

Figure 3. Input/output chart.

Use these questions to guide you:

> Suppliers: Who are our internal suppliers?

> Input: What services and supplies do they give us?

> Value: What value do we add?

> Output: What are the resulting supplies and services?

> Customers: To whom do we give these supplies and services?

You could take this activity to the next level by involving your team. Post a blank input/output chart on a wall near your office. Encourage your team members to fill in the information for the system. After a week, facilitate a discussion about systems thinking for your group. Add another step and ask for ideas for improvement at any point along the chart. A week later invite the same people to meet to discuss their ideas. What are your big take-aways from this activity? How can you use this to continue your development?

• **Systems thinking for society.** Consider a societal issue, such as homelessness or unemployment, and determine what would be involved if everything would be considered to solve the problem.

CROSS TRAINING

You will find related ideas at these crossover skills:

• Adapt to Situations

• Lead Ventures

• Manage Projects

• Initiate Process Improvement

READING FOR THE FINAL STRETCH

- *The Fifth Discipline: The Art and Practice of the Learning Organization*, by Peter Senge

- *Thinking Fast and Slow*, by Daniel Kahneman

SKILL 36

Plan and Organize Tasks

Your ability to plan and organize tasks is a skill that will keep you busy and respected during any job you might have. Today's business atmosphere is one of change, a flood of information, chaos, and overload. It requires you to determine specific tasks required for the job; group, prioritize, and sequence the tasks; establish goals and a realistic timeline; and begin the work. It helps to be organized in general. Have the right information at your fingertips. Have a clear plan of action every day. Tidy up your desk and emails so you can find what you need when you need it. These actions will keep you organized and make you a better planner.

It's important because your ability to organize yourself and plan ahead will have an impact on your career success. Your employer is paying you to think, plan, and organize so that everyone around you can do a better job too. Make planning and organizing a good habit so that when you are lucky enough to receive an assignment for planning an entire project, you'll be ready.

Hurdles to Overcome

- How aware am I of the critical need to plan for the future?

- Why should I worry about what other departments think when I have to get my own work done?

- I am just not an organized person, so how can I be expected to plan anything?

Your Path to Success

- Conduct planning sessions to create a vision, mission, and goals that align with those of your organization

- Explain the timing of planning and how delays can affect the future

- Predict what might drive changes in customer purchases, supplier goods, leaders' expectations, and other things that support your work

- Anticipate changes in your own department to see beyond current commitments

- Use tools to analyze and synthesize data and information before planning

- Involve everyone that needs to be involved in creating a strategy

- Gather input and data that inform plans

- Create order out of chaos

- Handle new situations with no past plan or method to proceed

- Coordinate and organize projects in a logical process to efficiently achieve results

TIPS FOR PEOPLE IN A HURRY

- **Your move after next.** Are you always prepared with a response when asked, "What's next?" A chess player always knows the move after next. As you work, be in the habit of thinking ahead to what's next, and what's next after that. Be prepared like a chess player so that you can verbalize your intent. Plan ahead.

- **Schedule it.** Do you feel as if there isn't enough time to get the important things done? Schedule them. Yep. Just as you schedule a dentist appointment or a haircut, schedule those things that are important but perhaps you don't like to do, such as completing your expense account. Schedule it!

- **Declutter!** Disorganized surroundings can distract even the best planner. Organize your stuff. Get distracted? Turn off your phone and email to focus on important tasks for a period of time.

- **To do.** Maintain an ongoing to-do list and don't put things off until tomorrow.

- **Don't do it.** You might be good at creating a to-do list, but how good are you at your not-to-do list? Evaluate how you spend your time. Do you need to do everything on your to-do list? Even more, do things pop up that you feel obligated to do? I'm not talking about being selfish, not being kind, not helping someone out. Instead, look at things for which you have created your own must-do and decide if it is really necessary.

PRACTICE SPRINTS

- **SWOT analysis.** Although generally used during a strategic planning session for gathering data, a SWOT analysis may be used for many things. SWOT stands for **s**trengths and **w**eaknesses that are internal to the organization and the **o**pportunities and **t**hreats external to the organization. It's a great way to see what you are up against as you plan and organize a task. Given the rapidly changing environments in which all organizations operate, understanding how to conduct a SWOT analysis has gained a higher level of importance. Turn to https://ideas.bkconnection.com/skillsforcareersuccess for a SWOT worksheet. Then meet with several of your coworkers who are involved in revising strategy to conduct a preliminary SWOT analysis. Answer these questions:

> What are our internal strengths and weaknesses?

> What are our external threats and opportunities?

This analysis may take several meetings. Compile your results and analyze what you have learned in order to effectively create and organize your plan. As a group, decide how a SWOT analysis can be helpful.

- **Pre-SWOT analysis.** For fun and practice, conduct a SWOT on something in your personal life. Examples could include whether you should embark on a side hustle, pursue a degree or certificate, volunteer for a local cause, or coach a youth sports activity. What did you learn from this activity that can help you conduct a SWOT at work?

- **Organized chef.** Select a particularly complicated dish and prepare it for your family. What did you do to put order in your preparation? How did the recipe help or hinder your efforts? What external distractions or problems prevented you from being as effective as possible? What could you have done differently to be more efficient? What did this exercise teach you about complexity and chaos while planning and organizing?

- **Life plan.** Do you have a life plan? Planning and organizing your own life is good practice for doing the same at work. A life plan is a way to articulate what's important to you. It presents your personal priorities and establishes goals and specific actions you can take to reach them. It also uncovers roadblocks and the support you will need. How is a life plan like the planning required of you on the job?

STRATEGIES FOR THE LONG RUN

- **Evaluate your strategic-thinking skills.** Based on information by the authors of *Becoming a Strategic Leader*, this eight-question assessment will give you an idea of strategic-thinking areas to improve. Rate yourself on a 1–5 scale, with 1 being "considerable improvement needed" and 5 being "no improvement needed." Share your ratings with your supervisor and obtain feedback about your scoring. Put a plan together to develop those skills on which you rate lower than a 4.

- ☐ Scan the environment for forces and trends that could impact the organization.
- ☐ Ensure that all necessary information is considered.
- ☐ See things in new and different ways.
- ☐ Be able to select the truly key facts or trends from a large amount of data.
- ☐ Understand your own biases and do not let them interfere with your thinking.
- ☐ See relationships between seemingly disparate data.
- ☐ Ask probing questions about causes and effects
- ☐ Offer original, creative ideas.

Even if you aren't creating a strategic plan, you should be planning strategically.

- **Focus on the future.** To plan and organize, you need to be able to look to the future and predict what will happen that will drive change. These changes may affect how you plan, so you need to take them into consideration. Look to changes in technology, political trends, demographics, the economy, talent availability, marketing methods, competition, and others. Read recent publications that can shed some light on these, such as *Harvard Business Review, Fast Company, Forbes, Wired, Bloomberg Business Week, Entrepreneur, Fortune, Inc., The Economist,* or *Consumer Reports.* Identify at least seven things that you think might affect your organization. Meet with your mentor to discuss your concerns.

- **Visit Gettysburg.** There is no better place to stimulate your thinking about strategy, planning, and organizing than a trip to Gettysburg. Make it a family vacation in the summer and walk the battlefields with a guide who will help you feel what it was like. This is also a great place to go for a team-building event.

CROSS TRAINING

You will find related ideas at these crossover skills:

- Practice Systems Thinking
- Stay Organized
- Manage Projects

- Manage Time
- Set Goals
- Champion and Manage Change

READING FOR THE FINAL STRETCH

- *Getting Things Done*, by David Allen
- *Becoming a Strategic Leader*, 2nd ed., by Richard Hughes, Katherine Colarelli Beatty, and David Dinwoodie

Set Goals

Your ability to set goals is key to setting yourself up for success for almost anything you will do in life. Setting goals includes several steps. The first is of course deciding what it is you want to accomplish. That becomes the starting point. You should consider setting goals in your personal life as well as establishing goals at work. Goals that are in writing are more likely to be accomplished, and goals that are written in the SMART format (later in this section) are more likely to be accomplished effectively and on time. While you set your goals, think of subgoals, such as what you need to learn or what you need to change before tackling your goal. Determine if there are any roadblocks that might slow up your goal achievement. On the positive side, identify who can help you accomplish your goals. Make a plan for how you'll achieve your goal. Be sure to keep your plan in front of you every day. Your plan might be just a simple action list and even a part of your daily or weekly to-do list. Do whatever it take to establish and achieve your goals.

It's important because setting realistic goals helps to ensure you will achieve them. Your employer needs you to set and complete your own goals that are aligned with the organization and help it to accomplish its strategic imperative.

MASTERING THE SKILL

Hurdles to Overcome

- How aware am I that goals are good for me and my organization?
- How can I continue trying to reach goals when I keep missing deadlines?
- I set a goal once and it didn't work; why didn't I accomplish it?

Your Path to Success

- Set priorities for yourself and your organization and help others to do the same
- Logically establish priorities to manage your long-term and immediate projects
- Coordinate projects in a logical order to efficiently achieve your goals
- Prioritize by understanding importance and urgency
- Translate vision into goals and action
- Plan, write, and set clear and reasonable goals

TIPS FOR PEOPLE IN A HURRY

- **Ponder two quotes.** Eileen Caddy (a founder of the Findhorn Foundation in Scotland) said, "Set your sights high, the higher the better. Expect the most wonderful things to happen, not in the future but right now. Realize that nothing is too good." She also said, "A soul without a high aim is like a ship without a rudder." When you pair those two quotes, what meaning emerges for you? How can you implement your thoughts?

- **Need a goal?** Set a goal for something you want to accomplish. How will you know that you accomplished it? You need a measure of success. Establish a goal and its measure of success. How does it feel to know you reached your goal because you can measure it?

- **Set a life-changing goal.** If you were asked to set a life-changing goal, what would it be?

- **Overwhelmed by the goal?** Break the goal down into smaller, more manageable pieces. Sometimes these chunks are called objectives that support the goal. Schedule time to do a small chunk. Then start at the time you designated.

PRACTICE SPRINTS

- **Identify a personal goal.** List a personal goal at the top of a page. Beneath the goal make two columns. Label the first column "objectives" and the second "completed actions." In the first column list all the steps (objectives) you need to take to reach your goal, and in the second column list all the actions that will tell you if you have been successful in the first column. For example, your personal goal is to visit Europe with your family three years from now and you expect it to cost $24,000. Some of the activities in the first column might be "save money" and "determine an itinerary." Your second column might include "put away $600 every month," "buy a travel book to explore possible countries," or "talk to people who have made the trip." Your first column is a list of objectives that need to be completed. Your second column lists the actions and determines whether you actually did them. Setting goals is a good practice, but activities have to follow up or nothing happens.

- **Begin with the end in mind.** One of Stephen Covey's 7 Habits is to "begin with the end in mind." This habit is about setting long-term goals based on your values. Covey recommends formulating a "personal vision statement" to document your perception of your own vision in life. Meet with your supervisor and ask for advice about how to establish a personal vision statement. Ask others about their personal vision statements.

- **SMART goals.** Every goal you set should be SMART. It should be specific, measurable, attainable, relevant, and time-bound. When you ensure that your goals are SMART, they have a higher level of being understood by everyone involved and have a greater chance of being accomplished. Practice setting a SMART goal for something that you have been meaning to do at home, such as clean the garage, plant a tree, organize a closet, or take a load to a donation center or charity. Compare your goal with the SMART features. Does your goal meet all the criteria? Why is each criterion important?

- **Distinguish urgent from important.** You will always operate within the tension caused by urgent and important goals. Urgent tasks require immediate attention. Important tasks contribute to your long-term mission and goals. Urgent tasks almost always win your attention unless you have guarded time for the important goals. Important tasks rarely need to be completed today, but urgent tasks do. You will find yourself pushing important tasks back one more day. Guard time to work on important tasks. Prioritize important over urgent at least as often as urgent tasks usurp your time. Use the Eisenhower Urgent vs. Important decision matrix at https://ideas .bkconnection.com/skillsforcareersuccess to identify your own use of time and to determine how you can reduce the amount of time you spend on urgent goals and increase the time you spend on important goals. Share your finding with your coach for additional ideas.

- **Learn to say no.** Sometimes a part of accomplishing goals is your ability to say no to other things that are less important than reaching your goals. There is an art to saying no. You need to think about it before you say yes or no. There are ways that you can meet the obligation halfway for those times when you don't want to say no. And there are guidelines for times when you absolutely must say no. See https://ideas.bkconnection.com/skillsforcareersuccess for guidelines. Print or download them so they are nearby when a "no" occasion arises.

- **Select a challenge.** Identify a challenge that you've always wanted to do—for example, run a half marathon, learn to tango, or learn gourmet cooking. Plot a timeline to accomplish your challenge. During your challenge, track your thoughts and feelings along the way. Determine what works for you and what doesn't. How are you motivated? What gets in your way of progress? How do you manage your time? Is it better to do this with a partner or alone? At the end of the timeline, did you meet your challenge? What did you learn about yourself? What did you learn about your performance? What does this tell you about how you learn? About your ability to assess yourself? How can you put what you learned into practice at work?

- **Learn about priorities.** You will always have a number of goals at different levels of completion. Deciding which goals are more important or time sensitive than others is crucial. An earlier activity in this section mentioned urgent versus important goals, but priorities go beyond that. Check the number of goals you have. If you find yourself with too many goals, you're going to feel overwhelmed and are less likely to accomplish any. It's better to choose a few top priorities to provide focus when conflicting goals come up. You will probably complete one top priority over two minor goals. Time of day is a factor too. Complete your top priorities when you are at your best. If you have a large goal such as becoming fit, or achieving your project management certification, or being selected for a position in a foreign country, list all the things you need to do to accomplish the goal. Share your list with your manager and ask for advice. You might ask these questions: What did I forget? Is my goal clear? What risks will I face? Who can help me achieve this goal?

- **Help set department goals.** Your manager probably sets goals for your department on an annual basis—perhaps more often. The goals align with your organization's goals. Volunteer to be a part of this process. Before you take on the assignment, read a good book about goal setting, read and reread and become very familiar with your organization's current strategic plan, and ask your supervisor for a copy of the current department strategy and goals. This should prepare you to learn more.

CROSS TRAINING

You will find related ideas at these crossover skills:

- Plan and Organize Tasks
- Be Accountable
- Initiate Process Improvement
- Lead Self

READING FOR THE FINAL STRETCH

- *Ready Aim Fire? A Practical Guide to Setting and Achieving Goals*, by Erik Fisher and Jim Woods

SKILL 38

Be Resourceful

Your ability to be resourceful is the skill that will pull you out of a problem when necessary. Resourcefulness is how you accomplish what is desired when you do not have everything available that you expected to have. It is how you redefine what's possible. Resourcefulness is a skill that does not stand on its own. It is related to many other skills, and it is those skills, including networking, flexibility, negotiating, problem solving, and taking risks, that will be a part of your design for resourcefulness. It's hard to see the positive in any chaotic situation, but that's what it takes to be resourceful.

It's important because your career will be filled with challenges and you will need to prepare to be resourceful. Your resourcefulness will be viewed positively, and you will be seen as a can-do employee who manages the project no matter what issue you are facing.

MASTERING THE SKILL

Hurdles to Overcome

- How aware am I about my negativity, frustration, pessimism, finger-pointing, and lack of cooperation when things don't go as planned?

- I follow the rules, but how do these other people break them and do something wild and crazy and then get rewarded for being resourceful?

- What am I supposed to do—I'm just an employee?

Your Path to Success

- Overcome adversity by redefining what you really need to get the job done

- Find opportunities in an ever-changing situation and thrive when others think there is no way

- Know where you can find assistance and support when things aren't going as planned

- Stay focused on long-term goals even when obstacles stop you

- Be agile so that you can change direction when necessary while at the same time keeping the goal in mind

- Do not give up, no matter how many obstacles you face

TIPS FOR PEOPLE IN A HURRY

- **It's a gift.** When presented with a negative situation, immediately think, "This is a gift; what can I do with it?"

- **Who, me, positive?** Positivity is critical to show your resourceful side. Identify what it takes for you to stay positive. It might be a thought, a phrase, a memory. Once you identify what it is, practice it at all times, not just at work.

- **What's your station?** Tune in to what you say to yourself when you encounter a difficult situation; now tune into what you would rather be thinking.

- **Your five-year future.** Visualize your situation five years from today and what you can do that will prepare you for the job you will have at that time. What resourcefulness will get you there?

PRACTICE SPRINTS

- **Train wreck.** Think of a recent situation where everything seemed to go wrong. Think back to what happened. How do you think you reacted? How do you wish you had reacted? What opportunities did you miss? Who did you reach out to for help? Who could you have reached out to but didn't? How did you treat those around you? What do you wish you had done differently? Did you think about the entire system and how one change might create a problem elsewhere? How was your resilience? Who was working on the project with you? After you reflect on what happened, contact the person you remember on the project. Share your thoughts and ask how realistic you are being. Ask for additional advice and write it all down. At the end of the discussion, ask the individual for honest and candid comments. They will help you grow.

- **Positive or negative.** Think back to the events of the past couple of days. When did you respond positively? When did you respond negatively? What was the difference? What does it take for you to stay positive? Once you are armed with an answer, talk to someone who can help keep you on the positive track. Consider working with an accountability partner who will keep you on the straight and narrow. Practice this behavior at all times, not just at work.

- **Trio to try.** The next time everything seems to be falling apart, try these three ideas to give you time to think about it. First, take a timeout whenever you become frustrated. Step back, relax, and refocus on the resources you have available to you to help. Second, list all the negatives surrounding the situation and then next to each identify one or two ways that you can turn that negative into a positive. For every negative there is a positive. Finally, break the project into smaller portions and find ways to be successful with these smaller chunks. Give it a little time. Reward yourself and your team as you push through to the end.

- **Not Humpty Dumpty.** Too often when we need to be resourceful we begin to blame others or the system. What could instead trigger you to think about all the opportunities you have to show what you can do? What could switch you to a will-do-at-any-cost outlook? What can switch your thinking to all the people, resources, and options that are available to put things back together again? Don't be Humpty Dumpty. You can put things together again. What can prepare you for your next Humpty moment? Brainstorm ideas with someone who understands you as a person. Get prepared for the next fall.

STRATEGIES FOR THE LONG RUN

- **Start with one piece of the pie.** Resourcefulness is a skill that is related to many others. Review the following related skills that make up resourcefulness. Complete the self-assessment and rate your skills as master, average, or learner. If you don't rate as a master in all, turn to the chapters that are related to each of these skills and brush up on them by reviewing the development assignments.

  - ☐ Find opportunities in changing situations
  - ☐ Reach out to a broad network for support
  - ☐ Expect the unexpected
  - ☐ Stay resilient
  - ☐ Boast a positive can-do attitude
  - ☐ Stay focused on long-term objectives
  - ☐ Use a systems thinking approach
  - ☐ Change direction when necessary

☐ Demonstrate problem-solving skills

☐ Understand the value in taking risks

☐ See yourself as a lifelong learner

What are your top three? Which three need the most work? What do you need to do to present the whole pie?

- **Think about it.** It is hard to see the positive in a chaotic situation that you did not expect, but that is exactly what a resourceful employee is good at. You know how to get results even when the challenges seem overwhelming. How do resourceful leaders think? What thoughts help them see things differently instead of giving up? How can you turn your responses to these questions into a plan for your development?

- **"Never, never, never give up."** This quote by Winston Churchill is a good one to remember as you embark on your journey to improve your resourcefulness. The list in the first bullet point certainly provides plenty to work toward and to improve. Pick a quote or slogan that can be your mantra. Possibilities could be one of these: See the glass as half full; Just do it; Henry Ford's quote "Whether you think you can or you can't, you're right"; Prove yourself to yourself, not others; Helen Keller's quote "We can do anything we want to if we stick to it long enough"; or choose your own. What does your quote mean to you? How does it represent the person you want to be known as? How does it represent resourcefulness to you? How do you see living your life so that it represents this quote? Post this quote someplace where you will see it every day—on your monitor, framed on your desk, or taped to your mirror.

CROSS TRAINING

You will find related ideas at these crossover skills:

- Practice Resiliency

- Display Self-Confidence

- Practice Creativity, Innovation, and Appropriate Risk Taking

- *First, Break All the Rules: What the World's Greatest Managers Do Differently,* by Marcus Buckingham and Curt Coffman

SKILL 39

Demonstrate Problem-Solving Ability

Your ability to solve problems is key to your organization's success. Problems will occur; that's a given. How quickly and effectively organizations solve them will be dependent on their employees to analyze problems, assess the impact, determine alternative solutions, and select the best solution for the entire organization. Problem solving demonstrates an ability to exert control over unforeseen situations. Organizations rely on their employees to identify and solve problems. Don't let problems create a roadblock for your organization.

It's important because your organization expects you to solve problems as they arise. A problem left to languish or solved thoughtlessly will only grow and become a bigger problem for others throughout your organization. Learn and practice a practical problem-solving process that includes all the basic steps to define the problem, examine the data, identify alternatives, and implement the best solution. Skilled problem solvers demonstrate competencies such as logic, inquiry skills, creativity, resilience, systems thinking, and solution generation.

MASTERING THE SKILL

Hurdles to Overcome

- Problems are always there; why do we think we can solve them?

- Why do the same problems happen over and over again to me?

- How can I be expected to solve problems when it is just too hard?

- This is the way it's always been around here. Why should I bother?

- How can we solve problems when management won't let us implement anything different?

Your Path to Success

- Identify problems, threats, and trends early

- Create order out of a large amount of disorderly information to better define a problem and its causes

- Succinctly develop a problem statement and differentiate problems from symptoms

- Test the validity of information, using research, inquiry, and investigation skills to clarify situations

- Use idea-generation tactics, such as brainstorming, to produce a large number of ideas before selecting the best to implement

- Create an implementation plan replete with timeline, actions, and who has responsibility

- Balance logic and rationale research with your creative and novel solutions

TIPS FOR PEOPLE IN A HURRY

- **Stop solving; define first.** Most problem solvers begin by listing possible solutions. STOP! Effective decision making depends on defining the problem or the difference between what is and what should be.

- **Have a solution ready.** Practice being the problem solver, not the critic.

- **State a question.** Try to state most problems in the form of questions. "How can we reduce the number of errors in reports?" is better than "Develop a plan to improve quality," because it prevents a baked-in solution.

- **Take a break.** Often when you are bogged down with a problem, taking your mind off it helps you to refocus. For an immediate problem, take a walk around the block. For one with a longer timeline, go home and sleep on it.

- **Find a different perspective.** If you need a creative solution, try looking someplace else. Visit a toy store, hardware store, zoo, or dollar store. Just look and consider how something you see might be a potential solution.

PRACTICE SPRINTS

- **SOLVE every problem.** You will find that problems are solved more effectively when you use a standard procedure, because it helps you remember all the steps required to reach the best decision. Many processes exist, but most follow similar steps. The SOLVE process will help you remember the steps:

  1. **S**tate the problem: clearly define the issue in a question format if possible.

  2. **O**btain information and data: gather data about the circumstances, who was affected, and reasonable expectations.

  3. **L**ist possible alternatives: work with others to brainstorm (see skill 49) possible solutions without judging the ideas.

  4. **V**erify ideas and select the best: examine the pros and cons of possible solutions to determine which will work the best, when, and how to implement it.

  5. **E**valuate: monitor the implementation and modify it if required.

- **Hire someone.** Many things you do can be considered a way to solve a problem. For example, organizations that hire employees are solving a problem of needing a person to complete a defined job. You can learn about problem solving by volunteering to serve on a hiring team. Learn from the process. How did the hiring team define the need? What tools did they use to obtain information about the candidates? When it came to discussing the candidates, what criteria were used to make the decision? How did the team verify its final decisions? What kind of plan was put in place to monitor and evaluate the final selection? How was any of this information incorporated into the next hiring opportunity? What did you learn about problem solving during your time on the team?

- **Define the problem.** Einstein once said, "If I had 60 minutes to solve a problem, I'd spend 55 minutes defining it and 5 minutes solving it." That's pretty strong support for investing time at the front end of problem solving. It is true that being in a hurry can lead to a wrong move and that you'll probably have to do it over again. The next time you have a problem to solve, invest your time wisely up front in defining the problem. How do you define the problem? Start by listing what you already know or what you assume you know. Check out those assumptions and whether they are accurate. Determine what other information you need. This may be a good time to enlist others—especially those who are affected by the problem—since they may think of things you didn't. Search for the information you need, and remember that as you are searching you may uncover additional items you need to learn more about. Also, as you discuss the problem with people, look for patterns in how they describe the problem. Begin to identify causes of the problem. If you can reach the root cause of the problem, you will ensure that you are solving the right thing. Refer to the Five Whys tool in Problem Solving at https://ideas.bkconnection.com/skillsforcareersuccess to help you. Combine all your information and write a problem statement or questions. Then determine if you can solve the entire problem or if you need to address one aspect of the problem at a time.

- **Brainy idea.** Spend time focused on what your brain does while you are solving problems. To start, your brain perceives a problem and starts sending messages that something is wrong. It checks your memory to determine if there is a recollection of what you have now labeled a "problem." Your brain also searches for relevant information that may apply to your current problem. And at the same time, your brain is reviewing and discarding aspects that are not similar to past problems, thereby making a list of things that are different about this problem. Finally, your brain gathers all this information and defines the problem with a more specific label. It does all this in a matter of seconds or less. Compare what your brain does with the SOLVE process. There are similarities, but your brain doesn't have all the information to make the best decision. Without more information, a snap decision may occur, and it will not likely be the best. You need to help your brain out! What do you need to implement to ensure you and your brain solve the problem in the best way? Also look for the barriers in your brain—the cognitive blocks that impede your ability to correctly solve problems. We all have blocks that can be perceptual, emotional, intellectual, environmental, or cultural. What blocks get in the way of problem solving for you?

STRATEGIES FOR THE LONG RUN

- **Practice solving.** Identify a long-term problem that has plagued your department for a while. Ask your supervisor if you can put a team together to try to solve the problem. Use the SOLVE process above. Check the Problem Solving Tools at https://ideas .bkconnection.com/skillsforcareersuccess and use either the Five Whys tool or the Cause and Effect tool to try to determine the root cause of the problem. You need to solve the root cause of a problem, not just the symptoms.

- **Teach kids.** Volunteer to teach kids of any age problem-solving skills. You could volunteer to do so at an elementary school, at a YMCA, for a church group, in a 4-H club, for a Girl Scout group, or any other youth group. The experience will require that you learn all you can about how to solve problems, including the difference between a symptom and a cause, how to use a problem-solving process, what problem-solving tools are available, and many other things about problem solving. If you can teach it, you will know it.

- **Turn obstacles into opportunities.** Change the way you think about problems. When a problem crops up, tell yourself that the obstacle you are facing is actually an opportunity. Think about how that changes how you perceive the problem. What new perspectives do you see?

- **Help with new products.** Volunteer to work on a product development team for your organization. Even if you can't do it full time, identify key meetings that you could attend. Before you request this assignment, identify what you could contribute to the team and how.

CROSS TRAINING

You will find related ideas at these crossover skills:

- Make Key Decisions
- Resolve Conflict
- Collaborate with Others
- Adapt to Situations
- Stay Organized

READING FOR THE FINAL STRETCH

- *What Do You Do with a Problem*, by Kobi Yamada

Achieving Results

Jane Friedman has 20 years of experience in the publishing industry. She has written several books about writing, is a *Publishers Weekly* columnist, and is a professor with the Great Courses. Her expertise has been featured by the *New York Times*, the *Washington Post*, NPR, PBS, CBS, and the National Press Club. She has delivered keynotes and workshops for the *Writer's Digest* annual conference, Stockholm Writers Festival, San Miguel Writers Conference, Frankfurt Book Fair, BookExpo America, and Digital Book World. She's held positions as a professor at the University of Cincinnati and University of Virginia and is the recipient of numerous awards.

And that's a dramatically shortened version of her biography. Needless to say, Jane has numerous talents in the publishing arena. She is also the author of *Electric Speed*, a free newsletter published for authors and others in the publishing business. A recent post of hers in that newsletter caught my eye, where she wrote:

> I was grateful to secure a salaried job in publishing immediately upon graduating from college. But after three years in the same role, I became antsy for something new.
>
> I applied to countless jobs. Most of the time I never got an interview.

Then an internal position opened up at my company—in a different department—and I applied and interviewed.

I wasn't hired.

A second internal position opened up, an even better fit. I applied and interviewed. This time, I thought I had it.

Nope. I was crushed.

A third internal (and desirable) position opened up just a week later. I remember staring at the description, pinned to the announcements corkboard in the company lunch room, feeling dejected. What would be the point of applying? No one wanted me.

The next day when I went down to lunch, I stared at the posting again. OK, what did I really have to lose by trying (except to suffer another rejection)?

I got the job. Later I learned that I'd almost secured the other position, too.

It's unbelievably tempting to give up after a string of rejections. But sometimes, we're on the brink of success. That's why I ask writers: What would you do if you knew that—eventually—you would succeed? (Friedman 2020)

After a couple of rejections, Jane definitely succeeded. We've all heard stories of famous authors whose books were turned down:

- **Gone with the Wind**, by Margaret Mitchell, was rejected by almost 40 publishers before it finally hit the shelves. The Pulitzer Prize-winning novel has maintained a legacy of popularity. In fact, according to a recent Harris poll, the novel is the second most popular book in America, after the Bible.

- **The Wonderful Wizard of Oz**, by L. Frank Baum, was rejected for publication so many times that he kept a journal called "A Record of Failure" made up of all the rejection letters he received. Those publishers were proved wrong, though. The book has been translated into multiple languages and was adapted into more films, musicals, and miniseries than anyone can keep track of.

- **Harry Potter and the Sorcerer's Stone**, by J. K. Rowling, was rejected more than 10 times by a variety of publishing houses. Only after one agent's daughter nagged him into publishing it did the book become an international sensation.

- **Chicken Soup for the Soul**, by Jack Canfield, experienced 144 rejections. The book became a best seller, then a series, and now a multiarmed franchise...that actually sells soup.

- **And to Think That I Saw It on Mulberry Street**, by Dr. Seuss (Theodor Geisel), received 27 rejections from publishers. In fact, he had almost given up on writing altogether when he ran into an editor friend on the street, who asked to take a look—and the rest is history.

Achieving results requires many of the skills I share throughout this book, such as being organized, advocating for yourself, and setting your own goals. But more important than anything, as shown by these authors and Jane Friedman, to achieve results you need to persevere and be courageous and optimistic. Your role to achieve results in your organization requires you to manage projects, attend to details, be decisive and accountable, and sell your ideas to those who can fund them. Like Friedman, ask yourself, "What would you do if you knew that—eventually—you would succeed?"

Vision without execution is hallucination.

—THOMAS EDISON

SKILL 40

Manage Projects

Your ability to manage projects is not a new skill. Project management is one of the best ways to achieve results. Project management practices, principles, and processes were used to execute the Taj Mahal, Pyramids of Gaza, the Panama Canal, moon landings, and to explore options for the COVID-19 vaccine, and almost every other key outcome you have experienced. Project management has been considered a certifiable profession since the mid-20th century. A project is a temporary onetime event with a clearly defined beginning and end, a defined scope, and identified resources. Managing projects is your ability to apply the knowledge, skills, tools, and techniques required by each project. This would include such skills as establishing a schedule, identifying milestones, creating a budget and communication plan, and developing risk management and change management plans. There are many skills and tasks that fit under each of these topics—in fact, too many to be able to create a checklist of all you need to do to be a good project manager. Instead, you'll work in a dynamic environment, so think about how you can be a superlative professional in every way.

It's important because project management defines a plan and organizes an event with the maximum quality at the lowest cost. It tracks the process and manages change so that your organization can advance its goals as well as retain and learn from the experience. You have the ability to manage a high-visibility venture that has a defined set of directions. As a result, you will learn many skills that will help you throughout your career.

MASTERING THE SKILL

Hurdles to Overcome

- How aware am I of my limitations that will prevent me from being a great project manager (PM)?

- What can I possibly do with a large project with multiple cross-functional stakeholders and external technical vendors when everyone is upset because they don't go the way I want them—who needs the headache?

- Would I be setting myself up for failure without a mentor or other experienced PM to learn from?

- Why would I want an anxiety-producing assignment like this when I can stay in my own swim lane and not be bothered?

Your Path to Success

- Practice basic leadership skills

- Exhibit excellent communication and critical thinking skills

- Understand change management, process improvement, and risk management

- Practice system thinking and problem solving

- Be extremely organized

- Manage all elements of your projects: resources, time, money, scope, and customer satisfaction

- Exhibit strong business acumen and understanding of your organization

- Demonstrate accountability, a solid work ethic, initiative, and time management skills

TIPS FOR PEOPLE IN A HURRY

- **Shadow sooner.** If you anticipate you'll be a PM in the near future, find someone you can shadow to prepare for this all-encompassing assignment.

- **Practice consensus.** One of the most important elements of project management is reaching consensus. Learn how. Practice every chance you get before you start a project.

- **Don't take meeting notes.** What?!? It is nearly impossible to facilitate your team and take good meeting notes at the same time. Ask a nonparticipant to take notes so you can focus on the discussion. If you hold virtual team meetings, consider using a tool that can record the conversation for future use.

- **Know who's watching.** Be sure you know who is interested in your project and keep them über-informed.

- **Rate yourself.** One of the most important behaviors for managing projects is to see them through to completion. Rate yourself on a 1-to-5-point scale about your past status for completing projects. Are you satisfied with your rating?

PRACTICE SPRINTS

- **Use templates.** Many PMs use templates to save time, but there is a better reason. A template helps ensure that you are using a tried-and-true format and that you will not forget important elements. You might use a template for meeting agendas or meeting minutes or the project plan. Your organization may have software that it uses, or you could meet with several people who have experience as PMs and ask what works best for them.

- **Communicate with your team.** You know the importance of communication, of course, so why emphasize it for project management? Several reasons. You will likely have management's attention, and they want to have status reports. You will be working with a team, often cross functional and perhaps your first time working with people from another area. Keeping your team on track will be important for the published timelines and milestones. Things will change throughout the project, and you will need to keep everyone informed. All communication is important, but with project management it is even more important for several reasons. Keep the process on track by maintaining a regular meeting schedule and follow up immediately with meeting notes. Be sure the meeting notes include action items and who will do what by when. Following up after many discussions is also important. Keep your team informed if anything changes or if anyone has concerns. And of course provide status reports to everyone who needs them—it will probably include more people and at a higher level than you normally communicate with. Get feedback from your supervisor or coach about the content, length, and tone before you send your first couple of reports. Project management is a great opportunity to learn how to communicate with senior leaders in your organization.

- **The project management process.** A project management process is a template that suggests how to complete a project successfully. There are many variations, including those by the Project Management Institute (PMI; PMI.org) in the United States and PRINCE (PRINCE2.com) in the United Kingdom (UK). PMI divides projects into five process groups: initiating, planning, executing, monitoring, and closing. Meet with someone who has been a project manager and ask for the different tasks that must be completed under each of the five groups. List them in order and find ways to gain skills and knowledge in each.

- **Practice using the tools.** It takes more than a good PM to complete a project on time and within budget. Project managers use tools to complete their work efficiently and effectively. Three tools you may not have used that are staples in the project manager's tool kit are a Gantt chart, PERT chart, and WBS diagram. Gather information about each and find a way that you could use them in the work you do today. A Gantt chart breaks a large project down and organizes it into a series of smaller tasks. A PERT (project evaluation and review technique) chart is used to plan and schedule the project and to track the implementation phase. A WBS (work breakdown structure) chart is used to visualize the scope of the work by breaking a project into individual components so they can be scheduled effectively. Try them out with something that you do on a regular basis.

- **Manage risk.** Risk is a measure of the potential inability of a team to achieve its objectives as planned. A risk management plan examines the probability and the consequences of failing and creates mitigation strategies. Get experience by volunteering to develop a risk management plan for a project in your organization. Stay in touch with your supervisor for support throughout this project.

STRATEGIES FOR THE LONG RUN

- **Get certified.** If you enjoy managing projects and you anticipate this to be a part of your work in the future, begin to work toward project management professional (PMP) training and certification. This industry-recognized certification will help you understand the functionalities of managing projects. Because the certification is considered the global standard of excellence in project management, it can increase your earning potential. Some estimate that PMP certification holders earn 25 percent more than their noncertified peers. If you are not prepared for the PMP exam, attempt the Certified Associate in Project Management exam. The CAPM certification is a good choice for you if you have minimum project management experience but want to continue to pursue project management in the future. (Note that the PRINCE2 certification was developed by the UK government and is more appropriate if you work in the UK.)

- **Learn the lingo.** Although project management requires many of the skills excellent employees require to do their jobs, there are additional tools and techniques that might not be used in other tasks that they complete. Here's a list of tools, techniques, and other terms you may not have come across. All are used in project management. Research each term and learn how it is used in project management: deliverables, Gantt chart, PERT chart, stakeholder, WBS, project scope, mitigate risk, constraints, governance, project schedule, project charter, project sponsor, and project manager role. There may be others, and you can track them as you complete your research.

- **Long-term team project.** Ask your manager for an opportunity to lead a long-term project. Offer a suggestion if your manager doesn't have one in mind—perhaps an improvement project you would like to tackle. Invite others to work on it with you. Be realistic about the investment of time and effort.

CROSS TRAINING

You will find related ideas at these crossover skills:

- Practice Systems Thinking
- Plan and Organize Tasks
- Collaborate with Others
- Model Corporate Expectations
- Initiate Process Improvement
- Champion and Manage Change

READING FOR THE FINAL STRETCH

- *Managing Projects: A Practical Guide for Learning Professionals*, by Lou Russell
- *PMBoK Guide: A Guide to the Project Management Body of Knowledge*, by the Project Management Institute

SKILL 41

Attend to Details

Your attention to details is equally as important as your ability to see the big picture. In fact, you may be expected to hold both the big picture and all the details in your mind at the same time. Attention to detail, such as catching typos or incorrect dates, is a skill that can be developed even if it does not come naturally to you. Every person sees details differently. Some don't notice minutiae while others don't see things that are big enough to crush them. Usually the details you miss are unimportant anyway—but not always! And that's the catch. You need to attend to the details especially when they matter, such as reading a contract, proofing your résumé, writing a proposal, taking the correct medicine dose, using the right building materials, and combining and measuring the right ingredients.

It's important because attention to detail prevents errors, saves time, keeps you out of legal trouble, ensures safety, and makes you look professional. Attention to detail makes workplace success easier and more certain. Details matter!

MASTERING THE SKILL

Hurdles to Overcome

- How aware am I of all the details I miss?
- How could I possibly handle all the details when I'm a big-picture person—and proud of it?
- How can I attend to details when the boss and my colleagues are constantly distracting me?

Your Path to Success

- Recognize that details can be small or large, common or unusual since we all pay attention to different details
- Understand that details can make or break your ability to analyze a situation and make decisions
- Be present in the moment to enable yourself to focus on content and data
- Check your own accuracy diligently
- Take responsibility for any detail errors that slip through and correct them
- Model skills that support your detail attention such as organization, focus, and accountability

TIPS FOR PEOPLE IN A HURRY

- **Use bullets.** If you write lots of emails or directions, start delivering your messages in bullets. They are easier to write clearly (start each with a verb or a noun), they don't require that you use the correct conjunction, and they are easier to edit. And yes, do reread and edit them.
- **Break it down.** If you face a detailed document such as a contract or a task with many moving parts, break it down into chunks of information that are easier to digest.

- **Practice order to enable details.** When you are organized, it halves the job of attending to the details. Organize every element of your workspace—physical and electronic. Order will prepare you for the details that come your way. Order your calendar, plan your day, and make lists. Organization allows the space for details.

- **Stop multitasking.** Some experts tell us multitasking is impossible for the human brain. Instead, what is happening is that you are task-switching, causing a lack of focus, wasting time, and losing details. Do one thing at a time.

PRACTICE SPRINTS

- **See what's out there.** Get up from your desk and look out a window that you don't usually look out. Pay attention to the details you see. Take as long as you wish.

——*Stop reading this exercise until you return from the window.*——

Now come away from the window. Read the remaining directions in the final bullet in this section.

- **Details in the execution.** Pull a group of your peers together to identify skills and knowledge that will make all of you good execu- tioners. Here's a starting list of some of the skills required for effec- tive execution: establishing priorities, setting goals, organizing, delegating, working across departments, planning, measuring, scanning the environment, understanding customers, and making predictions. Once you have the list, identify the details you need to address for each and what it looks like in "my" job. Finally, circle all the things that each of you needs to improve. Who needs to improve the same things? Work together to identify several things you can do to improve your attention to detail. Plan to meet again until you have improved your ability to attend to details. Finally, add these skills to your development plans. Share your results with your super- visor and get input about how to gain the skills that will help you attend to the details.

- **Edit it backward.** It's almost impossible to edit your own writing. You know what each paragraph should say. Your brain knows. So, your brain automatically fills in missing words and corrects incorrect words. The best way to edit your own work is to read it backward. Not literally word for word, but sentence by sentence or paragraph by paragraph. Doing it this way slows you down and gets your brain's attention. If you have an important document, try editing it backward before submitting it. You can't trust yourself to edit your own work. Your brain knows what it is supposed to say!

- **Create a checklist.** Pilots must pay attention to details as a matter of safety, and that's why they depend on checklists. I have created a personal checklist that I use before I submit a manuscript to a publisher to ensure I've examined several bad habits that float into my writing as my brain goes into its creative mode. Do you have routine times when you need to pay attention to a set of details? Perhaps it's the details of opening and recording a Zoom call or the details of closing your family cottage for the winter. For those instances, create a checklist and use it. Keep it available each time since you will probably find times to add to it or clarify some of the points.

- **Complete cryptoquotes.** A cryptoquote is a short encrypted text word puzzle. Each letter represents a different letter of the alphabet. The message itself is usually a funny saying or a famous quote. Solving the puzzle requires that you switch back and forth between looking at the big picture (the whole sentence) and looking at the details (whether two letters could exist side by side in a real word). Many daily newspapers have these puzzles. Try one and force yourself to jump back and forth between the big-picture message and the details of the letters. Which part is easier for you? Can you understand why both the big picture and the details are important?

- ***Continued from the first bullet:*** Return from the window and close your eyes. Imagine in your mind all that you saw. Grab paper and a pencil and list all that you can remember in about five minutes. Did you run out of things to add to your list? Take your list and return to the window. Find 50 things that you did not notice the first time. What do you notice about the things you missed? Were they things that you don't usually think about? Were they very detailed or large and massive? Were they colors or something you could count? Were they stationary and easy to overlook, or were they so large that they didn't seem like a detail. Noticing what you didn't notice is a clue to you about the details you may need to pay extra attention to. Often your brain doesn't think these things are important. What has your brain decided isn't important? How can you remember to look for those unimportant important things?

STRATEGIES FOR THE LONG RUN

- **Clarify meeting details.** You can gain a reputation for running excellent meetings, eliminating confusion after the meeting, and getting results. It's all in the details. Follow these guidelines for a detail-pleasing meeting:

  > Write all action items in the same format: "who, will do what, by when" works well.

  > Assign key accountability for each action to only one person.

  > Recap all actions at the end of the meeting.

  > Email the actions to everyone within two hours (if possible) of the meeting.

  > If you haven't received notice about completion 24 hours prior to the next meeting, follow up.

  Make these guidelines your meeting mantra so that everyone understands and completes the details. Invite your supervisor to attend one of your meetings to provide additional ideas.

- **Practice presence.** You may not have a detail orientation because you are not present, are not paying attention. Your world is filled with distractions, pressures, and stress-causing activities. You should begin by determining why you aren't present. Are you bored, over-worked, depressed, anxious, or ambitious? All could prevent you from being present. Some say that we aren't designed to live in the present and that human psychology is wired to live in the past and the future. Although animals live in the present for survival, human survival depends on learning and planning: learning from the past and planning for the future. Living in the moment can help you attend to details. Yes, you need to examine why you aren't present, but you can practice presence now. Here are three things you can try:

> Go for a walk where you have never been, such as to a park, through a different neighborhood. Walk slower than normal and attend to what's around you. Try not to think of your destination. What do you see, hear, smell, and feel as you walk?

> Go to a store that is out of your normal routine, such as a hardware store, toy store, or craft shop. Look at all the things you've never seen before. Pick them up. Imagine how you might use them. Check how well they are made. Think of who in your life might use these items. What does it feel like to be in a store filled with strange things? What details do you see? Focus on being in the store.

> Go to a social gathering where you will know few people. Challenge yourself to meet and remember something important about as many people as you can. What questions do you ask to learn something about new acquaintances? What physical feature reminds you of their names? How did you feel as you focused on their stories?

Review your presence practice. Were you tired at the end? Staying focused and being present can be hard work. How many more details do you think you remembered by being present than if you were not? What can you do in the future to be more present?

- **Write an operational plan.** Let your supervisor know that you would like to participate in the development of an operating plan for your department in support of the next (or current, depending on the timing) strategic plan's goals and objectives. Depending on the expectations, an operational plan usually incorporates detailed action plans that, when completed, are the foundation for achieving the vision and the mission for your organization's strategic plan.

CROSS TRAINING

You will find related ideas at these crossover skills:

- Stay Organized
- Show Self-Awareness
- Improve Weaknesses
- Be Accountable

READING FOR THE FINAL STRETCH

- *The 7 Habits of Highly Effective People: Powerful Lessons in Personal Change*, by Stephen Covey
- *Improve Attention to Detail*, by Chris Denny

SKILL 42

Make Key Decisions

Your ability to be decisive is one of the skills organizations look for in employees they want to promote. But it is not just whether you can make fast decisions; it is whether you can make wise decisions. That means doing the preparation before making the decision, such as using a methodical decision-making process, gathering data that informs the decision, involving everyone who needs to contribute ideas, and being able to sell your idea backed with solid data and a rationale that others can buy. Although speed is usually important, it is critical that you are not hasty, but that you know when you have enough information to state a wise decision and move forward.

It's important because your leadership expects that you will be able to make key decisions as they arise. Your decisions should be well informed and time sensitive. You will require critical thinking skills to sort through all the information required to uncover what is valid and important to the decision you reach. Critical thinking will also help you review all data, content, and information to deduce the best conclusion.

Hurdles to Overcome

- Why should I make a decision since only I will be blamed if it isn't the right one?

- How can I figure out all the underlying issues and how they affect everything in the organization I will need to know to make a decision?

- How can I make a decision when there is always something more to analyze?

Your Path to Success

- Understand and practice your critical thinking skills

- Make comprehensive decisions that consider the system in a timely way

- Differentiate between critical and less important issues affecting a decision

- Seek advice and perspective from others

- Gather information required to make your decisions

- Use critical thinking skills to make logical, ethical, informed, and unbiased decisions

- Consider the entire system and understand how decisions will affect the entire organization

TIPS FOR PEOPLE IN A HURRY

- **Your decision process.** Wondering about your decision-making process? Do something that scares you that you've never done before. How did you respond?

- **Evaluate arguments.** When making decisions, review arguments from others to determine not only the pros and cons but also the strength of the arguments.

- **Consider evidence.** Closely review all evidence to determine where it originated and how reliable it is. Is the evidence from a biased news source or a researcher?

- **Match your organization.** Decide what elements must be included in decisions to match your organization's vision and values.

PRACTICE SPRINTS

- **Force Field Analysis.** If you struggle with difficult decisions, learn more about Force Field Analysis, a diagnostic tool developed by Kurt Lewin. The tool assesses two types of forces: driving and restraining. This effective, structured decision-making technique will improve the quality of your decisions and increase your chances of successful implementation. See the tool and an explanation of how to use it in the website materials at https://ideas.bkconnection.com /skillsforcareersuccess.

- **The last decision.** Review the last decision you made that should have been better. What happened? What part was satisfactory? What part was unsatisfactory? With whom can you discuss what you could have done better? Schedule time to discuss issues such as whether you made the decision too quickly, who you could have used as an information source, what signs you missed, or what you should try next time.

- **Bias detection.** Decisive people are able to detect prejudiced opinions of others. You can practice this skill. Listen carefully to practice identifying others' assumptions and biases. Determine if comments are valid by asking questions such as Who does this benefit? or Does the person appear to have an agenda? or What is this person overlooking or ignoring that doesn't support the claim? or How is this person trying to sway listeners' perception? or Is this person overselling or using unnecessary language to convince listeners? In addition, think about how this activity can help you identify your own preferences. How can you consciously set aside your own biases and partialities?

- **Group decision making.** You may find yourself in a situation where a group must make a decision. Consider how many people are involved, how much time is available, and the relative importance of the decision. Several tools you may use include multivoting, affinity diagrams, and a countermeasure matrix.

    1. Multivoting, sometimes called nominal group technique, is a method to shorten a list of ideas to a manageable number through a series of structured voting steps. It is good for a team to use to rank-order a list and limits the power of those with strong opinions. It usually produces a sense of closure, but a drawback is that it doesn't allow for development of the ideas.

    2. An affinity diagram is a tool used to organize a large number of ideas into logical groups based on a natural relationship among the ideas. It encourages balanced input, considers everyone's ideas, and reaches consensus on categories. It is best used when facts seem to have no structure and is good for large or complex issues. It may be too regimented for some since a portion is completed without speaking and some people are uncomfortable with the silence.

    3. A countermeasure matrix is a tool that documents causes, solutions, and implementation priorities of a problem and provides input for developing an action plan. It encourages the use of critical thinking and what to do. The drawbacks are that it needs to have the right people involved, and it is difficult to get balanced participation.

Learn more about these tools and how to use them in the website materials at https://ideas.bkconnection.com/skillsforcareersuccess. Be prepared to use one of the group decision-making tools the next time it is required of your team or group.

- **Advanced tools.** If you have basic skills in making decisions, you may want to explore several tools that give you different ways to compare or confirm your decisions. Several tools are listed here. Complete your own research for each to determine which ones might serve you and the kind of decisions you make.

    > **Decision matrix:** A tool that lists values in columns and rows to identify and analyze relationships.

    > **Weighted criteria:** A decision-making matrix that compares alternatives on one axis with weighted (prioritized by importance) values on the other.

    > **T-Chart:** An organizing tool that compares two facets of a solution, such as pros and cons.

    > **Decision tree**: A branching model that sorts through decisions and their consequences.

    > **Cost benefit analysis:** Estimates the value of options by evaluating the best approach to achieve the benefit at the best cost.

    > **SWOT analysis**: A two-by-two visual that shows strengths, weaknesses, opportunities, and threats of an idea, problem, or solution.

    > **Pareto chart:** Vertical bar chart that shows values and a line graph that plots the cumulative total. It is the basic tool for displaying the 80/20 principle.

- **Critical thinking skills.** A specific skill that is important to many actions and that gets more attention daily is critical thinking. Critical thinking is your ability to analyze a situation and the related facts, data, and evidence to make better decisions. Critical thinking should focus solely on factual information and is done objectively, without influence from personal opinions or biases. Review these seven skills required for critical thinking. Check off those that you need to shore up. Then create a plan for how you will achieve expertise.

- [ ] **Identifying and organizing:** the ability to identify the situation and the factors that influence it and then organize them in categories that will reveal connections, themes, or hierarchies such as the strengths and weaknesses, or opinions and facts.

- [ ] **Researching:** the ability to find the source of the information and conduct an independent verification.

- [ ] **Identifying biases:** the ability to identify your own and others' biases and not let them cloud your judgment.

- [ ] **Inferring:** the ability to summarize and assess the information and use it to draw conclusions or to extrapolate potential outcomes, without jumping to conclusions.

- [ ] **Solving problems:** the ability to organize your thoughts and to apply all the problem-solving steps.

- [ ] **Determining and displaying relevance:** the ability to recognize what information is the most important and to find a way to display it so the relationship between statements and data can be seen.

- [ ] **Asking questions and curiosity:** the ability to ask provocative, open-ended, and "why" questions.

- **Think system.** You will rarely have all the information you need to make a perfect decision. If you have to make a decision with limited input, accept the consequences and be agile enough to make a quick move. One thing you should always consider is the bigger picture. How will this decision affect those beyond me, such as customers, the department that supplies you with information, or your boss's boss? Who will your decision affect? Make a diagram with you positioned in a center circle. Draw lines out from your circle that lead to those you are directly connected to. Then draw lines from each of these to the next level of connections. This is a picture of all the departments and people who are affected by your decision. What can affect decisions in your organization? Does your organization have a clear governance system that prevents confusion over decision rights? What competing priorities might exist in your organization? Are task forces managed so that they produce only what they were supposed to when they were supposed to? Any of these could be a red flag, and you should check them out as you make decisions. Invite your boss to coffee for a discussion about decisions in your organizational system.

CROSS TRAINING

You will find related ideas at these crossover skills:

- Demonstrate Problem-Solving Ability
- Display Self-Confidence
- Adapt to Situations
- Model Corporate Expectations
- Lead Others
- Practice Systems Thinking
- Champion and Manage Change
- Sell Ideas

READING FOR THE FINAL STRETCH

- *Decisive: How to Make Better Choices in Life and Work*, by Chip Heath and Dan Heath
- *Don't Overthink It: Make Easier Decisions, Stop Second-Guessing, and Bring More Joy to Your Life*, by Anne Bogel

SKILL 43

Be Accountable

Your accountability is a way to set you apart from many. Accountability refers to a commitment to take responsibility and do what it takes to get results when you say you will. Seems pretty simple. It's common sense. Either you do it or you don't. Well, it seems that accountability continues to be one of the areas where employees don't live up to their employers' expectations. Why is that? Many employees don't understand what accountability is, why it's important, or who is responsible. What do accountable people do differently? To be accountable, you need to accept that accountability starts with you. You are accountable for all that you do—or don't do. You are accountable for making all deadlines—or missing deadlines. The key word is "all" since accountability is not a onetime event. It is similar to trust. You are either trustworthy or not. You are either accountable or not. Accountability shouldn't be viewed simply as getting tasks completed on time. View it as the way you want to operate all the time.

It's important because accountability is the road to the organization's results and its competitive advantage. Accountability is important for you because it aligns you to the business strategy and inspires your self-confidence. And most important, accountability is a good reputation to maintain for your career success.

MASTERING THE SKILL

Hurdles to Overcome

- How aware am I that I agree to things and am not clear about the details of exactly who, what, when, how, and where?

- What can be done to improve accountability when no one accepts ownership of it?

- We go off-site to a nice resort, we have great conversations, everyone agrees to accept responsibility to accomplish tasks by the quarterly meetings, but no one does—so why should I?

Your Path to Success

- Accept ownership and take initiative to achieve your results

- Recognize that only one person can be accountable

- Ensure clarity of direction for every task you take on

- Take responsibility before a deadline is missed to figure out a new solution

- Control your own fate and do not make excuses

- Willingly accept responsibility, additional duties, and obligations

- Manage expectations and clearly understand desired results for your assigned projects

- Have courage to always communicate the truth—even if projects or tasks aren't going as planned

- Collaborate and cooperate with others who may be a part of your solution

TIPS FOR PEOPLE IN A HURRY

- **Set a date.** When you are assigned a new task, project, or duty, be sure to clarify the specific date and time it is due. "Next week" is not specific!

- **Repeat.** When you are given a task, get in the habit of repeating the expectations. Restate what, when, where, and how. Lack of clear communication may be the main reason for accountability failure.

- **Focus on ownership.** A *Forbes* article (Schroeder 2020) states that trusting employees with ownership of their work is the most important element of creating a culture of accountability. Take ownership. Show your supervisor you can be trusted.

- **Model accountable language.** Walking your talk is the fastest way to mature your accountability. But if you slip up, stop, acknowledge it, and double down on your commitment. Do what you say.

- **On time every time.** Set an on-time goal for yourself. Punctuality is an element of trustworthiness.

PRACTICE SPRINTS

- **Clarity, clarity, clarity.** The best way to ensure your own accountability is to be sure that you are very clear about expectations. What results are expected? What's the due date? What time? In what form should the project be delivered and where? Don't know? Ask!

- **Why take ownership.** Accountability may be the single biggest differentiator between successful and unsuccessful employees. Accountability means that you will take ownership for your results. You believe you are in control of your own fate, and you don't make excuses. Simon Sinek, author of *Start with Why*, contends that we should know why we are passionate about what we believe. Take time to write a statement about why you are passionate about being accountable. You may share it with someone if you wish. More importantly, however, how does what you wrote connect to what you will do to be passionate about your accountability?

- **When it hits the fan.** Being accountable doesn't mean that things won't go wrong. They will. When things go awry, you need to tap into your problem-solving skills, determine what's going wrong, and fix it. You also need to communicate immediately with the person who assigned accountability to you. Finally, apologize to anyone who was negatively impacted, establishing corrective actions and setting dates for adjustment. That's not so difficult. Often events will be out of your control, and the sooner you inform others, the better. Your accountability won't be damaged if you keep the lines of communication open. Accountability requires that your actions rise above your excuses.

- **Responsibility assignment matrix.** A responsibility assignment matrix is sometimes called a RACI chart. It organizes the activities and decision-making authorities that each person has. The acronym stands for the four categories on the chart.

  > **Responsible** is the person who completes or performs an activity.

  > **Accountable** is the person who is ultimately accountable for completion and can vote yes or no; ultimately signs off on the project.

  > **Consulted** is the person who needs to provide information that contributes to the activity.

  > **Informed** is the person who needs to know about the decision or the action.

  The value in this tool is that it clarifies roles and responsibilities in complex projects. Go to https://ideas.bkconnection.com/skillsfor careersuccess for an example of a RACI chart. When could you implement a RACI chart to clarify who is responsible for what?

- **Ownership + initiative.** There is no easy recipe for accountability. But something that comes close is the combination of ownership and initiative. If you take ownership to get results on your projects and then also take initiative to ask for more, it means that you are willing to determine your own role in other problems and look for ways you might be able to help solve them. Take initiative now. Go ask your boss how you can help.

STRATEGIES FOR THE LONG RUN

- **From within.** Although accountability can be defined by external actions that we can see and measure, true accountability comes from within. Accountability is intrinsic. It is a willingness to accept ownership of the results. This is not something that can be assigned like a project. You have to choose ownership. You have to choose accountability. What do you need to choose to do? Establish an accountability partnership with someone else who wants to increase accountability behaviors.

- **What's your stage?** The Center for Creative Leadership (CCL) states that employees go through three distinct stages of individual commitment to accountability (Browning 2012):

  > Engaged employees are fully involved in and enthusiastic about their work and are supportive of the organization.

  > Empowered employees make their own decisions with regard to their tasks. Their actions and abilities are aligned with the organization's interest. CCL sees empowerment as a developmental transition.

  > Accountability requires a deeper relationship between the employee and the work, allowing the employee to make decisions and own the consequences.

  Which stage are you in, and what will it take to move you to full accountability?

- **Accountability culture.** The culture of accountability exists when all team members hold each other accountable for their commitments in a positive and productive manner. Many believe that accountability is only possible when everyone is working within an accountability culture. Whether you think that is true or not, it certainly makes it easier to be accountable. You may have experienced accountability in a negative and punitive manner in the past. Perhaps when you've been told you will be "held accountable," it sounds more like a threat. That's because many of us have experienced a situation where accountability lurks at the back end of a commitment you've made. Perhaps the mandate of being "held accountable" was not accompanied by clear and specific expectations. Well, it doesn't have to be that way. Accountability should be about high performance and not fear, stress, or discomfort. The secret is to ensure everyone understands up front what they are agreeing to—what they will be held accountable for. They should not be awaiting an attack at the back end. What can you do to help create an accountability culture in your organization? Discuss the idea with your mentor.

CROSS TRAINING

You will find related ideas at these crossover skills:

- Communicate Clearly
- Collaborate with Others
- Set Goals
- Demonstrate Problem-Solving Ability

READING FOR THE FINAL STRETCH

- *Winning and Accountability*, by Henry Evans
- *131 Ways to Win with Accountability: Best Practices for Driving Better Results*, by Henry Evans and Elaine Biech
- *Accountability: Taking Ownership of Your Responsibility*, by Henry Browning

SKILL 44

Sell Ideas

Your ability to sell your ideas effectively is one you will use often. Persuading someone to give your idea a chance may not be easy. Even though you may call it a pitch, you can't just go in and toss your idea as you'd pitch a baseball. You will need to do some research and groundwork before you schedule your appointment. Part of your preparation is to anticipate the difficult questions and prepare responses to them. Practice your pitch with someone and develop a one-page overview that you can leave behind if the person wants to think about your idea. Schedule a time that is good for the person you are selling to. For example, is the individual a morning person? Meet in the morning. Use your best eye contact and body language, ask for input, and listen carefully. You should be doing less talking and more listening—which means you need to have a tight presentation.

It's important because your ability to sell an idea is a career builder and will open doors for you. Whether you like it or not, you are a salesperson. We all sell, from ideas to products and services. Your ability to persuade and sell can affect another's beliefs, intentions, and behaviors.

Hurdles to Overcome

- How can I be expected to sell an idea when I have a shoot-the-messenger type of supervisor?

- How often do I yell, blame, or become depressed because it's not going my way?

- Who me? Sell? Do you really think I want to be a sleazy salesperson?

Your Path to Success

- Be able to deliver a solution-oriented, succinct statement that clearly describes what you are promoting

- Appreciate that everyone is a salesperson in one capacity or another

- Lead masterful sales conversations

- Use questioning techniques to uncover needs and to reach buy-in

- Understand the buyer, personality types, and how to overcome comments that prevent a sale

- Share the credit with others

- Measure every idea's value before deciding to promote it

- Creative, off-the-wall ideas excite you when you can see the benefit of a change

- Even if it is damaging, know the data to understand what you are selling

TIPS FOR PEOPLE IN A HURRY

- **Wish I would have said.** Identify the last two times you needed to promote or defend your ideas. How well did you do? What did you say? What do you wish you would have said? How quick were you to respond? Did you need more time to think about it?

- **Know when to hold 'em and when to fold 'em.** Knowing when to speak up and when to let it go is critical. How do you make this critical decision?

- **Pitching an idea?** Getting ready to pitch an idea to your boss? Don't bother unless you can clearly state the need—not your need, but the need for your boss or the organization.

- **Watch ads.** Tune in to the advertisements on television. What techniques do you see that might work for you?

- **Call in a favor.** Who have you built a relationship with that could help you sell your idea?

- **Identify the desires.** If you are looking for an idea to sell, or how to sell the idea you already have, uncover what the person needs. Present it as a desire, not just a problem. Ask "What are the possibilities?" or "What do you hope will happen?," then connect your proposal.

PRACTICE SPRINTS

- **Show me the money.** The next time you need to promote an idea to a colleague or your supervisor, lead with the outcome you desire, "show me the money" Jerry Maguire style. Begin by deciding exactly what you want the outcome to be. What are you promoting? What should it look like when complete? Decide on your complete message. Write it down. Then meet with the person and tell them what you want.

- **Show caution with spur-of-the-moment ideas.** Often you do not have time to think about whether to support or deny an idea. Meet with a coworker and brainstorm a list of what to consider before making the call. For example, even though it may appear to be time sensitive, can it wait 15 minutes while you weigh the pros and cons? Or how does this correspond to your organization's values? How does it correlate to your organization's vision? How does the idea support balance between your organization and your personal interests?

- **Answer the 5 Ws for selling.** You have a good idea, and you need your supervisor's permission before you start. To be sure you are prepared, act like a news reporter and answer the 5 Ws first:

  1. Why is this a good idea? Before you think about anything else, define the needs in your supervisor's language. Why does the organization need your idea? Does it increase the bottom line? Save money?

  2. Who will have responsibility and accountability? Who will be affected?

  3. What are the details? Be prepared to answer questions. Be sure to consider what concerns and objectives your supervisor will have.

  4. When will you implement your idea, how long will it take, and how long before you see a return on the investment?

  5. Where in the organization will your idea be experienced? Think about the big picture and use your systems thinking skills.

  Wrap your answers in a story. Your narrative needs to be memorable and interesting. Also be sure to select the best time to pitch your idea.

- **Create a compelling message.** Selling your idea depends on your communication skills. A compelling message that will get your listener's attention will focus on how the idea will help the individual or the organization. What problem is keeping them up at night that you can solve?

- **Make it negotiable.** First, design your presentation so that you don't get an immediate "no." Once someone makes a negative statement, it is difficult for them to change their mind without losing face. Before presenting your ideas, plan for possible alternatives and your backup position. Have a few ideas in your pocket. You can ask for more than you really need, to create some negotiating room. Be careful with this technique so that it isn't viewed as deceitful when it comes to negotiating. Practice your presentation and the negotiation of it by role playing with a colleague. Ask your colleague to challenge you with questions and issues that you might hear as you sell your idea. Ask for feedback about how you presented and what you could do better.

- **Create an info sheet.** Plan to develop a one-page overview that you can leave behind if the person wants to think about your proposal. On a single page include a brief overview of your idea and the benefit to the organization or the person you are selling to. Include data and a very brief action plan with a timeline and examples if possible.

STRATEGIES FOR THE LONG RUN

- **Take a class.** Selling your ideas is a skill you will use in every job. Take a class that focuses on personality style and that discusses the best way to sell to each style. Robert, a top salesperson in his company his entire career, says that the real key to selling is to adapt to the person you are selling to. This is true for selling your ideas to people who are internal to your organization too.

- **Your reputation is at stake.** Selling or defending ideas is serious business. You need to walk a fine line between being too aggressive and being too relaxed. You need to ensure that you do not get a reputation for leaning one way or the other. Consider these questions as you find your way through this sticky wicket:

  > How do you know when to stay out of an issue and when to get involved?

  > Is there something you shy away from (for example, conflict)?

  > Do creative, off-the-wall ideas scare you enough so that you ignore them?

  > Even if it is damaging, do you want to know the data?

  > Do you defend ideas of others equitably?

  > Do you give credit where credit is due?

  > Are you able to deliver a solution-oriented, succinct statement that clearly describes what you are promoting?

  > Do you have a measure for which ideas should be promoted and which should be left on the drawing board?

Meet with your coach and your supervisor to discuss these issues. Ask in particular if they can describe the behaviors that would be too aggressive and those that would be too relaxed.

- **Aristotle the salesman?** Want to study more about sales? Check out these thoughts. In the fourth century, Aristotle identified three essentials of persuasive communication: logos, ethos, and pathos. You need Aristotle's three persuasive essentials to be successful in selling your ideas:

  1. Logos, or reason, is the ability to articulate points clearly. To appeal to reason, you may use logical arguments, data, consequences, or scientific proof.
  2. Ethos, or credibility, is the ability to convey integrity and goodwill. To appeal to credibility, you may use your authority, expertise, communication skills, or body language.
  3. Pathos, or emotion, is the ability to influence emotion in listeners. To appeal to emotion, you may tap into tradition, mental images, relationships, or stories.

  Many persuasion theories exist, and most are influenced by the research of the psychologist Robert Cialdini. His six principles of persuasion include:

  > Reciprocity: giving first without any expectation of return
  > Consistency: committing to behave in the same way as in the past
  > Social proof: doing something because others are doing the same
  > Authority: deferring to experts or others with credentials
  > Liking: finding commonalities or genuinely liking another
  > Scarcity: demonstrating a shortage of items or time to act

  Which of these techniques might you use as you sell your ideas? How would they resonate with your supervisor or others you need to influence?

- **Ask for participation.** When selling an idea, save time to get input from the other person. Research shows that we are all more open to ideas when we feel as if we are a part of the idea, its development, and its implementation. You could ask questions such as these: How do you see this aligning with what we are already doing? How do you recommend we implement the action? What would you like to accomplish with this? Create a habit of asking for input to increase your chances of making a sale.

CROSS TRAINING

You will find related ideas at these crossover skills:

- Advocate for Self
- Maintain Composure
- Display Self-Confidence
- Exhibit Technology, Analytics, and Data Knowledge

READING FOR THE FINAL STRETCH

- *Influence: The Psychology of Persuasion*, by Robert Cialdini
- *Secrets of Closing the Sale*, by Zig Ziglar
- *To Sell Is Human: The Surprising Truth about Moving Others,* by Daniel Pink

Organizational Alignment

I t was the late 1980s, and I had been in business for several years. My company, ebb associates inc, owned an office building that was always buzzing with employees who had exciting ideas. The company had grown quickly, and everyone's responsibilities were still not sorted out. As the president of the company, I had maintained the role of creating, developing, and producing the majority of the custom-designed consulting solutions we sold. This involved starting with a blank piece of paper to create the program that would take the company from where it was to where it wanted to be.

A few of the required steps included assessing the current situation, identifying the knowledge and skills required to accomplish the organization's goals, gauging the resources available, and specifying responsibilities for everyone throughout the organization from the CEO to the newest hired employee. The biggest task was designing the unique training required—something that was realistic, relevant, and efficient.

To design, I needed to focus on all the details and the big picture at the same time. The office environment was hectic and dynamic; it was filled with people who were talking and turning out products—exactly what you would want in an office. Unfortunately, the exciting setting was not one in which I could focus. Not wanting to dampen that productive atmosphere, I started to look for an alternative so that I could focus on new projects. I found a corner table where I could work undisturbed for a couple of hours at my local Hardee's. I started showing up for a late lunch twice a week.

To accompany my work, I always ordered the same lunch: a chicken sandwich and Diet Coke with no ice. What's significant is that Hardee's didn't sell Coca-Cola products; Hardee's sold Pepsi products. I knew that, but as a staunch Coke enthusiast I continued to ask for Diet Coke, and the ensuing conversation was always the same: "We don't have Diet Coke. We have Diet Pepsi." To which I'd sigh and respond, "I suppose that will have to do." I'd pay for my lunch and get to work on the design of the day.

One day an employee I hadn't seen before took my order and surprised me with, "No, that won't do. Here's your sandwich, and I'll be right back." What happened next surprised everyone. He ran out the back door and into the grocery store next door. He purchased a bottle of Diet Coke for me and delivered it to the table where I sat with my chicken sandwich and my work.

At the time, Hardee's slogan was "We're out to win you over." This young employee took his company's vision to heart. His actions were aligned to Corporate's expectation: "win me over!" He was modeling Hardee's expectations to build a loyal customer base. You will need to support your organization by demonstrating business acumen and promoting your organization's vision and values. Your organization's ability to be agile requires you to take initiative like the Hardee's employee to make process improvements, champion change, and be creative, and to take appropriate risks. Your organization needs you develop loyalty—just like the Hardee's employee that I encountered; he had aligned himself to his company's vision of "We're out to win you over."

You don't make progress by standing on the sidelines,
whimpering and complaining.
You make progress by implementing ideas.

—SHIRLEY CHISHOLM

SKILL 45

Demonstrate Business Acumen

Your acumen for business is the basic understanding of how your organization, and the industry it operates in, works. Learning about your organization's products or services, how your competitors compare, and industry trends is knowledge that can set you apart from your colleagues. Knowing your organization is critical. But what specifically do you need to know, and how do you gain that knowledge and experience? Start with understanding what it is going to take to lead for success. For example, do you know what is valued in your organization? What behaviors, beliefs, and actions underlie your organization's success? What prevents success? Devote time to learning how your organization is organized and operates: its internal structure, key officers, primary products and services, and present and future goals. Understand the important priorities, values, and strategies of your CEO, division heads, and your direct supervisor. It takes time and determination to learn and implement; you will be rewarded for doing so.

It's important because your leaders expect you to know about the business and the industry. Your ability to talk the language of the C-suite regarding finances, challenges, customers, competition, and innovation is critical to your chances of working on exciting projects, being considered for promotions, and mingling with the movers and shakers in your organization. You need to be organizationally savvy to know how to think, influence, and add value within your organization.

MASTERING THE SKILL

Hurdles to Overcome

- How aware am I of everything that is going on around me as I work, who my customers are, and who receives my products and services?

- Why should I learn about the business when I don't want to be a business owner?

- How do I learn whether my organization is profitable, meeting its goals, achieving its mission, or competitive?

Your Path to Success

- Can explain and manage contradictory requirements and competing priorities in your organization

- Stay current with trends in the global market as well as economic and political trends

- Understand how your organization produces revenue

- Understand how to measure the margins produced by your products and services

- Describe your organization's operational processes

- Stay informed about external conditions and competitors' moves that might affect the organization and the industry as a whole

- Can intelligently discuss operations beyond your own area, including finance, products, and services
- Manage your budget, control expenses, and maintain cash flow
- Exhibit strong generalist skills

TIPS FOR PEOPLE IN A HURRY

- **Go beyond.** No matter what your corporate culture, every organization views favorably those who take initiative.
- **Stay informed.** The *Wall Street Journal* is one of the best ways to stay in touch with what is happening in the economy and the industry. Subscribe to it; read it.
- **Know your leadership team.** Learn more about your senior leaders and what is important to them.
- **Give yourself a promotion.** Imagine that you have the job of someone who is two levels above you. What do you need to learn to take over that position?
- **Be there.** Never give up a chance to attend an organizational meeting led by your senior leaders. Listen and determine how you are directly connected to their message.

PRACTICE SPRINTS

- **Account for sales and profit.** Meet with someone from accounting. Ask them to give you an overview of how each group/department in the organization contributes to sales and profit. After your discussion, summarize what you learned on one page of paper. List each group in a column down the left side of the page. Add two more columns. Label the first column "Costs" for the expenses the group generates. Use simple word descriptors (salaries, benefits, IT services), not actual dollar amounts. Label the second column "Contribution to Profits" and list how the group contributes to sales. Again, use simple word descriptors (informs public, serves customers). Continue to work on this summary sheet. When you perfect it, it will be a good tool for you to use to explain to others how each group within the organization contributes to sales and profits.

- **Know your financial terminology.** Brush up on your financial comprehension. An understanding of how the business operates means that you understand and can translate the financial terms. Several of these are completed. Fill in the meanings for the rest.

  > Assets are economic resources that a company owns.

  > Liabilities are the debts or expenses a company owes.

  > Equity

  > Balance sheet

  > Income statements

  > Chart of accounts

  > General ledger is a document that contains all the accounts of an organization.

  > Cost-benefit analysis

  > Expenses are the costs incurred in the process of earning revenues and conducting business.

  > Incurred expenses

  > Operating expenses

  > Revenue

  > Financial statements are the four statements that show the end results of an organization's financial condition: balance sheet, income statement, statement of cash flows, and statement of owners' equity

  > Gross profit margin formula is (Sales Revenue—Cost of Goods Sold) / Sales Revenue and shows overall markup of goods sold.

  > Earnings yield

  After you have completed what you can, meet with your supervisor or coach to determine how your organization uses this terminology and which are the most meaningful and why.

- **How your organization works.** Organizations are usually more complex than we imagine. In many organizations the path from A to B is rarely a straight line. There is the formal organization depicted as an organizational chart with seemingly straight lines from one place to another. There is also an informal organization where all the paths intersect and do not flow in a straight line. Once people are added to the processes, the entire system becomes more complicated, since they play the roles of gatekeeper, expediter, resistor, guide, influencer, informal leader, and others. Don't make the mistake of underestimating the complexity of the organization. Meet with your supervisor or coach and ask, "What is important for me to know about this organization, and how can I continue to learn more?"

- **Study your strategy.** Read your organization's strategic plan. What are the priorities? What resources are going to be needed? Project what skills and knowledge will be necessary. Learn about your organization's culture. What values are advocated? What values actually play out? What is rewarded? How is learning viewed? How is change managed? Learn what employees think about the organization. Read at least the last two engagement surveys. Is the organization getting better or worse? In what areas?

- **Tap the call.** If possible, listen to your CEO's quarterly conference calls with Wall Street analysts, or get a summary from your public communications department or organization website. This quarterly call provides a current report on your organization's operations and financial performance, and your CEO's priorities and plans.

- **Study your department business.** Meet with your manager to learn more about the business element of your department. Read your department business plan and then ask questions such as these: What are the goals? How are the goals aligned to the organization? How are the goals aligned to the C-suite strategy? How will the results be measured? What will be different if we are successful? What resources are required? What risks does our department face and what is the mitigation plan? Following your discussion, offer to help achieve the department goals.

- **Join an industry association.** Join one of your industry's associations. It will become a resource for you. Attend the conferences. Read the publications. Use the website. You will continue to learn and grow. And you will meet people with whom to network. If the association doesn't have the answer for you, your new network of professionals will be able to lead you in the right direction. Joining an association is an opportunity for you to affect your own destiny, an opportunity for you to invest in you. Learn who else in your organization belongs to the association so that you can double your learning by discussing what you learn.

- **Know your organizational drivers.** Meet with your supervisor or coach and plan a discussion about organizational drivers. Drivers are situations—or differences—that prompt an organization to develop alternative plans. External drivers may include economic, customer, market, regulations, public perception, or human resources. Internal business drivers may include systems changes, technology, shareholder, financial, leadership, structure, or cultural shift. Ask your supervisor these questions to initiate the discussion:

  > What are the key drivers that would cause us to revise strategy?

  > What drivers currently seem to be critical to our organization?

  > How critical are these differences?

  > What impact will these differences have on us?

  > What measures do we use to determine when it is time to make changes to address the drivers?

  > What drivers are affecting our customers? How do we help our customers respond to their business drivers while appropriately responding to our own—or is that important?

  > How does our organization monitor drivers?

  > What is my responsibility to support the organization as we monitor drivers and develop alternative plans as a result?

Continue to learn more about drivers by studying your competitor's drivers. What might your competition do that would have an impact on your organization? Meet with someone in another department to continue your discussion and learning about organizational drivers.

- **Mini MBA.** Meet with two or three managers whom you respect and ask for recommendations for books or classes to gain business acumen. Create a development plan incorporating what you learned. It might be a good idea to use the action plan template at https://ideas.bkconnection.com/skillsforcareersuccess so you can record your actions, your timeline, and a notional budget. Review your plan with your supervisor. You could request resources and time to take courses if necessary.

CROSS TRAINING

You will find related ideas at these crossover skills:

- Lead Ventures
- Set Goals
- Practice Systems Thinking
- Be Accountable
- Model Corporate Expectations

READING FOR THE FINAL STRETCH

- *Seeing the Big Picture: Business Acumen to Build Your Credibility, Career, and Company,* by Kevin Cope

Promote the Organization's Vision and Values

Y our willingness to promote your organization's vision and values provides direction for employees. The vision is an aspirational statement that presents what your organization wants to accomplish. A statement of values provides guidance to you and other employees as you go about completing your work. You must consider your organization's vision and values whenever you are making decisions, solving problems, or taking action of any kind. Your demonstration of doing this is a stronger message than any for promoting your organization's vision and values.

It's important because a vision and values statement gives employees a higher purpose for their jobs. A vision can help your organization attract top talent and establish an attractive brand. A vision ensures that everyone is aspiring to the same goals and feeling the success of reaching them. The values influence how the organization hopes to achieve its goals. They establish a kind of code of conduct for all employees to follow.

MASTERING THE SKILL

Hurdles to Overcome

- How can I focus on the vision and values when the operational systems and processes take so much of my time?

- Why should I sell the vision and values? That's leadership's job.

- Vision, values, mission—aren't they all just words the marketing department created to keep us in our place?

Your Path to Success

- Accept personal compromises when necessary to support your organization's vision and goals

- Be a resourceful, influential, and insightful organizational ambassador

- Consistently set the example for living according to your organization's vision and values

- Discuss the organization's vision with passion and authenticity

- Consider the values and vision when you're making decisions

- Hold yourself accountable for living the vision and modeling the values

- Clearly define how the values support reaching the mission and vision

- Ensure that other employees have clear priorities and that they see how they are connected to your organization's vision

TIPS FOR PEOPLE IN A HURRY

- **Culture match?** Examine your organization's culture. How does it model the organization's vision and values?

- **Review your decisions.** Think back to the decisions you made today. Write them down. How do your decisions rate when held up against your organization's vision and values? Observe your leaders making decisions. What line of sight do they seem to use? What can you learn from them?

- **Create your story.** Many people in an organization have a story about what the organization has done for them. Create your own story and be prepared to tell it to others in and outside the organization.

- **Role model.** Be a role model for your organization, even when you are not on the job. This benefits both you and the organization.

- **Speak up.** Reward others when you see them modeling the organization's vision or values.

PRACTICE SPRINTS

- **Align personally.** Life is much easier if your personal vision and values are aligned with the organization's vision and values. Don't have a personal vision and values statement yet? Go to https://ideas .bkconnection.com/skillsforcareersuccess for templates to examine your values and your personal vision statement.

- **Sell values and vision.** Imagine that you need to sell your values and vision to another organization. How would you do that? What techniques would you use? What words would you use? Selling focuses on features, benefits, and value. What features or elements of your vision and values are unique? What benefits do the values and vision produce for you? When selling value, you start with what's important to the other person. So what value do the values and vision produce for the person you are selling to?

- **The wisdom of Mark Twain.** Mark Twain said, "Good judgment comes from experience. And where does experience come from? Experience comes from bad judgment." What experiences have you had recently that conflict with your organization's vision and values? What caused that "bad judgment"? Was it warranted for any reason? What lesson can you learn from Mark Twain?

- **Be from Missouri.** Missouri is the Show-Me State. Meet with your coach or mentor and ask how to define what it means to "promote your organization's vision and values." Ask for advice about how to "show" and demonstrate both. How does your coach or mentor promote the vision and values? Do they have any concerns?

- **Values symbols.** Identify the rituals, symbols, ceremonies, customs, practices, signs, or other outward visuals that you believe represent your organization. Make a list of as many as you can think of. How do these relate to the vision? The values? Schedule a meeting with your supervisor to discuss these outward symbols.

- **Orientation presentation.** Volunteer to write and give a presentation of the organization's vision and values at the next new employee orientation. Clear it with your supervisor, of course.

- **Promote a vision.** Ask two friends whom you trust who work at different companies to discuss how their leaders promote the vision at their companies. Ask what is acceptable, what works, and what doesn't work.

- **Be the organization.** You represent your company no matter where you are. Your company expects you to speak positively about the organization, just as it will speak well of you and the rest of the workforce. Negative comments about your organization, individuals, or products could be a career changer—for the worst. Learn about your organization's rules for giving interviews for surveys, to news reporters, or even just casual comments at a social event. What are your organization's guidelines for being a corporate spokesperson?

STRATEGIES FOR THE LONG RUN

- **Prepare for disagreement.** Whenever you sell anything, anticipate criticism. When your sell/promote your organization's vision and values, be prepared with body language that shows you are listening and give the other person enough time to explain what they mean and why. Acknowledge their comments, even if it is just that you "understand where the person is coming from." Make statements that show you are open to suggestions and ideas. If you feel you need time to think about the disagreement, tell the person that these were good points and you'd like to think about them. Ask if you can continue the discussion at another time. Schedule another time after you've had time to think about the discussion.

- **Observation day.** Take a day to focus on what is happening around you. Ask questions and listen to your colleagues, employees in other departments, your boss, and others. Ask about your organization's strategic initiatives and their thoughts. Do their thoughts align with your organization's vision? Ask about what they see as the most important reason for your organization's existence. Do their statements align with your organization's values? Where do you fall on these same questions? How do you align with your organization's vision and values? Do you need to rethink your stance about your organization? Do you need to strengthen your views? How do your current actions promote your organization's vision and values? How can you stimulate more support? Meet with your mentor to discuss your experience.

- **Identify barriers.** Once you are familiar with your organization's vision and values, identify what you think might be barriers to excellence. For example, what unwritten rules exist that might prevent people from demonstrating the values the organization proclaims? Discuss this with your manager or mentor.

- **Sponsor a contest.** Talk with the head of your department to sponsor a Why We Love Our Job contest. Employees create their own short (one to three minutes) video presenting a dance, song, cheer, or another creative activity that includes the organization's vision and values.

CROSS TRAINING

You will find related ideas at these crossover skills:

- Resolve Conflict
- Model Corporate Expectations
- Practice Political Savvy
- Sell Ideas

READING FOR THE FINAL STRETCH

- *It's the Manager*, by Jim Clifton and Jim Harter

Initiate Process Improvement

Your ability to initiate process improvement is a valuable skill for your organization and for you as an individual. Your organization may use the term "continuous process improvement," meaning that you don't just examine processes occasionally but that it is an ongoing effort to improve processes that produce products and services. Systems thinking and process improvement are naturally related. If you are introduced to process improvement and already practice systems thinking, you will readily see the value of process improvement, since it requires that you examine everything, like systems thinking, that affects the process. Process improvement focuses on business-related goals that need improvement.

It's important because a philosophy of continuous process improvement requires everyone to be aware of how all tasks and processes can be more efficient and effective. This ensures that products and services offer higher value to the customer. Your process improvement skills ensure that you will have the ability to adopt a systematic approach for ongoing efforts as you identify and analyze problems and ultimately make improvements that benefit the entire organization and its customers. Initiating process improvement can be a real career boost; make it a requirement for your career development, not an option.

MASTERING THE SKILL

Hurdles to Overcome

- How aware am I of addressing things as if nothing is related?
- How can I possibly think of an entire process when I am just too disorganized?
- Why do all problems hit me at the same time? How can I be expected to juggle all those details?
- What can I do about improving processes? Isn't that management's job since they see the big picture?
- Why does process improvement have to be so laborious?
- Why make process improvements when it will all be back to the same old way tomorrow?

Your Path to Success

- Have a process focus when discussing actions and results
- Ensure a thorough understanding of every problem by relying on systems thinking when you solve problems
- Observe relationships and synergies in practices and procedures
- Use cause-and-effect relationships to explore outcomes
- Understand the value of measuring and data when you make enhancements or changes
- Think of work as a flow of events
- Identify and address the root cause of all problems you encounter

TIPS FOR PEOPLE IN A HURRY

- **Go beyond.** Every organization appreciates those who take initiative to look beyond the tasks in their job descriptions. Think long-term about what is needed to benefit your department or your organization.

- **Small and doable.** Narrow your focus to one area in your department. What is one small thing you could do to make an improvement?

- **Once ain't enough.** Giving one suggestion once does not necessarily cause change. You may need to repeat it several times or perhaps to several people. You aren't necessarily being ignored, but perhaps you need to find another way to offer it. Everyone is busy, and it is up to you to be persistent, use proper arguments, go through proper channels, and offer data. It is impossible to think that suggesting your idea once is all it takes. Don't think that your organization doesn't consider new ideas without giving everyone a fair shot.

- **Data is critical.** Data provides the detail that verifies you are ready to make improvements. Data can be collected at all stages of the process improvement effort. What data is available to you? It could be buyer behaviors, price changes, customer trends, user numbers, quality stats, satisfaction numbers, or hundreds of other things. Make a list of the data you use to do your job.

- **Rate your improvement.** Think of something that you improved recently. It can be personal or work related. How successful were you? What caused your success or lack of success?

PRACTICE SPRINTS

- **Bring a solution.** Don't take a problem to your supervisor without a possible solution or an offer to work on it. It would be rare for you to uncover an issue that management doesn't know about. It is more likely that they know but don't know how to fix it or haven't had time. Identifying a problem is just the first step. It would be valuable to your organization if you would take the second step, which is to create a possible solution and to offer to gather more data and information. Make a habit of finding solutions, and you'll become your organization's solution superhero. Think of one solution you can take to your supervisor today.

- **Process improvement.** Continuous process improvement is a philosophy organizations adopt. You'll need to understand several key elements that make up an organizational process improvement design. To be most successful, top management must lead the effort for the organization. The focus is on improving processes. Customer needs (internal and external) drive the need for improvement. It occurs throughout an organization. Process improvement utilizes the full potential of all employees. Decisions must be based on facts and data. Results are achieved through teamwork and by paying attention to variation, standards, redesign, and automation. List each of these essential elements of process improvement and identify how you could learn more about each. How has your organization adopted continuous process improvement? Discuss your plan with your mentor.

- **Practice PDCA.** Plan, Do, Check, and Act, or PDCA, designed by Walter Shewhart and popularized by W. Edwards Deming, is the methodology used for process improvement and is displayed as cyclical. Whether your organization uses a five-step or eight-step process, all processes are based on the same PDCA cycle. The plan step is the preparation, in which you identify the process to be improved and the approach you'll use. The do step involves implementing the plan and collecting data. The check step is the critical step of studying the results to determine what worked and what didn't and is the point of deciding if you corrected the root cause. The act step uses analysis to determine what happens next. If the root cause was found and corrected, the improvement will be standardized. If not, a new plan will be initiated. Practice PDCA on a personal situation such as improving your batting average, improving your ability to get to work on time, or improving how you save for retirement. Discuss your plan and results with someone in your personal life.

- **Flowchart fanatic.** A flowchart is probably the most valuable of all the process improvement tools. It is a visual representation of the flow of process steps using standard symbols connected by arrows. To construct a flowchart, identify major steps of the process and use the symbols to show what happens in each step. You will also need to define the boundaries of the process—that is, the start and end points of the process. Go to https://ideas.bkconnection.com/skillsforcareer success for guidelines and more details about constructing a flowchart. Select a process to chart. Invite colleagues to join you. Once you have completed the activity, discuss what you all learned about the process you chose. What problems did you encounter as you constructed your flowchart? How could flowcharts be useful to you in your team or department? What lessons did you take away from the experience?

- **Visit quality.** Schedule a visit to your quality department. Before you go, create a list of questions you want to ask about continuous process improvement.

STRATEGIES FOR THE LONG RUN

- **Process improvement team.** Request that your supervisor add you as a member to a corporate Lean Six Sigma or process improvement team. Be sure to share what you learn with the rest of your department or team. How can you use process improvement in your role?

- **Lean Six Sigma.** Consider taking a Lean Six Sigma class at your local community college to become more familiar with problem-solving tools, quality concepts, and total quality techniques. What would it take to be certified? Learn more about yellow, green, or black belt certification. Ask your supervisor whether your organization sponsors classes for certification.

- **Learning community.** Form a community of practice with others who are interested in continuous process improvement. You could share ideas, knowledge, and skills in person or online. Try meeting once a month and encourage sharing stories and concepts between the meetings.

- **ASQ.** Consider joining the American Society for Quality (ASQ). It is a global community of quality professionals dedicated to promoting and advancing quality tools, principles, and practices in their workplaces and communities. Learn more at ASQ.org.

CROSS TRAINING

You will find related ideas at these crossover skills:

- Demonstrate Problem-Solving Ability
- Manage Projects
- Practice Systems Thinking
- Lead Ventures

READING FOR THE FINAL STRETCH

- *The Quality Toolbox*, by Nancy Tague
- *The Goal: A Process of Ongoing Improvement*, by Eliyahu Goldratt

Champion and Manage Change

Your ability to manage change is important since change is a constant for organizations that want to maintain a competitive advantage. Organizations need to keep up with the rapid pace at which their sectors are evolving or risk losing out to their competitors. This requires change, and change requires managing and championing to achieve the strategic and operational objectives. Organizations that are most successful with change are able to minimize the discomfort, disruption, and disequilibrium change creates for employees and customers. You can help your organization balance the importance of managing today's work with the transition into the future.

It's important because change affects everyone in an organization, whether directly or indirectly. An organization's need for change may conflict with its employees' needs to maintain their sense of personal security. It's important for you to learn about your organization's change to prevent negative thoughts. You can help balance the conflicting interests between what the organization requires and what you and other employees can offer.

MASTERING THE SKILL

Hurdles to Overcome

- How often do I complain, grumble, or whine when something changes?
- Why am I stuck in today and unable to see the value in change?
- How often do I find myself in the middle of my organization's rumor mill and even spreading rumors myself?

Your Path to Success

- See things from a big-picture corporate perspective
- Be ready to take on new challenges, solve problems, and adjust as necessary
- Support activities required to position your organization for the future
- Adjust to and advocate for changes your organization experiences
- Take risks but also be realistic about everything that needs to be completed
- Express eagerness to learn and develop from discovery, experimentation, and new experiences
- Support others through the change by building sponsorship for the effort
- Model a resilient, adventurous, and optimistic attitude toward change

TIPS FOR PEOPLE IN A HURRY

- **Ready for change.** Inventory the strategies you use to cope with change. Observe your colleagues' change strategies. Which strategies can you adopt that are the most helpful?

- **Avoid grumblers.** Others' negativity and complaining will have a negative effect on you and your ability to manage change. Surround yourself with those who see positive value in the current changes.

- **Describe change.** List three words that describe how you address change. What does that say about you? Which words would you change?

- **Thoughts about change.** What's the first thing that goes through your mind when someone mentions change? Is it positive and exciting? Or is it negative and resisting? What do you want it to be?

- **Change champions.** Decide what you think is expected of a change champion. How can you play that role?

PRACTICE SPRINTS

- **Ready, set, change.** Change cannot be managed with a one-size-fits-all strategy. Change is personal. A champion of change has numerous tactics available to create support for the change effort. The resistance toward change is often an attempt to maintain the status quo. As a champion of change you can help management establish a positive message about the current change, and you can persuade your colleagues to join the change effort for the right reasons. These measures will champion change:

  > Address personal concerns first

  > Link the change to other issues people care about

  > Establish clarity around the purpose, goals, and realities of the change

  > Be available and visible so you can communicate progress and results

> Create a mechanism for candid, two-way discussions

> Tailor the information to others' expectations

> Deliver training on resiliency and how to build the skills to support the change

> Extend opportunities to celebrate and reward successes

- **Dr. Seuss and you.** Read Dr. Seuss's book *Oh, the Places You'll Go!* Like the characters in the book, you have choices about change. You can choose that (1) change is either difficult or fun, (2) change can be scary and confusing or an opportunity, (3) change can be something that you hope will go away or something that awakens responsibility, and (4) change can be an exciting open road or a speed bump to avoid. What choices will you make? How can you share this book and its message with your team or your colleagues?

- **Answer their questions.** Change champions communicate. Every employee wants four questions answered. Prepare for how you would answer these four questions if someone asks you. Expect to change your answers regularly—after all, it is change.

  > What is happening?

  > Why is it happening?

  > How will this affect me and my job?

  > What's the plan for getting there?

- **It's hard work.** The status quo is easy. Change is hard. You have to make a personal choice to change, then you need to determine what and how to change, and finally you need to manage the change. Identify someone you know who has made changes, perhaps someone who lost weight or purposefully changed jobs. Interview the individual to learn more about how it was done and what you can implement.

- **Communicate change.** It's unlikely that you will communicate too often during a change initiative. Guidance at https://ideas.bkconnection .com/skillsforcareersuccess provides ideas for you to consider and tips to create a communication plan. Print the page and discuss your own ideas with your supervisor or whoever is in charge of your change effort. Volunteer to help create a change communication plan.

- **Master the people side.** People often focus on the project management side of change. But that's not enough. You need to be aware of how people will react to change, what's behind their reactions, and what you can do to manage it. To manage and champion change, you will want to attend to your interpersonal skills, listen to new ideas, reach out to your network, focus on solutions, communicate the realities and the positives, ask for help when you need it, and encourage engagement from all. Which skills will you need to shore up, and how will you do that?

STRATEGIES FOR THE LONG RUN

- **Understand change responses.** Everett Rogers, a professor of sociology, researched human reaction to change and introduced a model that predicts human reactions to change. His model has become a standard reference in guiding organizational change processes. Understanding how people respond to change is key to a change strategy.

  > **Innovators** make up 2.5 percent and are the first to embrace the change; they are proud of being adventurous.

  > **Early adopters** make up 13.5 percent of the population and like to take on new challenges. They are trend setters who stay informed and are generally influential members of organizations.

  > **Early majority** make up 34 percent of all individuals. They are thoughtful about change initially and become positive about the change based on observations. They then become deliberate acceptors of the change.

  > **Late majority** make up 34 percent of the population who are skeptical about change. They may accept the change only because of peer pressure.

> **Laggards** make up 16 percent of all individuals who hold on to the past and resist change. This outlook becomes problematic if they reject the change completely. (Rogers 2003)

As a champion of change, place yourself in the position of those whom the change affects. Determine what you can do for each person, no matter what category they might be in.

- **Beg to be on the team.** Your very best learning experience is to jump into the middle of the action. The best way to do this is to be assigned to be a member of one of your organization's change management or implementation teams. Do all you can to advocate for membership on one of these teams. You will learn about change!

- **Prepare for change impact.** The pace of change will continue to get faster. You can be prepared with a skill set to address the constant churn of change. You could use these examples to prepare:

  > Practice resilience or the ability to adapt well to difficult events that disrupt your life

  > Maintain a positive attitude and look for the good in everything

  > Demonstrate flexibility and adaptability in everything that comes your way

  > Learn new skills within and beyond your job function

  > Schedule time to reflect on the exciting future and the positive options available

  > Learn or relearn time management skills

- **Ahead of the game.** Be a change advocate by anticipating future change. You can gain an advantage for your organization and yourself by keeping an eye on the future to predict what might affect your organization. Scan the environment, solicit information from knowledgeable sources, and follow futurist predictions. Imagine how your information could affect your department or organization. Have conversations with your manager and others from other organizations. Predict what may happen so that you are prepared for changes ahead.

CROSS TRAINING

You will find related ideas at these crossover skills:

- Communicate Clearly
- Promote the Organization's Vision and Values
- Practice Systems Thinking
- Manage Projects
- Exhibit Technology, Analytics, and Data Knowledge
- Adapt to Situations

READING FOR THE FINAL STRETCH

- *Leading Change*, by John Kotter
- *Leading Continuous Change: Navigating Churn in the Real World*, by Bill Pasmore

Practice Creativity, Innovation, and Appropriate Risk Taking

Your propensity for creativity, innovation, and appropriate risk taking plays a part in how your organization creates new products and services to enable employees and customers to do tasks better or do things they couldn't before. Creativity is the act of conceiving something original or unusual. Risk taking is the act of doing something with an uncertain outcome. "Appropriate" risk taking means that research and thoughtful consideration preceded the risk to reduce the amount of uncertainty and to ensure relevance. Both creativity and risk are required for innovation to occur—or the actual production of products, services, methods, processes, markets, or anything that has never been produced before.

It's important because innovation is the path to an organization's success. It allows businesses to improve services, solve problems, increase productivity, create new products, market the business, and surpass competition to the marketplace. Creativity, or thinking outside the box, is important because it is a key ingredient in identifying new ideas. Without creativity, innovation is nearly impossible. Likewise, risk taking is required to set the creative idea in motion, otherwise nothing will happen and the creative idea will remain a concept only. Research by the Center for Creative Leadership shows that although 94 percent of global executives say innovation is important, only 14 percent believe their organizations are effective at it (Horth and Mitchell 2017). Personally it is important for you to be creative and take risks. This demonstrates boldness without limiting your opportunities for development.

MASTERING THE SKILL

Hurdles to Overcome

- Why do I freeze when I hear the word "innovation," associating it with change, extra work, and loss of jobs?
- How can I possibly be expected to be creative when I am so practical?
- How can creativity be better since new ideas rarely work and I don't have time to be creative anyway?
- Why am I overly cautious and afraid of failure?
- What prevents me from taking risks or trying something different?

Your Path to Success

- Exhibit persistence, courage, confidence, flexibility, and a future-oriented perspective
- Show openness to probe for different interpretations and perspectives of problems
- Ask many questions, including those that challenge the status quo
- Persevere through obstacles or criticism when you believe you are right
- Generate ideas and experiment with unconventional methods

- Have a visionary perspective of change, even when opposed

- Don't give up when things become difficult; enjoy uncertainty

- Experiment and try new things to demonstrate personal and professional risk taking

- View failure as your opportunity to learn

TIPS FOR PEOPLE IN A HURRY

- **Widen your spectrum.** The next time you are facing a dilemma, ask "What's good about it?" followed by "What if we . . . ?"

- **Fail fast.** Although a well-used phrase, there is value in moving rapidly, celebrating success or learning from failure, and implementing lessons learned. How do you fail fast?

- **Take a risk to lunch.** Select a restaurant where you've never eaten, perhaps an ethnic restaurant where you will be unfamiliar with the food. How did you feel when you entered?

- **Search for barriers.** Look at your department through your innovation lens. What barriers are preventing employees from being creative and innovative? Fear of failure? Only one right answer? Judgmental attitudes? Lack of time? Unwillingness to change? Risk aversion? Others?

- **Read and create.** Read a newspaper that prints an opinion with which you disagree. It will help you appreciate different perspectives and widen your views. It will challenge your status quo.

PRACTICE SPRINTS

- **Try design thinking.** Ask your supervisor to assign you to lead a team or be a member of a team that will use design thinking elements. It will give you experience with experimenting, prototyping, getting customer input, trial runs, and other aspects of design thinking. Be sure that you will have a chance to learn about risk and creativity during the decision-making process.

- **Rate your creativity.** You can learn and practice creativity like any other skill. Assess your creativity behaviors on a 1–5 scale, where 1 means that you never or rarely practice it and 5 means that you do this easily. Rate yourself and place a number in the box.

  ☐ I am open to and welcome new experiences and ideas.

  ☐ I practice connecting unrelated concepts, words, ideas, and associations to everything.

  ☐ I don't try to fit in—I stand out.

  ☐ I work to refine and clarify my ideas.

  ☐ I probe problems for deeper understanding.

  ☐ I frequently ask, "What if we could do it?" or "What if there were no barriers?" or "What would it take to . . . ?"

  ☐ I ask lots of questions and am curious about everything.

  ☐ I like to brainstorm and build off others' ideas.

  Creativity can be learned. Start by examining the behaviors and how often you practice creativity skills. What kinds of situations inspire your creativity? How could you build more of them into your work? Explore your personal feelings about creativity. Note your ideas here—with a crayon.

- **Try brainstorming.** With your supervisor's assistance, search for a situation where you could lead a brainstorming activity. Brainstorming is an idea-generating process that suggests that the more ideas generated, the greater the chance that one will prove to be a high-quality solution. Introduce these rules to your team to ensure success:

  > Generate as many ideas as possible

  > Suspend judgment, believing that all ideas are good

  > Encourage freewheeling—the wilder the ideas, the better

  > Build on each other's ideas

  > Post all ideas as they arise

  > Allow enough time, to get beyond first thoughts

  > Encourage humor and playfulness

Facilitate the brainstorming session and offer the ideas to your supervisor to select those that could be implemented.

- **Review a past innovation.** Think of some unpopular idea, product, project, or concept that you supported or argued for. Evaluate what happened. Was it a success or a failure? What made it so? What would you do again? What would you change? Who can you discuss the scenario with who could provide insight on what happened and why? This is of course going to be easier for you if the project was successful. On the other hand, it will be a more valuable review and discussion if the project failed or if your idea wasn't chosen. Ask someone why they think that happened and what you could have done differently.

- **Take a risk.** Businesses need to take risks regularly. You need to take risks too. According to Bruce Deel (2019), refusing to take risks becomes a barrier that prevents you from fulfilling your purpose in life. Everyone needs to tailor a risk for themselves. Don't be afraid to take a calculated risk that will get you closer to your purpose. How? Follow these four steps that can be used for any planned risk. Use the four steps to design a calculated risk to find your purpose:

    R Research the details about your purpose and related topics, talk to your coach and mentor, review the data, and think about the pros and cons.

    I Identify possible negative outcomes, what might go wrong, and how you will respond.

    S Set milestones but be ready to change. Set goals that have dates and are dependent on each other as well as a contingency plan. Focus, refocus, and focus again to reach success.

    K Know when to do it. If you have done your research, know the possible drawbacks, and have clear goals, then just do it! Scary, yes, but only until the risk pays off.

    The risks you are taking should serve both you and your organization. Start small and work up to others. Everyone is created for a purpose. You probably will need to take several risks before finding your purpose.

- **Your innovation style.** Innovation requires a number of different subskills. All are related to both creative ability and willingness to take risks. Innovation skills include:

  > Sustainers are practical and reality oriented and measure new ideas against standards.

  > Modifiers tend to make incremental improvements.

  > Visionaries are great at originating ideas but may not be able to create an implementation plan.

  > Synthesizers blend numerous ideas together and are usually highly creative.

  > Challengers tend to be well-developed risk takers, but don't necessarily have original ideas.

  > Planners look for ideas that can be easily implemented, and although relatively risk-averse and not very original, the skill is necessary from a practical perspective. (Levitt 2002)

  Each of these styles adds value, and all are needed to create innovation. Identify which behaviors and skills you use the most. Should you develop others? What project would help you become more innovative?

- **Learn innovation.** Register for a class that will enhance your creativity or your risk-taking ability depending on your needs. For creativity, you might consider a poetry writing, pottery, or glassblowing class; for risk taking, consider scuba diving, snowboarding, or drag racing. During your learning, focus on how you manage your stress of being outside your element. How can you translate what you are learning about yourself to your job?

- **Innovation advisory board.** Select a team of experienced people who demonstrate risk taking and creativity. Ask them to provide insight into your efforts and advice about what you could do to improve your ability to create options that could be considered innovative. You will likely have the most success if you select people who have diverse roles throughout your organization. Meet with them as a group or one-on-one. Share your candid perceptions and ask for their honest ideas about what you could do differently.

- **Request a rotation.** Ask your supervisor for a rotation in a department known for its innovation, such as marketing, research, or the creative department.

CROSS TRAINING

You will find related ideas at these crossover skills:

- Be Resourceful
- Demonstrate Problem-Solving Ability
- Adapt to Situations
- Market, Sell, and Develop Business

READING FOR THE FINAL STRETCH

- *Six Thinking Hats*, by Edward de Bono

SKILL 50

Market, Sell, and Develop Business

Your ability to market and sell in order to attract and retain customers is an important relationship you need to develop. Knowing how to market and sell to current and future customers can be fun and exciting. You need to learn what customers want and need, stay informed about your competition, and know what it means to invest in innovative options for change in the future. You can discover this by connecting directly to your organization's customers or by meeting with your colleagues in sales and marketing. What you can do will depend on the size of your organization. Key to this is to think about customer loyalty. Understand your role in attracting loyalty. Figuring out how to attract and retain loyal customers is not always easy.

It's important because developing new business and keeping your current clients satisfied help your organization stay in business. An inability could cause the organization to stagnate and eventually go out of business. Understanding how to market, sell, and develop new business is critical to every organization.

MASTERING THE SKILL

Hurdles to Overcome

- How aware am I of my limited knowledge of how the business side of our organization works?

- What is the difference between developing business and being a shady salesperson?

- Why can't I just do my job? Isn't it up to sales and marketing to develop new business?

- Why should I listen to customers? All they want to do is complain.

Your Path to Success

- Spend time with potential customers to see their perspective

- Stay on top of the competition and how it affects your organization

- Have an understanding of what it takes for your organization to stay in business

- Invest time to think about innovative ideas and discuss the possibilities

- Create a marketing strategy and plans

- Market and sell your organization's products and services

- Gather information from your organization's front line and salespeople to better understand what they need to sell and market to customers

TIPS FOR PEOPLE IN A HURRY

- **Tied to the bottom line.** Determine how your day-to-day choices affect your organization's bottom line. List five things you do every day that affect the bottom line.

- **Repeat business.** The easiest business sale is repeat business. The second best is word-of-mouth business. If you were the senior leader of your organization, what would you do that would increase repeat and word-of-mouth business?

- **Your competitors.** What are your competitors doing that your organization could do better?

- **Giveaways.** What could your organization give away that would attract attention to your organization—even if the "free" part is temporary. Consider everything—services, products, or both.

PRACTICE SPRINTS

- **Google says.** Before developing business for your organization, learn what others are reading. Use a search engine to learn the perception of your organization. What did you learn? What are the strengths you can start with? What negatives must you overcome? How does this help you understand your organization and how to develop business?

- **What customers desire.** Research shows that customers want several things to happen when they receive service:

  > Respect for their time

  > To be listened to

  > Admission of mistakes

  > Honesty and candor

  > Appreciation

  Identify how these translate into the customer service policy for your organization. Is there room for improvement? Would it help sales? Decide what you need to do about it.

- **Develop new ideas.** You can give your organization an advantage over the competition by having new ideas to sell. Do you know how to identify or develop new ideas? A worksheet at https://ideas .bkconnection.com/skillsforcareersuccess provides some guidance about how to analyze the market, review customer needs, scan the future, and check your own ideas. Review the concepts to determine how you or your team could identify new ideas, services, or products that would grow the business. Be sure to consider how you can connect your brand with today's headlines. Meet with your sales and marketing departments to share your ideas.

- **Ask a customer.** What would your customers do if they were in your position? Get into the buyer mindset. Ask a customer or two, "What would you do?"

- **Study your website.** Review your website from your customers' perspective. Does it say exactly what you do for them? Is the language free of jargon? Do your images paint a picture that a customer would understand? Is your message clear? Now examine the websites of a couple of your competitors. How do they compare? Share what you discover with your supervisor.

- **Make a sales call.** Request to shadow a member of the sales staff for a day. Respect the sales staff in your organization since their results pay your salary. Bring what you learn and new ideas back to your team.

- **Retain loyal customers.** One of the most important aspects of sales and marketing is the relationship with your customers. What determines customer loyalty? What can you do to attract and initiate the relationship? What can you do to maintain the relationship? Figuring out how to attract and retain loyal customers is not easy. Chip Bell (Bell and Patterson 2011), customer service expert, states that five drivers work with most customers, most of the time. Turn to https://ideas.bkconnection.com/skillsforcareersuccess to learn more. Loyal customers feel committed to the organization and connected emotionally. Review Bell's five drivers for earning customer loyalty. Then discuss with your marketing and sales department what they do to build loyal customers. What is your role in developing business for your organization?

- **Read customer satisfaction reports.** Take time to review your organization's customer satisfaction reports for the past three years. What did you discover? What trends do you see? What consistencies do you see about what customers like and what they would like to change about your organization? What is your role in improving your customers' satisfaction?

MARKETING IS NO EASY TASK

Marketing and selling are complex skills. You need to know the right thing to say at the right time and in the right way. Consider the following items. Note your thoughts and then meet with your supervisor to get another perspective.

- Check out the information. You will want to have accurate content and data during important times of marketing or selling.

- Know your stuff. Be sure you are backing the claim up with data. Numbers are always good.

- Be selective in who you deliver the information to. Make certain it is the person who can do the most with it.

- Formulate a succinct message. Use only the most descriptive words, in the most logical sequence, in the shortest format possible.

- Choose the right time. Know what critical issues are in front of the person or group to whom you communicate and select the right time of the day—even the right day of the week is sometimes important.

- Be aware of the emotions in the situation. Even if you are 100 percent right, be prepared for the emotions that may erupt and play out in your mind and how you will respond.

- Getting cold feet? Nervous? Remind yourself that you are doing this for the good of the entire organization.

- **Move to marketing.** Request a rotational assignment in the marketing or sales department or customer service. Once you are there, scan the internal and external environments for ideas, trends, and ways to leapfrog the competition. Explore new concepts before the technology is available. Try to predict what the youngest generation you serve will want five years from now. During your rotation opportunity, ask the most creative person in the department to mentor you.

CROSS TRAINING

You will find related ideas at these crossover skills:

- Sell Ideas
- Exhibit Technology, Analytics, and Data Knowledge
- Attend to Details
- Display Self-Confidence
- Practice Creativity, Innovation, and Appropriate Risk Taking

READING FOR THE FINAL STRETCH

- *Marketing Made Simple: A Step-by-Step Storybrand Guide for Any Business*, by Donald Miller
- *It Starts with Clients: Your 100-Day Plan to Build Lifelong Relationships and Revenue*, by Andrew Sobel

SKILL 51

Exhibit Technology, Analytics, and Data Knowledge

Your knowledge of technology and analytics is more important today than ever. As COVID-19 swept through the world, it also caused extensive changes in the world of business. Technology became a powerful savior. Remote digital teamwork became the norm, not something that was done if necessary. Technology became the default engine for both education and conferences that went virtual during this time period. And most people became experts at using Zoom as they held meetings from home with their colleagues. The world changed in a few short weeks. Technology goes beyond delivering information and getting people together. Your technology requirements are likely to branch into more areas sooner rather than later.

It's important because, at its most basic level, technology ensures you and your organization will be more productive. Digital skills were once a niche skill set but are now a workplace essential. Technology ensures that your organization communicates more effectively, can be more competitive, and delivers computational accuracy. Your recent experience with the technical requirements caused by the COVID-19 pandemic emphasized the importance to move quickly and be ready for whatever happens. Nearly every job relies on different tools, programs, and processes. You will be a more competitive candidate if you have the technology skills that are common in your industry.

MASTERING THE SKILL

Hurdles to Overcome

- How aware am I about what my organization is doing to improve my colleagues' data literacy?

- All those numbers, data, and dashboards . . . it's just too complicated for me. Or am I just making an excuse?

- How clear am I about the meaning of big data and other terminology and what it means to my organization?

- How can I be helpful when I am falling behind in understanding AI, AR, VR, and all the rest of the alphabet soup that creates today's technology world?

Your Path to Success

- Help your organization use predictive analytics to forecast the future

- Practice creative thinking

- Gain experience with business analytics

- Determine how your organization can use artificial intelligence (AI), augmented reality (AR), and virtual reality (VR)

- Depend on the 5 Vs of big data: volume, velocity, variety, veracity, and value

- Perceive the value of digital marketing and how it develops business for your organization

- Value data integrity

- Understand visualization principles and use data visualization to tell a story

- Be knowledgeable of the analytic spectrum: descriptive, diagnostic, predictive, and prescriptive data

- Have knowledge of data security issues such as detecting, deterring, and mitigating threats

- Understand how to gather, organize, analyze, and interpret data

- Make it a priority to stay informed and be on the cutting edge of technology

TIPS FOR PEOPLE IN A HURRY

- **Acronym clarity.** Go online and read articles about AI, AR, and VR. Think of how your department might use one of these technologies.

- **Your data.** Think about how you use data daily. How do you use it to make decisions? Are you asking the right questions?

- **Skepticism is good.** Your leaders depend on the accuracy of data. When presented with data, challenge what you see. Dig into the numbers, the sources, and the relationships to look for information and additional data to confirm or disprove the initial report.

- **Robot boss.** In October 2017 Saudi Arabia granted citizenship to Sophia, a humanoid robot developed by Hanson Robotics, making it the world's first robot citizen. Imagine you have a robot for a boss. What's good about it? What's not?

PRACTICE SPRINTS

- **Be an observer.** Observe the changing business environment outside of your work. Think about the new products you purchase. What are your friends and family discussing and buying? What changes do you see in advertising on television and online? What digital options exist today that weren't available two years ago? What are the implications for your job and future evolutionary changes that may be required?

- **Use new technology.** How is your company using new technology? What are you doing with VR or AR? What should you be doing? How can you leapfrog other organizations? Since 2017 a Wisconsin company has been offering to implant a tiny radio-frequency chip in the hands of its employees, between the thumb and the forefinger. Although Sweden is the focal point of this technology, Three Square Market is the first U.S. company whose employees use the device (which is the size of a grain of rice) to check in for work, open doors, charge company food purchases, log in to computers, and so forth. The chip acts as a barcode for the employee's body. It does not have GPS capabilities, but it raises other ethical issues. As you consider new technology for your company, what ethical issues will need to be addressed?

- **Visit your experts.** Identify your organization's experts. Visit them, share what you know, and ask them what you want to know. Then ask for advice about where and how you can learn more.

- **Display the data.** Be sure to consider how to present your data in a way that best displays what you want to communicate. Choose your graph carefully. Just because a pie chart is the first choice on Excel does not mean that it is the best. Consider these options:

  1. Composition of the entire data set: pie charts, stacked bar charts

  2. Distribution of one variable: columns, scatter charts, bar charts

  3. Relationships on two scales: bubble charts, scatter charts

  4. Comparisons: bar charts, timelines, line charts, scatter charts

  5. Distribution of multiple variables: heat maps, bubble charts

  6. Connections and relationships: Venn diagrams, connection maps, heat maps

- **Stay up to date.** Unlike other skills you may have gained, your technical skills will change rapidly. To stay current, refresh your skills with continuing courses offered by your organization, actively use your skills as often as possible, and volunteer for design or implementation projects.

STRATEGIES FOR THE LONG RUN

- **Become data literate.** Data literacy means that you have data, domain, and business expertise as well as a technical understanding of the data. Technical literacy means that you understand the tools and technology. Analyst literacy means that you understand the analytical techniques and can tell a story with the data. If you need some basic definitions, get a copy of *A Non-Geek's A-to-Z Guide to the Internet of Things*, by Tamara Dull. You can download it for free at https://www.sas.com/content/dam/SAS/en_us/doc/whitepaper1 /non-geek-a-to-z-guide-to-internet-of-things-108846.pdf. It contains 38 pages of easy-to-understand definitions that will put you on the track to data literacy.

- **Ask for training.** Learn on the job and be proactive by asking your supervisor to enroll you in as many technology courses as are important to learn for your department. In exchange, offer to coach others in your department about what you learn.

- **Establish an expert team.** If you ever needed a network, technology is the subject and now is the time. Bring together a team of technology experts depending on your organization's needs. You may want to start by scheduling one-on-one meetings with each expert for a tech talk to determine what they are doing to build a data-driven workforce. Ask about the existence of a road map to achieve the organization's data goals and what the organization is doing to close the data literacy skills gap. Also ask if they would be willing to form a small team to increase awareness throughout your organization.

CROSS TRAINING

You will find related ideas at these crossover skills:

- Network with Others
- Practice Creativity, Innovation, and Appropriate Risk Taking
- Manage Projects
- Market, Sell, and Develop Business
- Practice Systems Thinking

READING FOR THE FINAL STRETCH

- *Data Story: Explain Data and Inspire Action through Story*, by Nancy Duarte
- *Big Data for Beginners: Understanding SMART Big Data, Data Mining & Data Analytics for Improved Business Performance*, by Vince Reynolds
- *Life after Google*, by George Gilder
- *The Visual Miscellaneum*, by David McCandless

PART THREE

CROSSING THE FINISH LINE

Build Character

How important is character? Character can be a catchall word that describes your traits and behaviors. It may also carry a judgmental decision, as in "you have character" alludes to a belief that you are honorable, credible, reliable, and honest. Your character is important because it creates your reputation and how people deal with you. Good character helps you gain respect, build relationships, and get the job that you want.

Steve Stephenson, owner of Applied Mechanical Resources in Virginia Beach, has owned his HVAC company for 20 years. Like many companies, he faced difficulties during the COVID-19 pandemic, but one thing he was not concerned about was whether his employees would provide the excellent service his company is known for. Why? Steve hires for character.

Steve defines character as starting with honesty: "You've got to have honesty first; it's number one." He also looks for integrity, compassion, humility, and initiative. How does Steve hire for character? He says during the multiple interviews, as many as seven or more, he has with candidates, he asks the usual questions, but also asks about their family life and what they like to do with their free time. This gives him an idea about whether they are team players, whether they are willing to jump in and do what is needed to get a job done, and how they support and care about others. During their conversations, Steve observes their eye contact, whether they are smiling, and whether they make the effort to choose appropriate words.

How does hiring for character pay off for Steve? He says he has a great team. They model integrity, with high values and standards that match the corporate values of supporting each other and providing good service to the customer. They demonstrate humility through their willingness to learn, to admit to their errors, and to come to work whenever they are needed, after all HVAC systems break down on Sundays and at night. Steve says they check their ego at the door. They show initiative by never asking about hours, offering to work weekends, and being eager to learn all they can. They show compassion by caring about each other and by showing empathy toward customers and ducks. Ducks? Yes. The day that I interviewed Steve, several members of his team were working on an AC unit at a shipyard. There was a mallard sitting on a nest of eggs that was quite upset about their proximity to her. They had just called Steve to ask what they could do, and the team decided to put up a temporary plywood barricade so that they would not disturb mama duck. That's a demonstration of compassion.

And of course they are honest in all that they do. How important is character? It can mean the difference between getting the job you really want and settling for something less.

This chapter is different from those in Part Two. Each of those chapters focused on a group of skills, and each skill was accompanied by suggestions for how you could learn and practice the skill. I'm not sure that anyone can "teach" you how to build your character. You have arrived where you are today, and the character you present is what you have built based on your family, education, and the choices you made throughout your life.

Character isn't something you are born with. You develop it along life's way. You can change your character, but it must be an intentional focus on qualities and traits that you must nurture within yourself. We are all a product of our thoughts, behaviors, and habits. Your character is built over time. Every decision you make every day will either enhance or detract from your character. How would you rate your character score at the end of each day?

WHAT IS YOUR CHARACTER?

This chapter focuses on the character traits that most organizations value in their employees. What is valued most is different from organization to organization. Are you thinking that character is the same as personality? Although character and personality may be related, they are distinct. Generally, your personality traits can be observed by others; character traits are not immediately obvious to others. Personality traits such as being assertive or happy are readily on view; character traits such as honesty or authenticity may take time to experience. Usually your personality includes surface-level traits, and your character encompasses subsurface, inner traits that you develop over time.

According to leadership guru John Maxwell (2010), character means that you have aligned your moral compass in all areas of your life. Your character is built on the choices you make. Character is your ability to make choices that create the person you want to be. Your character projects your deep-seated beliefs that you have developed over time.

Your character traits can be considered the principles that guide your life and arise from your core values. The words we use to identify values, character traits, and personality qualities often cross over. And sometimes you might see character traits that can be taught, such as self-confidence, goal focused, listening, self-awareness, productive, collaborative, organized, and resilient. These have been identified as skills in this book.

You will read many articles and opinions about character traits, and each will present a slightly different perspective. Organizations differ in what character traits they value. However, the one thing that is consistent is that only you can define and build your character. A person with good character chooses to do the right thing because it is the right thing from their perspective. You need to know which character traits are most valued by your organization and whether this is in alignment with what is most important to you. This chapter's focus is on building character that most companies would like their employees to display through their thoughts, words, and actions.

WHY YOUR CHARACTER IS IMPORTANT

Character is important to your career advancement. You are hired for a job based on your talents—the skills and knowledge you have acquired—as well as the potential your future employer believes you have. You also arrive with the character that you have been forming all your life. Your talent might get you hired, but your character will ensure you keep your job. In fact, John Maxwell believes that lack of character is the greatest threat to your job.

The key choices you make during your employment will set you apart from your colleagues—either positively or negatively. And most of those choices will be based on character traits, not necessarily the skills you employ. What do your choices say about your character when you choose these:

- Avoid delivering constructive feedback rather than exhibit the courage it requires to tell individuals how they could be better?

- Take shortcuts rather than conscientiously demonstrate credibility by following the process?

- Cover up an error rather than admit a mistake and establish integrity?

- Continue to do what you've always done instead of being flexible and trying something innovative?

Besides your own job security and career advancement, character is important to your employer. Good character sets the example for new employees that are hired. It builds self-respect and confidence among the workforce. Treating everyone with respect and compassion builds engagement among the workforce. Trust and authenticity in the workplace create a positive work environment with high morale. An organization known for its good character will earn a reputation within the community that the organization chooses to do the right thing. It will be recognized as a good place to work.

EXPLORING CHARACTER

Even though building character can be difficult to comprehend, the concept needs to be practical so that you can determine your own development plan. This chapter will not "teach" character, but it will do other things that will be more useful to you:

- Introduce and define the top 11 character traits that most organizations desire in their employees

- Describe what actions support and create those traits
- Present a process necessary to build character
- Help you examine your current character and determine your preferred character
- Offer ideas for how you can create your preferred character
- Provide guidance for ensuring your preferred character stays on track

Because character is different from the 51 skills we discussed in Part Two, this chapter has been designed differently. It will address character from the perspective of developing character traits, which are harder to define in a SMART objective than are skills. Defining a character trait is about what's inside that makes you who you are and isn't always specific or measurable. And it certainly isn't time-bound, given that many character traits are attributed to you by others. Character needs to be lived. We can define what character looks like. We can clarify what someone with a particular character trait might do. And we can describe what effect character has on others. Changing your character, however, is something only you can do.

TOP 11 TRAITS

Organizations throughout the world list over 100 character traits. It can be difficult to narrow them down to a practical working list. Which are the most important? Some traits relate to each other, and some may be subsumed by broader traits. Let's define the 11 character traits that most organizations desire in their employees. You will also find actions that support and deter the creation of each trait.

Since organizations differ, the character traits are presented in alphabetical order to avoid any hierarchical assumptions. Each trait is defined by how you demonstrate it in the first column and what you do that detracts from the trait in the second column.

Authenticity defines those who understand and accept themselves and others. You are vulnerable, transparent, and genuine, and you learn from your mistakes. Authenticity means that you understand what motivates you and can express your emotions clearly. You are able to be your true self.

ENHANCES AUTHENTICITY	DETRACTS FROM AUTHENTICITY
• Have an accurate perception of reality • Display a genuine and open persona • Send transparent messages • Think before you act	• Judge others • Are unable to accept or learn from mistakes • Are self-deceptive • Display egotistical behavior and brag

Compassion represents those who are personable, sincere, kind, generous, patient, tolerant, nonjudgmental, considerate, forgiving, and fair. Compassion means you show empathy, express gratitude to others, treat others with dignity, reject stereotypical thoughts, and accept mistakes.

ENHANCES COMPASSION	DETRACTS FROM COMPASSION
• Tolerate differences and errors • Are sensitive to others' feelings • Take a peaceful approach to anger and insults	• Lack awareness of impact on others • Exhibit a derogatory sense of humor • Are critical of and impatient with others

Courage describes those who act decisively to address difficult problems and persevere through them. Hemingway called courage "grace under pressure." Courage also encompasses tenacity, fortitude, endurance, determination, and in some cases willpower.

ENHANCES COURAGE	DETRACTS FROM COURAGE
• Take the lead on unpopular but proper actions • Confront conflicts promptly • Maintain determination • Carry on in spite of fear or danger	• Avoid conflict • Are fearful about trying new actions • Give up at the first sign of difficulty • Choose the path of least resistance • Feel powerless

Credibility is bestowed on you by others. You can't claim you are a knowledgeable, credible source. It must be earned. In that light it encompasses your actions, such as following through, meeting deadlines, being conscientious, admitting your mistakes, and using ethical and principled considerations to guide your decisions.

ENHANCES CREDIBILITY	DETRACTS FROM CREDIBILITY
• Follow through on promises • Meet timelines and deliver quality • Admit your mistakes • Continue learning to be competent • Model ethical behavior	• Focus on personal interests first • Produce questionable results • Break promises and makes excuses • Take credit for others' work

Flexibility means that you are willing to try different things. It includes a willingness to suspend your own agenda, regroup, and try new approaches. You are able to change your stance and get into others' comfort zones. You are resilient, tolerant, accepting, and open to change.

ENHANCES FLEXIBILITY	DETRACTS FROM FLEXIBILITY
• Adapt to others' needs • Listen to others' ideas • Allow things to flow naturally	• Are stubborn, rigid, and selfish • Take a firm stand and resist change • Quickly disagree with new ideas

Humility describes one who is respectful of others and has a modest self-opinion. You can easily empathize with others and are willing to accept advice from anyone and assist everyone. You listen carefully without judging, graciously accept credit, and willingly extend credit to others.

ENHANCES HUMILITY	DETRACTS FROM HUMILITY
• Treat others with respect • Are willing to say "I don't know" and learn • Express gratitude • Bestow credit on others • Are genuinely happy about others' success	• See self as too good for others • Think you deserve more • Take credit for more than you merit • Display a know-it-all attitude • Lack respect for those of lower stature • Are arrogant, boisterous, and conceited

Initiative is a trait that combines several positive characteristics, including doing what needs to be done without being told, doing the right thing without asking for permission, demonstrating the ability to think and take action when necessary, and making improvements because it is the right thing to do. Initiative demonstrates a sense of self-drive and is a game-changing habit for advancing your career. It is one of the top character traits employers look for in new hires.

ENHANCES INITIATIVE	DETRACTS FROM INITIATIVE
• Exhibit a drive to achieve	• Wait to be told what to do
• Improve things without direction	• Do not think or plan ahead
• Lead the way to complete projects	• Ignore needs of others
• Do the right thing without hesitation	• Take the easy route
• Trust your instinct	• Complain but are risk averse
• Follow through to completion	• Keep a low profile

Integrity is a trait built on moral principles and is generally attributed to you by others. It encompasses a number of subcategories. Integrity means that you have a consistently strong alignment between knowing and doing what's right. Integrity includes being honest, ethical, loyal, reliable, and responsible.

ENHANCES INTEGRITY	DETRACTS FROM INTEGRITY
• Achieve results on time	• Tell white lies
• Exhibit truthfulness and candor	• Cover up problems
• Model organizational values	• Are self-promoting and deceitful
• Take responsibility for actions	• Break established norms
• Don't bend the rules or push the limits	• Don't maintain confidentiality

Optimism means that you choose a positive attitude and enthusiasm. You are pleasant to be around and have a sense of hopefulness and confidence about the future. You encourage others to do the same through modeling.

ENHANCES OPTIMISM	DETRACTS FROM OPTIMISM
• Have high energy	• Communicate negatively
• Are goal oriented	• Complain
• See the good in everything	• Look for the worst in everything
• Encourage others	• Criticize, whine, and nitpick

Passion is having an intense desire to advance and sponsor a belief or cause. Passion is accompanied by energy, tenacity, perseverance, and persistence. Passionate people demonstrate self-discipline to stay with a goal or desired achievement, have zeal to accomplish goals, and keep moving forward.

ENHANCES PASSION	DETRACTS FROM PASSION
• Are ambitious	• Lack enthusiasm
• Are motivated to advance your career	• Are unmotivated, lazy
• Have strong initiative	• Are self-centered
• Endure in the face of adversity	• Take the easiest route

Trustworthiness is the ability to be trusted and trust others. It means that you are open, dependable, accountable, reliable, accepting, and honest in your communications and actions. Trustworthiness also means being thorough. It means that you do not steal from your employer—either physical supplies or time when you are supposed to be working.

ENHANCES TRUSTWORTHINESS	DETRACTS FROM TRUSTWORTHINESS
• Value openness and trust	• Create excuses; cheat
• Do what you say you will	• Miss deadlines; are unreliable
• Mean what you say	• Lack caring for others
• Live the truth	• Appear afraid of life

BUILDING YOUR PREFERRED CHARACTER

But how do you build character? You must start by knowing what you value. In earlier chapters you were encouraged to identify your personal core values on a worksheet at https://ideas.bkconnection.com/skillsforcareer-success. If you haven't already done so, it would be helpful to do so now. Your values form the foundation of your character. Based on your values, you must do the right things—the walk-the-talk mantra.

You will not perfect your character. It is unlikely that character is something that can be attained to 100 percent perfection. There is also the issue of balance. For example, is it possible to be too optimistic? Too humble? Too flexible? The answer is yes. You can take a character trait too far. All of us have work to do to improve our character. If you think you don't, you probably need to seek advice and insight from those around you.

A process. Building character is hard work. This five-step process is a way for you to start building your character. Notice that you need to tap into several of the character traits discussed to be successful with your plan.

1. **Recognize you have a need.** Perhaps you are struggling with and admitting you need to make a change. You need to take responsibility for your problems. To address this first step you need to have a healthy dose of two of the character traits we discussed: **humility** and **initiative**.

   > Think back to feedback you've received. What constructive feedback is related to your character?

   > What positive feedback is related to your character?

2. **Examine your current character.** You can start by reexamining your guiding principles and core values. How well are you living up to the values that you espoused. Decision making, goal setting, organizing, and planning are all easier when you live a life based on your values. Your values are the foundation of your character. Practice one of the character traits during this step: **authenticity**.

   > Use the worksheet at https://ideas.bkconnection.com/skillsfor careersuccess to clarify your core values.

   > Reflect on your core values. How well are you living up to them?

3. **Define your preferred character.** Select the character traits that you want to define you: your preferred character. You will need to be honest with yourself. Can you reliably and honestly select those that you want to define you, even though you know you need to make improvements? Selecting your preferred character traits requires **integrity**.

   > Review the core values you chose. How do they align with your preferred character?

   > Your company may have guiding principles or a selection of character traits that it wants to emphasize. If they align with your preferred character, do you want to include them in your defined character?

4. **Consciously decide to live the character you choose.** Live with a clear identity of who you are. Building your character won't just happen. You must be disciplined. Create intentional habits and internalize your intentions. You need to confront your fears and acknowledge that it will not be easy. Building character is hard work. Facing your weaknesses requires another trait from the list: **courage**.

   > Identify ways that you can stay focused on your preferred character traits. For example, select one character trait to focus on for a week. What did you learn about yourself?

   > Write down a trait and list the actions you can take that demonstrate it.

   > Wear a rubber band on your wrist to remind you of your commitment.

5. **Hold yourself accountable for the change you desire.** This will require self-reflection along the way. As you make choices, both good and bad, you'll want to reflect on why you made the choices you did. An accountability partner can help you through the difficult changes. You need to have willpower, tenacity, perseverance, and persistence to stick to the changes you desire. You will be practicing another character trait from the list: **passion**.

   > Keep an accountability journal to review your successes and those things you wish you'd done differently.

> Observe everything you are practicing; character is built on large defining moments in your life, as well as the minutiae you must address every day. What are both the large and the small things you are doing to build your character?

> Constantly push yourself by enlarging your goals to be more challenging.

You can't discount the effect poor judgment may have on your character. When you do things that detract from your character, it may take immeasurable effort to build it up again. It just isn't worth that one slip of the tongue, the poorly timed eye roll, or an angry email. Every choice you make either builds or tears down your character. Every day should be a character-building day by making the best choices possible.

PRACTICE SPRINTS

Prepare for your preferred character with a few practice sprints. Perhaps you were one of the lucky few who were raised in a family and attended a school where everyone modeled good character. If so, you have a head start. If not, there is no time like the present to get started.

Although these are not skill-building activities as printed in the rest of the book, they can provide inspiration and get you started. As you peruse the practice sprints, consider this guidance throughout:

- Create a habit to make every day better than the day before.
- Choose your colleagues wisely; they can be a strong influence on you and help you stay on track.
- Work on yourself as hard as you work at your job. You may be surprised at how improving aspects of your character will improve your enjoyment of your work, as well as your results.
- Give, give, give. Nurture relationships that are meaningful to you. You will get back more than you give.
- Do the right thing even when it seems as though the world is conspiring against you.
- Don't give up.

Building character is personal. Therefore, you will find that your supervisor, manager, coach, or mentor is required for very few of these practice sprints. That is not to say that you shouldn't involve them. You certainly can if you desire. Most of these sprints have been created so that you can try new things and reflect on what you experienced and learned.

Authenticity

Your ability to understand and accept yourself, demonstrate transparency and vulnerability, and be your true self.

- **Practice being you.** We all spend time creating an image of what we think we're supposed to be. But what if you were just you? Begin by appreciating who you are. Think about the character you now possess—not what you do and not what you desire. Who are you? Are you kind to the garbage collector, caring toward your grandmother, helpful to your neighbor? What do you appreciate about you? We all have experience of playing the role that we think others expect of us. Allow yourself to be vulnerable. Try to erase that role and take time to be aware of how you feel and what you are thinking. There is no right or wrong in this exercise. Just show up and be and pay attention to what that means. What do you appreciate about you that you can practice today—all day?

- **Stay true to you.** Once you've identified your authentic self, what you believe, and how you want to be, review any discrepancies that may exist. Determine opportunities when you can practice authenticity. For example, pause and be certain that each decision you make is the best and that you are not being swayed by internal or external pressures. Also, be honest in every conversation, even when it doesn't matter very much. A white lie to make someone feel good probably won't hurt, but it does send a message to your subconscious that dishonesty is acceptable. You need to decide. It may be better to say nothing. Speaking the truth demonstrates that you are responsible for your own beliefs. Staying true to you requires that you listen to your intuition and that you constantly strive to be better. Author and researcher Brené Brown (2010, 50) says that "authenticity is the daily practice of letting go of who we think we are supposed to be and embracing who we actually are." Developing authenticity takes time.

Compassion

Your desire to treat others with dignity and to express empathy, sincere gratitude, and tolerance.

- **Self-coaching for compassion.** We all want to be compassionate and sensitive. But it doesn't just happen. Become your own coach. On the left side of a piece of paper write down all the things that you do that you believe display compassion. On the right side write down all the things that you do that get in the way of displaying compassion. Review your results. How can you move more things out of the right-hand column? Are there additional things that should go in the left column? Try some of your suggestions and revisit this page in two weeks to reassess. How are you doing?

- **Compassion intention.** Establish a Compassion Intention Day. Determine the date that you will focus on finding opportunities to say thank you and to help others who need you. For example, when you receive a snarky email from a colleague, tell yourself that you recognize that this person has pressures that you may not know about. Determine how you can show compassion to the driver that cuts you off in traffic, to the barista that makes an error on your coffee, to the person who shoves in front of you in line, or how you react when your spouse snaps at you. Each of these people may have had a terrible day that you know nothing about. Spend the day focused on others, not yourself. Tell yourself that, just like you, the other person is seeking happiness and fulfillment in life. What can you do to add happiness to others' lives? Perhaps just a smile is required. You can do that. Smiles are free. Reconcile your experience at the end of the day. Who can you discuss your day with to explore your compassion intentions?

Courage

Your ability to act decisively to face agony, intimidation, or danger.

- **Until courage is a habit.** A lack of courage based on fear can cost you when it interferes with your sleep or digestion or even a relationship when you didn't stand by someone you knew was right but in a perilous situation. A lack of courage can cost you in how you come across to others as well as your own self-perception. How can you practice courage? Try these three steps to be more courageous.

First, notice your body reactions every time you are facing fear; say, "Oh, yeah! I knew that would happen" and produce a remedy. For example, if speaking unnerves you and your throat dries out, say, "Ah, just what I expected," and take a swallow of water. If facing your boss's anger unhinges you, recognize the whoosh in your brain and force it out so you can listen better. Choose the discomfort of the fear over the disillusionment you'll feel later for not having the courage to go forward.

Second, identify why your lack of courage is unfounded or senseless, and how it is wasting your time and costing your health. Write these down.

Third, once you are ready, do not hesitate. Just do it. Remind yourself of what you've written in step two. Also add how great it will feel once the first step is taken. For example, I have a fear of water, and once I've gotten to this point I begin a swim by jumping in the deep end first. I've done this for years and the rest of my time in a pool is glorious because I face the fear and remove it first. Add supporting mechanisms along the way. You can find role models, identify others who will support you, or identify a "security blanket" such as a charm or a favorite saying. Practice steps one through three the next time you know you will be called on to be courageous.

- **A week of courage.** Decide on a week to practice courage. Day one: identify what it means to you to be more courageous. What does having courage mean to you? Day two: determine in what instances you want to have more courage and why you want to be more courageous. Day three: create a list of all the reasons you have *not* to be more courageous. Determine how the positive reasons to change can be strengthened and how the negative reasons can be weakened. Day four: act on all the times you want to be more courageous—disagreeing with a bigot, speaking up in a meeting, giving difficult feedback to your boss, supporting an unpopular but good idea, asserting yourself during a conflict, or any of the other reasons you know that being courageous is the right thing to do to build your character. Day five: check in with yourself. How'd you do? What did you learn about your courage? What do you need to continue doing? Stop doing? Increase doing? Repeat day four, five more times. Check in with yourself on day ten. What did you learn about yourself and courage as a result of this exercise?

Credibility

Bestowed on you by others and earned by being knowledgeable, conscientious, and principled.

- **Build competence and accountability.** Credibility has two parts. First, that you are competent and that people turn to you for answers. Second, that you are accountable and that people know they can depend on you for the best answers in a timely manner. Decide how you can build both of these elements separately. Find a coworker with whom you can discuss competence and accountability. Both of you should want to build your credibility.

  Competence: Work together to determine how you can expand your competence. Certainly taking classes might come to mind first. Also consider reading your industry's journals, shadowing someone in a related department for a day, attending conferences, doing a job swap, learning more about your organization's needs and problems, studying your organization's competition, volunteering for difficult tasks, or taking on a challenge.

  Accountability: Create a list of all the things you and your coworker should and should not do that demonstrate accountability. For example, the things you should not do might include blaming others, blindsiding employees, or trying to cover up something. The things you should do include keeping everyone informed, telling the truth, taking personal responsibility, admitting mistakes immediately, and moving on. You might think that taking ownership of mistakes would decrease your credibility. It doesn't. In fact, just the opposite occurs. You gain credibility. Commit to your coworker a step you will take next week to increase your competence and accountability.

- **Expand your credibility.** Build your credibility by creating and sharing ideas. Where do your ideas come from? Start by identifying thought leaders in your industry who could be your role models. Then, continue to learn all you can about your organization and industry. Solve problems. You don't need to have all the solutions, but you can build credibility by convening others to address issues and identify solutions. Then write about what you learn in a company newsletter. You could also start a blog for your organization or to share with others on the internet. Start by identifying a dozen key topics you could write about. Create several short 500- to 800-word articles with just three short points. Obtain feedback from others and then publish the articles.

Flexibility

Your ability to be an agile thinker and doer.

- **Challenge your cognitive flexibility.** The environment changes rapidly every day, so it is critical that you develop your ability to be agile and flexible. Practice your flexibility in three ways: personally, with other people, and on the job. First, you can begin by simply changing your daily routine: take a different route to work, eat lunch at a different time, exercise in a different way or location, use a map instead of GPS, eat at a restaurant you've never tried, or sit in a different location for dinner. Second, work closely with someone on your team who thinks very differently than you. Perhaps they are very analytical and detail oriented, whereas you are a creative, big-picture thinker. Think about where you differ, but more importantly identify ways that you can move into the other person's comfort zone, such as slowing down your speech if you speak faster or making more or less eye contact to match the other person's eye contact. Author Anaïs Nin said, "We don't see things as they are; we see them as we are." This is the challenge of practicing flexibility— to be able to see things as they are as well as how others see them. Third, practice flexibility on the job. Identify a task that you do and look at it from a different perspective. How many different ways could you do it? What if you did it backward? What if you removed or combined some of the steps? What if you shared part of it with someone else? Are you getting anxious just thinking about doing it differently? That says a lot. Challenge your views and habits. Perhaps take a creativity class or read a creativity book to help you see that there is more than one way to do anything.

- **Find the gray.** Black-and-white thinking is good in many ways, but when your organization needs to solve a sticky problem, needs an innovative idea to surpass the competition, or needs to find a way to negotiate with a challenger, you need to find creative solutions that are neither black nor white. Think of someone whose beliefs or values you do not agree with. Why might they think that way? What is it that they value that you don't? If you are flexible enough to understand their viewpoint and admit that they have a plausible rationale, it will be easier for you to adapt to thinking differently, easier to communicate with others, easier to resolve problems, and easier to identify innovative solutions. Question your own thoughts and messages. Don't be tenaciously locked into one perspective. Study your thoughts. Do they really serve the character you are trying to build? What's the gray between your perspective and another's? What thoughts and words will show your flexible side? Character building is all about choosing. Flexibility is a key area of choice.

Humility

Your ability to empathize with others, accept advice from anyone, and accept credit graciously.

- **Practice humility.** Think back over the past week. Were there opportunities when you could have practiced humility but did not? Did you try to one-up someone? Did you pass up an opportunity to thank someone? Did you avoid accepting responsibility for a mistake or problem? Did you avoid providing help to someone who needed it? Did you forget to give someone credit? Did you "tell" instead of "ask"? Did you practice honesty in what you said and left unsaid? Did you find something to be grateful for this week? Will these situations present themselves again? If yes, write them on a list or in your scheduler to remind yourself to be grateful; the opportunity will be available again and you will receive a second chance.

- **Practice here-and-now humility.** Author and organization development guru Edgar Schein (2013) identifies three types of humility. One is the humility you feel around elders and dignitaries. The second is the humility you feel in the presence of those who awe you with their achievements. The third is the here-and-now humility. Although rarely observed in business, it is the most relevant for you if you want to achieve great things. It challenges the typical power play as it models that "my status is inferior to yours at this moment because you know something or can do something that I need in order to accomplish some task or goal. I must be humble because I am temporarily dependent on you." It is your ability to make everyone feel psychologically safe to contribute ideas, to disagree, and to be a part of the solution. What does humility mean to you? How do you practice humility? What can you do to expand your practice of humility?

Initiative

Your ability to do what's right without being told.

- **Skill or will?** Initiative is extremely hard to explain and extremely important to your career advancement. It is difficult to explain to someone else because so many things are bundled together. It is extremely important to your career, because without it you are not likely to go anywhere! It isn't a skill, but helps to define other skills. It is a part of your professional image, and at the same time it helps your organization achieve its goals. Initiative is important at home and at work. It is seeing something that needs to be done and doing it. Initiative doesn't always have to be a physical task. You might take initiative to ask a difficult question at the right time or offer to help someone else or ensure that you provide status updates before they are due. Create a list of 10 ways you could show more initiative at work. Create a second list of 10 ways you could show more initiative at home. If you have difficulty identifying 20 items, ask your boss and your spouse. I am sure both would be happy to help you.

- **What do they avoid?** You know those things around the house and the office that everyone avoids? They are tasks that aren't fun, are often repetitious, may be dirty, and usually result in not learning anything new or challenging. For example, at home it might be straightening up the hall closet or ordering the junk drawer. At work it might include scanning, shredding, filing, cleaning up data, or merging duplicates. Heck, even cleaning the refrigerator or the microwave in the breakroom would be appreciated! Pick one of these to show initiative that everyone else will value. Don't tell anyone of your intentions; just start doing it. Reflect on what happened. Why did you select the task you did? How did you feel about starting the task? How did you feel while you were in the midst of the task? Did your feelings change as you reached a difficult part or because it took longer than you anticipated? What happened after you finished? How did people respond? What did you learn about initiative from this exercise?

Integrity

Your ability to demonstrate consistent and uncompromising observance of moral principles and ethical values.

- **Whose truth in quotes?** Honesty and integrity are givens. Or are they? Spencer Johnson, physician and author of *Who Moved My Cheese?*, said, "Integrity is telling myself the truth, and honesty is telling the truth to other people." How do you rate yourself on each: honesty and integrity? Your rating isn't for sharing. It is for contemplating, though. What are you doing to yourself when you aren't honest with others or with yourself—even if you are the only person who knows? What do you wish you did differently? Tom Peters, management guru, stated, "There is no such thing as a minor lapse in integrity." Is Tom being too harsh? What are your thoughts about this quote? What do you need to do to make integrity your personal mantra? List at least five things now and add one each day this week. You will have a dozen reminders by the end of the week.

- **Change your image.** If you are working on the character trait of integrity, you will need to do some serious soul-searching. What do you do that suggests you do not always act with the highest levels of integrity? You might say that it is just others' perceptions. However, perceptions are their reality. You can't rate your integrity as "somewhat." Integrity is like truth and pregnancy: You can't be somewhat truthful. You can't be somewhat pregnant. Either you are or you aren't. So let's go back to your soul-searching. List all the reasons people may believe you do not model integrity. You probably know what they are. It can be scary to put them on a piece of paper. Remember, this activity is for you to do alone. Are you overly ambitious? Do you hold back the entire truth? Do you treat people differently, perhaps playing favorites? Do you blame others when something goes wrong? Do you take all the glory? Do you share information that was intended to be kept confidential? Well…you get the idea. After you have completed your list, you have a decision to make. What are you going to do about it? Write those things down too. Now you have an action plan. Implement it.

Optimism

Your choice of positive over negative, enthusiasm over boredom, success over failure.

- **A glass half full.** If you have trouble seeing the glass as half full, you could be losing out. It seems that most successful people are optimistic. Positive thinking increases your self-confidence, encourages others to support you, and even improves your appearance. Without optimism, your life may remain stuck in the same place. Boost your optimism by practicing affirmations, getting over the past, being thankful, finding something pleasant to do every day, remembering your accomplishments, focusing on the small things, giving others hope, being generous, practicing an encouraging attitude, noticing what's going well, choosing positive colleagues and friends, and finding the good in whatever happens. Take this list of general things you can do and identify at least one specific step you can take to fill up that glass. For example, you could create an affirmation that you say daily or create a new one each day and write them in a notebook. For getting over the past, look at who you might hold a grudge against and forgive them—if not in person, then at least in your mind. Each weekend create a new list of ways you will practice optimism the following week and fill up your glass.

- **Morning to night.** Looking at a long list of things to do to improve can be overwhelming. So this practice idea takes a different perspective. It suggests that you practice optimism all day long! Yes! Practice optimism from the time you awake until you go to sleep. Sure. You can do it. Begin each morning by reviewing your plans for the day. Positively see the exciting things you will accomplish. Delight in your first human interaction, first cup of coffee, and the opportunity to go to work. During the day show interest in others, hang around optimistic people, practice forgiveness, and smile—often. A University of Kansas study found that smiling, even if you don't feel like it, reduces your stress (Kraft and Pressman 2012). In addition, smiling draws people in and you are likely brightening their day too. Near the end of your day, note all that you experienced, learned, and improved. Celebrate your accomplishments. Before you go to sleep, review all the things that you completed and enjoyed, and that went well for you. Your subconscious will grab these events and influence your thoughts as you sleep. It's a full day of optimism, but what better way to build a habit?

Passion

Your desire to invest energy and action in what you believe.

- **Find your passion.** Being passionate provides you with energy and power because you are working on something that excites you. How can you find it? Think about what you loved doing as a child. Did you sell to your neighborhood, perform in plays, read? What do you enjoy doing now? Do you like to meet new people, bake, exercise? What part of your job do you love doing—organizing events, working in teams, supporting the mission, making customers happy, mentoring others, researching a project? What are you doing when you lose track of time—writing, working on a particular project, volunteering? What would you do if money wasn't an issue? Once you have a list, identify several items and develop your passion around them. For example, if baking is your passion, don't open a bakery yet; instead, bake for your neighborhood and experiment with new creations. If writing is your passion, don't start with a book; instead, ask for more writing tasks at work or start a blog. If you love to organize, ask your boss for more project-type work. Give your passion time and let it evolve, then set goals. Do you want your passion to lead to a different role at work? If your passion is your hobby and you keep it as such, the passion for your hobby will overflow to the job, adding passion throughout your life. At some point you should reevaluate your progress and what you plan to do. If you can't decide, it may be time to hire a coach to help you work through the decision process.

- **Passion needs your involvement.** Being passionate about anything means that it is meaningful to you and it raises your enthusiasm to a higher level. It doesn't mean that it will just appear. Sometimes you need to work harder than other times to maintain the passion. It means that you are willing to take initiative and be a self-starter because you believe in what you are doing. To be passionate you need to make it a priority. Writing goals that support what you are doing can serve as a reminder to move forward and to track your progress. Don't wait for something to happen. Create it. Your passion is internal, so if you aren't feeling it, look for what would ignite it. Skills that support your passion include resilience, self-discipline, planning, goal setting, results orientation, collaborating with others, and attending to details. Examine these skills and the ideas throughout this book. What do you need to improve that will increase your passion? It's also possible that your passion for this particular cause has waned. If so, consider what you need to do. It is also possible that passion isn't a character trait that you require. If that's the case, review the character traits you chose.

Trustworthiness

Your ability to be trusted and trust others because you are open, dependable, accountable, reliable, accepting, and honest in all you do.

- **Build trust.** Trust is the cornerstone of trustworthiness, although it is not all there is to trustworthiness. Trust must occur both ways. The four general ways to build and strengthen trust are listed. Number the behaviors from 1 to 4 in order of what you believe is easiest for you, with 1 as the easiest and 4 the most difficult.

☐ Honesty and candor: "I say what I mean." "You will always know where I stand."

☐ Accessibility and openness: "I'll tell you all about me." "Let's keep our agenda open and have fun."

☐ Approving and accepting: "I value people and diverse perspectives." "You can count on being heard without judgment or criticism."

☐ Dependability and trustworthiness: "I do what I say I will do." "I keep my promises." "You can count on me."

What you perceive as easiest are the strengths that are natural to you. They are the natural ways you go about building trust with others. Those that are more difficult are important to others who do not have the same characteristics as you and who value those trust-building skills. These are probably the ones you need to improve. To build character and be trustworthy, you need to practice all four. Who is good at these skills? Observe them and how they build trust. Identify specific things that they do and decide how you could implement the same.

- **The trustworthy 12.** Read the trustworthy 12 actions listed here and rate yourself on each. What grade would you assign yourself on these actions? Be a hard grader. Remember, you are grading these for your character. Any slip-ups can deter your character building.

☐ Your words and actions are congruent, avoiding mixed messages

☐ You keep your commitment in word and deed

☐ You mean what you say

☐ You are predictable and don't let your emotions get in the way

☐ You keep confidences and guard against gossip

☐ You act in ways that support the values of your organization

☐ You are a straight shooter, discussing issues with individuals rather than with others

☐ You are a sounding board on sensitive issues for others

☐ You are honest and candid even when the outcome is not in your favor

☐ You accept accountability for your own actions and the results of those actions

☐ You are transparent with no hidden agendas

☐ You are on time—always

Review your results. In order to focus, select only two or three actions to work on. Create a plan for how you will improve them. Your plan should include when you think you aren't achieving what you want and why. Then add what you plan to do to improve and how you will measure success. Review your list in one month to determine your progress.

ENSURE YOUR PREFERRED CHARACTER STAYS ON TRACK

You need to find ways to hold yourself accountable to keep your preferred character moving forward. How can you do that? Begin by following the process presented to you earlier in this chapter. The plan will guide you to decide what character traits you want to improve. Once you have your plan, use some of the practice sprints to coach yourself. Find ways to stay focused, such as these techniques.

Stay Focused

Techniques are available to keep you focused, such as your goals, action plans, and how you hold yourself accountable.

- Review your goals periodically.
- Don't do too much at once—really! Choose just one or two things to start with and give yourself time. It took your whole life to build your current character. You have ingrained habits that you may be trying to change. That's hard work!
- Track everything you are practicing. Your character is built on large defining moments in your life, as well as the small details you must

address every day. Both are equally important. Define them to keep you more aware.

- Regularly push yourself by enlarging your goals to be more challenging.

- Be sure you have the resources available to address your plans. Time will be the number one resource you require. You may also need money for a course or two. Be sure you have your manager's support on any of the activities you choose.

- Hold yourself accountable.

- Celebrate your success.

Remind Yourself

Everyone is busy, and new tasks come your way every day. It's easy to get sidetracked from the important work of building your character. Establish ways to remind you of what's important.

- Keep your plan in front of you. Don't bury it in a file on your desktop. Print it or put it on your phone where you'll see it every day.

- Wear a lucky charm or something that will remind you of your goals. Some people wear a rubber band on their wrists. Others wrap a ribbon around the pen they use. Still others wear a bracelet or pin. When my son, Thad, was in first grade, his teacher was a terror, invoking fear in several of the kids. Thad loved dinosaurs, so we made a wristband displaying the head of a ferocious tyrannosaurus rex. It became his talisman that he looked at to give him courage.

- Develop a daily question to ask yourself at the end of each day. It might focus on a specific trait you are improving or just be a general question about how you are doing.

PRACTICE REFLECTION

Since your character is focused on who you want to be, it is critical to do some deep thinking about what you are doing, what works, and what doesn't. Reflecting is an important step when building character.

- Use self-reflection to confirm the choices you made.

- Maintain an accountability journal and use it to track your goals, review your successes, and list those things you wish you'd done differently.

- Think about why you may have done something you wish you could change. It happens to everyone, but the key is to figure out why it happened and what you can do to prevent it from happening again.

- Schedule meetings with yourself at least quarterly to review your plan and ensure you are on track.

- Periodically review your original character traits and your values. Is everything still aligned? How well did you match them to the person you want to project? Is refinement required? It's OK to change your mind. The only person who knows who you want to be is you.

- Don't give up. You will falter along the way. Guaranteed. It's your life and you need to be your best.

Involve Others

You don't have to do it alone. Think of who can help you.

- Building your character may be a personal task for many of you. On the other hand, there are many reasons for you to use your coach or mentor to work on some of the specifics. How much, or how little, you wish to share with them is up to you.

- Select an accountability partner to help you through the difficult changes.

- You may also wish to consider your spouse or significant other. That's for you to decide.

No one said this would be easy. You need to have willpower, tenacity, perseverance, and persistence to stick to the changes you desire. Creating the character that defines you may be the most important thing you do for your own development. Stick with it. It's important.

Reading for the Final Stretch

➜ *Change Your Questions, Change Your Life*, by Marilee Adams

➜ *Principles*, by Ray Dalio

➜ *Principles for Success*, by Ray Dalio

➜ *Behave: The Biology of Humans at Our Best and Worst*, by Robert Sapolsky

➜ *Talent Is Never Enough*, by John Maxwell

➜ *Leadership Trust: Build It, Keep It*, by Christopher Evans

➜ *Drive: The Surprising Truth about What Motivates Us*, by Daniel Pink

➜ *Humble Inquiry*, by Edgar Schein

Talent might get you hired,
but character ensures you'll keep your job.

—ELAINE BIECH

Don't Allow Your Career to Run Amok

D ebra McKinney has spent most of her professional life in the field of talent development with a focus on corporate learning strategy. She was employed by the Bolívar Group, based in Bogotá, Colombia, South America, founded in 1939. With more than 20 companies and over 20,000 employees currently, the group has activities in Latin America centered principally in finance, insurance, and construction. It is highly respected for its financial soundness, tradition, and strict adherence to ethical principles.

As the director of the Bolívar Group's Center for Leadership Development, Debra created, managed, and continuously improved the Future Professionals program. The program was originally developed to attract and retain outstanding university students to the Bolívar Group. Every semester, students in areas of study of interest to the group at selected universities were invited to an on-campus session presented by a company representative and students currently taking part in the program. Interested students applied directly.

Students were accepted into the program when they were halfway through their studies. Groups of 5–15 students entered the Future Professionals program each semester, with a weeklong onboarding process before classes began. During the student phase, they worked as interns one full day a week, and full time during university vacation periods. They also received four hours of in-house training a month, which focused on the companies and their products and services, as well as personal and professional development topics. Students rotated among companies in the group every semester, depending on their skills, performance, development, and areas of study.

Upon graduation, students received an offer of full-time employment in one of the companies of the group, with an open-ended contract and an agreement to stay for at least two years. Debra and her team kept tabs on each cohort for the length of their two-year employment period. They also kept in touch with all by holding a large "homecoming" type of get-together (often at her house) every year. Students who left before the minimum two years paid a fine, which was stipulated in the contractual agreement. Over the lifetime of the program, more than 50 percent of the participants remained with the companies, occupying professional and managerial positions. Most of the earliest professionals currently occupy senior technical, senior executive, and C-level positions.

This is one of the most impressive programs of its kind, and we can glean valuable lessons about people entering the workforce for the first time. For example, what did the Future Professionals do to ensure their success? And what did others do that undermined their own success?

Debra shared that the outstanding Future Professionals exhibited common behaviors that ensured their success on the job, including:

- **A high degree of professionalism.** They kept commitments, met deadlines, followed up, asked appropriate questions, avoided excuses, and requested feedback on performance.

- **Friendly and courteous.** They treated everyone with respect, whether in person or online. That included fellow workers at any level, contractors, customers, maintenance, security, and the sales force.

- **Problem solvers.** They offered innovative and creative suggestions and proposals persistently but respectfully and followed up through the proper channels.

- **Self-control.** They were prudent and humble in interpersonal interactions: thinking before reacting, accepting that one might be mistaken, avoiding excessive public reactions, and apologizing for an error.

Unfortunately that wasn't the case for all. Debra shared that some Future Professionals also exhibited unproductive behaviors that created obstacles to their advancement, including:

- **Inability to learn from others.** There was a lack of appreciation for the ability to learn from anyone; a lower level in the hierarchy or less education does not mean others have little to offer you. For example, the corporate university receptionist, who studied philosophy in college at night, once told Debra that young professionals often treated her like a piece of furniture. They have something new employees don't: experience!

- **Blaming others.** They were quick to place blame for problems, mishaps, or errors. They didn't comprehend that if they made a mistake, they needed to report it to the person in charge as soon as they realized it and offer a possible solution.

- **Unrealistic expectations.** They lacked an appreciation for job requirements, their performance, and the company. They expected promotion without proving themselves on the job more than once.

- **Inability to accept and address conflict.** They took real or imagined slights personally, escalated situations, were unwilling to offer or receive apologies and move on, and were unable to offer constructive alternatives.

Debra says that after 20 years of the Future Professionals program, "it is clear to me that the problems young professionals face which negatively affect the job are more frequently related to personality or character, rather than lack of knowledge in their field." She says that often there is a great deal of bad decision making, which is the result of not looking ahead to the consequences from the organization's point of view, not realizing the rules are the same for everyone and apply to all, believing that having graduated from a good university somehow makes you a better human being, or the inability to realize that work is part of "real life" and that what you do leads to real consequences. "Aww, Mom!" and "Please, Professor . . ." don't work on the job, and no one cares much about whatever personal drama is going on in your life. Everybody has problems.

Sadly, Debra shared that some of the Future Professionals exhibited behaviors that were actually harmful to their careers, including these:

- **Willful poor decisions.** They failed to consider the consequences of their actions for the organization, such as legal or regulatory aspects, customer satisfaction, or security. Sometimes they tried to go around the rules and processes, failed to properly inform themselves before acting, or ignored specific instructions.

- **Small or large ethical transgressions.** This included lying, covering up their improprieties or those of others by action or inaction; doing something because everyone else was doing it; exaggerating or minimizing results; "faking it"; passing on gossip; and appropriating or "borrowing" company resources.

- **Inappropriate corporate representation.** Some employees posted recordings on social media, participated in radio call-in shows, or used television interviews to speak poorly of the company, its products or services, or other employees. This is ill-advised behavior and at times even illegal. Today's "good buddy" may be your future boss. Companies watch over their reputation on digital media.

- **Failure to protect confidential information.** At times employees made impromptu comments to others in social situations, such as weddings or parties. These comments would get back to the company through someone who was a friend or family member of someone at the company. Sometimes these situations even revealed confidential company information, such as a new product launch. Some employees also exaggerated their roles.

- **Treating people differently.** This includes being servile to their superiors or other useful people and being mean, dismissive, or rude to people they considered inferior or unimportant.

CAREER TRIP-UPS

Debra's experience with the Future Professionals program is similar to almost any new employee experience in any organization in any country. The Hay Group surveyed 450 leaders and 450 graduates (Goleman 2015). Seventy-six percent of the managers reported that entry-level employees are not ready for their jobs. What's missing? They need to be more adaptable, resilient, collaborative, empathetic, better listeners, better communicators, and self-disciplined. On the other hand, 70 percent of the graduates believe that their technical skills are more valuable than their soft skills, and 69 percent believe soft skills get in the way of doing their job well.

The majority of this book has focused on what it takes to succeed at work: refining your interpersonal savvy, planning and prioritizing work, achieving results, and building your leadership capability. Yet simply being decisive and accountable won't safeguard your career from taking a wrong turn.

Several of the examples from the Future Professionals program may seem clearly inappropriate and just "dumb" mistakes, but those dumb mistakes could follow your career. Young, new employees may not think about the consequences of posting something derogatory on social media and how it could come back to haunt them at a later time.

Other examples could be matters of self-esteem: not being able to admit to a mistake, or covering up an error and hoping it won't be discovered, or inflating their contribution to a project. Hopefully, others, such as addressing conflict, solving problems, attending to details, or setting goals, are skills that will be learned.

Some career trip-ups are more related to your character. If so, read Challenge 1 for more information. Trip-ups caused by a lack of character include defensiveness, untrustworthiness, arrogance, rigidity, and, of course, an unawareness of yourself. Uncover these blind spots in your character immediately.

But even knowing the skills required to do a good job can be a problem. Sometimes these skills can be overplayed or used at the wrong time or get mixed in without personality. Ambition is good, right? Well, yes, but you can also be too ambitious. This book lists self-confidence, selling ideas, creativity, and risk taking as valuable skills. Yet every one of them when pushed to the limits could be detrimental to your career.

Sometimes these behaviors turn into what the Center for Creative Leadership (CCL) calls derailers. Derailers are behaviors that prevent your progress. A derailer is a weakness that needs to be improved if you are going to realize your potential. If it is not improved, it can limit your progress. A derailer can be linked to a talent that you take to the extreme, but multiple other strengths cannot compensate for it. What makes it worse is that other people focus on and even emphasize your weaknesses in any type of competitive situation, such as job promotions or hiring situations.

CCL, the pioneer in the topic, has studied derailers since 1983. It periodically updates its research with subjects throughout the world. Most of its studies contrast individuals who make it to the top of organizations with those who derail. The most remarkable thing about the CCL research is the consistency of the derailers over these studies. The research shows five characteristics observed in derailed leaders (Scisco, Biech, and Hallenbeck 2017):

- Have problems with interpersonal relationships
- Fail to hire, build, and lead a team
- Fail to meet business objectives
- Are unable or unwilling to change or adapt
- Lack a broad functional orientation

It also found that leaders can avoid derailment and expect long-term success by developing and strengthening their skills in these areas: interpersonal skills, adaptability, team leadership, and focusing on results.

You might say, "Well, I'm new. Shouldn't new employees be given a break?" After all, it takes new employees time to figure out the landscape, understand this thing called a job, and create a new professional persona. That could be true, but if you look at the case of the Bolívar Group, students were the best of the best and given two years to work and go to school with special courses and plenty of time to learn the business side of life. They still exhibited amateurish behaviors that threatened their careers.

Debra identified two other derailers exhibited by the young employees at the Bolívar Group: hubris and overextension. She describes hubris as:

The people in our program were outstanding students, leaders, went to top-level schools, and had been told all along by family, professors and others that they were amazing. True, perhaps, but when you get into a company, you're just one of the unwashed masses, and all the rules apply to you, and your possible "amazingness" does not qualify you for special consideration. There are a lot of other equally amazing people, who may be amazing for reasons other than having had a fine education and being "academically" smart. None of this makes you a better human being, nor more eligible for all of the perks. A company is different from a university; things work differently, the objectives are different, timelines are different and almost everyone has more experience than you. As Marshall Goldsmith said, what got you here, won't get you there.

 ## WHAT GOT YOU HERE

Marshall Goldsmith has written a practical book titled *What Got You Here Won't Get You There*, which is basically about what stands in the way of your next achievement. The book is a fast read, down to earth, and practical. Goldsmith identifies 20 transactional flaws. Get together with a coworker and review the 20 flaws. Rate them from 1 to 20, beginning with the flaw that is the most problematic for each of you. Share your lists with each other. At a second meeting suggest ways that you could improve your flaws—especially those that you rated as the most problematic. Here are six of the flaws Marshall identifies:

- Adding your two cents' worth in every discussion
- The need to rate others and impose your standard on them
- The need to share your negative thoughts
- Claiming credit that you don't deserve
- Clinging to the past
- Failing to express gratitude

Debra describes overextension as:

Some of those in the program thought they could do everything. It was typically that they were working their first challenging job (because they have good qualifications); have side gigs (since that's a symbol for this generation); most have a significant other; most still seriously keep up with another activity (music, sport, volunteering); and some have family responsibilities beyond what is usual for their age. All of these responsibilities led some to greatly overextend themselves resulting in poor decisions, because they thought they could handle it all. They didn't ask for help in time nor did they heed advice. There weren't a lot of these situations, but each case was shockingly stupid and led to their expulsion from the program (and even out of the university) or their job, if already full-time employees. I had furious supervisors, crying students and parents, and even angry university reps all visiting my office. Fortunately, most of them learned a hard lesson and went on to have other opportunities at other organizations.

So if you are new to the world of work and your organization, once you know and understand your organization's culture, it's time to put your professional persona on. Many derailers in addition to the key ones CCL has found for leaders exist. Some are character flaws or are connected to your personality. You need to change those earlier rather than later. Research over decades suggests that it's very difficult to change core aspects of your personality after age 30—not impossible, just difficult.

BEHAVIORS TO LEAVE AT COLLEGE

If this is your first job, here's a reminder that you are no longer in college and you need to demonstrate a new set of behaviors. No matter how good you were in school, you need to leave some of your behaviors in school.

BFFs. Some of your best friendships will develop in the workplace, but it is inappropriate to broadcast them. Don't post pictures of your friends on Facebook. In some instances it can lead to claims of favoritism.

Personal privacy. In college, everything was woven together. On the job, you are expected to maintain some modicum of separation. It's probably OK to talk about the football game you attended with your friends over the weekend, but not the drunken brawl that kept you up until 4 a.m. the next morning.

SoMo. If you are addicted to Facebook, LinkedIn, WhatsApp, WeChat, Twitter, TikTok, Lasso, Instagram, YouTube, or a host of others, use them with caution. Of course, your organization realizes that some of them are useful for connecting at work. However, going on Facebook 20 times a day will probably interfere with your work. Learn your organization's guidelines and maintain them.

Body language. How you communicated in school may not be acceptable on the job: avoiding eye contact, eye rolls, a weak handshake, and checking your phone will all be interpreted by those around you—and not with much respect. These are probably habits at this point, so you'll need to make an extra effort to change.

Disorganization. Was your messy dorm room a badge of honor? It won't fly at work. Clean up your space every afternoon before you leave work.

Tardiness. Being late to class may have been cool in college, but it's not acceptable for work. Lateness is viewed as unprofessional, inconsiderate, and disrespectful.

Victim mentality. Does it always seem as though you get the short end of the stick? As though the universe is conspiring against you? It's not you; it's them taking advantage of you? It's time to stop blaming others, practice gratitude, and find a healthy dose of self-confidence.

It's not about you. Your job starts with you, but it's not about you. You are not the center of your boss's universe. You need to work with others. Brush up on your interpersonal skills, especially when dealing with the boss you dislike and the baby boomers who seem to have all the information.

AVOID POTHOLES AND BAD DIRECTIONS

As I alluded to earlier, sometimes you can have too much of a good thing. You think you are doing everything that is expected, and wham! Something comes at you out of nowhere. For example, you may think keeping your head down, keeping your nose to the grindstone, and getting your work done is enough, but not so. Perhaps you feel you should be judged on your performance. But that's only part of your job. You also need to pay attention to your relationships with your coworkers, building your networking skills, and collaborating with others. Here's a short list of how some of these directions that you took to heart can turn into work potholes if you aren't careful:

- Risk taking can become dangerous and irresponsible without the data
- Helpful can easily become micromanaging or meddling
- Self-confident can become entitled or arrogant
- Analytical can be seen as resisting change
- Precise can become risk averse
- Achieving goals can turn into overly ambitious
- Political savvy can be viewed as mistrustful
- Charismatic can be seen as manipulative
- Diligent or hardworking can be seen as perfectionism
- Creativity can be viewed as flakey or you can't make up your mind

How can this happen? In some cases you might think you are doing the right thing. In other cases you may have had a performance review and were told you needed to be more decisive. You take the feedback to heart and you produce decisions too rapidly without data or without taking others into consideration.

SKILLS YOU DIDN'T THINK YOU'D NEED

If you want a great career, you need to develop yourself. But what you develop yourself for is dependent on what you are doing and your place in life. When you were in college you needed study skills, money management skills, self-care skills, and time management skills. While you were taking classes you thought you would be using all the knowledge you learned in your classes—English, calculus, chemistry, accounting, or economics—on the job. But that likely wasn't the case. Several skills are required on the job that were not even offered in your college curriculum. Consider this partial list and catch up now.

Work ethic. That starts with showing up. The number one reason employees are fired is absenteeism. Of course, it goes beyond just showing up on Monday morning to include abusing vacation policy. Instead, you need to hustle, stay late, arrive early, and do what it takes to stand out. You'll know what to do by observing and taking cues from those who are respected and more experienced than you.

Sales. A part of any job is to sell. You will sell your solutions, your ideas, your initiatives, and yourself for the next promotion. To sell successfully you need confidence in your skills and potential and to be able to persuade people during a conversation. Sales encompasses other skills, including psychology, communication, empathy, and debate.

Receptivity to feedback. Receiving, accepting, and acting on criticism even when it seems unfair is a key skill for your development. Go one step further and actively seek out critiques that will help your projects succeed and you to grow. Use the feedback to determine what you can do better next time. Employers watch for those who learn from feedback and continue to grow.

Gratitude. Be appreciative. Recognize what others do for you. Say thank you. Build an attitude of gratitude.

Networking. Yes, networking is a skill. Even though we discuss this as a skill elsewhere in the book, it is also listed here because it's not a skill you immediately think of as a requirement on the job. Networking goes beyond attending a conference for you to grip and grin. It means being available when your colleagues need help or meeting someone in another department who will be key to your next project.

Political savvy. Again, not something that you thought you would need, but it is critical to know what your leadership values, who the informal leaders are in the organization, and who respects whom and why. It helps you to know who the powerful people are and how to practice subtle self-promotion.

Personal judgment. Having situational awareness is critical so that you know what is going on around you, increasing your ability to be vigilant to changes and threats. Your judgment will also determine how people have different preferences, styles, and needs. Adapting to each is to your benefit so that you can better understand their needs, how to communicate with them, and focus on what's most important to them.

Email proficiency. Did you grow up with email, so it seems just common sense? Unfortunately, it's not common sense to lots of people. The quick guidelines to judge your use of email are as follows: Respond to your emails within 24 hours. Use the correct name of the person you are addressing, and double-check that it's spelled correctly. Use a tool like Grammarly for error-free grammar. Don't hit "reply all" unless absolutely necessary. Use the copy and blind copy functions appropriately (not to sneak information to someone inappropriately). Use an appropriate greeting and signature line.

DON'T STUMBLE AND FALL

As you see, your career can be on track and yet you might stumble and fall at any turn. What's the least you can do to prevent a mishap? Well, start with the basics. You want to be successful in your career. Your employer needs you to be successful too; and by the way, if you are working for a smaller company, your behavior has a greater impact on productivity, morale, and the overall health of the business. A good employee's attitude and work ethic can be infectious. As an employee you should ensure that you are accountable, take initiative, display optimism, and model good communication skills.

Being Accountable

Reliability is important no matter what your job or company. If it was instilled in you as a child, it is easier to understand the importance of showing up on time and performing your assigned duties. You need to be able to work without your supervisor hovering over your desk. It means that you are disciplined enough so no one needs to tell you not to make personal phone calls, borrow office supplies for home, surf the internet, place a personal online order, or text and tweet. Tied to accountability are all the character traits in Challenge 1: have integrity, honesty, and credibility. Your employer should be able to count on you to show up, do your job, stay focused, be prepared, and do what you said you'd do when you said you'd do it.

Taking Initiative

What's the most important behavior employers look for in employees? Every person I interviewed or spoke with in preparation for this book stated "taking initiative." Their words were "do what they need to do without being asked," "don't wait to be told what to do," "look around and see what's needed," "bring me a solution, not a problem," "go the extra mile," and "take some initiative, damn it!" Whether it is offering solutions to problems or volunteering to help someone or taking 100 percent responsibility for mistakes that weren't entirely your fault, your employer will take notice of your initiative. It counts—a lot! Don't wait for someone to tell you what to do. Don't complain about problems. Don't find reasons why you can't do something. Managers can't be everywhere, so it's your responsibility to speak up, pitch in, follow through, and just do it. Your manager will notice when you go beyond your own job to look out for your colleagues and the organization's interests. Do what isn't being done.

Displaying Optimism

A smile alone won't get the job done, but a positive attitude and a pleasant disposition produce a well-rounded employee that others want to work with. Your good attitude is on display every morning when you walk in the door or get on your first phone call. Customer service reps are taught to smile when on the phone with a customer because you can "hear" a smile on a call. Your optimism shows through every time you face a problem with a can-do attitude, or pleasantly agree to a change because it is better for the customer, or happily suspend your agenda to support your team. Your approachability index is a throwback to the "plays well with others" note on your kindergarten report card. You are not expected to be a pushover; you're expected to learn assertiveness skills without discouraging your coworkers. Remember: emotions are contagious.

Modeling Excellent Communication

We've been communicating since birth. Therefore, we should be good. Right? Wrong. We are all still learning to improve our communication every day. Communication is essential in virtually every job. Improving communication skills is vital to becoming a successful employee. Your good ideas will fall on deaf ears if you can't deliver them effectively. Your inability to understand others will end up in unnecessary conflict. Your hastily written email may cause a disaster. Your lack of clarity will confuse your manager. You won't be considered for plum projects or prestigious promotions without excellent communication skills. Say good things about people and your organization, or don't say anything at all. Clean up all of your bad communication habits now, or you will top out in a role you may not like. And your poor communication skills reputation will follow you throughout your career. Sound ominous? It's a reality if your communication fails you.

CAUTION YOUR TONGUE

Take care with your communication to ensure that it is constantly building partnerships in order to grow the business. One of the greatest stumbling blocks of potentially successful employees is that they speak destructively about their organizations, their management, or other team members without thinking about the results. If you are guilty of this major blunder, make changes quickly in this area. How? You need to change a bad habit and turn it around. Before talking about someone else, get in the habit of asking yourself four questions before speaking:

- Will this comment help our organization?
- Will this comment help our customers?
- Will this comment help the person to whom I am speaking?
- Will this comment help the person about whom I am speaking?

If you cannot answer yes to all four questions, don't say it. There is a big difference between being honest and candid, on the one hand, and gossiping destructively, on the other. After reading this activity, ask one of your coworkers or your supervisor or even your direct reports to observe your communication for a week. At the end of the week, take the individual or individuals to lunch and ask them for their observations—especially those that they think could be destructive. Listen carefully to what they say.

Lessons Learned from the Bolívar Group

Debra suggests also adding these practical reminders to your skill set:

- **There are many opportunities to learn.** As you progress in your career, degree programs become less important than earning professional certifications, keeping up to date in your field and industry through wide-ranging reading, and learning new topics in areas that complement your field of activity.

- **It's a globalized world.** The United States is one of the few places in the world people can consider themselves well educated without speaking a second language. In addition to language skills, you need to be conscious of the dos and don'ts of cross-cultural communication. You will interact with people from many parts of the world in person and online. In addition to being more employable, you will open many doors to a more interesting life.

- **Be a team player.** Before worrying about promotion, concentrate on being a "good member," such as a good team member or a good meeting participant. If you are not a good member, it is unlikely you will be considered for a leadership position. Leadership is not a job. You may be a leader in one situation and a part of the group in another.

- **Learn to sell.** Everyone needs to know how to sell: your ideas, projects, initiatives, and yourself. Commercial skills will always open doors, even if you are not in sales or marketing. Today we are all a part of the gig economy.

WHAT'S NEXT?

Are you aware of what you need to improve? Awareness is step one. Seriously ask yourself what you are going to do about it. What's your next step? If you need clarity about what others see, ask them: current and past supervisors, peers, subordinates, clients, your coach, and friends. At work you may be more professional, but friends see you when you are comfortable and have your guard down.

Tell them that you want to improve and need candid and honest input. What do they see when you are not at your best? Most people will be reluctant to tell you the worst. To get them to open up you may need to share comments you've received in the past. Then listen, listen, listen. One casual remark or excuse from you is likely to shut down the discussion. Remember that there may be specific situations that trigger your behaviors. Identify them. Also notice how you react under stressful situations. Stress taxes your cognitive resources and prevents you from exerting the self-control you need in the moment.

You may also want to identify assessments that are available to you, such as 360-degree multiraters, performance appraisals, or other assessments that are listed in Challenge 3. Talk to your supervisor or someone in HR to learn what's available to you.

Now you need to make changes. As with so many other recommended actions in this book, you need to get out there and do something different from what you are doing now. Identify the positive behaviors you want to substitute for your current behaviors. Then plan when you will start making the changes. Change is difficult, so you need to prepare yourself ahead of the troubling situations when you can. You may also want to identify a self-reminder. For example, if you are working on being more reserved and professional during meetings, write question starters (such as, "tell me more about how you could…") in your notebook or take notes instead of interrupting. To remember the change, you might switch your watch or a ring to the other hand, and the discomfort will be a reminder.

Breaking habits that you've lived with is not easy. If you are serious about career advancement, don't take the ideas in this chapter lightly.

WHAT WILL TRIP UP YOUR CAREER?

How carefully and seriously did you read this chapter?

If you don't think it pertains to you, you are heading for failure. All of us can use the lessons in this chapter to improve ourselves so that our career isn't disrupted, isn't derailed, or doesn't run amok.

Keep your career on track.

Reading for the Final Stretch

→ *Be Your Own Mentor,* by Anne Bruce

→ *The Extraordinary Leader: Turning Good Managers into Great Leaders,* by John Zenger and Joseph Folkman

→ *What Got You Here Won't Get You There,* by Marshall Goldsmith

→ *Changing Yourself and Your Reputation,* by Talula Cartwright

Talent is cheaper than table salt. What separates the talented individual from the successful one is a lot of hard work.

—STEPHEN KING

CHALLENGE 3

Managers Support Employee Development

Some of the most talented minds in robotics worked at the National Robotics Engineering Center (NREC) at Carnegie Mellon University (CMU). In 2015 some of NREC's best and brightest employees started leaving. In the beginning it was only a few software developers, but then entire teams left. Eventually the center's director left.

Soon, many of the scientists that were working on vehicle autonomy, including developers, grants specialists, and commercialization specialists, were gone. Intellectual property was streaming out the door. Where was it going? Well, not far. It seems that Uber, the ride-sharing start-up company, had moved into a renovated building that at one time housed a chocolate factory—and shared the parking lot with NREC. Uber had initiated a multi-year project to create driverless cars and needed talent.

At final count, Uber had snatched about 50 Carnegie Mellon specialists, almost half of its staff in about a month, including many from NREC's highest ranks. NREC was a logical place for Uber to search for talent. Ten years prior in 2004 when the U.S. Defense Advanced Research Projects Agency

(DARPA) held its first Grand Challenge contest to locate the best autonomous vehicle, CMU made it the farthest in a Humvee named Sandstorm. NREC continued to rack up years of experience, working with commercial companies, NASA, and the military to design a broad range of systems from autonomous ground combat vehicles to automated strawberry-sorting systems.

An agreement was established between Uber and CMU so that some of the departed NREC employees could remain part time to finish their projects. Still, the absence of talent presented new challenges for NREC. In the end, the lab's budget was slashed and entire projects folded. Promised joint projects between Uber and CMU were never launched. The AI lab had to rebuild its bench strength with new hires.

How did this happen? Shouldn't CMU have seen this coming? Well, not at the time. In the past, universities anticipated losing top researchers and scientists to competitors, other top universities, or think tanks, but not necessarily to corporations, and certainly not in a single hiring spree. But times have changed and this occurs more often. Most organizations face a skills gap due to changes in technology, demographics, globalization, and disruption. Developing talent is an essential solution from two perspectives:

- Organizations ensure that they have the knowledge, skills, and attitudes required to get their products and services out the door.

- Organizations are more likely to retain their skilled workforce, since employees' desire for development is a critical ingredient for job satisfaction.

This chapter addresses the manager's role in developing employees. The organization benefits because it has the talent it requires. Employees benefit because they receive the development they desire and feel a valued part of the organization—encouraging them to remain with the organization.

Are you reading this as a manager or someone who wants to acquire your manager's support? In either case, developing employees isn't just important, it's vital. Let's dig deeper into the reasons.

Developing your employees benefits your organization; to win in the marketplace, your organization must help your employees maintain relevant skills. Developing your employees improves their performance, increases productivity, improves adherence to quality and safety standards, and reduces your organization's skills gap. Employees who receive the skills they need build their confidence, improve the match to their job, and enhance their overall performance. In addition, investing in your employees demonstrates that you value your employees, increasing their satisfaction and improving their chances for staying on the job. This reduces employee turnover and enhances your organization's brand and reputation, thus appearing more attractive to new recruits.

Managers who take a personal interest in employees and their development build loyalty, and loyalty increases productivity. Talented employees want to be appreciated; they want to advance; they want to gain skills to be more valuable to their organizations. Coaching, training, mentoring, and all of their variations are paths to skill development. But it starts with the organization and its managers. If you are a manager, it starts with you.

REAL MANAGERS DEVELOP OTHERS

Let's face it, managers are busy. As a manager, one of the most important roles you play is to develop your people. The pace of change is so prevalent it hardly bears repeating; however, it is this trend that has exacerbated the need for organizations to identify and signal the skills they need as well as develop options to upskill and reskill their employees. It is your job as a manager to translate that message to your employees and to create mechanisms to develop them (Biech 2018a).

Technology ensures that you and your employees can access all the information you need when and where it's needed. However, you need to support your employees by ensuring they are tapping into the most helpful and accurate content. You can help your employees identify what skills and knowledge they need and then ensure that they acquire the development that is necessary.

START WITH THE BASICS

Once you know employees' learning needs, you are in a position to make an immediate and lasting difference in their performance. Start by developing your coaching and development skills. What are the most beneficial developmental skills you should have? Start by ensuring that you are skilled with the basics: keep employees informed about the organization's strategy and direction, improve your coaching skills, discuss your employees' development with them, give them feedback on a regular basis, and encourage a growth mindset environment (Biech 2017).

Communicate the Organization's Strategy and Direction

What does your organization need your employees to know? Topics will include changing customer expectations, competitive threats, and opportunities on the horizon. Help your employees stay in touch with your organization's needs. Employees can keep their careers aligned to the organization with this information. As your organization pursues new opportunities, employees should know about and have the option of developing the skills that will be required. Be sure that you have shared a copy of your organization's strategic and business plans with your employees. Discuss their contributions to the organization's success. Share information about current operations across the organization. Be transparent about the challenges, including new supplier relationships, new strategies, impact of industry trends, economic conditions, and other things your leaders are discussing. Invite questions and ask for suggestions. Actively see learning opportunities in other parts of the organization. You could swap employees with another department or encourage them to rotate into one of your customer's departments so they can learn more and be more helpful.

Improve Your Coaching Skills

The one management skill that will make the greatest difference is coaching. Improving your coaching skills demonstrates that you are serious about developing your employees. The purpose of coaching is threefold. First, it helps the employee develop skills. Second, it helps employees understand what the organization needs and how they fit into the organization's goals. And third, it gives managers a clearer picture of what each employee wants, what they want to improve, where their strengths lie, and what their long-term goals are. A coaching discussion sends a message to the employee that you care about their development.

Discuss Their Development

Hold regular one-on-one meetings with each employee to discuss and understand their developmental needs. Explore their current performance and identify areas to improve. Encourage them to keep their individual development plans (IDPs) up to date and help them identify ways to close any skill gaps. Ask them for ideas about how they would like to learn or upgrade their skills. Different people will want different things. Don't assume that everyone wants to be a leader.

Give Constructive Feedback

Feedback should include specific recommendations for future improvement and development. When feedback is delivered regularly and tied to examples on a daily basis, it helps your employees learn incrementally. Your feedback should be both constructive changes and reinforcing comments, and it should be timely. When executed well, delivering feedback can impact employee performance by more than 25 percent. Don't miss opportunities to guide your employees by holding back your feedback; share it as soon as possible. Use feedback as a tool for growth and recognition. Employees want to know how they are doing.

Mind Their Mindsets

Your employees should have a foundation for a successful growth mindset. Carol Dweck has spread the word about her decades of research on achievement and success. A growth mindset means that people believe that they can develop almost anything through dedication and hard work. The added value for you and your team is that when your employees tap into their growth mindset, it creates a love of learning and resilience—perfect traits for a successful function. With a growth mindset, your employees are poised to accomplish almost anything they want. A growth mindset teaches that all great people have these qualities, since a growth mindset creates motivation and productivity and enhances relationships.

CAREER DEVELOPMENT PLANNING

Supporting your employees to develop themselves may be the most important part of your job. It consists of assessing individuals' interests, values, and capabilities; exploring their options; establishing goals; and encouraging employee development to fulfill your employees' aspirations and meet the organization's needs. The career development process may be initiated by your employees or you. Your organization may use a specific process or template. Most career development processes follow a similar format to this one:

1. Help your employees articulate their career aspirations and identify your employees' strengths and development needs. This may require using assessment tools. Discuss results with your employees to help them identify needs and gaps.

2. Provide options for career goals and developmental activities, noticing what the individual needs and what the organization needs, such as competency requirements or future roles that your organization will need.

3. Assist them in developing a realistic IDP. Typically, an IDP offers the necessary features: set goals, list actions, identify resources, establish target dates. See Step 3 for more IDP information. For more details you might also use "My Career Development Plan," found in part 4 and at https://ideas.bkconnection.com/skillsforcareersuccess, or use one of your own.

4. Establish ideas to help your employees get experience with the skills they need to develop. This book includes hundreds of pages of activities for over 50 skills. As your employees implement their plans, you need to follow up with them. Hold regularly scheduled meetings with them to monitor their progress, and provide ideas and support for development.

CAREER DEVELOPMENT DISCUSSION GUIDE

Here's a quick guide to opening discussions with employees to learn more about what they like to do, what excites them, and what they want to do in the future.

Current Goals

- What is your greatest strength?
- What do you like best about your job?
- What skill would you like to improve?
- How do you learn best?

Future Goals

- Where do you see yourself in 3 years? 10 years?
- What part of your job would you like to do less of in the future?
- What job or role most excites you?
- What is your ultimate career goal?

Support

- How can I help you in your current job?
- How can I help you to achieve your career goals?
- What development do you think would help you achieve your goals?
- Who else can help you achieve your goals? (Biech 2018b)

Assessment Options

Assessments aren't a requirement for developing career plans, but they can be very useful. Your employees have the ability to use the statements in "Hurdles to Overcome" and "Your Path to Success" in each skill as a self-assessment. You could use an assessment to help both you and your employee identify what the employee needs to improve. Check with your HR department to learn about any ethical or legal issues involved in selecting and administering assessments in the workplace. This list comprises some of the major types of assessments. The multirater, sometimes called a 360-degree assessment, is used most often, but others might be useful in various situations.

- **Multirater.** Multirater assessments collect feedback from multiple reviewers, including the individual, the manager, coworkers, and sometimes customers, to gain insight into the development needs of an individual.

- **Intelligence.** Intelligence assessments typically consist of verbal and math questions to assess general intelligence and problem-solving skills.

- **Personality.** Personality assessments ask preferential questions and assess aptitudes and personality style. Some target specific job categories, such as sales, or competency areas, such as leadership.

- **Aptitude.** Aptitude assessments ask questions to determine if an individual has the potential to complete a specific role without prior knowledge, experience, or training. Employers may use them to make hiring decisions.

- **Skill or ability.** Skill or ability assessments provide an objective evaluation of an individual's ability to complete a job or task. These assessments measure current skills.

- **Interest.** Interest assessments, sometimes called career assessments, help individuals match preferences to specific jobs, job categories, or professions.

Develop Employees' IDPs

Make IDPs an expectation, not a choice. IDPs require that you have discussions about career goals with your employee. IDPs provide a blueprint for each employee and are especially useful since they record and track goals, identify developmental strategies, and document accomplishments. They generally identify long- and short-term plans and provide an opportunity for you to add your comments and support.

Discussing each employee's interests and career goals is a conversation that identifies the activities the individual can do to ensure growth. The IDP Discussion Guide for Managers is located at https://ideas.bkconnection.com /skillsforcareersuccess. Learning employees' perspectives about what they want to achieve in their careers helps managers find the best fit. Many employees may be uncertain about what they want to do, and the discussions become good clarifying events. An IDP lays out a plan for each employee and is the vehicle that ties personal development to your organization's strategic goals. You can review Step 3 for more information about the IDP purpose and process. Investing time to discuss your employees' development plans is always a win for the employee and the organization.

Development Activities

Organizations need to focus on developing employees for key roles, which means being knowledgeable of the many development methods available. An environment in which people have access to the tools, resources, professional support, and experiences to develop necessary skills will broaden their perspectives. You have a variety of approaches you can use to develop talent in your employees. Listed are approaches available to you:

- **Formal learning programs:** certifications, courses, academic assignment, advanced degree education, immersive classes
- **Informal development:** coaching, mentoring, online personal development courses
- **Job-related opportunities:** stretch assignments, committee and task force involvement, action learning
- **Outside the job, but in the organization:** rotational assignments or attending meetings in other departments as an observer, job shadowing
- **Volunteering:** instructing at a community college, providing community service, participating in a loaned executive program
- **Self-study:** research projects, reading, study groups
- **Networking activities:** professional associations, online and social supported networks (Biech 2017)

SPECIFIC EMPLOYEE DEVELOPMENT DISCUSSIONS

Employee development discussions are a way to keep employees' development and their career plans on track. Perhaps you use a nine-box model that compares employee performance with their potential to determine high-performing employees, to conduct succession planning, or to determine a bonus structure or other things. The Center for Creative Leadership suggests a similar structure to identify four types of development conversations you might have with employees who are in different places in their performance and potential (see figure 4). When you know each of your employees well enough to be able to plan an appropriate constructive conversation with them, you show them that you care enough to tailor discussions to meet their needs.

Top talent employees meet or exceed performance expectations. They learn quickly, are accountable and credible, and are ready for more responsibility. They deliver superior results.

Solid performers also meet or exceed performance expectations. They are accountable, professional, and good contributors who deliver consistent results.

Potential performers are expected to deliver more to the job than they currently do. They may not have been in their positions long enough to demonstrate their full value.

Underperformers are not meeting performance expectations and need to improve. They currently need to focus on their assigned responsibilities in order to determine their full value (Smith and Campbell 2014).

	Solid performer discussion	Top talent discussion
Performance	Under performer discussion	Potential performer discussion
	Low	Potential

Figure 4. Designing employee development discussions.

As you might imagine, each of these employees requires a different type of discussion. For each type of employee, your discussion might consider these suggestions:

- **Top talent.** Focus on what you can do to invest in them.

  Share your perceptions and recognize their high performance with specific examples. Identify their aspirations, what roles interest them, and what motivates them. Most important, focus on how you can support them with development and experiences for future roles.

- **Solid performers.** Focus on retaining them.

  Provide recognition for their accomplishments and share appreciation. Focus on their current positions and offer to help them grow. Share with them potential opportunities in the next two years. Most important, focus on how to engage and retain them.

- **Potential performers.** Focus on how to provide them with more experience.

  Open a discussion about their concerns with a transition, job understanding, corporate support, or other things that could move them to be more productive. Often these employees are new to their jobs. Focus on the steps they need to take within the next few months and identify how you can provide support.

- **Underperformers.** Focus on the specifics of moving them from poor to solid performers.

  Be very clear about the performance issues and what needs to happen for individuals to retain their positions. Focus your attention on specific steps they need to take over the next few months. Offer ongoing support, monitoring, and coaching.

Before you hold these discussions, plan what you will say. You will want to examine any data that is available to you. List observations you've made about the individual and what you know about the individual, such as past performance, career interests, and observations from others. Anticipate how the person will respond to your discussion. Finally, be prepared to offer developmental opportunities, resources the person can tap into beyond you, and how you will suggest creating accountability for the individual's development. After your discussion, be sure to reflect on what happened, what lessons you learned, what went well, and what you would do differently next time.

ONGOING EMPLOYEE DEVELOPMENT SUPPORT

Employee development is an ongoing, never-ending action for you. Therefore, I have created a list of ongoing, never-ending ways to support your employees' development. These short idea bursts are meant as reminders and thought starters for you. They are grouped into three categories: support their development, build their confidence, and recommend developmental exercises.

Support Their Development

You can do a great deal to support your employees' development. No matter how small, they will notice it.

Keep employees in the loop. You can tell them about a job opening, a spot on a cross-functional team, or a temporary role. Suggest networks that will link them to others for learning and growth. This could include mentors, coaches, professional associations, or a learning community of practice. Each offers an opportunity for your employees to learn more about the entire organization and become more informed and valuable to the organization.

Be a great role model. Probably the best thing a manager can do is to demonstrate that learning is important. Accept feedback and be open to bad news. Remember the value and importance of this act. Be sure to invest in your own learning. Top it off by sharing what you are learning with your employees. They will feel privileged that you shared with them.

Invest in your employees. Whether it is spending money so the employee can attend a conference, or allowing time to meet with an onsite book club, managers need to invest in their employees' futures. Invest your time in them by asking them for their ideas, listening to their concerns, respecting their suggestions, and maintaining all confidential information.

Offer development beyond the job. Well-rounded employees are a benefit to your organization. Employees learn new skills and obtain a better understanding of how the organization works if they have opportunities to develop in other departments or even other organizations. Tools that you have available include shadowing someone else, a stretch assignment, rotational assignment, job swap, or others.

Help them focus on skills and knowledge they need. There is so much to learn and not enough time. You can help your employees cut through the noise and information by letting them know what is necessary from a talent development professional's perspective and from the organization's perspective.

Remove barriers. If the organization's processes challenge employees' development, you need to find a way to run interference for them. Make introductions, bridge departments, and find ways to help employees continue to learn.

Help them get ahead. Coach your employees about what is required to get ahead in the organization. Inform them about career plans and develop their leadership skills. Help them understand the politics and other expectations the organization and the leaders have.

Coach in the moment. You need to be able to coach on the go and while things are happening. It includes asking just three questions (Biech 2018a):

- What went well?
- What didn't go as well as you would have liked?
- What will you do differently next time?

Accept mistakes. No one wants things to go wrong. No one plans it. But when things do go wrong, it is a great opportunity to reflect, learn, and try it again. Accept mistakes and make certain that learning has occurred as a result.

Seek learning opportunities. Check in with your employees regularly to determine what skills they want to enhance. Things occur beyond the IDP, so encourage them to keep their IDPs and career plans up to date. Then seek opportunities for all employees within your department or outside.

Outfit them with practical tools. Expanding your employees' practical skill sets is a key to developing the talent your organization needs. Fitted with practical skills, they will also be able to accept a larger workload. Some of these skills include time management, decision making, communication skills, critical thinking, process improvement, organizational skills, prioritization, and meeting management skills. Check this book out for tools to develop your employees' skills.

Build Their Confidence

Confident people have an aura about them that makes others want to be a part of what they are doing. They are admired by and inspire confidence in others. According to the Mayo Clinic, low self-esteem impacts almost every aspect of our lives (Neff, Hsieh, and Dejitterat 2005). I am certainly no confidence expert, but here are a couple of thoughts that are helpful to me.

Practice confidence daily. Think of self-confidence as something you can develop if you practice every day. It starts with ensuring your employees know everything there is to know about their profession. Nothing builds confidence like knowing your stuff and having a positive mindset. Help them find themselves in their work.

Stay ahead of change. Keep your employees informed about change and make sure that they have a plan for their future. Develop their skills and knowledge to maintain their place on the cutting edge. By doing so you are providing the kind of development opportunities your employer and your participants expect and deserve.

Delegate work. Strengthen employees' competence and confidence by delegating tasks or an entire project. Delegation doesn't mean just dumping a project on someone. Manage the process to achieve the best outcomes. Provide support and guidance. Establish goals and schedule milestone meetings.

Allow them to struggle. Sometimes the best help is no help. If you are coaching your employees, be discreet about when you may or may not help them. Sometimes struggling is the best way to learn. Pushing employees to figure out the answer may be just the growth experience that they need. That does not mean that you never help or that you allow the struggle to go on too long. Balance giving the right answer with learning responsibility. Stretch assignments are good.

Increase their credibility. Help your employees build credibility by getting them involved in real business challenges. Allow them to work closely with the organization's business lines. Show them how to ask the right questions and measure the right metrics: "What business problem does this solve?" "What metric will validate results?"

Conduct stay interviews. Instead of exit interviews—those held after employees have decided to leave—conduct *stay interviews* to learn what it will take to have them stay. See an example format at https://ideas.bk connection.com/skillsforcareersuccess.

Recommend Developmental Experiences

Thousands of experiences exist to develop employees. Try new things regularly.

Offer experiences with you. Offer rotations to other departments. Allow them to shadow you for a day. Take your employees to a meeting of your peers and manager so they can see the topics and the level of conversation that occurs.

Pair employees with mentors. Mentors are helpful in many ways. Encourage your employees to seek mentors. Help your employees feel comfortable before their first meeting with a potential mentor.

Connect employees to your organization with meaningful work. Provide critical types of information to your employees to ensure they feel connected. An analysis of over 300 potential drivers of engagement by CCL and other organizations found that a connection between work and organizational strategy is a critical driver of discretionary effort among employees.

Involve them. When planning for the year, or even for the month, ask employees to identify how they would like to contribute and what they would like to learn. This helps them choose and experience learning on the job. It also avoids employees volunteering only for the tasks they are already qualified to complete.

Volunteer. Encourage employees to seek challenges outside work. Other areas of their lives often provide challenges equal to those found on the job. They can find plenty of leadership opportunities in nonprofit, social, or professional organizations. Schools, sports teams, and other youth events often need volunteers to help.

There are many other things you can do to develop your employees: recommend books, offer a seminar, partner them with other managers, provide coaching, or help them find a mentor. The "Ideas to Develop Your Employees" can be helpful as a reminder.

IDEAS TO DEVELOP YOUR EMPLOYEES

This checklist provides you with quick and easy ways to develop your employees (Biech 2018a). Add your own ideas to personalize it. You can download a copy at https://ideas.bkconnection.com /skillsforcareersuccess.

Find Out Who They Are

☐ Meet with each person about once a month to talk about longer-term goals and new ideas they want to implement

☐ Meet with employees once each week to learn about their progress on their current projects, updates, and any struggles they are facing

☐ Listen to them

☐ Provide opportunities for 360-degree feedback options or other assessments

☐ Identify specific books for each employee that will help them understand their strengths and learning needs

☐ Help them find a mentor

☐ Introduce them to communication styles (for example, the DiSC or Myers-Briggs Type Indicator)

☐ Provide performance metrics and create constructive conversation

Help Them Explore Their Professional (and Personal) Opportunities

☐ Have all employees read a leadership book, and hold a monthly discussion

☐ Demonstrate how to seek feedback

☐ Introduce them to someone who can connect them to other experiences—such as someone in another department

- [ ] Provide constructive feedback, always asking whether they like or dislike certain tasks or parts of the job
- [ ] Ensure that everyone has an IDP and uses it appropriately

Show Them How to Learn

- [ ] Teach them how to network
- [ ] Coach them
- [ ] Allow them to struggle
- [ ] Ensure they have opportunities to experiment, fail, and learn
- [ ] Create an ownership mentality by trusting them, providing experiences, and giving them authority
- [ ] Share your own mistakes
- [ ] Link them to a professional association or network
- [ ] Provide a way all employees can share what they are learning

Give Them New Experiences

- [ ] Turn over a small part of your job to them
- [ ] Have them give a presentation to another department about what your department does
- [ ] Invite them to conduct a brown bag lunch presentation about the department for the rest of the organization
- [ ] Ask them to run a meeting in your absence
- [ ] Find a project for them to lead
- [ ] Take them as a guest to one of your meetings with the next level up
- [ ] Offer development options beyond the job
- [ ] Trade employees with other departments for a month
- [ ] Trade employees with suppliers or customers of your organization

Explore Ideas for Development

- ☐ Use your meetings to share new skills or knowledge
- ☐ Delegate something you really like to do (not only what you don't like to do)
- ☐ Identify an employee for a stretch assignment instead of giving it to someone who already can do the job
- ☐ Define the organizational politics and culture and show them that "politics" isn't a bad word
- ☐ Discuss how to navigate organizational politics
- ☐ Lead them to classes, conferences, online learning, or other opportunities to develop them; spend the money to help them learn
- ☐ Assign someone to complete the work of employees who are away learning; this is beneficial for two reasons: (1) it provides a developmental opportunity for someone, and (2) the learner will not return to a stack of work
- ☐ Help identify volunteer opportunities outside your organization
- ☐ Arrange for an employee to shadow someone in another department or a step or two up the chain

Develop Yourself

Oh, and most important, develop yourself first. Be a model for life-long learning to build trust and to demonstrate credibility: accept feedback, be open to bad news and change, and invest in your own learning.

CREATE A LEARNING ENVIRONMENT

Ensure that you have created a learning environment so your employees know that you value and support learning. You won't need to do much to convince your employees that learning is good. They come to you ready to learn. What are signs that employees know they have landed in a learning culture? (Biech 2018a)

Create a safe space for failure. We all know that the best learning occurs right after you make a mistake. You can embrace failure to ensure that improvement occurs. Reinforce it by encouraging employees to diagnose what happened. Give employees time to reflect, develop, and share what could be better next time. This allows learning to occur, builds expertise, and promotes both individual and organizational learning. I do a fair amount of work with the navy, which uses an after action report, usually called an AAR or postmortem, to explore projects from the start to the end. The purpose is to review what was expected and what actually happened. The learning is found in the difference between the two.

Align employee goals to organizational needs. Employees want to feel that they are part of the organization. They want to feel that they are contributing to the organization. If your organization uses employee journey maps or learning paths, they should be tied to development plans. It is clear that alignment benefits the organization, but employees get value from it too. Delivering training to support the organizational needs sends a strong message that the organization cares about their future.

Add Ingredients for an Irresistible Situation

Establishing a learning-infused environment is a start, but if you stop there it is like setting the table with your best china and silverware and never serving the gourmet meal. What can you include on your menu that adds the ingredients for an irresistible learning situation for your employees? What can you do to inspire them to value lifelong learning? Here are a few things to get you started.

Provide opportunities beyond the job description. Give employees the joy of breaking free from the compartmentalized setting that most employees operate within in their departments. You know that to develop employees for larger roles in the organization, they need to understand how everything in the organization works—together. Create opportunities for employees to try on new roles and responsibilities outside their job function. Create opportunities for job shadowing or job rotations.

Give permission. Organizations can be rigid in their structures and processes. This can make it challenging to implement changes and improvements that may cross department lines. A part of your job is to see across department lines to remove barriers and to design a more fluid approach to learning and working. Work among and between departments and functions to take the barriers away and watch employees find new ways to solve problems, growing and developing along the way. Help departments establish cross-functional teams where necessary.

Support networking. Find ways to help employees locate contacts that can help them grow. Introduce them to other professionals that can act as mentors or coaches. Pay for their membership to join professional associations. Offer training courses and workshops internally and keep tabs on those offered outside your organization. Create networks and social sharing options for your organization. Keep employees informed of networking events. Connecting to a network offers a way to get additional support, advice, and information on how to grow professionally and personally.

Pay for developmental options such as classes, certification, and assessments. Offer certification and university courses. Employers know that when their people have passed either of these, the employees will have the basic knowledge that is covered in both. Offer multirater, single-rater, and self-assessments so that employees have the opportunity to receive feedback to determine specifics about what they need to develop.

Teach them how to set goals. Much of what has been described here will be less than useful unless employees know how to establish their developmental goals. Goal setting should be a part of your DNA. Goals are the path to accomplishment. Without goals, employees may receive lots of development but still be off track. Steps 1–4 at the beginning of this book provide additional information if you need it.

Developing employees accomplishes two goals. First, it keeps employees energized about and engaged in their jobs. Second, it ensures the organization will have people ready to move into positions when the situation arises. This demonstrates that the organization is interested in its employees' development so that it can promote from within. All of this leads to a higher level of engagement and productivity and a positive outlook about their future with the company. Determine how your leadership can help champion a learning atmosphere where your organization has skilled employees who feel valued and respected.

Questions to Ponder

? Reflect on the learning environment in your department. Do new employees view it as an environment that will nurture their development and growth?

? How do you communicate that employees are responsible for their own development and that the talent development department is there to support them?

? Decide how you define and model excellence for your employees. Ask your team how they think you model excellence. Are they the same? If not, should they be? Help your staff decide how they each define their own excellence and whether they are satisfied with it.

? Learn how you can help align learning to your organization's requirements. Take a leading role to help your employees see how they align with the organization. Why is this important to your employees?

? Ensure everyone's IDP is up to date. How do your colleagues do this?

? If you have not had career conversations with all your employees, use the 4Cs to Develop Others, found at https://ideas.bkconnection.com/skillsforcareersuccess, to initiate them.

Reading for the Final Stretch

→ *The Coaching Habit: Say Less, Ask More, and Change the Way You Lead Forever,* by Michael Bungay Stanier

→ *A Coach's Guide to Developing Exemplary Leaders,* by James Kouzes, Barry Posner, and Elaine Biech

- → *ATD's Foundations of Talent Development: Launching, Leveraging, and Leading Your Organization's TD Effort*, by Elaine Biech
- → *90 Days, 90 Ways: Onboard Young Professionals to Peak Performance*, by Alexia Vernon
- → *Talent Conversations: What They Are, Why They're Crucial, and How to Do Them Right*, by Roland Smith and Michael Campbell
- → *Employee Development on a Shoestring*, by Halelly Azulay
- → *Developing Employees*, by Harvard Business Press authors

The degree to which I can ... facilitate the growth of others ... is a measure of the growth I have achieved in myself.

—CARL ROGERS

PART FOUR

SUPPORT FOR THE RACE
TOOLS AND ACTIVITIES

BALANCING CAREER AND LIFE GOALS

Most of us spend our time in the eight general categories of this life circle. Just because the slices are equal on this graphic does not indicate that they are equally important, nor should you think that you should spend an equal amount of time on each.

Definitions for Each Area

- Fun—vacations, hobbies, pleasure reading, travel
- Relationship—friends, current or future life partner
- Career—job satisfaction, work, career path, education
- Family—children, parents, relatives
- Social—sports, activities, clubs
- Health—exercise, diet, vitamins
- Financial—savings, investments, home, retirement plan
- Creative—Self-space, spiritual, artistic, community, sharing with others

Identify a goal that you wish to reach in each of the categories. For example, if you have been telling yourself you need to get in shape, you may wish to create a goal such as, "By May 13, I will visit the gym three times each week."

Options

Rate your satisfaction with each category on a 1–7 scale. Then develop goals for the two or three categories that you rated the lowest. If these categories do not work for you, change them to something more meaningful.

MIND MAPS

Create a mind map of the opportunities for personal growth. Use a mind map to visually organize information. Start with an idea in a circle in the middle of a sheet of paper. Branch out with lines to connect to other ideas.

Put "Opportunities to develop" in the center circle. Begin to add ideas around the outside and place them inside the circles also. You may begin with several general categories such as "experiential activities," "training," and "nonwork." You may also list more specific categories such as "listening," "public speaking," and "email," which might all roll into the more general category of "communication." Don't forget creative, out-of-the-box ideas, such as learn to make cotton candy, enroll in opera lessons, try out for a play, take a cooking class in Tuscany, or get a real estate license. Use your mind map to create an individual development plan for yourself.

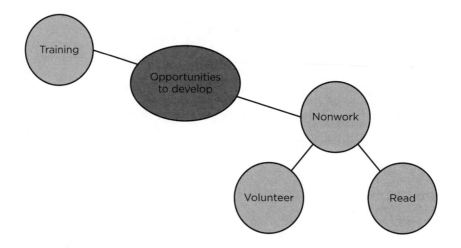

INDIVIDUAL DEVELOPMENT PLAN

Your IDP provides a disciplined approach to thinking through your career goals, relating your development to your organization's long term plans, and identifying specific actions for you to take. Your IDP is a flexible guide that should be reviewed no less than semi-annually and updated as necessary to reflect your current work situation and your organization's needs. Your organization might have its own IDP format, and if not, you can begin with this template.

Complete the contact information first. Ideally you will list your long-term and short-term goals next. On page 2 you can complete the development that you need in order to reach these goals. You will see a separate page of examples. This is where you list training, education, and development activities (formal and informal) to develop the competencies you will need to meet your goals. In some cases you will be aware of classes or volunteer activities; however, in other cases you may need to research ideas for how to develop certain skills. Be sure to ask your supervisor for development ideas.

You'll find more complete instructions and examples for creating your IDP in Step 3.

INDIVIDUAL DEVELOPMENT PLAN (IDP) YEAR _____

Name	Department	Position/Title	Location/Site	Initial Date

Years in Position	Phone Number	Address

Programs/Tracks: __Leadership __Sales __Academic Degree __Intern __Other (specify)

Short-Term (1-2 years) Developmental Goals	Relationship to Corporate Goals
•	
•	
•	

Long-Term (3-5 years) Developmental Goals	Relationship to Corporate Goals
•	
•	
•	

The IDP is a planning document to foster the identification and communication of my personal and professional development goals balanced with the knowledge and skill requirements of the organization. I understand that the IDP is not a binding contract, either to the organization, my supervisor or me.

Employee Signature (Required)	Date	Comments

The developmental goals are achievable and serve the interests of this organization. The IDP is approved to the extent that workload and budget allow. Assignments may be rescheduled. Modifications may be made to accommodate changing circumstances but must be approved by the supervisor.

Supervisor Signature (Required)	Date	Comments

Mentor Signature (Optional)	Date	Comments

DEVELOPMENT PLAN FOR _____

DEVELOPMENTAL OBJECTIVES	SKILL AREA	CLASS OR ON-THE-JOB ACTIVITY	START DATE	END DATE	HOURS	PRIORITY (1, 2, 3)	TUITION OR COST	INDIRECT COST (SALARY/ TRAVEL)
a								
b								
c								
d								
e								
f								
g								
h								
i								
j								
k								
l								
m								
n								

Skill Areas: 1 = Professional, 2 = Personal, 3 = Leadership, Management, 4 = Certification, Qualification, 5 = Performance

DEVELOPMENT PLAN FOR 2025 (EXAMPLE)

DEVELOPMENTAL OBJECTIVES	SKILL AREA	CLASS OR ON-THE-JOB ACTIVITY	START DATE	END DATE	HOURS	PRIORITY (1, 2, 3)	TUITION OR COST	INDIRECT COST (SALARY/ TRAVEL)
a Use process to manage conflict	5	Conflict Mgmt Class	2/3	2/3	8	1	0	$250
b Improve EI skills	1	EI Seminar 103	Q2	Q2	24	2	$930	$1,200
c Interview and select a mentor	3	Use approved process	Feb	Mar	6	2	0	$200
d Create objectives with mentor	3	Meet bi-monthly	Mar	Dec	20	2	0	$600
e Complete budget certification	4	Attend BCF-203	Q3	Q3	16	1	$895	$480
f Identify future skills to improve	2	Peer coaching group	Jan	Dec	36	1	0	$1,000
g								
h								
i								
j								
k								
l								
m								
n								

Skill Areas: 1 = Professional, 2 = Personal, 3 = Leadership, Management, 4 = Certification, Qualification, 5 = Performance

MY CAREER DEVELOPMENT PLAN

Use this worksheet to capture your career development plan. Work through the activities that are presented in the beginning of the book in Steps 2–4 and summarize your plan here.

Career Focus and Ideal Job:

Stay Aligned

Values	Character Traits	Strengths

My Principal 1–2 Year Goal:

Objectives, Strategies, and Actions	Resources	Date
Support Objective 1:		
Strategy/Action:		
Strategy/Action:		
Strategy/Action:		
Support Objective 2:		
Strategy/Action:		
Strategy/Action:		
Strategy/Action:		
Support Objective 3:		
Strategy/Action:		
Strategy/Action:		
Strategy/Action:		
Support Objective 4:		
Strategy/Action:		
Strategy/Action:		
Strategy/Action:		
Strategy/Action:		

Required Development:

1. _____

2. _____

3. _____

Potential Obstacles:

RESOURCES AND REFERENCES

ATD Research. 2018. *Lifelong Learning: The Path to Personal and Organizational Performance*. Alexandria, VA: ATD Press.

Azulay, H. 2018. "Networking with Integrity." ATD, August 29, 2018. https://www.td.org/insights/networking-with-integrity.

Bailey, C., and A. Madden. 2016. "What Makes Work Meaningful—or Meaningless." *MIT Sloan Management Review*, Summer 2016.

Bell, C., and J. Patterson. 2011. *Wired and Dangerous: How Your Customers Have Changed and What to Do about It*. San Francisco: Berrett-Koehler Publishers.

Bennis, W., and B. Nanus. 2003. *Leaders: The Strategies for Taking Charge*. 2nd ed. New York: Harper and Row.

Biech, E. 2017. *The Art and Science of Training*. Alexandria, VA: ATD Press.

Biech, E. 2018a. *ATD's Action Guide to Talent Development: A Practical Approach to Building Your Organization's TD Efforts*. Alexandria, VA: ATD Press.

Biech, E. 2018b. *ATD's Foundations of Talent Development: Launching, Leveraging, and Leading Your Organization's TD Effort*. Alexandria, VA: ATD Press.

Booher, D. 2011. *Creating Personal Presence: Look, Talk, Think, and Act Like a Leader*. San Francisco: Berrett-Koehler.

Booher, D. 2014. "Securing Executive Support." In *ASTD Handbook: The Definitive Reference for Training and Development*, edited by E. Biech, 627–634. Alexandria, VA: ASTD Press.

Brassey, J., K. Coates, and N. van Dam. 2019. "Seven Essential Elements of a Lifelong-Learning Mind-Set." McKinsey & Company. February 19, 2019. https://www.mckinsey.com/business-functions/organization/our-insights/seven-essential-elements-of-a-lifelong-learning-mind-set.

Brown, B. 2010. *The Gifts of Imperfection: Let Go of Who You Think You're Supposed to Be and Embrace Who You Are*. Center City, MN: Hazelden Publishing.

Browning, H. 2012. *Accountability: Taking Ownership of Your Responsibility*. Greensboro, NC: CCL.

Burke, W., K. S. Roloff, and A. Mitchinson. 2016. "Learning Agility: A New Model and Measure." White Paper. Teachers College, Columbia University.

Cialdini, R. 2008. *Influence: The Psychology of Persuasion*. 5th ed. Boston: Allyn and Bacon.

Dalton, M. 2014. "Tactics for Learning from Experience." In *Experience-Driven Leader Development,* edited by C. McCauley, D. DeRue, P. Yost, and S. Taylor. San Francisco: Wiley.

Deel, B. 2019. *Trust First: A True Story about the Power of Giving People Second Chances*. New York: Optimism Press.

Diamandis, P., and S. Kotler. 2020. *The Future Is Faster Than You Think: How Converging Technologies Are Transforming Business, Industries, and Our Lives*. New York: Simon and Schuster.

Duval, S., and R. Wicklund. 1972. *A Theory of Objective Self-Awareness*. Ann Arbor: University of Michigan, Academic Press.

Dweck, C. 2017. *Mindset: The New Psychology of Success: How We Can Learn to Fulfill Our Potential*. New York: Random House.

Dweck, C., and K. Hogan. 2016. "How Microsoft Uses a Growth Mindset to Develop Leaders." *Harvard Business Review,* October 7, 2016. https://hbr.org/2016/10/how -microsoft-uses-a-growth-mindset-to-develop-leaders.

Encyclopedia.com. "50 Cent." Last modified June 16, 2020. https://www.encyclopedia .com/people/literature-and-arts/music-popular-and-jazz-biographies/50-cent.

Eurich, T. 2018. "What Self-Awareness Really Is." *Harvard Business Review*, January 4, 2018. https://hbr.org/2018/01/what-self-awareness-really-is-and-how-to-cultivate-it.

Folkman, J., and J. Zenger. n.d. *The 11 Components of a Best-in-Class 360-Degree Assessment*. Orem, UT: Zenger | Folkman.

Franklin, B. 2016. *Benjamin Franklin's Book of Virtues*. Carlisle, MA: Applewood Books.

Friedman, J. 2020. "A Note from Jane." Electric Speed Newsletter, March 7, 2020. https://mailchi.mp/janefriedman/electric-speed-128?e=807579498a.

Gallup. 2016. *How Millennials Want to Work and Live*. Washington, DC: Gallup. https:// www.gallup.com/workplace/238073/millennials-work-live.aspx.

Godin, S. 2019. *Stop Stealing Dreams: What Is School For?* Hastings on the Hudson, NY: Seth Godin.

Goleman, D. 2015. "Help Young Talent Develop a Professional Mindset." September 13, 2015. Retrieved at http://www.danielgoleman.info/daniel-goleman-help-young-talent -develop-a-professional-mindset/

Goodman, T., ed. 2016. *Forbes Book of Quotations*. New York: Hachette Book Group, Inc.

Groysberg, B., J. Lee, J. Price, and J. Cheng. 2018. "The Leader's Guide to Corporate Culture." *Harvard Business Review*, January-February, 44–57.

Hallenbeck, G. 2016. *Learning Agility: Unlock the Lessons of Experience*. Greensboro, NC: CCL Press.

Heifetz, R., and M. Linsky. 2002. "A Survival Guide for Leaders." *Harvard Business Review* 80(6): 65–74.

Horth, D., and M. Mitchell. 2017. *How to Treat New Ideas*. Greensboro, NC: CCL.

Isaacson, W. 2003. *Benjamin Franklin: An American Life*. New York: Simon and Schuster.

Kouzes, J., and B. Posner. 2017. *The Leadership Challenge: How to Make Extraordinary Things Happen in Organizations*. Hoboken, NJ: John Wiley and Sons.

Kouzes, J., B. Posner, and E. Biech. 2010. *A Coach's Guide to Developing Exemplary Leaders*. Hoboken, NJ: John Wiley and Sons.

Kraft, T., and S. Pressman. 2012. "Grin and Bear It: The Influence of Manipulated Positive Facial Expression on the Stress Response." Association for Psychological Science, July 30, 2012. www.sciencedaily.com/releases/2012/07/120730150113 .htm.

Levitt, T. 2002. "Creativity Is Not Enough." *Harvard Business Review*, August.

Maxwell, J. 2010. *Talent Is Never Enough*. Nashville, TN: Thomas Nelson Publishers.

Merrill, D., and R. Reid. 1994. *Personal Styles and Effective Performance*. Boca Raton, FL: CRC Press.

Neff, K., Y. Hsieh, and K. Dejitterat. 2005. "Self-Compassion, Achievement Goals, and Coping with Academic Failure." *Journal of Self and Identity* 4 (2005): 263–287.

Rogers, E. M. 2003. *Diffusion of Innovations*. 5th ed. New York: Free Press.

Schein, E. 2013. *Humble Inquiry: The Gentle Art of Asking Instead of Telling*. San Francisco: Berrett-Koehler Publishers.

Schroeder, B. 2020. "If You Want to Maximize Your Career, You Need to Embrace Freedom and Accountability: Seven Insights to Guide Your Way." *Forbes*, January 14, 2020. https://www.forbes.com/sites/bernhardschroeder/2020/01/14/if-you-want-to -maximize-your-career-you-need-need-to-embrace-freedom-and-accountability--seven -insights-to-guide-your-way/#11483148896c.

Scisco, P., E. Biech, and G. Hallenbeck. 2017. *Compass: Your Guide for Leadership Development and Coaching*. Greensboro, NC: CCL Press.

Senge, P. 2006. *The Fifth Discipline: The Art and Practice of the Learning Organization*. New York: Doubleday.

Smith, R., and M. Campbell. 2014. *Talent Conversations: What They Are, Why They're Crucial, and How to Do Them Right*. Greensboro, NC: CCL Press.

Thomas, K. W., and R. H. Kilmann. 1974. The Thomas-Kilmann Conflict Mode Instrument. Mountain View, CA: CPP, Inc.

Toffler, A. 1984. *Future Shock*. New York: Random House.

ACKNOWLEDGMENTS

I owe thousands of thank-yous to everyone who helped to shape this book. A few of them are noted here.

Charlotte Ashlock, Dianna Booher, Linda Growney, Debra McKinney, Julie Righter, Cat Russo, Lisa Shannon, and Kathryn Stafford for an initial review of the content, the title, and the additional thoughtful guidance. Thank you for your time, your thoroughness, your ideas, and your advice. You'll see your words woven throughout this book.

Charlotte Ashlock, Ronda Davis, Jane Friedman, Dennis Padilla, and Steve Stephenson for graciously allowing me to tell your tales. We always learn more from real-life stories.

Debra McKinney for making Challenge 2 come alive with your real-world experience and examples. What a delight you are and oh, so wise.

Lesley Iura for a hundred things, starting with believing in this concept. Thank you for being as excited about this book as I am. Your expert counsel is always a joy. Edward Wade for turning my vision into reality. You're the best. Melody Negron for giving all the details their marching orders.

ATD, CCL, ISA, and all past and current employees and members. You lead the world in learning. I've learned so much from my association with all of you.

Justin Brusino for making things happen—in numerous ways and multiple places.

Dan Greene for patiently seeing me through book #86.

INDEX

compassion: character and, 422, 430; defined, 422; intention and, 430; practice of, 430

competence, 432

competency goals: knowledge and skills, 52–53; learning and, 51–52; planning and, 51–53; practice and, 53; for skill development, 38

competing commitments, 65–66

conferences: lifelong learning and, 15; self-leadership and, 281

confidence building, 19, 476. *See also* self-confidence

conflict resolution: anger diffusion, 201–202; skills, 199–204; Thomas-Kilmann Model, 200, 201, 203

conscientiousness style. *See* analytical style

constructivism, 11

controlling style: adapting to, 124–125; of author, 108; illustrated overview of, 125f; jargon of, 123; persuasion and, 166

Cope, Kevin, 377

Cottrell, David, 228, 273, 291

courage: character and, 422, 427, 430–432; conscious decision and, 427; defined, 422; habit of, 430–431; practice of, 430–432; steps, 431; week of, 431–432

Covey, Stephen, 113, 182, 314, 347

COVID-19: Barra and, 181; technology, analytics, data and, 409–410

Cowart, Lynn, 120

Creating Personal Presence (Booher), 250

creativity: brainstorming and, 399–400; design thinking and, 398; skill, 396–402

credibility: accountability and, 432; character and, 422–423, 432–433; competence and, 432; defined, 422–423; expanding, 432–433; practice, 432–433

cryptoquotes, 344

Csikszentmihalyi, Mihaly, 218

curiosity, 22

customers, 14

Daisley, Bruce, 238

Dalio, Ray, 444

Davis, Ronda, 25–26

de Bono, Edward, 402

decision making: bias and, 350–351; critical thinking and, 352–353; force field analysis, 350; group, 351; skill, 348–354; strategies, 352–354

de Geus, Arie, 21–22

delegation, 230, 285, 288, 476, 479

Denny, Chris, 347

derailers, 450–452

design thinking, 398

details: cryptoquotes and, 344; multitasking and, 343; operational plan and, 346; skill of managing, 341–347; window exercise, 343, 344–345

development, career: celebration and, 69; failures and, 68; goal setting for, 37–39; habit of, 66; help seeking for, 67; narrowing needs in, 36–37; overview, 3–4; reading recommendations, 67; reflection and, 68; skill development, 38; what we know, 69–70. *See also* Association of Talent Development; managers, employee development by; personal development strategy; individual development plan

development plan. *See* personal development strategy

Diamandis, Peter, 70

differences, 121, 126, 152, 182, 193–198, 199, 290, 422

dispositional flexibility, 265, 457

diversity, equity, and inclusion. *See* differences; people, appreciating

do, delegate, or dump, 230

dominance style. *See* controlling style

dreams: jobs and, 86–87; lifelong learning and, 15

Dr. Seuss. *See* Seuss, Dr.

Duarte, Nancy, 414

Duckworth, Angela, 76, 83

Dull, Tamara, 413

Dweck, Carol, 83, 467; mindset of growth and, 20; power of yet and, 78

early adopters/early majority, 393

easygoing styles, 125f

Edison, Thomas: on potential, 14; on success and failure, 75

education: Franklin and, 9–10; leadership and, 289; selling ideas and, 365

Eichinger, Robert, 283

Einstein, Albert: challenges faced by, 43–44; problem solving and, 327

Goldsmith, Marshall, 134, 223, 451, 461

Goleman, Daniel, 223, 449

Graham, Dawn, 71

Grant, Adam, 192

gratitude, 455

gratitude journal, 222–223

Grenny, Joseph, 267

Grit (Duckworth), 76

growth mindset: attitude adjustment and, 81; beliefs and, 82–83; defined, 77; fixed mindset compared with, 77; focus on, 20; habit and, 80–81; KSAs and, 79; for lifelong learning, 19–20; mastering, 78; skills, 77–83; stretch project and, 82; success and, 78

Gurvis, Joan, 267

habits: *Atomic Habits*, 24; of career development, 66; of courage, 430–431; growth mindset and, 80–81; *Tiny Habits*, 80

Haines, Allen, 145

Hallenbeck, George, 94, 291, 296, 450; on agile learning, 16; *Learning Agility* by, 24

Harry Potter and the Sorcerer's Stone (Rowling), 76, 332–333

Harter, Jim, 382

health: balance and, 235; vitality and, 20

Heath, Chip, 354

Heath, Dan, 354

hubris, 450–451

humility: character and, 423, 426, 434–435; defined, 423; here-and-now, 435; need and, 426; practice of, 434–435

humor, 195–196

IDP. *See* individual development plan

ikigai (reason for being), 20

image, professional: change "but" to "and," 250; digital presence and, 249; dress for success, 249–250; elements of, 247; integrity and, 436–437; positivity and, 251; professional presence and, 250; reading recommendations, 253; responsibility and, 251–252; skill of, 247–253; strategies, 251–253; stress management and, 252

impromptu speech, 216–217

individual development plan (IDP), 2, 7f; discussing draft with supervisor, 47; draft, 45–46; finalizing, 47–48; guidance, 45–48; managers' employee development and, 470–471; overview, 45; reading recommendations, 44; responsibilities related to, 46–47; worksheets, 489, 490f, 491f, 492f

industry associations, 376

influence, 118; skill of, 161–167; style and, 123, 163

initiative: character and, 424, 426, 435–436; defined, 424; modeling corporate expectations and, 271–272; need and, 426; practice, 435–436; taking, 456–457

innovation: advisory board, 401–402; brainstorming and, 399–400; design thinking and, 398; review past, 400; skill, 396–402

innovators, 393

input/output chart, 303–304, 304f

integrity: character and, 424, 427, 436–437; defined, 424; image and, 436–437; networking and, 56–57; Peters on, 436; practice of, 436–437; preferred character and, 427

interpersonal relationships: Barra and, 181–182; building, 183–187; collaboration, 188–192; conflict resolution, 199–204; differences of people and, 193–198; networking, 205–210

jobs: dream, 86–87; learning on, 17; lifelong learning and, 14, 17; retrofitting and inventing, 31; swapping, 303

Johari Window, 133

Johnson, Ellie, 105

Johnson, Spencer, 436

Jordan, Michael, 75

journaling: gratitude and, 222–223; leadership, 278–279

judgment, avoidance of, 111

Kahneman, Daniel, 305

Kaiden, Sue, 71

Kamen, Dean, 297–298

Kaplan, Karen, 211–212

Kay, Katty, 140

Kaye, Beverly, 41, 120

Kirkland, Karen, 99

knowledge: competency goals and, 52–53; lifelong learning and, 14; stretching, 20

knowledge, skills, and attitudes (KSAs), 79

Kotter, John, 395
Kouzes, James, 483

laggards, 394
language, foreign, 154
late majority, 393
leadership: candy bar wrapper example of, 275–276; CCL, 359; education and, 289; journaling, 278–279; of others, 284–291; systems thinking and, 301–302; ventures, 292–296. *See also* self-leadership
Leadership Brand (Ulrich), 287
leading others: commitment and, 287–288; delegation and, 288; engagement research and, 288–289; expectations and, 286–287; high potential leaders and, 290; skill of, 284–291; volunteer, 291
leading self. *See* self-leadership
leading ventures: skill, 292–296; strategic planning and, 294–295
Lean Six Sigma, 387
learning: agility, 93; competency goals and, 51–52; expansion of, 26; Franklin and, 10; managers' employee development and, 480–482; mobile-enabled, 87; self-confidence, 137–138; social, 69; tactics, 17–19; what to learn, 26; willingness for, 271. *See also* experience, learning from; formal learning opportunities; lifelong learning
Learning Agility (Hallenbeck), 24
Lencioni, Patrick, 192
Leslie, Jean, 57
Lewin, Kurt, 132
life: audit, 112; balancing, 33–34
lifelong learning, 7f; accountability, 22–23; actions supporting, 19–23; action tactics, 17; advantages, 12–13; aspiration and, 22; barriers to, 23; classes and, 15; commitment, 21; components of, 12; conferences and, 15; confidence building and, 19; curiosity and, 22; customers and, 14; dabbling in, 14–15; defined, 10–11; dreams and, 15; experimentation and, 14, 15; feeling tactics, 17; Franklin and, 9–10; habits and, 80–81; jobs and, 14, 17; knowledge and, 14; learn to learn, 21–22; mentor and, 15; mindset of growth for, 19–20; networking and, 15, 17; opportuni-

ties, 16–19; organization and, 10–11, 13; other's tactics, 17–18; personal benefits of, 12; planning and, 14; podcasts and, 15; practice of, 13–14; preparation, early, and, 21; preparing for, 19, 21; process improvement and, 14; professional benefits of, 12–13; professional organizations and, 14; reading recommendations, 24; research on, 11; self-awareness and, 22; self investment and, 27; skills supporting agile, 16; tactics, 17–19; theories associated with, 11; thinking tactics, 17; upholding your organization, 22; virtual learning and, 15; vulnerability and, 22
listening, 94, 97, 150, 151, 152–153, 192, 194, 201, 207, 209, 280, 381, 474; active listening, 152–153
Livermore, David, 198
Lombardo, Michael, 283

Madden, John, 286
maintaining composure: anti-perfectionism and, 215; QUICK plan, 217; skill, 213–218
managers, employee development by, 463; activities, 471; assessment options, 469–470; basics, 465–467; confidence building, 476; discussion guide for, 468–471; experiences recommended for, 477; format for, 468; goals and, 469, 482; ideas for, 478–480; IDPs and, 470–471; learning environment for, 480–482; networking and, 481–482; ongoing, 474–480; overview, 464–465; permission and, 481–482; reading recommendations, 483–484; specific discussions, 471–473, 472f; supporting, 474–475
Manoogian, Sam, 99
MAPP career assessment, 33
marketing and sales: customer desire and, 405; customer retention and, 406; idea development and, 405–406; skill, 403–408, 455
Martineau, Jennifer, 105
massive open online courses (MOOCs), 21
Maxfield, David, 267
Maxwell, John, 196, 419, 420, 444
McCandless, David, 414
McCauley, Cynthia, 57
McKinney, Debra, 445–448, 450–451

ABOUT THE AUTHOR

Elaine Biech is a consultant, facilitator, and author of the *Washington Post* number one best seller *The Art and Science of Training*. With four decades of experience and 85 published books, she has been called "one of the titans of the training industry" and the "queen of talent development publishing." She delights in supporting leaders to execute their vision, building teams to maximize their performance, and guiding organizations to address large-scale change. She is a dedicated lifelong learner who believes that excellence isn't optional and that we all have the potential to reach our goals and live our passion.

Elaine is the recipient of numerous professional awards including the 2020 Association for Talent Development (ATD) Distinguished Contribution Award, the ATD Bliss Award, ATD Torch Award, and ATD Staff Partnership Award. She served on ATD's board of directors and executive board, the board of governors and executive board of the Center for Creative Leadership, and ISA the Association of Learning Provider's board of directors. She was selected for the Wisconsin Women Entrepreneur's Mentor Award and received ISA's highest award, the Spirit Award. She was selected as the inaugural Certified Professional for Talent Development (CPTD) Fellow Honoree by ATD's Certification Institute. Elaine is a consummate talent development professional who has been instrumental in guiding the talent development and consulting professions throughout her career.

ABOUT ATD

Unleashing human potential is important work. For nearly 80 years, the Association for Talent Development (ATD) has supported those who develop the knowledge and skills of employees in organizations around the world. We know that getting employees up to speed, trained, and ready to tackle today's increasingly demanding business landscape is no small task. As a professional membership organization, we offer research and resources on best practices, tools, courses, and programs to help talent development professionals level up.

Our 30,000 members come from more than 120 countries and work in public and private organizations in every industry sector. We support talent development professionals who gather locally in volunteer-led U.S. chapters and international member networks, and with international strategic partners.

We're in this together to help create a world that works better.

For more information, visit www.td.org.

Berrett–Koehler
Publishers

Berrett-Koehler is an independent publisher dedicated to an ambitious mission: *Connecting people and ideas to create a world that works for all.*

Our publications span many formats, including print, digital, audio, and video. We also offer online resources, training, and gatherings. And we will continue expanding our products and services to advance our mission.

We believe that the solutions to the world's problems will come from all of us, working at all levels: in our society, in our organizations, and in our own lives. Our publications and resources offer pathways to creating a more just, equitable, and sustainable society. They help people make their organizations more humane, democratic, diverse, and effective (and we don't think there's any contradiction there). And they guide people in creating positive change in their own lives and aligning their personal practices with their aspirations for a better world.

And we strive to practice what we preach through what we call "The BK Way." At the core of this approach is *stewardship,* a deep sense of responsibility to administer the company for the benefit of all of our stakeholder groups, including authors, customers, employees, investors, service providers, sales partners, and the communities and environment around us. Everything we do is built around stewardship and our other core values of *quality, partnership, inclusion,* and *sustainability.*

This is why Berrett-Koehler is the first book publishing company to be both a B Corporation (a rigorous certification) and a benefit corporation (a for-profit legal status), which together require us to adhere to the highest standards for corporate, social, and environmental performance. And it is why we have instituted many pioneering practices (which you can learn about at www.bkconnection.com), including the Berrett-Koehler Constitution, the Bill of Rights and Responsibilities for BK Authors, and our unique Author Days.

We are grateful to our readers, authors, and other friends who are supporting our mission. We ask you to share with us examples of how BK publications and resources are making a difference in your lives, organizations, and communities at www.bkconnection.com/impact.

Dear reader,

Thank you for picking up this book and welcome to the worldwide BK community! You're joining a special group of people who have come together to create positive change in their lives, organizations, and communities.

What's BK all about?

Our mission is to connect people and ideas to create a world that works for all.

Why? Our communities, organizations, and lives get bogged down by old paradigms of self-interest, exclusion, hierarchy, and privilege. But we believe that can change. That's why we seek the leading experts on these challenges—and share their actionable ideas with you.

A welcome gift

To help you get started, we'd like to offer you a **free copy** of one of our bestselling ebooks:

www.bkconnection.com/welcome

When you claim your **free ebook**, you'll also be subscribed to our blog.

Our freshest insights

Access the best new tools and ideas for leaders at all levels on our blog at ideas.bkconnection.com.

Sincerely,
Your friends at Berrett-Koehler